Public Opinion in the 21st Century

Let the People Speak?

The New Directions in Political Behavior Series

GENERAL EDITOR
ALLAN J. CIGLER
University of Kansas

PUBLIC OPINION IN THE 21st CENTURY

Let the People Speak?

Russell Brooker

ALVERNO COLLEGE

Todd Schaefer

CENTRAL WASHINGTON UNIVERSITY

WADSWORTH
CENGAGE Learning™

Australia • Brazil • Japan • Korea • Mexico • Singapore • Spain • United Kingdom • United States

WADSWORTH
CENGAGE Learning

Public Opinion in the 21st Century: Let the People Speak?
Russell Brooker, Todd Schaefer

Publisher: Charles Hartford

Sponsoring Editor: Katherine Meisenheimer

Senior Development Editor: Jeffrey Greene

Editorial Assistant: Kristen Craib

Project Editor: Reba Libby

Editorial Assistant: Deborah Berkman

Senior Art and Design Coordinator: Jill Haber Atkins

Senior Photo Editor: Jennifer Meyer Dare

Executive Marketing Manager: Nicola Poser

Cover Image: © Bob Daemmrich / The Image Works, Austin, Texas: Houston City Councilman Gordon Quan speaking at a rally at the Texas Capitol. He is an Asian-American and recognized as one of the top lawyers in the U.S. January 11, 2005.

For product information and technology assistance, contact us at **Cengage Learning Customer & Sales Support, 1-800-354-9706**

For permission to use material from this text or product, submit all requests online at **www.cengage.com/permissions** Further permissions questions can be emailed to **permissionrequest@cengage.com**

Library of Congress Control Number: 2005927841

ISBN-13: 978-0-618-37620-9

ISBN-10: 0-618-37620-8

Wadsworth
20 Channel Center Street
Boston, MA 02210
USA

Cengage Learning is a leading provider of customized learning solutions with office locations around the globe, including Singapore, the United Kingdom, Australia, Mexico, Brazil, and Japan. Locate your local office at **www.cengage.com/global**

Cengage Learning products are represented in Canada by Nelson Education, Ltd.

To learn more about Wadsworth, visit **www.cengage.com/wadsworth**

Purchase any of our products at your local college store or at our preferred online store **www.cengagebrain.com**

Printed in the United States of America
3 4 5 6 7 14 13 12 11 10

Contents

PART IV. THE PEOPLE SPEAK: EXPRESSING PUBLIC OPINION IN PRACTICE   259

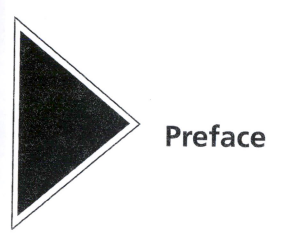

Preface

PUBLIC OPINION has become increasingly important in American and even world politics in recent years, making understanding it equally important. At the same time, studying and teaching public opinion can be quite challenging. It's easy to get lost in the minutiae of methodology or the details of certain aspects of the subject and thus lose the proverbial forest for the trees.

We wrote this book to provide a comprehensive, yet brief and accessible, introduction to the study of public opinion. It encourages critical thinking about a "big picture" understanding of public opinion through the use of unifying themes, while providing overviews of the literature on various subtopics of public opinion. Numerous provocative, hands-on exercises are included to engage students.

THEMES

There are two basic underlying themes of this book. The first is public opinion as expression of the popular will and public opinion as a process of communication between the leaders and led. We call this theme the *democratic dialogue*. Who speaks, what do they say, and does the government listen? Whose opinions are most important in shaping public policy? How do they make their opinions known? How do we know—and how do governmental decision makers know—what those opinions are?

The second theme of the book concerns the proper role of the public in democratic government in theory and practice: namely "Vox Populi, Vox Dei"—

is the voice of the people the voice of God, or at least the voice of reason and wisdom? We call this theme the *democratic dilemma*. Are we capable of governing ourselves as democratic theory dictates? How much influence *should* public opinion have in developing public policy? How well can "we, the people" make wise, informed decisions in an increasingly complex world? These questions are at the root of the scholarly debate between those who portray the public as irrational, ignorant, or incompetent and those who claim the public, with all its shortcomings, is essentially wise and rational.

APPROACH

This book addresses public opinion as a *political* phenomenon that is integrated into the political process. While political scientists enjoy measuring and analyzing it, public opinion is important because of its role in the political world. What people believe, and what they do about those beliefs, affect the creation of public policy. What opinions—and whose opinions—get expressed, either through voting or other types of political participation, makes a difference. To explore this theme adequately, we include material on how the people voice their opinions. We describe how citizens—and which citizens— contact their representatives to express their opinions and how those officials respond to them.

We are inclusive in our treatment of methodologies. In addition to extensive coverage of survey research, the book also examines several other quantitative and qualitative methods. These include what we call "informal" methods of public opinion research that officials use to gauge the opinions of the people through analyzing elections, listening to lobbyists, reading mail, and listening to constituents. Unlike some books on public opinion, we cover political participation along with politicians' own use of polls and other measures of opinion.

TEACHING OBJECTIVES

Pedagogically, the book has four main objectives. The first is obvious—to teach students about American public opinion. This is the principal goal of any textbook on public opinion. The second objective is to stimulate students to think critically about public opinion, both in theory and practice. We hope students will be provoked into thinking about the citizenry's role in government both through active learning components and examinations of the scholarly and normative debates surrounding the topics in each chapter, which are incorporated in the unifying themes.

The third objective is to teach students how to engage in quantitative and qualitative data analysis. Quantitative analysis is usually more challenging for students. The book employs a good deal of quantitative data throughout the text. Public opinion, political participation, and voting behavior are typically studied quantitatively, and students cannot understand the concepts without understanding the numbers. Although the book assumes only a minimal understanding of statistics on the part of students, it will guide them in developing their quantitative analytical abilities to interpret the data.

In addition to a considerable number of statistical tables and figures on public opinion, political participation, and voting, there are exercises from the 2002 and 2004 American National Election Studies. Several data sets are included, complete with suggestions for exercises that use them. The data sets are on the book's Web site.

The fourth objective is to help the students apply the book's concepts to specific real-world contemporary issues. Several issues are used as illustrations, and exercises are included that will engage students in the issues. Another aspect of the book that differentiates it is the inclusion of several Interactive Learning Exercises on the Web site. These exercises engage and challenge students to apply the concepts they learn to "real world" manifestations of public opinion, from data analysis and critical thinking exercises to stand alone simulations. These exercises are designed to show students that public opinion is a real force that political decision makers must take into consideration as they develop public policy.

CONTENT

We begin the book with an overview of public opinion and explanations of our two themes of the *democratic dialogue* and the *democratic dilemma*. In the first chapter, we define (or show how difficult it is to define) public opinion. We also review the views of influential theorists and scholars on what public opinion *is* and how important it *should be*. The next two chapters are about the various methods of ascertaining the public's opinions. The first of these chapters covers survey research. Survey research, often called "polling," is the most important method in public opinion research (some political scientists have said it has "hegemony" over the field), so we devote an entire chapter to it. We include the rapidly developing field of Internet surveying and two variants of survey research—deliberative polling and survey-based experiments.

The next methodology chapter deals with other types of research. Some of these, such as laboratory experiments and analysis of mail, are quantitative. The other, mainly focus groups and in-depth interviews, are qualitative. We devote much more space to qualitative methods than usual because we think that qualitative methods are valuable tools for learning about public opinion and are under-used today. In the ongoing methodology debate of social scientists on the merits of quantitative versus qualitative methods, we are not taking sides. They are both important, and we explain both. Certainly political candidates think focus groups are useful for learning about public opinion; they use them regularly. The last part of this chapter is concerned with what we call "informal" methods of research; they are important because candidates and politicians use them and rely on the information they gain from them. After all, one of the main reasons public opinion is important is because of the effect it has on people in the public policy development process.

The next three chapters are devoted to individuals' organization and acquisition of their opinions. Chapter 4 covers how people structure their political thinking, focusing on the two main conceptual tools of party identification and ideology. Understanding these tools is key to understanding much about American political behavior. Chapter 5 discusses political socialization, or where and how people develop the opinions they eventually express. Chapter 6 examines the relationship between mass media and public opinion. It not only includes discussion of the effects media messages may have on people's opinions, but also how the media cover public opinion expressions like polls and protests, and how well the media do at educating the public and providing a diverse range of ideas.

The following two chapters chronicle the history of public opinion since it was first measured systematically in the 1930s and people's opinions today. Chapter 7 traces the history of American public opinion for the last seventy-plus years using four issue domains: 1) economic or social welfare issues; 2) racial issues; 3) social issues; and 4) defense and foreign policy issues. Chapter 8 looks at Americans' opinions today, with special emphases on economics and financial inequality, gender issues, and racial issues.

Chapters 9 and 10 are devoted to the process of converting public opinion into public policy. Chapter 9 explores ways that the public conveys its opinions to governmental decision makers through various forms of participation, while Chapter 10 analyzes how those decision makers learn, and attempt to influence, the opinions of their constituents.

In the following two chapters, we explore more fully the twin themes of *democratic dialogue* and *democratic dilemma*. Chapter 11 delves into the vital question of whether the public is capable of self-governance. The chapter is organized around the two main sides in this "public competency" debate, and also addresses the extent to which Americans support democratic values in theory and practice. From the normative question of whether the government should listen to the people, Chapter 12 explores the more empirical question of whether it actually does so. In similar fashion, this chapter reviews three main lines of research into this particular question, all with different answers. Indeed, we hope the material in these chapters helps students realize scholars have their own disagreements on these issues, thus further stimulating them to develop their own opinions and learn to weigh arguments and assess evidence.

Chapter 13 examines presidential approval, an especially conspicuous case study of the relationship between public opinion, its measurement, and public officials.

Finally, we conclude with a brief chapter that attempts to revisit the main themes and set the stage for the role of public opinion in the future. We hope by this point the book has proven itself in helping both students and faculty engage the subject matter.

SUPPLEMENTS

On the book's Web site, we have included numerous Interactive Learning Exercises. Organized by chapter, these exercises are designed to provide students with hands on practice and experience with the quantitative and qualitative methods of public opinion research and analysis. They include data analysis, critical-thinking exercises, and simulations.

ACKNOWLEDGEMENTS

We owe many thanks to many people. Because we live 2,000 miles apart, we know different people and will write our acknowledgements separately. I, Russell Brooker, would first like to thank Norman H. Nie, my mentor in graduate school and the author of my success in the real world. Norman taught me how to do public opinion research and started me on the road to learning statistics. I would also like to thank Sarah Wierdsma and Veronica Carrillo for their help in researching some of the topics, and Laura Cleary and Amanda Arkebauer for making PowerPoint behave itself. Eric Sanders downloaded the National Election Study databases. Paul Smith was vital in developing the Liberal-Conservative self-classification exercise. Jeana Abromeit helped me explain the gender gap. Stephen Sharkey provided important help and institutional support at Alverno College. Thanks also to Bob Dieringer and The Dieringer Research Group for helping me learn about a large number of things, including Sopwith University and drunk driving. My wife, Karen, deserves lavish praise for supporting me as I wrote this book in my "spare" time. Thanks also to Ed Fitz and other colleagues at The University of Chicago who, although not specifically involved with this book, are remembered fondly: Barney Fenster, Rebecca Lee Hatfield, Celeste Scarbelli, and Jeremy Warren.

I, Todd Schaefer, would like to thank my mentor-colleagues at Northwestern University, especially Ken Janda, who first taught me methods but more importantly provided sage advice on writing a text with Cengage Learning, and Ben Page, who introduced me to the worlds of public opinion and mass media and through his scholarship has struggled with many of the core issues in this text. Jerry Goldman also provided some helpful tips on the proposal process. I'd also like to thank my colleagues at Central Washington

University for listening to my trials and triumphs along the way, especially Jim Brown and Matt Manweller who gave me valuable feedback on certain sections. Linda Rubio and Jonika Brakstad provided random staff assistance. Lastly, my wife Kathy and two cats provided comfort, moral support, and well-needed R&R.

We both thank our colleagues who served us well as reviewers of this book. They made this a better book.

Gerald Kosicki, *Ohio State University*
Kenny J. Whitby, *University of South Carolina*
Mark Peffley, *University of Kentucky*
Stephen J. Farnsworth, *Mary Washington College*
Geoff Peterson, *University of Wisconsin-Eau Claire*

We would jointly like to thank Katherine Meisenheimer and Jeff Greene at Cengage Learning, Katherine had faith in us from the beginning and provided valuable help in the early phases of the process. Jeff shepherded us through the actual writing of the book in a supportive and patient manner. Also, we can't forget New Directions series editor Allan Cigler at the University of Kansas, who listened to a brief pitch of our ideas at a Midwest Political Science Association meeting and encouraged its transformation into a full-length book proposal, and now book.

R. B.

T. S.

PART

I

Introduction

A Decent Respect to the Opinions of Mankind

It is rare that the public sentiment decides immorally or unwisely, and the individual who differs from it ought to distrust and examine well his opinion.

—Thomas Jefferson[1]

[Public opinion:] a compound of folly, weakness, prejudice, wrong feeling, right feeling, obstinacy, and newspaper paragraphs.

—Sir Robert Peel[2]

Questions to Think About

Welcome to the world of public opinion! Each chapter will begin with a list of "Questions to Think About" to give you a preview of what will be covered and what to think about. In the first chapter of this book, we will examine the nature of public opinion and consider the opinions of contemporary students of the discipline. As you read this chapter, ask yourself:

- What is the proper role of public opinion in the functioning of a democratic government? How much influence should the people have?
- If you were designing the U.S. government, would you construct any barriers to democratic participation—to the people automatically enacting their opinions as public policy? Why? What would those barriers be?
- What is public opinion? How would you define it?

JUST WEEKS after the terrorist attacks of September 11, 2001, Congress passed, and President George W. Bush signed, the USA PATRIOT Act, giving the government wider investigative and judicial powers than it had possessed up to that point, including the power to eavesdrop on more people and to imprison suspected terrorists without bringing them to trial. The Act became law with lightning speed (most legislation takes many months, if not years, to come to fruition) and with relatively little deliberation. It also passed overwhelmingly, with a vote of 356–66 in the U.S. House of Representatives and 98–1 in the Senate.

The climate of opinion when the bill was enacted indicated that most people favored the Act; in fact, even into 2004, nearly two-thirds of the population (64 percent) said the Act "is about right" or "does not go far enough in restricting people's civil liberties in order to fight terrorism." Only 26 percent said the Act "goes too far."[3] Passage of the PATRIOT Act, then, would seem to be a simple case of democracy in action, of government responding to the people's will: The nation was attacked, people demanded action, and the government gave it to them.

Upon closer inspection, however, the case of the PATRIOT Act highlights a number of thorny issues about the role of public opinion in American politics. These include

- Majority tyranny, or the degree to which what the majority wants may threaten minority rights, including fundamental freedoms;
- Public knowledge, understanding, and deliberation about complex issues of public policy;
- The sudden emergence of new issues on the political agenda, and government response to *perceived* public moods or even *anticipation* of future public reactions, rather than to "real" public sentiment.

First, the Act arguably threatened certain fundamental democratic principles. Critics asserted that it violated the Fourth Amendment of the U.S. Constitution because it permitted unreasonable searches and seizures, and violated the Sixth Amendment because it did not give the accused a right to a speedy and public trial. These opponents said the fact that it had widespread public support did not matter. They said that the government, *even with the support of the overwhelming majority of the people*, did not have the legitimate power to violate Constitutional rights. The rights in the first ten amendments were added to the Constitution to stop the government from trampling on the rights of the people — even if the majority of the people wish it to do so.

Next is the issue of whether the public really supported the provisions of the PATRIOT Act, or even knew what the law entailed. On the one hand, it did seem that the bulk of the population wanted more security, even at the risk of losing some rights. A Fox News/Opinion Dynamics poll in mid-October, 2001, right before the Act's passage, found that 71 percent of the public was "willing to give up some personal freedom in order to reduce the threat of terrorism."

These data provide evidence apparently supporting actions like those in the Act. Yet other polls suggest that the public may not have been so supportive. A Gallup survey conducted at roughly the same time found 60 percent *opposed* to "making it easier for legal authorities to read mail, email, and tap phones without the person's knowledge," something that the PATRIOT Act actually did.[4]

The USA PATRIOT Act was also a lengthy and complex piece of legislation; the bill itself was 342 pages long. It is likely that many members of Congress did not fully understand everything that was in the law they were voting upon—much less members of the general public, who are usually far less informed. The bill's speedy passage and lack of debate made it even harder for the public to have a fully informed opinion about it.

Lastly, politics surrounding passage of the PATRIOT Act and antiterrorism policy more generally arose suddenly and developed extremely fast. Prior to September 11, terrorism—while a persistent and age-old problem—wasn't high on the list of priorities of most Americans or their elected representatives. Indeed, it is unlikely that on September 10 there were many people walking around with the idea in their heads that "we urgently need a new antiterrorism policy that gives more investigative powers to the government." Yet, the situation quickly changed, as concern about terrorism rocketed to the top of the nation's agenda. This made the opinion and policy environment very volatile.

Political leaders had to adapt to this new state of affairs. Most members of Congress, even those with reservations about the PATRIOT Act, knew they needed to do something, but such a rapidly emerging issue meant they had to act in an environment of uncertainty about what the people wanted exactly. Therefore, they were likely responding more to *perceived* public opinion— namely, that general sentiment that something had to be done about terrorism, and done now. What the public wanted to be done, and whether it supported specific elements of the PATRIOT Act, was unclear. Indeed, as indicated by the Gallup poll result discussed earlier, there is some evidence that the public might have disagreed with some of bill's specific measures for fighting terrorism. But given such a fast-moving issue, how could politicians know for sure?

Another element in the law's swift and overwhelming passage had to do with what policymakers believed public opinion might very well be in the future. Many elected politicians undoubtedly *anticipated* that opposing the bill, even on specific grounds the public might favor (like protecting freedoms), could come back to haunt them in the next election, especially if there were another terror attack. They knew that a vote against the Act would be hard to explain to voters, especially if an opponent chose to highlight it, which was likely, given the new importance of the issue.[5] On the other hand, if the new law turned out to be unpopular, they could always argue that improvements could be made, but that they had acted in the face of the new threat.

Indeed, part of the molding and selling of the bill by the Bush administration and its allies in Congress was to frame it in stark, nationalistic terms, making it hard to resist. Supporters implied that failing to support the Act would in effect be supporting terrorism. The very title of the bill—its official name was "Uniting and Strengthening America by Providing Appropriate Tools Required to Intercept and Obstruct Terrorism Act of 2001" (hence USA PATRIOT Act)—was designed so that its abbreviation would make a vote against it sound unpatriotic, like a vote against America itself.[6] So, symbolically at least, it was simply much easier to vote for the bill.

Despite a lack of complete certainty about the exact role of public opinion in passage of the USA PATRIOT Act, it is nevertheless clear that what the public thinks and wants concerning important issues like antiterrorism policy is a crucial part of understanding contemporary American politics. The plethora of polls and media coverage about the public's reactions to the September 11, 2001, attacks and their aftermath testifies to the importance of public opinion.

WHAT IS PUBLIC OPINION?

If public opinion is so theoretically important to democratic government, we should first define the term. Unfortunately, there is no universally agreed-upon definition of "public opinion." There are many definitions from which to choose. How one defines public opinion may in fact be influenced by what one thinks of public opinion in the first place, as the quotes from Jefferson and Peel at the beginning of the chapter suggest.

But even neutral, more analytic observers like academics disagree about what public opinion is. If you were to read every work on public opinion, you'd probably find a different explanation in each one. Much of this lack of consensus stems from the fact that public opinion is an abstract human concept like love, rather than a tangible, physical object like a chair. It is much easier to define what a chair is than what love is. A chair is something we can see, touch, and so forth, while love is more difficult to describe. Nevertheless, all but the most cynical of us would say that both chairs and love exist. Although probably not as important as love, in a similar fashion we infer public opinion's existence from people's statements and actions. In some ways, public opinion is analogous to Supreme Court Justice Potter Stewart's observation about pornography—that he couldn't exactly define it, "but I know it when I see it."[7]

What all of the definitions have in common is that they are about thoughts of the people concerning governments or governmental policies. For our purposes, we define public opinion as "the expressed attitudes and views of ordinary people on issues of public concern." Let us examine each of the component parts of this definition more closely.

Expressed Attitudes and Views: Public opinion must be voiced, or publicly expressed before it can be known or influential. If government is to listen, then the people must speak. If people keep their opinions to themselves, how can the government heed them? Attitudes and views are someone's preferences toward objects—favorable, unfavorable, neutral, no opinion, or whatever—but preferences nonetheless. Of course, there are conflicting definitions of what attitudes and views are, and both terms are sometimes used synonymously with opinions. In this book, we will use *opinions* to mean "observable, verbal responses or actions to issues or questions." In our usage, an *attitude* or *view* will refer to "a covert, psychological predisposition or tendency."[8] The distinction is not always clear in the literature, but we think it is a useful one. So in our formulation, attitudes and views are preferences that don't become opinions until they are expressed—until the people speak, in some form.

Ordinary People: Here we mean the general public, or "regular" people, not leaders such as members of Congress, lobbyists, or newspaper columnists. We say "people" purposely, referring both to citizens and noncitizens. In the United States today, both citizens and noncitizens have opinions that matter to the government. Although citizens tend to have much more power in politics, including the right to vote, the views of noncitizens may be important or relevant too, and worth considering or at least paying attention to. A good example might be what noncitizens think about immigration or visa laws, or what Muslim or Arab foreign nationals think about security issues after September 11, 2001.

Issues of Public Concern: For the purposes of this book, *public opinion* means *political* public opinion—opinions about public matters of policy, politics, and government. If the vast majority of the people believe, as the authors do, that the Chicago Cubs deserve to win the World Series, that is an admirable opinion, but it is not *political* opinion. Nor is public opinion—as we use the term—concerned with which stars were the best and worst dressed at the Oscars or which rock band is the greatest of all time. To be *political*, public opinion must deal with what the government, at some level, should do or not do.

However, the distinction between political and nonpolitical opinion is complicated by the fact that the dividing line is often unclear and is constantly changing. For many years, discrimination against women by businesses in pay and promotion was not a political issue, but now it is. In addition, until recently, private companies and government agencies were allowed to discriminate against homosexuals without committing a "political" act. Now, such discrimination is illegal in many jurisdictions, and the rights that should be accorded homosexuals are matters of debate; they are clearly "political." As shown in Box 1.1, smoking has changed over the years from a private act with only personal implications to a public, and political, issue.

We don't pretend to believe that our definition is superior to all others, or that one can't learn valuable lessons about public opinion from other ones. But our definition is simple, and the one that best fits our focus on how public opinion gets, or does not get, translated into public policy.

What is it that the public has opinions about? We have already stipulated that the opinions must be political to be counted as "public" opinion here, but now we will identify some more specific objects of public opinion. First, opinions may be about issues. In fact, this is the most common use of the term *public opinion*.

Box 1.1

Mind If I Smoke? What Is a "Political" Opinion?

In this book, we define public opinion as being limited to political issues. Often, it is clear what is political and what is not. Elections, for example, are political, and *Wheel of Fortune* is not. But what about smoking? Today, it would be considered a political issue, but a few years ago it was not. *Growing* tobacco has been a political issue for well over a hundred years. Government subsidies to tobacco growers had their origins in tobacco farmers' movements in the nineteenth century. But *smoking* tobacco has only recently become a political issue. Before the 1960s, movie theaters allowed smoking in all the seats, and restaurants did not have smoking or nonsmoking sections—the entire restaurant was the smoking section. Tobacco companies were free to advertise wherever they wished. Millions of Americans became familiar with the semiliterate jingle heard repeatedly on television and radio, "Winston tastes good, like a cigarette should." While some people did not like smoking and objected to smokers puffing near them, smoking was seen as strictly a personal decision, and not smoking around nonsmokers was seen as a personal courtesy. Cigarette advertising was seen as a strictly commercial issue.

In this book, we define public opinion as *political* opinion. If we were writing this book in 1955, we would not have mentioned smoking because it was not a *political* issue. But now it is. There are many laws that restrict smoking in buildings' common areas, restaurants, and even bars. There are also laws prohibiting the sale of tobacco products to customers under eighteen. Tobacco advertising is not allowed on television, radio, or billboards. There are even laws against certain cartoon characters advertising cigarettes; Joe Camel, for example, is not allowed to ask you to buy Camels. Some people and organizations, such as the American Medical Association, favor banning tobacco advertising altogether. A coalition of several states won a court judgment worth hundreds of billions of dollars against tobacco companies.

The point here is that what is a political issue changes with the times. What can be classified as *political*, and therefore as *public* opinion, changes as the issues change. It does not change automatically; people make it change. Smoking became a political issue because politically active groups made it political. As the facts became more widely known through a series of *Surgeon General's Reports* (especially after the 1964 report), pro-health organizations, such as the American Medical Association, the American Lung Association, and the American Heart Association, inveighed against smoking. New groups, such as Action on Smoking and Health (ASH), have developed. In the meantime, many companies, recognizing the tremendous costs to them in employee heath expenses due to smoking, have limited smoking on their premises, and some have supported more restrictive legislation.

This expansion of what counts as *political* is also seen in other issues. Domestic abuse (in the form of wife-beating and child abuse) is now seen as a criminal, and therefore *political*, issue rather than strictly a family issue to be worked out within families. In addition, some issues that have always been seen as political are now seen as more political. For example, drunk driving has been illegal since before there were cars to drive, but only within the past thirty or so years has the political system aggressively attacked the problem and politicians been held responsible for drunk driving violations. This increased emphasis has happened largely through the efforts of anti-drunk driving organizations such as Mothers Against Drunk Driving (MADD).

What is *political* opinion, and therefore *public* opinion, changes over time in response to the political forces of the day.

How does one feel about abortion? About taxes? About foreign affairs? A type of issue may be a specific bill or law in Congress; for example, what is one's opinion on the USA PATRIOT Act mentioned above?

One form of issue opinion is the amount of money that might be spent on a program. Two people might have the same opinion on public education—that it is a good thing. But one might want to spend more money on it than the other.

Second, opinions may be about politicians or governmental organizations. What does one think about the president, the governor, or a senator? How does one feel about Congress or the Drug Enforcement Administration (DEA)? Opinions could also be about political nongovernmental organizations, such as the American Civil Liberties Union (ACLU). A variant of these opinions is how one evaluates a politician or organization: how well is the president handling the economy? How good is the DEA at keeping illegal drugs out of the country? How well is the ACLU protecting Constitutional freedoms?

One obvious type of question about evaluating politicians is how people plan to vote in the next election. That is certainly one of the most common areas of research in American public opinion.

Third, opinions may be about groups in society. The groups may be demographic, such as African Americans, the elderly, or the poor; or the groups may be occupational or ideological, such as police, professors, conservatives, or Democrats.

A fourth type of opinion is people's views of the political system and how they fit into it. For example, do people feel that they have influence in the system? Do they think that officeholders care about their opinions? Do people "believe" in the system, or are they alienated from it?

PUBLIC OPINION IN PRACTICE

Demonstrating a different view of public opinion, political communication scholars Robert Entman and Susan Herbst argue that "'public opinion' is a useful fiction that actually refers to several different phenomena. . . ." They identify four "referents" of public opinion, or ways that public opinion is manifested in contemporary politics: mass opinion, activated opinion, latent opinion, and perceived majorities.[9] Although their conception is much broader than our definition, these four referents provide useful insights into how public opinion may affect public policy, and so it is useful to discuss them in detail.

Mass Opinion

Mass opinion is the simple aggregation or summation of individual opinions and preferences, as measured through opinion polls, direct public votes on issues, or elections. This is the form of public opinion most observers mean when they refer to "public opinion." Indeed, it is the one we usually use in this book. Sometimes, mass opinion is clear, informed, and hence potentially powerful in politics and policymaking, but at other times it is vague, uninformed, or malleable. It is the most democratic form of public opinion, but not always the most influential.

Activated Public Opinion

Activated public opinion is the opinions of the active, engaged, and informed segment of the population. These are party loyalists, interest group leaders and participants, citizen activists, people who write letters to the editor or to elected representatives, and so forth. In theory, the entire population, or at least a large part of it, should be activated, but in practice on a number of issues it may not be. Furthermore, since the activated public's opinions tend to be more stable, and they are more vocal and involved, politicians may have greater incentive to listen to their voices rather than to the mass public.

Latent Opinion

Latent opinion is potential or eventual public opinion—or where public opinion will end up on an issue after it goes through a crystallization and deliberation cycle. V. O. Key, one of the most influential students of twentieth century public opinion, knew that latent opinion was difficult to measure but at the same time was important in the policymaking process.[10] Smart politicians know how to read, anticipate, and intuitively respond to latent opinion, or at least to what they think it will be. The earlier example of the PATRIOT Act illustrates this process—a process that may lead politicians to ignore the results of polls and other measures of short-term mass opinion.

On the other hand, politicians who do not accurately predict latent opinion can run into trouble. For example, in 1992 the media revealed that many members of the U.S. House of Representatives had formed a House bank in which they had checking accounts. Several House members had routinely written checks without sufficient funds in their accounts. Although the checks were "bad," the House bank had paid them. A public furor arose, with voters objecting to the fact that House members could write checks without money, while they, the voters, could not. This became known as the "House banking scandal," and many representatives who had written the bad checks were defeated in the next election. Another example, in Box 1.2, shows how anti-administration forces in Milwaukee County, Wisconsin, used a pension issue to force the resignation of the county executive.

Did the public have opinions about representatives writing bad checks before the House banking scandal? Did they have opinions on pensions for

Milwaukee County employees before the terms of the new pension decisions were revealed in the media? Probably not. Although the people reacted very strongly when they became aware of these "scandals," it is unlikely that many people had even thought about these issues beforehand. Furthermore, the officeholders in question likewise failed to anticipate that latent opinion would become mobilized, thinking instead the public didn't care. Otherwise, presumably, they would not have behaved as they did.

Again, latent opinion may eventually emerge or stay dormant, but it nevertheless may play an important role in the opinion-policy process.

Box 1.2

What Is an Opinion? The Curious Case of Tom Ament and Rapid Mobilization

What is an opinion? Can a person have a position on an issue without knowing it? Sometimes people have opinions, or attitudes, or predispositions on issues that have not arisen yet. This is what we mean by *latent opinion*. History is full of examples in which issues have arisen from "nowhere" and become important. Usually, these issues involve highly emotional topics that political entrepreneurs can use effectively, although usually temporarily. The case of Tom Ament provides one such example.

F. Tom Ament had served in Milwaukee County (WI) government since 1968 when the "pension controversy" erupted at the end of 2001. Ament had served as a county supervisor on the County Board from 1968 to 1992 and as county executive from 1992 to 2002. In Milwaukee County, the County Board is the legislative body, and the county executive is the head of the executive branch. Like most county governments in the United States, the Milwaukee County government fulfills its duties largely out of public attention. The city and state governments are noticed more by the citizens and covered more by the media. Two county supervisors called the Milwaukee County government "the invisible level of government."[1] At the time of his third election as county executive, Ament was seen as a bland but competent executive who faced no foreseeable challenge to his position.

After having been elected county executive in 1992, 1996, and 2000, Ament and other county officials reconfigured the county pension formula that determines how much county employees receive when they retire. The reconfiguring was deemed necessary to attract and retain county employees without raising their pay. The new formula was passed easily by the County Board in 2001. When reporters began calculating the new formula's effect, they found that Ament would see a great increase for himself. If he won re-election in 2004, as everybody expected him to do, he would be eligible for a lump-sum retirement payment of more than $2 million and an annual pension of $98,000. Other long-time county employees would enjoy similar pensions.

When the public became aware of the pension numbers, the "invisible level of government" became the most visible. People formed an organization, Citizens for Responsible Government, that collected signatures to recall Ament. The recall effort quickly collected the signatures of more people than had voted for Ament in 2000. In January and the first half of February of 2002, virtually every local news report included something on the recall effort and calls for Ament to resign. Ament offered to forgo his right to his lump-sum payment, but calls for his resignation did not abate. On January 18, 2002, the major Milwaukee newspaper, *The Milwaukee Journal Sentinel*, called for him to resign. On February 21, he announced his resignation, effective February 26. Although there was no recall vote on Ament, since he resigned, several of the supervisors who had voted for the new pension formula were recalled.

When Ament was elected for the third time in 2000, people assumed that he could be re-elected in 2004 if he wanted to be. By the time he resigned in 2002, virtually nobody was speaking publicly on his behalf. Public opinion, in the form of a certain recall election, had forced Ament to resign. In short, people were appalled and repelled by the prospect of Ament receiving a pension as large as the new formula would give him. We can easily say that people had a very clear opinion by the time controversy was at its height.

But did people have opinions on government pensions before that? Did people even think about government pensions? It is improbable that, before the controversy began, even 1 percent of noncounty employees in the public could have described the pension system. But within a few months, public opinion caused an overhaul of county government.

In measuring public opinion, we need to understand that there are opinions "out there" that we cannot see. If somebody had thought to conduct a telephone survey of Milwaukee County voters in September 2001, before the controversy began, it is very unlikely that any voters would have voiced any opinions on county pensions. This episode, then, shows that there are limits to our ability to measure public opinion—and that there are limits to politicians' ability to ignore it.

1. Bruce Murphy, "Daddy Dearest," *Milwaukee Magazine,* January, 2002. www.milwaukeemagazine.com/012002/daddy_dearest.html

Perceived Majorities

The English poet and political journalist Alfred Austin once quipped that "public opinion is no more than this: what people think that other people think."[11] Perceived majorities are what people—especially elites like policymakers and politicians, but also journalists and even members of the mass public itself—think public opinion is on some topic. These perceptions may or may not correspond with mass opinion, and indeed may be derived from sources quite different from polls or elections, such as media coverage.

Perceptions of majority sentiment can be powerful shapers of elite actions, as policymakers try to respond to what they think the public wants. As mentioned earlier, passage of the PATRIOT Act may have had a lot to do with perceived majority opinion: The media were inundated with stories about terrorism, and how life in America would "never be the same," how freedom would have to be curtailed for security, and so forth. Such coverage, coupled with the general climate of opinion about terrorism, may have given elected officials the perception that the public favored stronger antiterrorism measures, even ones like greater surveillance that (as we saw in a poll measure of mass opinion) the public might not have actually favored.

Given our definition and theoretical approach, this book will primarily concern the "mass opinion" form of public opinion. However, it is useful to keep Herbst and Entman's referents in mind when analyzing how public opinion works in practice.

THE APPROACH OF THIS BOOK

This book will examine the many facets of public opinion, using two main perspectives or themes. The first sees the relationship between public opinion (what the people want) and public policy (what the government does) as a democratic dialogue between leaders and led. We see the role of public opinion essentially as a communication process whereby the people speak, and the government either responds or does not respond—and it may respond in several different ways. The people then react to the government's actions, and the government reacts to their opinions. Of course, in reality the process is not that simple. Different members of the public will say different things to the government. The people may speak clearly or ambiguously. They may speak directly to government officials or indirectly through elections or interest groups. The governmental leaders may hear, or not hear, what the people are saying, or they may hear a distorted version of the public's messages. In addition, governmental leaders may also try to influence public opinion to conform to what they, the leaders, want to do anyway—in essence, telling the people what to say. We call this entire process of the people communicating their opinions to the government, and the government's response, the *democratic dialogue.*

The second theme focuses on the sticky question of how much influence the public should have in government, as opposed to political leaders, experts, and so forth. If government is to follow public opinion, it is important to ask whether the public is up to the job. Are ordinary citizens, in a postmodern, complex society, really capable of governing themselves? At root is the fundamental question that has hounded democratic philosophers since the time of the ancient Greeks: Is the public wise or foolish? If the public is ignorant, whimsical, indecisive, or otherwise incompetent, then is it really a good idea to listen closely to what the people want? We term this the democratic dilemma: Should the government listen to the people? How much, and when should they do so?[12]

THE PEOPLE SPEAK: PUBLIC OPINION AND THE DEMOCRATIC DIALOGUE

Public opinion has been important to politics in the United States from the very beginning. On July 4, 1776, the third day of its existence,[13] the American government approved the Declaration of Independence. The document was an explanation of Congress's decision to break away from Britain. In it, Thomas Jefferson, the author, recognized that when "it becomes necessary for one people to dissolve the political bands which have connected them with another . . . a decent respect to the opinions of mankind requires that they should declare the causes which impel them to the separation." The Declaration, then, was written for the purpose of addressing "the opinions of mankind" or, as we would say today, public opinion. But Jefferson was writing the Declaration to do more than justify the decision for independence. He also wanted to influence public opinion to support the new United States in the war against Britain that had started more than a year before. He wanted those people who supported the rebellion to stand steadfast in its support, and he wanted those who were undecided to take up arms against the tyrant King George that he described later in the document. He also wanted to sway the opinion of King Louis XVI and his court in France to provide aid to the rebellion—clearly opinion, if not quite "public" opinion.

Photo 1.1. The concept of public opinion appears prominently in the Declaration of Independence, the very document which justified the creation of the United States. *Library of Congress.*

The Declaration proclaims a government in which public opinion would be an ultimate standard upon which governmental policies would be measured. The essential argument of the Declaration is that the government should act on the behalf of its citizens—do as they think it should. In this book, we will accept Jefferson's challenge and look at the nature of public opinion and its role in the current American government. We will examine how public opinion is, or is not, translated into public policy, what we label the *democratic dialogue*.

In the Declaration, Jefferson explains the theory of government upon which rested the decision for independence and, more importantly, the legitimacy of democratic government. Since Jefferson so succinctly summarizes the democratic theory of government, and the vital role of public opinion, it is worth quoting him at length. You have probably read, and maybe been forced to memorize, the second paragraph of the Declaration, but it is worth one more reading. As you read it, think in terms of public opinion and responsive government.

> We hold these Truths to be self-evident, that all Men are created equal, that they are endowed by their Creator with certain unalienable Rights, that among these are Life, Liberty, and the Pursuit of Happiness—That to secure these Rights, Governments are instituted among Men, deriving their just powers from the consent of the governed, that whenever any Form of Government becomes destructive of these Ends, it is the Right of the People to alter or to abolish it, and to institute new Government, laying its Foundation on such Principles, and organizing its powers in such Form, as to them shall seem most likely to effect their Safety and Happiness.

According to Jefferson, then, people create governments to protect their human rights. In turn, those governments derive "their just powers from the consent of the governed." Whenever a government does not secure the people's rights, "it is the Right of the People to alter or to abolish it. . . ." The people are then right to institute a new government. This new government will be organized in such a way that the people, in their opinion, "shall seem most likely to effect their Safety and Happiness." In this entire prescription for proper government, and in the determination of improper government, it is the opinion of people that matters most.

These ideas were not original with Jefferson. He himself claimed he just wrote what was considered common sense by educated people of his time. Many of the ideas expressed in the Declaration can be traced back to an English philosopher, John Locke. Locke, writing in the late 1600s, argued that each man is "by nature, free, equal and independent," and thus cannot be "subjected to the political power of another without his consent."[14]

Indeed, the essential spirit of the Declaration represented a culmination of Western thought extending back to the ancient Greeks ("democracy" itself takes its name from Greek words meaning "the people rule"). Still, it can be argued that the foundations for the first modern democratic government—one that would actually allow the voices of ordinary citizens to have weight in political decisions—were laid on that day in 1776.

The Role of the Public in Democratic Government

If *democracy* means "rule by the people," government should abide by the popular will. In other words, public opinion is crucial to the conduct of democratic government; without it, democracy fails—by definition.

Of course, it is a sheer impossibility for government to do what *all* of "the people" want. Therefore, we must first understand democracy to be at work if government does what the *majority* wants. Since the majority, by definition, is most of the people, this is an easy democratic shortcut, although it also leads to important questions about the role of the minority or minorities, as the example of the PATRIOT Act shows.

It is also impractical, as the creators of the American republic realized, for the public to govern directly. The Framers accepted the basic idea of *representative democracy*—namely, that leaders make policy in the name of their followers. Therefore, the role of public opinion in a democracy is to provide the benchmark for the people's representatives to do what a majority of the public wants.

But how does the government *know* what the public wants? Clearly, the public must make their wishes known for democracy to be effective; they must communicate their concerns to policymakers. Likewise, the government must have a means for *listening*, or receiving the people's messages, so that it can enact the people's desires into governmental policies.

How much, and in what ways, public opinion affects governmental policies depends on many variables: Who speaks—everyone, or only a select few? Are they all equally important? Do politicians listen—and what do they hear? Do they obey? And finally, should they obey? These are some of the questions addressed in this book.

PUBLIC OPINION AND THE DEMOCRATIC DILEMMA

Eleven years after Jefferson and his colleagues in the Continental Congress wrote the Declaration of Independence, another group of men wrote the U.S. Constitution.[15] They incorporated the basic Jeffersonian idea of the government emanating from the people. The Constitution itself begins with the words, "We, the people...." Probably the most important aspect of the Constitution concerning public opinion is that it allows ordinary people the right to vote. In the Constitution, all the members of the national government are either elected directly by the people or chosen by those who are elected by the people. There are elections at regular intervals that nobody can postpone or cancel.

But despite believing in the basic idea of popular sovereignty, the Constitutional Framers saw the need to temper the impact of public opinion— to erect barriers between the will of the people and the actions of the government. The Framers thought that any government had to be based on the people—but many of them, however, had rather dim views of the people. They thought public opinion could be volatile, passionate, and shortsighted. They were afraid that if left unchecked, the people could create a tyranny of the majority and trample on the minority's rights; in the end, the people would destroy the very government that gave them power.

In *Federalist* No. 10, James Madison, often called the "father of the Constitution," summarized of the Framers' view on popular direct democracy, as opposed to representative democracy:

> [D]emocracies have ever been spectacles of turmoil and contention; have ever been found incompatible with personal security or the rights of property; and have in general been as short in their lives as they have been violent in their deaths.[16]

More rational, educated men were needed to stand between the opinions of the masses and the actions for the government. For example, Madison, also in *Federalist* No. 10, said that representatives of the people could "refine and enlarge the public views" and furthermore, he wrote, "It may well happen that the public voice, pronounced by the representatives of the people, will be more consonant to the public good than if pronounced by the people themselves. . . ."[17]

Madison was not proposing that the people walk away and leave governing to their representatives. In the same paragraph, he went on to say, "On the other hand, the effect may be inverted. Men of facetious tempers, of local prejudices, or of sinister designs, may, by intrigue, by corruption, or by other means, first obtain the suffrages, and then betray the interests of the people." [18]

Nevertheless, Madison, like the bulk of the Framers, did not think the public should have a *direct say* in matters of public policy. In *Federalist* No. 49, Madison argued against the idea of allowing disputes to be settled by appeals to the public convention and in favor of government intervention to control public passions:

> still, it [a hypothetical dispute] could never be expected to turn on the true merits of the question. It would inevitably be connected with the spirit of pre-existing parties, or of parties springing out of the question itself . . . [or] would be connected with persons of distinguished character and extensive influence in the community. The *passions*, therefore, not the *reason*, of the public would sit in judgment. But it is the reason, alone, of the public, that ought to control and regulate the government. The passions ought to be controlled and regulated by the government. [emphasis in original][19]

In *Federalist* No. 71, Alexander Hamilton perhaps best summed up the Framers' view of the proper relationship between popular opinion and government policies—that the government should be based on the "deliberate sense of the community" but not ruled by it:

> The republican principle demands that the deliberate sense of the community should govern the conduct of those to whom they intrust the management of their affairs; but it does not require an unqualified complaisance to every sudden breeze of passion, or to every transient impulse, which the people may receive from the arts of men, who flatter their prejudices to betray their interests.[20]

Influenced by Hamilton and others like him at the Constitutional Convention, the Framers erected a series of barriers to limit ordinary people's influence. The first was that most of the government was chosen indirectly, rather than directly, by the people; in other words, there was somebody standing between the people and the officeholders. In fact, in the Constitution, the people directly elected only the House of Representatives. State legislatures chose the Senate (although now we have amended the Constitution so that the people also directly elect senators). The Electoral College chose the president. The president chose judges, subject to confirmation by the Senate. The judges, once chosen, served as long as they wished, independent of Congress and the president—and therefore independent of public opinion.

Second, the government was, and still is, limited. Every power of the government—and by extension every desire of the people—must be included or implied in the Constitution. Even if public opinion desperately wanted the government to do something, the government would not be allowed to do it unless it were specified or implied in the Constitution. Over the years, there has been a great deal of debate about what is implied in the Constitution, but there is agreement that the government is limited, not only in its powers but in its ability to respond to the public's immediate wishes.

The third barrier to public opinion was the provision that the government was forbidden from doing several things. Section 9 of Article I lists many of them. The government, for example, could not tax exports, could not enact *ex post facto* laws (punishing people for crimes that weren't illegal at the time they were committed), and so on. Even if the people want the government to enact one of these forbidden laws, it cannot do so.

The fourth set of limitations appeared in 1791, when the first ten amendments to the Constitution were ratified. A long new list of prohibitions limited the government and, by extension, the will of the people electing the government. In the First Amendment alone, Congress was limited in five ways because it could make no law

- Respecting the establishment of religion, or prohibiting the free exercise thereof
- Abridging the freedom of speech
- Abridging the freedom of the press
- Abridging the freedom of the people peaceably to assemble
- Abridging the freedom of the people to petition the government for a redress of grievances.

The freedoms laid out in the first ten amendments are limitations on what the government can do, so they are "freedoms" held by the people. But, at the same time, they are limitations on what the people can do themselves by working through the government. The people, even an overwhelming majority, are forbidden from using the government for certain purposes. The First Amendment declares that, "Congress shall make no law. . . ." Theoretically, the people cannot sacrifice their rights, even if they want to.

The Constitution thus reflects an underlying tension between the desire to allow the people input into government and to ultimately hold leaders accountable on the one hand, and the belief that the public is not to be fully trusted with the reins of government on the other. As Jeremy Belknap, a member of the Constitutional Convention, put it: "Let it stand as a principle that government originates from the people; but let the people be taught that. . . . They are not able to govern themselves."[21] The Framers did not trust an elite to govern without popular consent, but neither did they trust the masses to make wise decisions, as their limits on popular input attest.

RECENT VIEWS ON THE ROLE OF PUBLIC OPINION

The balancing act laid out in the Constitution has outlined the issue of public opinion for the entire history of the Republic. For example, the debate over the quality of public opinion was renewed in the first half of the twentieth century, largely in the writings of two political commentators, Walter Lippmann and John Dewey.

Lippmann, echoing the views of the Founders, believed that the modern world was too complex for most people to understand and that ordinary people are not especially interested in politics and are not capable of knowing enough about political issues to help guide the government. They are particularly ignorant of matters of which they do not have personal experience, especially foreign affairs. According to Lippmann, ordinary people work only with stereotypes and are not capable of understanding politics. He said that the "primary defect of popular government" is that members of the public are characterized by "violent prejudice, apathy, preferences for the curious trivial as against the dull important, and the hunger for sideshows and three legged calves."[22] But even if the people improved their character, they still would not know enough to guide the government because they simply do not spend enough time learning about political issues to understand them. He calculated that well-informed people spent about half an hour a day reading newspapers. That, he claimed, is not enough to really understand government; reasonable division of labor should lead to the best-informed and most intelligent people guiding public policy. "It is not possible to assume that a world, carried on by division of labor and distribution of authority, can be governed by universal opinions in the whole population."[23] Lippmann favored establishing a network of expert administrators in "intelligence bureaus" who would be responsible for governing. Ordinary people would not be "burdened" with a great deal of information they could not use. "The purpose, then, is not to burden every citizen with expert opinions on all questions, but to push that burden away from him towards the responsible administrator."[24]

John Dewey on the other hand, following in the footsteps of Thomas Jefferson, believed that ordinary citizens were capable of making wise choices and effectively influencing governmental decisions, provided that good information and education were available. He believed public opinion could be the basis for true democratic government.

> Democracy is a way of personal life controlled not merely by faith in human nature in general but by faith in the capacity of human beings for intelligent judgment and action if the proper conditions are furnished. . . . For what is the faith of democracy in the role of consultation, of conference, of persuasion, of discussion, in formation of public opinion . . . except faith in the capacity of the intelligence of the common man to respond with common sense to the free play of facts and ideas which are secured by effective guarantees of free inquiry, free assembly, and free communication?[25]

He also argued that through proper education, training, and especially participation in public affairs, people would become fuller and more competent citizens.

Dewey thus recognized that the role of the citizen in the modern world was difficult, but at the same time he rejected rule by an elite, even if it were educated and benevolent, like the one Lippman advocated. Dewey argued that individual citizens need not be experts on everything, but "what is required is that they have the ability to judge the bearing of the knowledge supplied by others upon common concerns."[26] Indeed, he foresaw government listening even more closely to the people:

> That government exists to serve its community, and that this purpose cannot be achieved unless the community itself shares in selecting its governors and determining its policies, are a deposit of fact left, as far as we can see, permanently. . . . We have every reason to think that whatever changes may take place in existing democratic machinery, they will be of a sort to make the interest of the public a more supreme guide and criterion of governmental activity, and to enable the public to form and manifest its purposes still more authoritatively. In this sense, the cure for the ailments of democracy is more democracy.[27]

Two Divergent Views: George Gallup and Lindsay Rogers

With the advent of public opinion polling in the 1930s and 1940s, the debate over public opinion became more centered on the polls. There were many spokespersons on each side, but two individuals best summed up the opposing perspectives of the time—George H. Gallup and Lindsay Rogers. Gallup, the first famous modern pollster, and probably the most famous of all time, argued that polls could accurately measure public opinion and would therefore strengthen American democracy. Rogers, on the other hand, said that polls could not accurately measure public opinion, which, he said, was a good thing, because doing so would actually diminish American democracy.

Gallup, writing in 1948, believed that modern polling made it possible to achieve an important goal of democracy—to make "the will of the majority . . . ascertainable at all times."[28] He wrote that public opinion polls could take the guesswork out determining the people's will. Polls could improve democracy by

lessening the power of interest groups. Polls could show how members of interest groups, as opposed to their leaders, felt about issues—as well as show how
ordinary people felt. As he put it, "Public opinion polls can not only deflate the
claims of pressure groups and of minorities seeking special privilege, but, more
importantly, they can reveal the will of the inarticulate and unorganized majority of citizens."[29]

Gallup did not advocate turning over the government to polls. He said,
"The public cannot be expected to render sound judgments on problems or
issues about which they are ill informed" nor "have intelligent views regarding matters of a wholly technical nature."[30] He also said that political leaders
should not change principles in order to conform to polls, but the leaders
would govern more effectively if they understood public opinion. Indeed,

> great leaders will seek information from every reliable source about the people they
> wish to lead. . . . The public opinion poll will be a useful tool in enabling them to
> reach the highest level of their effectiveness as leaders. . . . The answer to the ques-
> tion [of whether the country will suffer when leaders pay too much attention to
> polls] is not that the country will suffer when its leaders begin to pay a lot of atten-
> tion to public opinion polls. The country will suffer when its leaders ignore, or make
> wrong guesses about the public's views on important issues."[31]

Lindsay Rogers, in a 1949 book *The Pollsters,* said that if Gallup really could
"ascertain" public opinion at all times, "it would be frightening." "Fortunately,"
he said, "it is not true."[32] Rogers said that pollsters really do not "ascertain"
public opinion through polling. First, polling is based on "the answers persons
give to strangers" [the interviewers]. Poll respondents are unlikely to feel comfortable with strangers and are more likely to reveal their "public" thoughts
instead of their "private" thoughts. Even if individuals answered honestly, they
could not be expected to give reasoned responses. "They have to give their
instantaneous reactions to propositions that they may have considered for the
first time." Second, public opinion is constantly changing, and measuring it is
like trying to measure the length of a jellyfish.[33]

Third, he said that polls give every respondent equal importance, which is
not at all how public opinion works. In real public opinion, some people are
more knowledgeable about some issues, care much more about certain issues,
and have much more influence than others over issues—but in a poll, each person is the same as every other person. Even people who have no information
about an issue but answer questions about it are counted in poll results, and
there are very many people who have little information. He said, "there is an
extremely large class . . . that is indifferent. It reads little and thinks less." And
since that class makes up a large proportion of the population, it counts for
much in polling. Fourth, because of most people's limited knowledge about
politics, extremely complex controversies must be reduced to very simple
terms, thereby distorting the issues. Questions must be reduced to "yes,"
"no," or "don't know." Rogers said, "Instead of feeling the pulse of democracy, Dr. Gallup listens to its baby talk."[34]

In the end, Rogers concluded that public opinion polling may be suitable for predicting election results. "But the method is not suitable for measuring public opinion on the foreign or domestic proposals that statesmen may make."[35] But Rogers did not regret the limitations of polling. In fact, he thought that public opinion as determined by polling *should not* have much influence in day-to-day policy decisions. He referred to the conviction of the eighteenth-century English political leader Edmund Burke that statesmen should use their judgment in governing and not be shackled by public opinion. Rogers quoted Burke favorably in his explanation of his role as a Member of Parliament:

> I knew that you chose me, in my place, along with others, to be a pillar of the state, and not a weathercock on the top of the edifice, exalted for my levity and versatility, and of no use but to indicate the shifting of every fashionable gale.[36]

The Democratic Dilemma Today

The implicit debate between the perspectives of Jefferson and Hamilton, Dewey and Lippmann, and Gallup and Rogers continues on in political science (and even in other fields that also study public opinion, such as sociology, psychology, and communications). The balancing between the sovereignty of the people and prudent checks on their will is not of historical importance only; it continues to be important even today, as the opening story about the PATRIOT Act demonstrates. Given the widespread focus placed by politicians, the press, and other observers on "what the public thinks," coupled with the vast powers of today's government and its potential for misuse by leaders with popular approval, how much influence the people's voice should have in government is even more of an issue than it was for the Founders.

CONCLUSION

The public is the vital backbone of our democratic process. But what role public opinion does—and should—play exactly in the American political system at the beginning of the twenty-first century remains unclear. Does the government listen to what the people say? How often, and in what ways, does what the people want become what the government does? Do "we, the people" speak wisely? Should governmental leaders listen to us, or should they follow their own inclinations or those of experts (whoever they may be)? We will explore these issues throughout the remainder of the book. But as a part of "the public," it's important that you struggle with these questions too and come up with your own answers.

Suggested Reading

Dewey, John. *The Public and its Problems*. Athens, OH: Ohio University Press, 1954.

Gallup, George. *A Guide to Public Opinion Polls*. Princeton: Princeton University Press, 1948.

Key, Jr., V. O. *Public Opinion and American Democracy*. New York: Alfred A. Knopf, 1961.

Lippmann, Walter. *Public Opinion*. New York: The Free Press, 1922.

Rogers, Lindsay. *The Pollsters: Public Opinion, Politics, and Democratic Leadership*. New York: Alfred A. Knopf, 1949.

Notes

1. Thomas Jefferson, in a letter to William Findley, March 24, 1801, accessed at http://memory.loc.gov/cgi-bin/query/r?ammem/mtj:@field(DOCID+@lit(tj090115).

2. Sir Robert Peel, source unknown.

3. Lydia Saad, "Americans Generally Comfortable With Patriot Act," *The Gallup Organization*, accessed at www.gallup.com, March 2, 2004, p. 2.

4. Fox News/Opinion Dynamics poll, October 17, 2001; Gallup Poll, October 19, 2001; both accessed from the Roper Center Archives on Lexis/Nexis. For a discussion of the possible ramifications of the PATRIOT Act on civil liberties, and the lack of deliberation in its passage, see Nancy Chang, *Silencing Political Dissent: How Post-September 11 Anti-Terrorism Measures Threaten Our Civil Liberties* (New York: Seven Stories Press, 2002), pp. 43–66.

5. Support for this model of Congressional voting behavior comes from R. Douglas Arnold, *The Logic of Congressional Action* (New Haven: Yale University Press, 1990); reasons for believing presidents also engage in this sort of action are found in Benjamin I. Page, *Choices and Echoes in Presidential Elections* (Chicago: U. Chicago Press, 1978). Obviously, given their dates of publication, neither of these sources give evidence supporting this conclusion with the PATRIOT Act specifically, but it seems a reasonable and relevant application given the circumstances.

6. See David Domke, *God Willing? Political Fundamentalism in the White House, the "War on Terror," and an Echoing Press* (Ann Arbor, MI: Pluto Press, 2004); and William Safire, "Acronymania: Creating Weird Titles to Spell Catchy Words," *New York Times Magazine*, February 24, 2002, p. 13.

7. Justice Potter Stewart wrote this in a concurring opinion for *Jacobellis v. Ohio* (1964), a case about indecency and freedom of the press. The complete quote is: "I shall not today attempt further to define the kinds of material I understand to be embraced within that shorthand description [hard-core pornography]; and perhaps I could never succeed in intelligibly doing so. But I know it when I see it. . . ."

8. We borrowed some of the language of this paragraph from Vincent Price, *Public Opinion* (Newbury Park, CA: Sage, 1992), p. 46.

9. Robert M. Entman and Susan Herbst, "Reframing Public Opinion as We Have Known It," in W. Lance Bennett and Robert M. Entman, eds., *Mediated Politics: Communication in the Future of Democracy* (New York: Cambridge University Press, 2001), pp. 203–225.

10. See V. O. Key, *Public Opinion and American Democracy* (New York: Knopf, 1961); and Entman and Herbst, "Reframing Public Opinion."

11. From Alfred Austin, *Prince Lucifer* (London: Macmillan, 1887), accessed at http://www.geocities.com/Athens/Oracle/6517/56.htm.

12. Of course, there are many kinds of "democratic dilemmas," and the term does not originate with us. For example, one set of scholars uses it to refer to the question of whether citizens can become politically knowledgeable (see Arthur Lupia and Mathew D. McCubbins, *The Democratic Dilemma: Can Citizens Learn What They Need to Know?* New York: Cambridge University Press, 1998). For a usage and discussion that is close to the one we use here, see Kay Lehman Schlozman, "Vox Populi," *The Brookings Review* Vol. 21, Issue 3 (Summer 2003): 4–7.

13. The Continental Congress voted for independence on July 2, 1776. Two days later, it approved the Declaration of Independence.

14. Quoted in James David Barber, *The Book of Democracy* (New York: Pearson, 1995), p. 368.

15. Six men signed both the Declaration of Independence and the Constitution.

16. Alexander Hamilton, James Madison, and John Jay, *The Federalist Papers* (New York: Mentor Books, 1961), p. 81.

17. Ibid., p. 82.

18. Ibid., p. 82.

19. Ibid., p. 317.

20. Ibid., p. 432.

21. Jackson Turner Main, *What the Anti-Federalists Were For* (Chicago: University of Chicago Press, 1981), p. 163.

22. Walter Lippmann, *Public Opinion* (New York: The Free Press, 1922), p. 230.

23. Ibid., p. 228.

24. Ibid., pp. 250–251.

25. From John Dewey, "Creative Democracy," accessed at http://www.Beloit.edu/~pbk/dewey.html, pg. 2. Originally published in *John Dewey and the Promise of America*, Progressive Education Booklet No. 14 (Columbus, OH: American Education Press, 1939).

26. John Dewey. *The Public and its Problems* (New York: Henry Holt Co., 1927), p. 209.

27. Ibid., p. 146.

28. George Gallup, *A Guide to Public Opinion Polls* (Princeton: Princeton University Press, 1948), p. 4.

29. Ibid., p. 5.

30. Ibid., p. 7.

31. Ibid., p. 8.

32. Lindsay Rogers, *The Pollsters: Public Opinion, Politics, and Democratic Leadership* (New York: Alfred A. Knopf, 1949), p. 3.

33. Ibid., p. 58.

34. Ibid., p. 17.

35. Ibid., p. 237.

36. Ibid., p. 217.

Measuring Public Opinion: Survey Research

"Polls are the worst way of measuring public opinion . . . except for all the others."

—Humphrey Taylor[1]

Questions to Think About

In this chapter and the next, we will look at ways in which political scientists learn about people's opinions. Here, we will examine surveys, also knows as polls. As you read this chapter, ask yourself:

- How would you ask a person for his or her opinion on an issue? Choose an issue and write a question. Ask somebody that question. How well did you learn that person's opinion?
- How many students at your college or university would you need to interview to determine the opinions of the student body on several political issues? How would you choose them?
- How do you think the students' political opinions at your institution compare to the political opinions of all Americans?

THE STUDY of public opinion is not a new phenomenon. Governments have paid attention to public opinion as long as there have been governments. Even the most oppressive tyrants need to know what the people are thinking, if only to oppress them more effectively. As the famous investigator of public opinion, V. O. Key, Jr., said, "Governments must concern themselves with the opinions of their citizens, if only to provide a basis for repression of disaffection."[2]

But the formal study of public opinion has developed only within the last eighty years or so. Scientific survey research, for example, was not used to study the attitudes and opinions of people until the 1930s. In this chapter and the next, we will examine the most important methods currently used for ascertaining and studying public opinion. In these two chapters, we will divide research methodologies into two main types: **survey research** (this chapter) and everything else (the next chapter). We give special attention to survey research because of its prominence in the study of political opinion.

As you read these chapters, think about the *democratic dialogue*. How public opinion is measured plays a vital role in the democratic dialogue of connecting what the people want with what the government does. For government to implement majority sentiment accurately, it must listen to the people and "hear" them correctly. Therefore, which indicators of public opinion that politicians rely upon in making their decisions, and even whether they consult measures of public opinion at all, are key questions for the strength of the public opinion-policy linkage.

Also think of the *democratic dilemma*. If political officials can measure public opinion, should they follow its counsel? How do they know if their reading is accurate? There are many subtle ways to unintentionally draw a biased sample or write a biased question. Should formal scientific methods, such as surveys, be trusted and informal unscientific methods, such as letters from constituents, be given less credence? Even if the data are *absolutely guaranteed* to be accurate (realistically an impossibility), should political leaders follow the people's will, even if they think another course of action would be preferable? Or should they, remembering Alexander Hamilton (from Chapter One), acknowledge that although "the deliberate sense of the community should govern" their conduct, they are under no obligation to comply "to every sudden breeze of passion or every transient impulse?"*

Before we start our explanation of survey research, let us begin with a story. It is the story of a magazine, *The Literary Digest*, and its effort to predict the outcome of the 1936 presidential election. It is a perfect bad example. That is, it demonstrates how bad methodology leads to bad, inaccurate results.

The Literary Digest was a popular magazine that had correctly predicted several elections before 1936. The magazine's method of ascertaining voters' intentions was to mail out "ballots" to millions of people and then count the "ballots" that were mailed back. In 1936, the magazine mailed about 10 million "ballots" to people who had telephones and owned automobiles. About two million people mailed them back. With great confidence, *The Literary Digest* announced that Alfred Landon would be the next president.

Have you ever heard of President Landon? We think not. Mr. Landon received 36.5 percent of the popular votes and only eight electoral votes (Maine and Vermont). Keep this story in mind. We will return to it later as we discuss mistakes to avoid when conducting survey research.

---

*Alexander Hamilton, James Madison, and John Jay, "Federalist No. 71," The Federalist Papers (New York: Mentor Books, 1961). p. 432.

The most common method, by far, for learning about public opinion is the sample survey. In a sample survey, researchers ask a few hundred or a few thousand people their opinions about the issues being considered. When applied to political use, such as in election campaigns, survey research is often called "polling," and survey research studies are called "polls." The key to understanding survey research is that a few people are asked questions, and their answers are generalized to a much larger population. Typically, around 400 to 3,000 people are included in surveys, and their answers are generalized to populations ranging from several thousand to several million people. Survey research works only if the small sample of people is representative of the larger population. Researchers care about the answers of the people they interview because those answers represent what all the people in the population would say if they were asked. For survey research to work, a small number of respondents must represent thousands or millions of people in a population.

TYPES OF SURVEYS

There are basically five ways to survey people: face-to-face interviews, telephone interviews, mail surveys, exit polls, and Internet surveys.

Face-to-Face Interviews

In face-to-face interviews, interviewers talk with respondents in person, usually in their homes. At one time, this was the most common type of surveying, but it is used much less today. Two important surveys that have traditionally used face-to-face interviews—we will often refer to them in this book—are the General Social Survey (GSS) and the National Election Study (NES). The advantage of face-to-face surveys is that the questionnaires can be very long (sometimes over an hour) and more complex because the interviewer can explain the questions to the respondents. In addition, the interviewer can use visual aids, such as pictures or scales. Scales are often used in many types of surveys, but they are easier to visualize in a survey where the respondent can actually see the scale. For example, in one type of question the respondent places herself on a "thermometer" scale in evaluating somebody, such as an elected official. The "thermometer" has 100 degrees. If the respondent really likes the official, she would place herself at "100," but if she really disliked the official, she would place herself at "zero." Although this respondent could place herself on the scale in any form of survey, it is easier in a survey where she could see a picture of a thermometer.

There are four serious drawbacks to face-to-face surveys. The first one is that the respondents are unlikely to give embarrassing or socially unacceptable answers because they do not want the interviewer to think badly of them.

Questions on race are especially sensitive in face-to-face interviews. Another problem is that the entire survey process could take a long time to complete, especially since a great deal of time is taken up driving to respondents' homes. A third problem is that there is very little control over the setting of the interviews. Research organizations trust their interviewers, but they cannot check up on them in a large proportion of interviews to see that they are asking the questions correctly.

But the most important problem with face-to-face surveys is their cost. Considering that interviewers have to drive to respondents' homes—and if they are not at home may have to drive back again—the cost of interviewers' salaries can skyrocket. Largely to save money, the NES has included telephone interviews in the last few surveys. The NES was conducted entirely by telephone in 2002, but the 2004 survey was conducted in person.

Telephone Interviews

The most common type of public opinion survey conducted today is a telephone survey. If you read about a poll in a newspaper or magazine or hear about it on television, it was probably conducted over the telephone. Almost all polls conducted by politicians and by media companies, such as newspapers and television networks, are conducted over the telephone. Telephone surveys have some advantages over face-to-face surveys, especially in their much lower cost and faster implementation. If speed is very important, telephone polls can be completed overnight. They also have the advantage that interviewers can be closely supervised so that a high quality can be maintained. Supervisors have the ability to monitor telephone interviews at random times, without the knowledge of the interviewers, so mistakes in interviews can be corrected quickly.

Telephone interviewing today is usually conducted with the assistance of computers. This type of interviewing is called Computer Assisted Telephone Interviewing (CATI). With CATI, interviewers read questions off the computer screens and enter the answers directly into the computer databases. The computer can assist the interviewers by automatically skipping irrelevant questions (such as not asking nonvoters whom they voted for); it can also allow the researcher to experiment with different question wordings by randomly asking different respondents different versions of questions.

The most important drawbacks to telephone surveys are their simplicity and short length. It is very difficult to receive meaningful answers for complex or long questions. People simply have a difficult time processing complex questions over the telephone. The interviewers can help, but they cannot show pictures over the phone. Another drawback is the short length. Whereas face-to-face interviews can last over an hour, telephone interviews seldom take more than twenty minutes. (Some telephone surveys do take forty to sixty minutes, but it is unclear how alert the respondents are by the end of the interviews.) Another problem is the unexpected intrusive nature of phone surveys; although it not true that every telephone survey takes place just as supper is beginning, it seems that way.

Preelection polls have an added limitation. Since many people who answer the questions about their intended vote will actually not vote, analysts need to "correct" for nonvoters. To do this, voters are asked if they are registered to vote and how likely they are to vote. In addition, projections of likelihood of voting can be based on respondents' past voting turnout (as revealed by the respondents) and demographic characteristics. Since nobody knows who is *really* going to vote, nobody knows precisely what the voting projections should be. Different methods of "correcting" for nonvoters have different advocates, but nobody knows for sure exactly which correction factors work best.

Mail Surveys

Mail surveys are seldom used today in political research. Although they can be less expensive than telephone surveys, their drawbacks are usually too great to overlook. The first main drawback is that they are slow; it may take several weeks to conduct a simple mail survey. Another problem is that the response rate tends to be very low, often under 30 percent, so that it is questionable how well the respondents represent the larger population. (Some advocates of mail surveys point out that telephone surveys also can have extremely low response rates. We will address response rates later in this chapter.) The third main drawback is that it is impossible to determine who actually answered the questions. Did the intended respondent answer the questions, or did his teenage daughter do it? Or did he get his buddies to help him and give consensus answers? It is impossible to tell.

Besides low cost, mail surveys have three main potential advantages. First, pictures or other visual aids can be included to illustrate the questions; just as with face-to-face interviews, respondents can see visual scales to help them conceptualize the questions. Second, respondents can answer the questions when convenient; they can also have time to consider the questions, and their answers may be more thoughtful. Finally, the questionnaires can be anonymous, so respondents can give embarrassing, socially unacceptable, but honest answers without fear of being identified. For example, in a recent survey conducted for a state department of transportation, people who had lost their driver's licenses, mostly for drunk driving, were asked how often they drove illegally. Since the questionnaires were not identified, the respondents knew they could answer the question without fear of repercussions. Most of them did report driving illegally, and 17 percent said they drove illegally every day.[3] This survey had the typical disadvantages of mail surveys in that the response rate was under 30 percent, and the researchers did not know for sure who answered the questions. However, the researchers were convinced that drivers without valid driver's licenses would not answer honestly on the telephone and thought that a mail survey would yield the most honest answers.[4] Of course, if the mail questionnaires are identified, as with ID numbers, this advantage disappears.

One variation of the mail survey is an in-class survey. If you wanted to sample 10 percent of the students in your college or university, you might try to find a representative sample of students—or you might want to find a representative sample of classes. You could hand out the questionnaire to each class and then collect them after the students have had time to complete them. In an institutional setting, this is often the best way to sample people. It tends to be quick and cheap—and almost always easier—and has the advantage that the responses are anonymous.

Exit Polls

Exit polls are administered to voters immediately after they have voted and are leaving the polling places. Polling precincts are sampled so that they are representative of the jurisdiction. Exit polls have an important advantage over preelection telephone polls because all respondents really are voters; nobody

"Yes, Myra, I do still love you. What I don't love, however, is this exit poll every damned morning."

© The New Yorker Collection 1992 Jack Ziegler from cartoonbank.com

Photo 2.1. Exit polls of voters leaving election polling stations are used to predict and analyze election results. Here, a young woman fills out a Los Angeles Times poll. © *Bob Daemmrich/The Image Works.*

needs to "correct" for likelihood of voting. Some practicing politicians place great faith in these polls. Dick Morris, a former political aide for President Bill Clinton, wrote, "Exit polls are almost never wrong."[5]

Exit polls are typically conducted for the media. In the 2004 election, the Associated Press and five television networks (ABC, CBS, CNN, Fox, and NBC) pooled their resources in the National Election Pool. They hired Edison Media Research and Mitofsky International to conduct the polls. Respondents were asked how they voted and for several demographic characteristics.

Sometimes, the sample sizes are very large; in 2004, for example, the National Election Pool sample consisted of 13,660 voters. The results are used for three main purposes. The first purpose is to give the media sources to "call" the election on election night. It may be disconcerting to watch a television network anchor say "CBS calls Indiana for Bush" when only 2 percent of the votes have been counted, but exit poll results tend to be accurate enough to reliably "call" states. However, there was some controversy over exit polls in the 2004 election. Some people said the results were too far off to be credible, while others claimed that they had been "adjusted" to be more in line with the vote totals.[6]

The second use of exit polls is to estimate how different demographic groups voted. For example, the 2004 National Election Pool showed that President Bush won 55 percent of the male vote while Senator Kerry won 51 percent of the female vote.[7]

Sometimes exit poll results have been used to challenge the results of elections. Dick Morris said when he was working for Vicente Fox, a presidential candidate in Mexico, he used exit poll results to claim victory. He said he released the results on election day to prevent the other side from stealing the election. In a presidential election in Ukraine on November 21, 2004, supporters of challenger Viktor Yuschenko used exit poll results to claim that he had won the election and that the official election results, showing Prime Minister Viktor Yanukovych to be the winner, were fraudulent.[8] A new election was held later, and Yuschenko won.

Internet Surveys

The fifth survey method is Internet surveys. The questions in an Internet survey may be much like those in mail surveys, but they are answered online. Internet surveys have some advantages and one big disadvantage.[9] The first advantage of conducting surveys over the Internet is that thousands of people can be contacted quickly. It is possible to contact more than 100,000 people in one day—something that would simply be impossible or intolerably expensive with other methods. If large numbers of people reply to the questionnaire, respondents in very small population subsets can be identified, such as, for example, black conservatives with Master's degrees. It is also possible to segment the respondents into very precise subgroups. For example, in a telephone survey it would probably not be possible to compare Protestant and Catholic white men with college degrees between the ages of eighteen and twenty-four because of small sample sizes. But it could be possible in an Internet survey if the total sample were 50,000.

A second advantage is that the respondents can see varied visual stimuli or hear music or campaign speeches. Researchers can vary the colors, the words, or the sounds in many different ways and get better ideas of how people respond.

A third advantage is cost. Although there can be a considerable expense for the computers and Internet access, as well as writing and programming the questionnaire, there are no expenses for postage or printing; in addition, it is extremely cheap to recontact potential respondents who do not reply. Multiple contacts are likely to increase the response rate. It is also very easy to reward respondents for sending back completed questionnaires. Whereas it can be very cumbersome and expensive to mail $5.00 to a respondent as a way of saying thanks, it is easy in an online survey to send a coupon for Amazon.com to give a potential respondent a tangible reason to respond. Fourth, an Internet survey can be an iterative process; if necessary, a researcher can easily follow up with questions after respondents send in their completed questionnaires.

Because they are essentially mail surveys, Internet surveys have some of the same characteristics of snail mail surveys. One of them, an advantage, is that the respondent can answer when it is convenient, not when an interviewer calls. Another advantage common to mail surveys is that the contact can be personalized. In addition, online respondents tend to answer much faster than snail mail respondents. Respondents also tend to give more complete answers to questions that require written sentences (open-ended questions) than they do when writing out answers by hand.[10] Another common characteristic with ordinary mail surveys, a disadvantage, is that the researcher cannot control who actually answers the questions. A difference from mail surveys is that responses are not anonymous; it is easy for a researcher to tell who sent the survey response. In fact, if a respondent sends in a completed questionnaire from work, an employer could intercept it.

The most important disadvantage of Internet surveys is that they are unlikely to be representative of people as a whole. Only those who complete questionnaires over the Internet, a small percentage of the American population, are eligible to participate in these surveys, so the samples are not representative of the entire United States. According to a 2004 telephone survey,[11] approximately 59 percent of American adults use the Internet; of these people a smaller proportion answer questionnaires online. People who do not complete questionnaires online have no chance of being included in an Internet survey. However, some researchers point out that nonrepresentativeness may not be as large a problem as it first appears to be. The demographics of an Internet sample are not necessarily unlike the demographics of the American public; several companies that conduct Internet surveys make sure that the demographics of their samples are generally representative of Americans. James Witte and Philip E. N. Howard[12] have noted that the Internet's advantages of extremely large sample sizes may compensate for the disadvantage of nonrepresentativeness. With extremely large samples, meaningful comparison can be made between subgroups of respondents, so that even if the sample as a whole is not representative, comparisons between groups within the sample may accurately reflect differences between those groups of people.

Witte and Howard also point out that the difference between the "unrepresentative" Internet and the "representative" telephone survey is not necessarily as great as it seems.[13] Because of the proliferation of cell phones and the public's declining cooperation rates with telephone surveys, the representativeness of telephone surveys is also questionable. We will discuss cooperation rates later in this chapter, but while nobody is now saying that Internet surveys are as representative as ones conducted by telephone, some researchers do say the gap is closing. Witte and Howard compare the status of Internet surveys today with the status of telephone surveys in the 1930s. You may recall that the "perfect bad example" of *The Literary Digest,* cited earlier in this chapter, involved sampling from lists of automobile owners and telephone subscribers, two groups of Americans who were nonrepresentative in 1936 but would not be nearly as unrepresentative today. As the Internet proliferates, Internet users will also become more representative of Americans as a whole.

In an effort to make use of the Internet's advantages, some commercial firms are developing lists of e-mail addresses from households that have given permission for the companies to use them as survey respondents. One such firm, Survey Sampling International, has a list of over 1.5 million American households' e-mail addresses. Although these lists are typically used by businesses, the people in the households are classified by party identification, so it is possible to survey only Republicans or Democrats.[14] Such a commercially prepared sample is not the same as a real random sample drawn by the most sophisticated methods, but it may be very useful, even with its limitations.

One exception to the problem of nonrepresentativeness would occur if a researcher had a list of all, or nearly all, the e-mail addresses of potential respondents. This would not be likely to occur for most surveys of public opinion, but it could occur if the population were more limited, such as the members of an organization or employees of a company.

Self-Selected Listener Opinion Surveys (SLOP)

If you watch much television, you are probably familiar with another type of survey—the phone-in or Internet survey in response to questions posed on TV shows. These surveys are sometimes called SLOP and are worthless for any purpose other than entertainment. Since only people who are watching the program and care enough to respond take part in the process, the survey respondents are not representative of any other larger population. Sometimes during sports telecasts, TV viewers are asked for coaching decisions, such as "Should the manager take the pitcher out?" We encourage you to participate in these exercises if you have nothing better to do with your time, but do not pay any attention to the results.[15]

CROSS-SECTIONAL SURVEYS VERSUS PANEL STUDIES

The overwhelming majority of public opinion surveys are cross-sectional studies. They are like snapshots of public opinion at one point in time. The advantage of a cross-sectional survey is that it can measure detailed opinion at one time. As long as a researcher wants to know the state of opinion at one time, a cross-sectional survey is perfectly adequate. However, if a researcher wants to explore changes in opinion, one cross-sectional study will not provide appropriate data. Two methodologies are used to study opinion change: time-series studies and panels.

A time-series study uses identical questionnaires or identical questions at different points in time. The National Election Studies and the General Social Survey are excellent examples of time-series studies. Identical questions are asked repeatedly over several surveys, and the answers can tell us how opinion has changed, or not changed, over the years. Time-series studies can also reveal how opinion has changed overall and for various population subgroups. But these studies cannot track who changed. For example, if we conducted two surveys that included abortion questions, we might find that the proportion of women who said abortions should always be available increased from 30 percent to 40 percent. We could then conclude that support for abortion had increased among women, but we could not conclude that 10 percent of women had changed their minds. In fact, 10 percent may have left the "always available" position, while 20 percent changed to that position, for a net increase of 10 percent. Or, a large number of older women with antiabortion opinions may have left the electorate and been replaced by younger pro-choice women. Even using two or more cross-sectional surveys, we cannot tell which one of these three, or more, possibilities actually happened.

But with a panel we can. The advantage of a panel study is that we can tell who changed their minds because we interview the same people two or more times. In the history of the National Election Study, there have been several major panel studies, including: 1956–58–60, 1972–74–76, 1992–94–96, and 2000–02–04. In a panel study, if the same question is asked twice, one can see how many people—and which people—changed their minds.

The major drawback of panel studies is the difficulty of finding the same respondents for each wave of the study. It is expensive to find people who have moved, and it is impossible to find everybody. Even when researchers are quite successful in re-locating and re-recruiting respondents, the number of willing respondents declines after only a few waves. Consider the 2000–02–04 NES panel survey as an example: 1,807 respondents were included in the 2000 survey, and 1,187 of them were successfully re-interviewed for the 2002 survey, for a repeat rate of 65.7 percent. In the 2004 survey, 841 were re-interviewed, for a total repeat rate of 46.5 percent.

THE POPULATION AND THE SAMPLE

Regardless of the method used, there are two important concepts to understand in survey research. The first is population. A population is all the people about whom one is gathering information. If one were interested in a presidential election, the population would be all the voters in the election. If one were interested in the opinions of women in Georgia, the population would be all the women in Georgia. The second concept is sample. A sample is all the people that one actually asks for their opinions. Typically, the sample is much smaller than the population. The reason that a sample is used is that it is almost always impossible or impractical to interview the entire population. The cost and logistics would also be prohibitive. Even in a town where only 5,000 people voted, it would not be practical to interview all the voters.

In surveying, a small number of people, usually between 400 and 3000, are asked for their opinions on issues. Researchers do not particularly care about the opinions of these specific select few or feel that their opinions are more important than those of other people. Rather, researchers care about their opinions because they represent what the larger population thinks. In statistical language, the opinions of these few hundred or so people can be generalized or *projected* to the entire population. Surprisingly, it takes relatively few people to create an accurate picture of the whole; the best national surveys, such as the National Election Study and the General Social Survey, consist of interviews of usually only about 1,500 to 3,000 individuals (the 2004 NES had 1,212 respondents).

PROBABILITY SAMPLING AND RANDOMNESS

However, to obtain accurate results, not just any 1,500 people will do; the people must be selected scientifically—that is, through probability sampling. The concept of probability sampling is very important in survey research. In fact, Herbert Asher says, "Probability sampling is typically cited as the number-one characteristic that makes a poll or survey scientific."[16] In probability sampling, we choose respondents randomly. In a sample that has been selected randomly, every person in the population has a known probability of being selected. The reason that randomness is so important is that a random selection is likely to be representative of the population from which it was selected, and its likely deviation from the characteristics of the actual population can be mathematically calculated. If a sample of people is selected randomly and then asked questions, we can be reasonably sure that the opinions expressed are going to be close to those of the entire population.

There are two basic ways to select a sample randomly. One is through **simple random sampling (SRS).** In SRS, a researcher has a list of people who could be questioned and assigns a random number to each one. The researcher then chooses a proportion of those random numbers and interviews the people to whom they have been assigned. For example, if you had 5,000 students at your university and wanted to interview 500 of them, with SRS you would randomly give each student a number from zero through nine. (Actually, you would have a computer do it; most statistical and spreadsheet programs have the ability to assign random numbers.) Then you would choose one number, such as 7, and interview every student to whom the computer had assigned that number.

The other principal method of random selection is **interval sampling.** Using this method, a researcher has a list of people and selects every *n*th person. For example, if you wanted to sample 500 students in your institution, and there were 5,000 students from which to choose, with interval sampling, you would select every 10th person.

But in almost all surveys involving public opinion, the researcher does not have a list of people who could be included in a sample. For example, there is no list of potential voters to assign random numbers to or from which to choose "every 3,000th one." When there is no list, however, researchers can still select random samples. In these cases, sampling can be accomplished using multistage selection. In an in-person survey, such as the National Election Study or the General Social Survey, the United States is divided into several areas, called Primary Sampling Units (PSUs). Some of those are chosen, with the likelihood of selection being proportionate to the population in each one (if there are 2 million in one and 4 million in a second, the second one is twice as likely to be selected). Each PSU that is selected is then divided into smaller regions, with some of those selected in the same manner. The smaller areas are then again subdivided into city blocks, or rural areas are chosen. The people to interview are selected from those final blocks or areas.

For telephone surveys, the country is divided into area codes and exchanges. (An *exchange* is the second three numbers of a telephone number. For example, the telephone number of the White House switchboard is 202-456-1414; the area code is 202, and the exchange is 456.) Within each area code/exchange permutation (such as 202-456-....) some *hundred series* are selected. There are companies that specialize in telephone samples and know which hundred series are most likely to have residential telephone numbers, as opposed to business or government numbers. The best hundred series are selected, and random two-digit numbers are added to them. For example, if 202-456 were the area code/exchange combination and "14" was the hundred series chosen, the random last two digits might be "14." If that happened, the final number chosen for the sample would be 202-456-1414. The number itself, not the people with the number, would be selected. The interviewer would then have to choose one of the adults in the household randomly to be interviewed. This process is called **Random Digit Dialing,** or

RDD. If the number were not in service or were a business or government number, another number, chosen the same way, would be substituted. (In this example, nobody from the number would be interviewed because the number is a government number.)

There are also nonprobability sampling methods. You could interview the first 100 people you meet, or you could go to a shopping mall and interview all the people at Barnes and Noble. You could get a sample size of 100, but you would not be able to project your data beyond those 100 people. You could not project the results from such a survey to the American public—or to any other public. In the Barnes and Noble example, the only people who had any chance of being included in your sample were those who were shopping when you appeared. Everybody else in the world would have had a zero probability of being selected for your sample. You could not even project the results of your survey to all Barnes and Noble shoppers.

There is another method for drawing survey samples that seemed to be probability sampling at one time but actually was not: quota sampling. In this method, the population under study is categorized according to important demographic variables such as gender, race, and income. Each interviewer is then required to interview a specific number of each kind of person. George Gallup explained quota sampling this way:

> An interviewer is sent an assignment asking him to interview a number of people, usually between 10 and 25. He is told to interview a certain number in each of four socio-economic groups in his community, how many men to interview, how many women, how many persons in each income level, how many farmers, if any, and so forth.[17]

Gallup wrote this paragraph in a press release on October 7, 1948, about the time he confidently predicted that Thomas Dewey would defeat Harry Truman for the presidency of the United States. Have you ever heard of President Dewey? Probably not. Gallup was wrong because quota sampling does not work. Even if voters are interviewed in the correct demographic proportions, selection of the respondents is not random. Interviewers tend to choose convenient or friendly-looking people to interview. After the 1948 election, Gallup abandoned quota sampling. Although the 1948 election does not give us the "perfect" bad example of polling, it does give us a very good one.

HOW SAMPLES CAN BE BIASED

A sample represents the larger population only if each person in the population has an equal, or known, probability of being included in the sample. If everybody in the population is not given an equal chance of being selected in the sample, we say the sample is biased. The most famous example of a biased sample is the *Literary Digest* sample of 1936—the perfect bad example that we discussed earlier in this chapter. Since the sample was taken from house-holds that had automobiles or telephones, those without them had zero chance of being selected in the sample. Since 1936 was during the Great Depres-sion, and only wealthier households had automobiles and telephones, the sam-ple was biased in favor of wealthier voters, who were more likely to vote Republican.

Another way that the *Literary Digest* survey was biased was that the survey respondents themselves decided whether they would send back the postcards. Those most interested in the election were then the most likely to respond. This self-selection bias was a problem because those who chose to participate were different in some way from those who chose not to participate. The responders were probably more Republican.

There are several other ways a sample could become biased. If you, for example, wanted to survey a random sample of the students at your college or university but selected your sample from a list of students that excluded trans-fer students, you would have a biased sample because transfer students would have no way of being included in the sample. If you used a list of students that was a year old, your sample would be biased because it would not include freshmen or students who had transferred into your school in the last year, and it would include seniors who had graduated in the last year, whom you would not want.

In the case of the multistage sample, selection methods used for the General Social Survey and the National Election Study, a sample would be biased if some cities or areas of the country were left out of the selection process; for example, if people in New England had no chance of being selected for the study, the sample would be biased. The sample would also be biased if the populations were estimated incorrectly, so if an area of 20 million people were incorrectly listed as having a population of 2 million people, its chance of being included in the sample would be only one-tenth as large as it should be. In the case of a telephone survey, if some area codes or exchanges were left out, the resulting sample would be biased.

Weighting Samples

Sometimes samples are biased through no fault of the researcher. For example, some people simply do not want to cooperate with surveys, and if enough peo-ple of one type do not respond, the sample becomes biased through what we call nonresponse error. There could be a survey of residents of a state in which 15 percent of the adults had less than high school educations, but 10 percent of the sample had this level of education. In fact, it is common for some kinds of people, such as those with less education, to be underrepresented in surveys because they are harder to find or are less likely to cooperate with interview-ers; other underrepresented types of people include ethnic minorities, men, and the young. But researchers are not helpless when the proportion of survey respondents does not match the proportion of people in the population. Researchers can adjust the sample of people by giving more weight to respondents in the demographic groups that are underrepresented and less weight to the respondents in the overrepresented demographic groups. According to the Pew Research Center,

> Most surveys—including those conducted by the Pew Research Center—attempt to correct for demographic biases through the use of statistical weighting, in which certain characteristics of the sample (e.g. education, race) are compared with known parameters of the population and then adjusted to match them. The result is typically to give slightly more weight to African Americans and Hispanic respondents, the less educated, males, and the young."[18]

Researchers weight the data by giving each respondent the inverse of his or her disparity in probability of selection. Here is an example: Suppose 20 percent of adults in a state have four-year college educations, but when we conduct a study of all the adults in the state, 30 percent of our sample is college educated. Since college graduates are oversampled by a 30/20 ratio, we simply give them a weight of 20/30. That is, we count each college graduate as 2/3 of a person. We would do the same for respondents in other educational categories. For example, using the percents from above, if 15 percent of the population did not complete high school, but 10 percent of our sample had that level of education, those members of the population would be underrepresented by a 10/15 ratio, and we would give them a weight of 15/10, or 1.5. The following Table 2.1 shows how weighting would work in this example.

TABLE 2.1. Example of Simple Weighting.
Sample Size = 1,000

Educational Level	Percent in Population	Sample Size		Over/Under Represen-tation	Weight		Weighted Number in Sample
		Number	Percent		Fraction	Decimal	
College Graduate	20%	300	30%	30/20	20/30	.667	200
Some College	28%	330	33%	33/28	28/33	.848	280
High School Graduate	37%	270	27%	27/37	37/27	1.37	370
Less than HS Grad	15%	100	10%	10/15	15/10	1.50	150
Total	*100%*	*1,000*	*100%*				*1,000*

Source: Hypothetical data.

In the end, when we apply the weighting, we have the same number of respondents, but they are included in the correct proportion. We have made this example very simple to show the logic of weighting, but in a real survey weighting can be very complicated. If one weights for several variables simultaneously—such as education, age, gender, and ethnicity—the logic is the same, but the mathematics are much more complex. In many of the following chapters, when we use examples from the National Election Study, we will use weighted data.

Sometimes, researchers intentionally create samples that are disproportionate. A researcher might do this to study a minority group in a population. For example, suppose a researcher wanted to compare the opinions of African Americans and whites in a particular state where whites made up 90 percent of the state's population, and blacks made up 10 percent. It would not make sense to interview 1,000 respondents to get a sample of only 100 blacks; comparisons of blacks and whites would be very difficult. It would make more sense to interview 500 black respondents and 500 white respondents. With 500 individuals in each sample, inter-group comparisons would make statistical sense. But if the researcher wanted to combine the 500 black and 500 white respondents to study the population as a whole, the combined sample would be biased in favor of blacks. The researcher could then weight the data so that black respondents would be given weights of 100/500, or .20, and whites would be given weights of 900/500, or 1.8.[19]

QUESTIONS AND THE QUESTIONNAIRE

After researchers choose the sample of people, they must ask the questions. There are two basic kinds of questions—open-ended and structured. An open-ended question asks a respondent to answer in his own words. An example is, "What is the most important problem facing the nation today?" The respondent can answer from a large number of perspectives and will put the answer in his own words. In a structured, or closed-ended, question, the respondent is asked to answer in the researcher's categories. An example is, "Do you approve or disapprove of affirmative action admissions programs at colleges and law schools that give racial preferences to minority applicants?" The respondent cannot explain her opinion of affirmative action; she can only approve or disapprove.

The overwhelming majority of questions in surveys is structured. They are easier to ask, easier to answer, and easier to compile and compare. It is also much easier to compare people's answers on structured questions; as a result statistical analysis is easier and more meaningful.

There are several rules in writing questions. We review some rules, but there is not enough room here to address all the important rules for question writing;

there are many textbooks on survey research. Here, we just want to emphasize that questions should be clear and unbiased. To be clear, the questions must be on topics the respondents are competent to answer, and they must be expressed in words the respondents will understand. It would not make sense, for example, to ask Americans questions about Chinese politics or ask questions containing technical language. In addition, all respondents should understand the question in the same way. It would not be good to ask if the respondents had written to an elected official "recently" because different people will interpret "recently" differently; it would be better to ask "in the last twelve months." To be unbiased, questions should not lead the respondents to answer one way rather than another; for example, one would not portray one response in a positive light and another in a negative light. One would also not ask a question and give a reason for one answer but no reason for another answer. You will note later in this book, when questions from the National Election Study are quoted, that respondents are not led to give one response rather than another.

How Questions Can Be Biased or Misleading

Though some standard question formats exist, avoiding bias when asking questions on opinions is not so easy. There are many ways to write a biased question. A question may be biased because it portrays one side of an issue more favorably. For example, one questionnaire, written by the American Civil Liberties Union (ACLU), included a question asking respondents to agree or disagree with a series of statements. One statement was:

> I believe government should not be allowed to invade anyone's privacy by wiretapping, Internet monitoring or other means without first demonstrating to a court that there is a "probable cause" to which the individual being targeted has committed a crime.[20]

In this question "invading privacy" is portrayed very negatively and leads the respondent to agree with the statement.

Another way a question can be biased is to link one of the possible answers to an authority figure. In a newsletter sent to constituents, a Republican congressman included a questionnaire about issues facing Congress. One question was:

> Should Congress make permanent President Bush's tax cuts, which include across-the-board income tax rate reductions, an expansion of the child tax credit, and marriage penalty relief?[21]

The question links tax cuts to President Bush, so that answers to the question might reveal more about the respondents' opinions of Bush than of tax cuts. (It also identifies the popular aspects of the tax cuts without referring to unpopular aspects.)

Sometimes, if a question is difficult to understand, survey results may not be accurate. For example, in 1992, the Roper Organization conducted a survey for the American Jewish Committee. One of the questions was as follows:

> Does it seem possible or does it seem impossible to you that the Nazi extermination of the Jews never happened?

The responses were:

Possible that it never happened:	22 percent
Impossible that it never happened:	65 percent
Don't know:	12 percent

When the results of this study were released, people were concerned that 22 percent of the survey respondents said it was possible that the Holocaust had never happened, and 12 percent did not know. Of course, the real problem was the question. With the double negative, a respondent had to say "impossible" to mean that the Holocaust had happened. The question was asked later with a changed wording: "Does it seem possible to you that the Nazi extermination of the Jews never happened, or do you feel certain that it happened?" With this wording, 91 percent said the Holocaust had happened.[22]

Sometimes a question may be worded fairly, but if the respondents are not competent enough to answer the question, the results will be meaningless. Take the following question from the same congressman as above:

> MBTE is an alternative fuel that can contaminate ground water and is a proven carcinogen. Some believe MTBE manufacturers should be shielded from lawsuits because Congress requires the use of an oxygenate in a reformulated gasoline. Others argue that MBTE liability provisions simply shift costs for clean up to water consumers. Should MTBE manufacturers be shielded from liability?[23]

This may be a reasonable question, but not for the large majority of the American public because very few Americans know what MTBE is or what the issue of legal liability entails.

A few years ago, one of the authors of this book was working on a survey for a city government. The mayor wanted to survey the citizens to get their opinions on issues and governmental performance. One official suggested to the researcher to ask the respondents if they thought the city fire department should buy more pumpers or hook-and-ladders. Your author assured the official that ordinary citizens have no idea what the fire department should buy; that is why they hire a fire department. The question was not asked.

Operationalizing Concepts

The most serious problem for survey researchers in writing questions is not avoiding obvious mistakes; competent experienced researchers can almost always avoid actual errors. A more serious problem in writing questions is operationalizing abstract concepts. Operationalization in this context means translating a concept into a survey question. For example, if one wanted to know about Americans' opinions concerning the federal government's responsibility, if any, to ensure economic prosperity and high levels of employment, there are a great many ways one could ask a question to ascertain those opinions. One could ask, for example, if the respondents feel the government does have such a responsibility in a simple Yes/No question. Or one could ask two questions, if the respondent thinks the government has a responsibility to ensure prosperity and if the government has a duty to provide jobs for all Americans. There are many questions that could be asked to obtain this information. In the National Election Studies, one particular question wording has been used for several years. The question asks each respondent to take a position from "1" to "7" on this issue, with "1" meaning that the respondent thinks the government does have a responsibility, and "7" meaning that the government does not have a responsibility. This question has been used in the NES for many years. The precise wording in the 2004 NES was:

> Some people feel the government in Washington should see to it that every person has a job and a good standard of living. Suppose those people are at one end of a scale, at point 1. Others think the government should just let each person get ahead on their own. Suppose these people are at the other end, at point 7. And, of course, some other people have opinions somewhere in between, at points 2, 3, 4, 5, or 6. Where would you place yourself on this scale, or haven't you thought much about this?

In the 2004 NES, 1,212 people were asked this question in a face-to-face format. Of these 1,212 respondents, 135 placed themselves at point "1" and 92 placed themselves at point "2." We think it is a safe assumption that none of those 227 people thought of themselves as having an opinion of "1" or "2" on this issue before the interview began, yet we have confidence that we know something about their opinion concerning responsibilities in the area of jobs and standards of living. The "1" and "2" are just convenient ways to classify these 227 people as having liberal positions on this issue. We are inferring the opinions of those 227 people because we believe, and have evidence, that people who are liberal place themselves at points "1" or "2."

Sometimes, it is not clear how a question should be worded, and apparently equally valid wordings yield very different answers. In 1987, a Gallup poll was conducted with 4,244 American adults to get their opinions about American politics. One of the questions inquired about each respondent's concern for the outcome of the 1988 election. The question was asked in two different ways, each to half the respondents. The question wordings and results are below.

So, after reading the results of these two questions, how many Americans cared a good deal about the outcome of the 1988 election? The answer is 54 percent or 76 percent or somewhere in between. We don't know any closer than that. Both these question wordings are "correct," but they give us very different answers. We do not have a solution to this problem. Welcome to the world of survey research!

TABLE 2.2. Alternate Question Wordings.

Version 1: "Generally speaking, would you say that *you personally* care a good deal which party wins the presidential election in 1988 or that you don't care very much who wins?"

Care a good deal	54%
Don't care very much	40%
Don't know	6%

Version 2: "Generally speaking, would you say that *you personally* care a good deal who wins the presidential election in 1988 or that you don't care very much which party wins?"

Care a good deal	76%
Don't care very much	20%
Don't know	4%

Source: From *The People, The Press and Politics* by Norman Ornstein, p. 117. Copyright © 1988. Reprinted by permission of Norman Ornstein.

Sometimes, issues have many facets, and there is no "one" way to ask about them. One example is affirmative action. Just what affirmative action entails is not certain; some say it involves more inclusive recruiting and training and attempts to "level the playing field," but others say it involves quotas and preferences, and is racism under a different name.

Lee Sigelman and Susan Welch compiled a series of questions and responses concerning affirmative action. They found that, depending on the specific question asked, between 23 percent and 96 percent of black respondents and between 9 percent and 76 percent of white respondents supported affirmative action. For example 76 percent of whites agreed that "affirmative action programs that help blacks get ahead should be supported," but only 9 percent supported giving blacks preference in getting jobs over equally qualified whites because of past discrimination against blacks. (See Table 2.3.) Although the data are somewhat dated, they do show that how one asks a question is important in determining how respondents answer it.[24]

Scales and Indexes

Some concepts are just too complex to be operationalized in one question. No one question quite captures the concept, but several taken together do approximate it. Analysts combine answers to multiple questions to develop scales; each respondent's score on the scale indicates how much that person has that characteristic. Sometimes, scales may be called indexes. In the National Election Studies, several theoretical concepts are addressed in scales. For one of those, Political Efficacy (the opinion that one can effectively participate in

TABLE 2.3. Alternate Operationalizations of a Concept (Affirmative Action).

	Respondent's Race	
Opinion	Black	White
Affirmative action programs that help blacks get ahead should be supported (1980-G)	96%	76%
Agree that after years of discrimination only fair to set up special programs to ensure that women and minorities are given every chance to have equal opportunities in employment and education (1978-H)	91	71
Favor affirmative action programs in employment for blacks, provided there are no rigid quotas:		
(1978-H)	89	67
(1988-H)	78	73
Approve of requiring large companies to set up special training programs for members of minority groups (1977-NYT)	88	63
As long as there are no quotas, makes sense to give special training and advice to women and minorities so they can perform better on the job (1978-H)	77	70
Employers should set aside places to hire qualified blacks and other minorities (1980-G)	73	51
Approve of requiring businesses to hire certain number of minority workers (1977-NYT)	64	35
Approve of requiring some corporations to practice affirmative action, sometimes requiring special preferences to minorities or women when hiring (1978-C)	58	35*
Approve Supreme Court decision allowing employer to set up a special training and promotion program for minorities and women (1978-H)	56	36
Support Court ruling allowing employers to favor women and minorities in hiring over better qualified men and whites (1987-G)	56	25
Support giving blacks preference in getting jobs over equally qualified whites because of past discrimination against blacks (1984-GJ)	49	9
To make up for past discrimination, women and minorities should be given preferential treatment in getting jobs and places in college as opposed to mainly considering ability as determined by test scores (1958-J, 1984-G)	23	10*

Source: Lee Sigelman and Susan Welch, *Black Americans' Views of Racial Inequality: The Dream Deferred* (Cambridge: Cambridge University Press, 1991), p. 129. Reprinted by permission of Cambridge University Press. *All respondents, not just whites.

Sources of original data: H = Louis Harris and Associates; G = Gallup Poll; NYT = *New York Times*; C = Cambridge Survey Research, summarized by Lipset and Schneider (1978); J = Lawrence Johnson and Associates and Metro Research Services, summarized by Lichter (1985); GJ = Gallup Joint Center Poll.

politics), the questions that are used to make up the scales are shown below. In each question, respondents are asked to agree or disagree with each statement and are classified into five categories: agree strongly, agree somewhat, neither agree nor disagree, disagree somewhat, and disagree strongly. You will notice that sometimes questions are asked so that "agree" means the respondent is high on the scale and sometimes "disagree" puts the respondent higher on the scale.

Political Efficacy (how powerful or influential the respondent feels)

- "I feel I have a pretty good understanding of the important political issues facing our country."
- "I consider myself well-qualified to participate in politics."
- "I feel that I could do as good a job in public office as most other people."
- "I think I am better informed about politics and government than most people."
- "So many other people vote in the national election that it doesn't matter much to me whether I vote or not." ("Disagree" is the efficacious answer.)

We can make a simple scale with the five efficacy questions by simply adding the responses. If we give a value of "5" to the most efficacious answer and a value of "1" to the least efficacious answer and then add the answers for all five questions, we will have a scale on which each respondent will have a score between a high of 25 (the respondent answered each question with the most efficacious response) and a low of 5 (the respondent answered each question with the least efficacious response). Then we can discover what kinds of people feel efficacious and what kinds of people do not. The following table shows the levels of efficacy for respondents in the 2000 NES classified by amount of education. Table 2.4 shows that 19 percent of all the survey respondents had very efficacious scores of 21 to 25 and 13 percent had the lowest scores of 5 to 10. The table also shows that people with more education tend

TABLE 2.4. Self-Assessed Political Efficacy Example of a Scale Made from Several Variables.

Score on 5–25 Scale	Total Sample	Educational Level				
		< HS	HS	SC/AA*	BA	MA+
21–25 (highest efficacy)	19%	6%	8%	17%	30%	40%
16–20	37	32	34	39	41	39
11–15	31	32	39	34	24	17
5–10 (lowest efficacy)	13	30	19	10	5	4
Mean	16.1	13.7	14.5	16.2	17.9	18.8
Sample Size	*1,423*	*129*	*390*	*433*	*310*	*161*

*SC/AA-Some College/Associate's Degree
Source: 2000 National Election Study.

to have higher levels of efficacy. The reason the table is included here is to show how using five variables can measure a concept, such as efficacy, better than using only one of those variables.

Question Order

In any telephone or face-to-face interview, questions must be asked in a specific order. The order can be important because every question that the respondent answers influences every question asked subsequently. Answers can change, depending on the order of the questions. For example, in a 2004 Gallup survey on the September 11, 2001, terrorist attacks, Gallup asked people whether the Clinton and Bush administrations had done all they could to prevent the attacks. The order of the questions was rotated so that half the time the Clinton question was asked first, and half the time the Bush question was asked first. The question was:

> Based on the information available to the Clinton/Bush administration before the terrorist attacks on September 11, 2001, do you think the Clinton/Bush administration did—or did not—do all that could be expected to prevent the terrorist attacks?"[25]

When respondents were asked about the Bush administration first, 48 percent said that it had done all it could to prevent the attacks, and 48 percent said it had not. But when the Clinton question was asked first, only 35 percent said the Bush administration had done all it could, and 60 percent said it had not (see Table 2.5).

If the question about the Bush administration is asked first, President Bush appears to be more vigilant than Clinton, but if the question about the Clinton

TABLE 2.5. Did the Clinton/Bush administration do all it could do to prevent the terrorist attacks? (Percent).

	Bush Question Asked First	Clinton Question Asked First
Bush Administration		
Did all it could	48	35
Did not do all it could	48	60
Unsure	4	5
Clinton Administration		
Did all it could	30	34
Did not do all it could	63	61
Unsure	7	5

Source: The Gallup Poll Organization: http://www.gallup.com/content/default.aspx?ci=11239.

administration is asked first, both Clinton and Bush appear to be about the same. Which is correct? Why are the numbers so dissimilar? Analysts can debate reasons for the difference, but, as David W. Moore of the Gallup Organization wrote, "Based on the available data, there is no definitive way to answer the question." Welcome once again to the world of survey research!

SAMPLING ERROR AND OTHER ERRORS

The first thing to understand in **sampling error** is that there is no *error*—that is, there is no mistake. Sampling error is simply the statistical variation that sample survey results will yield. The idea behind sampling error is that if, say, we took a sample of 400 Americans and found that 54.5 percent of them approve of the job the president is doing, we would not insist that *exactly* 54.5 percent of all Americans approve of the president. We would realize that the true percent for the entire population might be 54.7 percent or 52.1 percent or 55.9 percent. All those percents are reasonably close to the 54.5 percent that we received. If we have conducted the survey correctly, we would not expect to get *exactly* the right percentage, but we expect to be *close*.

Sampling error just tells us how close we would be to the actual percent in the real world, with a certain probability of accuracy. Sometimes, people refer to the sampling error as the "plus or minus percent." Usually, analysts use the 95 percent level of confidence. They say that a percentage is accurate plus or minus a specific number of percentage points 95 percent of the time. For example, if the survey of 400 respondents found that 54.5 percent of the respondents approved of the way the president was handling his job, an analyst would say that the true percentage was 54.5 percent, plus or minus 5 percentage points at the 95 percent level of confidence. That means that there is a 95 percent probability that the true percentage is between 49.5 percent and 59.5 percent. If we wanted to be more precise, we could interview more people. If we interviewed 1,100 people, we would be ± 3 percent instead of ± 5 percent. The following table shows the increasing precision that comes with each sample size. Basically, more interviews are better; the main disadvantage of more interviews is the added cost.

You will notice that with very small sample sizes, the error range is very large. If 52 percent of respondents in a sample of 50 respondents say they are going to vote Republican, we are 95 percent sure that the actual percent in the population who plan to vote Republican is 52 percent ±14 percent, or between 38 percent and 66 percent. Not exactly shocking news! We probably knew that before we conducted the survey. Small samples are usually not very useful.

You may also notice that with 400 respondents the error margin is ± 5 percentage points. That is why a sample of 400 is common for commercial surveys. Generally, academic surveys, such as the GSS and NES, include around 1,500–2,500 respondents. This is the point where the added expense of

TABLE 2.6. Calculating Sampling Error 95% Level of Confidence.

Sample Size	± "Error"
50	14
100	10
200	7
300	6
400	5
500	5
600	4
700	4
800	3.5
900	3.5
1,000	3.1
1,100	3
. . .	
2,400	2
. . .	
9,600	1

This table assumes that 50% of the respondents answered a question one way and 50% answered it another way. If the split is other than 50/50, the sampling errors are smaller (i.e., better).

interviewing more respondents becomes too large. The added expense grows larger as we add respondents. Notice how easy it is to reduce the error margin at first but how it becomes more difficult. In order to reduce the error margin from 14 percentage points to 5 percentage points, we need to add only 350 more respondents (from 50 to 400). But to decrease it from 5 percentage points to 1 percentage point, we must add 9,200 respondents.

The major reason to increase the sample size in a survey from 1,000 to 2,000 is not to increase the precision of the total sample; it is to increase the precision of subgroups within the total sample. If a total sample is 1,000, with 500 men and 500 women, the sampling error for the total sample is ± 3.1 percentage points, but it is ± 5 percentage points for men and for women separately. If there are 200 respondents with college educations, the sampling error is ± 7 percentage points for them. If an analyst wanted to examine college-educated women, the sample size would be very small, and the sampling error would be very large. But with a sample size of 2,000, typical for NES surveys, subgroups are larger, and the accompanying sampling errors are smaller.

But sampling error is not the only source of error in surveys. There are many other types of error—and these *really are* errors, or mistakes. The 1936 *Literary Digest* survey mentioned previously illustrated some common errors. First, *The Literary Digest* committed a *population specification* error. That is, the magazine specified the population of voters as those households that had cars and telephones. In fact, many people, especially the poor and lower middle class, possessed neither cars nor telephones. Second, the magazine committed *selection error* because from among the potential respondents with cars and telephones, the actual survey participants were not selected randomly; instead, those most interested sent back their postcards. This type of selection error is also called a *nonresponse error*. This simply means that the people who did not respond are different from those who did. If the people who did not respond were exactly the same as those who did, nonresponse would not matter because the respondents would be a good representation of all the people in the population. In the case of *The Literary Digest*, it is likely that the middle-class and upper-class Americans who had cars and telephones and were interested enough to return the postcards were more likely to be Republican than those without as much interest in the presidential campaign.

Two other errors that did not happen in the *Literary Digest* survey, but could happen, are *interviewer bias* and *processing errors*. Interviewer bias occurs when interviewers do not ask questions properly or suggest answers improperly. For example, an interviewer may not like the current president and may cause the respondent to rate the president's behavior in office unsatisfactorily. Processing errors occur when answers are simply recorded improperly; an example would be if a respondent evaluated the president's behavior as "good" but the interviewer recorded it as "excellent." In the *Literary Digest* survey, there were no interviewers, and although there may have been processing errors, they would not account for the inaccuracy of the survey's prediction.

Another possible error is *instrument error*. This type of error occurs when a question is biased or is not asked correctly. If the question leads respondents to answer one way, it is biased and does not give the researcher accurate results. We have listed some examples previously. To some extent, instrument error is unavoidable when asking about something other than demographics and very clearly understood issues like voting. There is no one right way to ask for someone's opinion on race, abortion, taxes, or any other important issues. There are many ways, some good and some bad, to ask about important issues. As we have seen, very small changes in question wording can yield vastly different question responses.

ADVANTAGES AND DISADVANTAGES OF SURVEY RESEARCH

Survey research is the method used most often to learn about people's political opinions. It is also the research method we will use most often in this book. The clearest advantage to this method is that, with careful random selection of the sample, the results of survey research can be projected to the entire population. If 55 percent of 400 survey respondents say that they approve of a program to improve public education, a researcher can be reasonably sure that about 50 percent to 60 percent of all the adults in the U.S. population would say they approve of the program. The main strength of survey research is that it enables a researcher to "project" or "generalize" to the entire population. There is simply no other way to learn what an entire large population, such as the American electorate, thinks.

Surveys use standardized questions that can be asked of many people in identical form so that analysts can compare people's answers. The same questions can be asked of people at different places at different times. Groups of people can be compared across space and across time. By asking men and women identical questions, we can compare their answers; we can even compare their answers in 1992 to their answers in 2004.

When used properly, surveys can describe the population or predict behavior very accurately. Much of the work of the U.S. Census Bureau involves sampling people, and the numbers generated from those samples have great credibility. The unemployment rates and inflation rates, for example, are derived from sample surveys. In elections, there are many polls that predict very accurately how the vote will go. There are some horror stories of wildly bad predictions, but reputable pollsters regularly predict election results within three or four percentage points.

Another important advantage of survey research is that it is fast and can be relatively inexpensive. For less than $20,000, one can find out approximately what the American public thinks about an issue—and one can do it in a few days.

But survey research has its disadvantages and its critics. The most common criticisms of survey research concern its superficiality, the lack of time respondents are given to reflect on the questions, the lack of information respondents have in answering the questions, the isolation of responses, and the equality of respondents.

Superficiality: Although a researcher can learn approximately how someone feels about an issue, the researcher cannot learn the complexity or subtlety of that person's opinion. Just as one advantage of survey research is that standardized questions allow easy comparisons between people and groups of people, a disadvantage is that standardized questions force respondents to place their opinions in a preset format that may not be appropriate for them. For example, if a survey respondent rates the president's behavior as "good" rather than "excellent," "fair," or "poor," it is not clear what "good" means or why the person gave the president that rating. Maybe the person thinks the president is "excellent" on the abortion issue, "poor" on taxes, "good" on foreign relations—or maybe the person thinks the president is pretty bad but is "good" compared to the person's expectation that he would be terrible. A respondent may have a very complex evaluation of the president—"good" just does not capture it.

Lack of Time to Reflect: Another problem with survey research is that interviewers record what the respondents say on the telephone with only a few seconds to respond to each question. And the interview is almost always a complete surprise to the respondents, so they have no time to prepare. (It is extremely unusual to warn respondents ahead of time that they are going to be surveyed, partly because the researcher usually does not know who will be surveyed ahead of time.) The first response may be a good indication of the respondent's opinion, or it may not be. Regardless, it is the one recorded.

Lack of Information Respondents Have: Survey respondents frequently do not know the background or context of many opinion questions. Interviewers seldom give more than one or two sentences, if that, of background information. The researcher cannot know the context that respondents use in answering the questions. For example, does each respondent understand the alternatives? Does the respondent know the implications of each response? When being asked about a proposed program, does the respondent know how much each program component will cost? Would the respondent answer the same if she knew how much her taxes would increase if her "favorite" alternative were actually enacted into law? Robert Weissberg[26] conducted a survey concerning proposed new programs and found that fewer respondents favored programs when they were told how much they would cost.

Isolation of Responses: In all sample surveys, interviewers talk with each respondent individually, one at a time. This is good in one sense, because no respondent can influence another respondent's answer. But in the political world, people do influence each other's opinions. We do not know if the respondents would answer the same way if given some time to think or discuss the president's program with friends. Critics of survey research have said that trying to measure public opinion by asking people for their opinions "assumes public opinion to be the aggregation of individual opinions recorded by trained, objective interviewers."[27] Many critics say that opinion is not really *public* unless people have opportunities to discuss their views with others. When people talk among themselves and read and hear others discuss their opinions, they are likely to become more informed. Robert Lane explained how people can refine their opinions by discussing them with friends and acquaintances at work:

> The hollering, the bantering, the kidding that Republicans take from Democrats and vice versa—these experiences bring the "way out" opinion nearer to the group norms, but while they homogenize opinions, they may also, in the American work culture, civilize them too.[28]

Equality of Respondents: It may be comforting for a good Democrat conducting survey research to count the response of each person the same—one person, one response. In some circumstances, such as elections, this makes sense. But in most other circumstances, it does not. In the real political world, people and their opinions are not equal. Some people have more informed opinions, and some work harder in the political system to convey their opinions to governmental officials. Some survey respondents simply do not know what a question means in a telephone survey, but they answer it anyway—and probably forget about it before they begin supper. But these respondents are counted the same as more informed respondents.

TWO VARIANTS OF SURVEY RESEARCH

Two variations on survey research have been conducted by political scientists. Both variations use basic survey research methodology but then add a new aspect. The first, deliberative polling, gives the respondents a great deal of information so that they can make more informed responses. The second, survey-based experimentation, uses modern computer technology to randomly separate respondents into different subgroups and ask them different questions.

Deliberative Polling

Deliberative polling addresses criticisms of the public that many public opinion analysts have made—that the public is so uninformed its answers to many questions are not meaningful. You may recall the discussion by Walter Lippman in Chapter One. Lippman said that people are ignorant of matters of which they do not have personal experience; he said that even well-informed citizens spend only a short amount of time each day learning about the issues of the day.

Proponents of deliberative polling acknowledge that if people do not have enough information on which to base their survey responses, they are unlikely to give very informed answers—and that if they did have more information, they would likely answer differently. The purpose of a deliberative poll is to provide survey respondents with information and then survey their opinions. According to the Center for Deliberative Polling, a deliberative poll "is a tool designed to measure what public opinion on major issues would be like if citizens had the time and resources to become better informed."[29]

In a typical deliberative poll, researchers use scientific random sampling to select a sample of American citizens and then administer a regular telephone survey to those people. Then the researchers send the respondents "carefully balanced" background information on several issues. After the respondents have had time to read the written material, they meet together face-to-face for a weekend, during which they meet in small groups and ask questions of experts on different sides of the issues. There are large-group question-and-answer sessions as well. After the weekend, the respondents are polled again. Their answers are compared to those before the weekend. According to James Fishkin, Director of the Center for Deliberative Polling,

The Deliberative Poll gives citizens a chance to become more knowledgeable about current issues and provides them with a public space to express their views. Having the information and time to thoroughly examine an issue in depth moves the conversation beyond the usual sound bites and into the gray areas of real experience. During small group discussions, participants learn from one another and come to better understand the reasoning behind opposing viewpoints.[30]

Beginning in 2003, the Center for Deliberative Polling has conducted online deliberative polls. In one poll, conducted from January 19 through February 26, 2004, a sample of 266 eligible voters deliberated about the candidates and issues current in the presidential primaries at the time. The respondents received information about the candidates and issues, and participated in moderated online discussions for an hour each week. In addition, they asked questions that were answered by experts. Their answers were compared to two control samples of 346 and 546 respondents who did not receive the information. The study found that the deliberative poll participants were able to improve their scores on information tests more than the control groups were; in addition, those who participated in the deliberative poll tended to become more internationalist in perspective when compared to the "control" groups. The study also found that participants' opinions toward President Bush did not change much (perhaps because he was already a known figure) but that they came to like John Kerry and John Edwards better, with Edwards gaining more than Kerry.[31]

Typically, participants in deliberative polls become more informed, and their increased knowledge is reflected in the thoughtfulness of their answers at the end of the process. For example, when asked about crime in one poll in 1994 in Britain, respondents were more likely to show awareness of the limitations of prison as a tool for fighting crime, an increased willingness to use alternatives to incarceration, and greater respect for procedural rights of defendants.[32] Respondents do not, however, usually change the basic directions of their answers; conservatives do not become liberals, and Democrats do not become Republicans. In the British example, support for the death penalty and the belief that prison is "too soft" did not change, while the percent who believed court rules should be less on the side of the defendants increased.[33]

Survey-Based Experiments

In the next chapter, we will cover the study of public opinion with laboratory experiments. Experiments in their simplest form are well known; participants are randomly assigned to different groups, with one group receiving one stimulus and another group receiving a different stimulus. The participants' behavior on some task is then measured, and the two groups' actions are compared. Most experiments are conducted in laboratory settings and involve the physical presence of the participants, or *subjects* as they are typically called. But sometimes survey research is used to conduct experiments. These studies are statistically projectable to the entire population if the survey respondents are chosen randomly. In one sense, survey-based experiments are not new; researchers have experimented with different question wordings for years. However, the development of computer interviewing has made experimentation with surveys much easier. With Internet interviewing and Computer Assisted Telephone Interviewing (CATI), researchers can randomly assign respondents into various classifications, in much the same way that subjects in laboratory experiments are randomly assigned to various groups. Survey-based experiments are often used in studying people's opinions on racial issues because race is an extremely sensitive topic in current American politics. Since experimental designs can be unobtrusively inserted into questionnaires, they can circumvent the tendency of people to give socially acceptable answers to the questions. That is, respondents can be asked questions as part of an experiment without realizing it.

There are several ways that experimental designs can be built into surveys. Martin Gilens[34] has compiled some of these methods. In the simplest type of survey experiment, respondents can also be asked different forms of a question. For example, in one study, respondents were asked questions about a hypothetical welfare mother. In one form of the question she was white, and in the other form of the question she was black. (In that experiment, almost identical percentages of white respondents thought the white and black welfare mothers would try hard to get jobs and try to have more children to get larger welfare checks.) Second, the environments in which respondents answer questions can be changed. In a survey, white respondents were asked to rate African Americans on characteristics, including negative stereotypes. Half of the respondents, randomly chosen, were asked about affirmative action beforehand. The researchers found out that white respondents who had been earlier asked about affirmative action tended to give more negative ratings than those who had not been asked about it.[35]

Third, respondents can be given different types of information. One study found that if some respondents were told the crime rate was declining while other rates were not, they were less likely to support spending for prisons than those who had not been told.[36]

In a fourth type of survey experiment, the *list experiment*, randomly chosen respondents are read one of two lists of items. In one example of a list experiment, respondents are read lists that they are told "might make people angry or upset." The items include increasing gasoline taxes and professional athletes earning large salaries. One list includes four items, and the second list includes the same four items plus "Awarding college scholarships on the basis of race." All respondents are then asked to tell the interviewer how many items, but not which items, upset them. The purpose of the experiment is to allow respondents to indicate that they are upset by affirmative action without having to actually say so. If respondents in the first group report that they are angry or upset by an average of 2.5 items and the respondents in the second "test" group indicate that they are angry or upset by an average of 3.0 items, the researchers would know that about half the respondents in the "test" situation are angry or upset by the additional item.[37]

A fifth type of survey experiment involves the interviewer reading one last agree/disagree question at the end of the interview. Before the question, half of the respondents—randomly selected—are complimented ("I just want to say that I've really enjoyed talking with you, and that your answers are very useful to us"). In one study, more respondents who had been complimented agreed with the statement than did those who had not been complimented.[38]

An organization has been formed to facilitate the use of experimental designs with large randomly selected samples. This organization, the Time-sharing Experiments for the Social Sciences (TESS), is funded by the National Science Foundation. With TESS, a researcher can use Internet or CATI technology to ask a few questions with an experimental design in a large survey. TESS calls this "time-sharing," and it saves researchers much money by spreading the set-up costs across several projects and by asking demographics only once for multiple studies.[39]

WHO CONDUCTS PUBLIC OPINION RESEARCH?

Four main types of organizations conduct public opinion research:

- Academic research organizations
- The media
- Politicians
- Commercial companies

Academic Research Organizations

Many colleges and universities have research centers. They conduct a wide variety of research, including political research. They may conduct research strictly for academic purposes, or they may conduct commercial research for paying customers. Generally, they are managed by professional researchers with student helpers who learn how to conduct research on the job.

Two of the most important academic research organizations are The Center for Political Studies at the University of Michigan and NORC at the University of Chicago (NORC is also known as the National Opinion Research Center). The Center for Political Studies is part of the Institute for Social Research. It has conducted interdisciplinary social and political research involving the collection or analysis of data from scientific sample surveys for more than 50 years. Its most important study for our purposes has been the American National Election Study. This study was first conducted in 1948 and 1952.

Since 1956 it has been conducted every two years at the time of congressional and presidential elections. (In addition, the Center for Political Studies has also conducted some "pilot" studies, usually in odd-numbered years, to improve its methodology.) The National Election Study is the premier source for political opinion over the last half century, especially as it relates to voting. The 2000, 2002, and 2004 National Election Studies are cited extensively in this book, and subsets of data from the studies are included on the *Public Opinion in the 21st Century* Web site for your use.

NORC has offices at the University of Chicago and in Washington, D.C. NORC's clients include government agencies, educational institutions, foundations, other nonprofit organizations, and private corporations. For our purposes, the most important study that NORC conducts is the General Social Survey. This survey was conducted almost annually from 1972 through 1993. It has been conducted biennially in even-numbered years since 1994. It includes questions on a variety of topics; although it is not principally a political survey, it includes many political questions.

Both the National Election Study and the General Social Survey use face-to-face interviews, although the National Election Study has recently used telephone interviews to supplement its sample. Part of the 2000 study and all of the 2002 study were conducted by telephone. The cross-sectional part of the 2004 NES was conducted with face-to-face interviews, but the 2004 segment of the 2000–2002–2004 panel study was conducted by telephone. Both studies include questions that use the same wording year after year, so that trends can be tracked. Although they phase questions in and out of the questionnaires to account for changing issues, they keep many questions the same, so that people's answers can be compared.

In addition to these two institutions, most large universities, and many small ones, have their own research centers. They typically conduct both academic studies and conduct paid studies for clients.

The Media

The media also conduct many political surveys. Almost all of the media surveys, other than exit polls, are conducted using telephone interviews. Media surveys typically are conducted to create articles for the media audiences. The larger media often run political polls during electoral campaigns and when major stories occur. Some major media collaborate on a regular basis; for example, *The New York Times* and CBS News frequently sponsor polls together, as do *The Wall Street Journal* and NBC News.

If you see a poll story in a newspaper, look for the "How Box." This is a box that explains how the survey was completed; it usually contains the dates of the interviews, the sample size, and the margin of error at the 95 percent level of confidence.

BOX 2.1

The "How Box"

Following is an example of a "How Box" that appears in newspaper poll stories to explain how the poll was conducted. This is from *The New York Times,* Friday, October 19, 2004, in connection with the article, "The 2004 Campaign: Surveys; Poll Shows Tie; Concerns Cited on Both Rivals."

How Poll Was Conducted

The latest *New York Times*/CBS News Poll is based on telephone interviews conducted Thursday through Sunday with 1,048 adults throughout the United States. Of these, 931 said they were registered to vote.

The sample of telephone exchanges called was randomly selected by a computer from a complete list of more than 42,000 active residential exchanges across the country. Within each exchange, random digits were added to form a complete telephone number, thus permitting access to listed and unlisted numbers alike.

Within each household, one adult was designated by a random procedure to be the respondent for the survey. The results have been weighted to take account of household size and number of telephone lines in the residence and to adjust for variation in the sample relating to geographic region, sex, race, Hispanic origin, marital status, age and education.

Based on the 2000 presidential vote, residents of heavily Republican counties, heavily Democratic ones, and politically competitive counties were weighted to their proper share of the population.

Some findings regarding voting are additionally weighted in terms of an overall "probable electorate," which uses responses to questions dealing with voting history, attention to the campaign and likelihood of voting in 2004 as a measure of the probability of respondents' turning out in November.

In theory, in 19 cases out of 20, the results based on such samples will differ by no more than three percentage points in either direction from what would have been obtained by seeking out all American adults. For small subgroups, the margin of sampling error is larger.

In addition to sampling error, the practical difficulties of conducting any survey of public opinion may introduce other sources of error into the poll. Variation in the wording and order of questions, for example, may lead to somewhat different results.

Complete results are online at nytimes.com/politics.

"The 2004 Campaign: Surveys, Poll Shows Tie: Concerns Cited on Both Rivals" by Adam Nagourney and Janet Elder from *The New York Times*, October 1, 2004. Copyright © 2004 The New York Times. Reprinted by permission.

Although media polls are not conducted in order to further academic research, academic researchers have access to their results and use them in their analyses, as you can see from the citations in this book. In addition, politicians frequently use media polls to gauge the state of public opinion.

Politicians

Politicians and political parties conduct polls regularly, during campaigns and at other times. In fact, along with media polls, polls sponsored by parties and politicians are some of the principal sources that political decision makers use to learn about public opinion—and are some of the main ways that officeholders gather public opinion that will be translated into public policy. However, research conducted by politicians is often undertaken in order to find ways to change public opinion rather than to learn it. Politicians use surveys to find words and phrases to use in selling their preferred policies to voters.[40]

Commercial Companies

There are many commercial research companies that work for media clients, political parties, and individual politicians. Some of these that conduct research for parties and politicians work for both Democrats and Republicans, while others work only for one party. These companies typically also conduct research for nonpolitical clients, such as regular business firms. Gallup is the most famous of these.

A CRISIS IN SURVEY RESEARCH?

With the explosive growth in the use of cell phones, as well as other devices like "caller ID," "privacy manager," "call forwarding," and ordinary answering machines, the future of telephone survey research is uncertain. Not so many years ago, a researcher could assume that practically all households had one telephone line, without privacy managers or caller ID. People either answered the telephone, or they did not. Now, caller ID is very common, and many people screen their calls. In one national study conducted by the Pew Research Center, 78 percent of the respondents said they had answering machines or voice mail, and 43 percent said they used them to screen telephone calls (and these are the people who responded to the survey; we do not know what percentage of the nonrespondents screen their calls—logic leads us to believe it is higher).[41] Although households with higher incomes were more likely to have these devices, a majority of the lowest-income households used them.[42]

Households often have two or more—and sometimes many more—telephone lines. One study conducted in 1997 and 1998 found that 31 percent of households nationwide had two or more telephone lines.[43] Developing telephone samples is harder than ever because households with multiple lines are more likely to be included in samples. In addition, more affluent households are more likely to have multiple lines.

The advent of cell phones is affecting survey research because cell phone owners dislike being called for surveys because they pay by the minute, and most polling organizations do not include cell phone numbers in their samples. According to a 2003 survey, 2.8 percent of households had wireless telephones but no landline telephones.[44] Although this is not a particularly large number now, it is likely to rise over the next few years, further affecting the quality of Random Digit Dialing telephone samples.

In addition to problems with samples, many sources have noted declining **response rates** over the last few decades. The Council for Marketing and Opinion Research conducts a periodic survey about the survey research industry's image, and it noted after its 2003 survey:

> The **refusal rate** for this survey has shown a steady increase throughout the years, but this year, the refusal rate took a sharper than usual increase. Refusals prior to the introduction were significantly higher. Respondents didn't even give the interviewer any time to explain the purpose of the call. This could be the result of an ever-skeptical public that believe that they will be sold something.

> When the interviewer has the chance of getting through the introduction and the respondent refuses, the reasons seem to be mostly circumstantial (i.e., inconvenient time, uninteresting or inappropriate topic) rather than a general reluctance to participate. The additional response that may be adding to the refusals is the fact that respondent[s] listed themselves on the national Do-Not-Call list, and don't understand that survey research is exempt.[45]

The Pew Research Center found that the response rates on two surveys, each conducted in 1997 and in 2003, declined for both. In the first survey, conducted "with commonly utilized polling techniques" the response rate declined from 36 percent to 27 percent. In the second survey, one that employed "more rigorous techniques aimed at obtaining a high rate of response," the response rate declined from 61 percent to 51 percent. The Pew Research Center remarked, "This decline results from increased reluctance to participate in surveys and not from an inability by survey organizations to contact someone in a household."[46]

On a more positive note, the Pew Research Center reported that although its response rates decreased, its findings were still representative of the American population. The Center concluded "that carefully conducted polls continue to obtain representative samples of the public and provide accurate data about the views and experiences of Americans."[47] In addition, the Council for Marketing and Opinion Research found that unethical selling under the guise of research, known as SUGGING, has declined.[48]

CONCLUSION: MEASURING OPINIONS AND DEMOCRACY

We began this chapter with a sarcastic quote about polling being the "worst way of measuring public opinion." Actually, public opinion surveying *is* a terrible way to study public opinion. The questions are superficial; if you don't believe us, try to write a question on abortion that would elicit your complete opinion. Now write a perfect question that captures your opinion on the government's proper relationship with the economy. Now do the same thing for another ten issues. Do you find, perhaps, your opinions are a little too complex to be reduced to one number—answer number 4, for example? But in survey research, we reduce real people's opinions to specific numbers.

There are many other problems with survey research, which we have outlined in this chapter. Sampling error, for example, assumes 100 percent response rates, which we *never* obtain. All analysis assumes that each person who answered a question understood it exactly the way the researcher meant it—which is, to say the least, implausible. And all survey research depends on the respondents' answers, which we know are often incorrect and sometimes dishonest.

Yet survey research is an excellent method of learning about people's opinions. Even with all the problems, experience has shown us that the answers *really do* reveal people's opinions. The information from survey research has been very useful for understanding how people perceive the political world. Survey research is the only way we can obtain information that we can generalize, or project, to the entire population. That is why we have devoted an entire chapter to the methodology—and why we will refer to it repeatedly in this book.

But before we return to survey research, we will examine other methodologies that are used to study public opinion. None of these other methods has the advantage of projectability to a larger population, but each has its own benefits. With laboratory experiments, researchers can control all the extraneous variables in order to measure the important study variables more clearly. Researchers can use analysis of mail to see how people think and write about politics, and to find when social movements begin. Qualitative research can overcome the superficiality problem of survey research by probing deeply into each person's understanding of and attitudes towards politics. It is to these other methods that we now turn.

Suggested Reading

Asher, Herbert. *Polling and the Public* (6th Edition). Washington, DC: CQ Press, 2004.

Fishkin, James F. *The Voice of the People: Public Opinion and Democracy*. New Haven: Yale University Press, 1995.

Manza, Jeff, Fay Lomax Cook, and Benjamin I. Page, eds. *Navigating Public Opinion: Polls, Policy, and the Future of American Democracy*. Oxford: Oxford University Press, 2002.

Warren, Kenneth F. *In Defense of Public Opinion Polling*. Cambridge, MA: Westview Press, 2001.

www ▶▶▶ Interactive Learning Exercise

Gathering Survey Research Data

An important part of learning about public opinion is finding out how public opinion data are gathered. In this interactive learning exercise, you can administer a public opinion questionnaire. Use the public opinion questionnaire from this book's Web site. There are four questionnaires from which to choose. There is an SPSS data file (without any data) for each questionnaire on the same Web site. All questionnaires are written in MS Word format. It is easy to customize each questionnaire and SPSS file for your own needs. Most of the questions in these questionnaires are taken from the National Election Study and General Social Survey questionnaires.

Notes

1. Humphrey Taylor, "Myth and Reality in Reporting Sampling Errors: How the Media Confuse and Mislead Readers and Viewers," *The Polling Report,* May 4, 1998. Cited in Kenneth F. Warren, *In Defense of Public Opinion Polling* (Cambridge, MA: Westview Press, 2001), p. 45.

2. V. O. Key, Jr., *Public Opinion and American Democracy* (New York: Alfred A. Knopf, 1961), p. 3.

3. Russell G. Brooker, Laura M. Cleary, and Richard W. Yob, *Evaluation of the Effectiveness of the Occupational Licensing Program* (Madison, Wis.: Wisconsin Department of Transportation, 2002). The study was conducted by The Dieringer Research Group, Inc., http://www.dot.wisconsin.gov/library/research/reports/safety.htm.

4. The reason the researchers thought that people without driver's licenses would not answer honestly is that they conducted some face-to-face preliminary interviews with drivers who had lost their licenses. These drivers told them that they would not answer questions honestly on the telephone but would in a mail survey if it were anonymous.

5. Dick Morris, "Those faulty exit polls were sabotage," *The Hill,* 2004, accessed at www.hillnews.com/morrris/110404.aspx.

6. Ibid., Steven F. Freeman, "The Unexplained Exit Poll Discrepancy," 2004, accessed at http://www.ilcaonline.org/freeman.pdf.

7. National Election Pool. From CNN Web site, www.cnn.com/ELECTION/2004/pages/results/states/US/P/00/epolls.0.html.

8. Dick Morris and Peter Finn, "Partial Vote Results Show a Tight Race in Ukraine Runoff," *Washington Post,* November 22, 2004, p. A15.

9. For other, similar, lists of advantages and disadvantages, see James Witte and Philip E. N. Howard, "The Future of Polling: Relational Inference and the Development of Internet Survey Instruments," in Jeff Manza, Fay Lomax Cook,

and Benjamin I. Page, eds., *Navigating Public Opinion: Polls, Policy, and the Future of American Democracy* (Oxford: Oxford University Press, 2002), pp. 274–275; and Donald R. Schaefer and Don A. Dillman, "Development of a Standard E-Mail Methodology: Results of an Experiment," *Public Opinion Quarterly* 62 (1998): 378–382.

10. Schaefer and Dillman, p. 382. Also see Duane Bachman, John Elfring, and Gary Vazzana, "Tracking the Progress of E-mail versus Snail-Mail," *Marketing Research* 8 (1996): 31–35.

11. The Dieringer Research Group, Inc., *2004 American Interactive Consumer Survey,* accessed at http://www.thedrg.com/d/nws/pr/aics_prod_desc.pdf.

12. Witte and Howard, p. 281.

13. Ibid., pp. 278–280.

14. Survey Sampling International, *Internet Sampling Solutions,* accessed at www.surveysampling.com.

15. After the second presidential debate in 2004 between John F. Kerry and George W. Bush, one of your authors found that several newspapers were sponsoring an Internet poll on who won the debate. Your author chose to respond to the poll sponsored by *The Indianapolis Star,* having delivered the *Star* when he was 15 years old. He found that 94.5% of the survey respondents said that Senator Kerry had won the debate. Of what value was that information? Zero. Nothing.

16. Herbert Asher, *Polling and the Public,* 6th ed. (Washington, DC: CQ Press, 2004), p. 69.

17. Quoted in Lindsay Rogers, *The Pollsters: Public Opinion, Politics, and Democratic Leadership* (New York: Alfred A Knopf, 1949), p. 105.

18. Pew Research Center, *Polls Face Growing Resistance, But Still Representative* (Washington, DC: 2004), p. 5, accessed at http://people press.org/reports/display.php3?PageID=813.

19. Weighting is also used for other purposes. For example, Paul M. Sniderman and Thomas Piazza (*Black Pride and Black Prejudice* [Princeton, N.J.: Princeton University Press, 2002]) weight respondents based on the number of adults living in each sample household. Since only one person from a household can be interviewed, people who lived in households with more eligible adults were less likely to be interviewed, so those respondents had greater weights. (See p. 183 for a more detailed explanation and for information on other weighting used in that study.)

20. American Civil Liberties Union, *National Crisis Survey on Freedom and Liberty* (New York, 2004).

21. Jim Sensenbrenner, *Keeping in Touch* 52 (April 2004).

22. Everett Carll Ladd, "The Polling Business: The Holocaust Poll Error: A Modern Cautionary Tale," *Public Perspective: A Roper Center Review of Public Opinion and Polling,* July/August 1994, accessed at http://edcallahan.com/web110/articles/holocaust. htm.

23. Sensenbrenner, 2004.

24. Lee Sigelman and Susan Welch, *Black Americans' Views of Racial Inequality: The Dream Deferred* (Cambridge: Cambridge University Press, 1991), pp. 128–129.

25. David W. Moore, "Which Administration Is More Culpable for Terrorist Attacks?," *The Gallup Poll Tuesday Briefing*, April 6, 2004, accessed at http://www.gallup. com/content/default.aspx?ci=11239

26. Robert Weissberg, *Polling, Policy, and Public Opinion: The Case Against Heeding the "Voice of the People"* (New York: Palgrave Macmillan, 2002).

27. Susan Herbst, *Reading Public Opinion: How Political Actors View the Democratic Process* (Chicago: The University of Chicago Press, 1998), p. 16.

28. Robert E. Lane, *Political Ideology: Why the American Common Man Believes What He Does* (New York: The Free Press, 1967), p. 241.

29. http://www.pbs.org/newshour/btp/dop_background.html.

30. Ibid. http://www.pbs.org/newshour/btp/dop_background.html.

31. http://www.pbs.org/newshour/btp/polls.html.

32. James F. Fishkin, *The Voice of the People: Public Opinion and Democracy*(New Haven: Yale University Press, 1995), pp. 207–208.

33. Ibid., p. 208.

34. Martin Gilens, "An Anatomy of Survey-Based Experiments," in Jeff Manza, Fay Lomax Cook, and Benjamin I. Page, eds., *Navigating Public Opinion: Polls, Policy, and the Future of American Democracy* (Oxford: Oxford University Press, 2002), pp. 232–250.

35. See Paul M. Sniderman and Edward G. Carmines, *Reaching Beyond Race* (Cambridge, MA: Harvard University Press, 1997).

36. See Christopher H. Achen, *The Statistical Analysis of Quasi-Experiments* (Berkeley: University of California Press, 1986).

37. In this example, the researcher would know that about half the "test" respondents were angered or upset by using simple mathematics. If the two sets of respondents were similar (which they would be because they were randomly assigned to be in the "test" or "control" group), and *all* respondents in the "test" group were angered or upset by the extra item, the average of the "test" respondents would be 1.0 items higher than the average for the "control" group. If half were angered or upset by the additional item, their average would be 0.5 items higher. For examples of this methodology, see James H. Kuklinski, Michael D. Cobb, and Martin Gilens, "Racial Attitudes and the 'New South,'" *Journal of Politics* 59 (1997): 323–349; James H. Kuklinski, Paul M. Sniderman, Kathleen Knight, Thomas Piazza, Philip E. Tetlock, Gordon R. Lawrence, and Barbara Mellers, "Racial Prejudice and Attitudes toward Affirmative Action," *American Journal of Political Science* 41 (1997): 402–419; and Martin Gilens, Paul M. Sniderman, and James H. Kuklinski, "Affirmative Action and the Politics of Realignment," *British Journal of Political Science* 28 (1998): pp. 153–183.

38. See Paul M. Sniderman, Louk Hagendoorn, and Markus Prior, "The Banality of Extremism: Exploratory Studies in Political Persuasion." Prepared for the annual meeting of the Midwest Political Science Association, Chicago, 2000.

39. For more on TESS, see http://www.experimentcentral.org.

40. See Lawrence R. Jacobs and Robert Y. Shapiro, *Politicians Don't Pander: Political Manipulation and the Loss of Democratic Responsiveness* (Chicago: University of Chicago Press, 2000), esp. Chapter 2.

41. Pew Research Center, *Polls Face Growing Resistance, But Still Representative* (Washington, DC: 2004), p. 9.

42. Ibid., p. 10.

43. Cited in Witte and Howard, p. 279.

44. Pew Research Center, p. 11.

45. Council for Marketing and Opinion Research, *2003 CMOR Respondent Co-operation and Industry Image Study Topline Summary*, 2003, p. 2.

46. Pew Research Center, p. 1

47. Ibid.

48. Council for Marketing and Opinion Research, p. 1.

Measuring Public Opinion: Other Methods

The best argument against democracy is a five minute conversation with the average voter.

— Winston Churchill[1]

Questions to Think About

In this chapter we will look at nonsurvey ways in which political scientists learn about people's opinions. As you read this chapter, ask yourself:

- What can you learn about a person's political opinions from a conversation that you could not learn from a survey?
- How important is the ability to project survey respondents' opinions to a larger population when compared to learning more in-depth information about a few people?
- How well do you express your opinion on an issue by checking a box?

THERE ARE other ways than survey research that political scientists use to study public opinion. In this chapter, we discuss four of them. Two are quantitative; this means that, like survey research, they involve numbers and numerical analysis. The others are qualitative; they do not involve numerical analysis. The four research methods are:

Quantitative Methods
- Laboratory experiments
- Analysis of mail

Qualitative Methods

- In-depth interviews
- Focus groups

IN ADDITION, we include a few methods that are not widely used by political scientists but are commonly used by practicing politicians to study politics. Because they lack methodological discipline, we call them informal methodologies. They are:

Informal Methods

- Elections
- Interest groups and lobbying
- Media
- Feedback from constituents

SINCE THESE alternative methodologies are less familiar than survey research, we will devote more space to citing examples of research using them. As you read these short summaries, keep in mind that we are only briefly summarizing studies that have much more in them than we can mention here. One of the main attractions of qualitative research is that it yields complex, subtle data—exactly the kind of data that cannot be summarized briefly in a statistical table or in a few paragraphs. In our summaries, we do not mean to describe the studies completely, only to give examples of the kinds of findings one can obtain from the research.

As we explore the four formal research methodologies, we see the dominance of survey research on the political science discipline. That dominance is revealed by the fact that practitioners of these methodologies regularly explain their research by comparing it to survey research. Practitioners of survey research, on the other hand, almost never explain their work by comparing it to other methodologies.

But before we begin discussion of these additional research methodologies, we remind you of the questions we asked in the previous chapter about how much government officials can and should pay attention to research findings. Concerning the *democratic dialogue,* do these other methodologies enable the people in government to "hear" the people better? Although these methodologies are not projectable to the larger population, they can reveal more in-depth opinions than surveys can. Do these types of research help officials hear and understand the people better? Concerning the *democratic dilemma,* should unprojectable research results be used to help government officials understand the public better?

Part of this chapter involves what we call informal research techniques. They include what all democratically chosen government leaders have done ever since there have been democracies (and probably before)—that is, elections, lobbying, media, and feedback from constituents. These "research methods" have a special place in democratic politics; in fact, they are either integral parts of the governmental framework (elections) or are protected by the First Amendment (rights of petition, press, and speech). Thinking about the relationship between public opinion and public policy, do these methods have some special priority over the more "formal" research methods? For example, is a legislator acting more responsibly or "democratically" to act in response to a survey, some focus groups, or a lobbyist?

OTHER QUANTITATIVE METHODS

Two types of **quantitative research,** laboratory experiments and analysis of mail, reveal different kinds of information than survey research does. These methods permit researchers to ask different kinds of questions than would be appropriate for surveys. The main problem with these methods is that, for the most part, they are not projectable, as surveys are. We cannot say, for example, that if X percent of subjects (as experiment participants are called) in an experiment respond in one way to a situation, then X percent, or any other percent, of all adults would respond the same way in the same circumstances. The sample sizes are typically too small, and study participants are typically not chosen randomly from the entire population being studied, for the study results to be projectable.

Laboratory Experiments

In **laboratory experiments,** study participants are divided into two or more groups and are given different stimuli. One or more groups is the *treatment* or *test* group that receives a stimulus that the other group, the *control* group, does not. The stimuli may be documents, explanations, exercises, or television advertisements. After the stimulus, or nonstimulus, subjects in each group are asked to perform a task or answer questions. The researcher wants to see if the stimulus leads subjects to behave differently from the subjects who have not been given the stimulus or have been given a different stimulus. The reason that researchers use experiments is that they can isolate stimuli and see their effects without the confounding effects of the rest of the environment.

Experiments in public opinion research have yielded some very interesting and useful results. Shanto Iyengar and Markus Prior[2] conducted an experiment to investigate the effect of political television advertisements on people's opinions of commercial television ads. In the experiment, they showed 9 TV ads to 1,553 people. The ads were shown in three locations in the Los Angeles area. The subjects were divided into three groups: (1) a control group that saw nine commercial ads; (2) a treatment group that saw one political ad and eight commercial ads; and (3) another treatment group that saw two political ads and seven commercial ads. Iyengar and Prior found that more-educated subjects rated the commercial ads more negatively if they had seen one or two political ads, while less-educated subjects rated the commercial ads more negatively only if they had seen two political ads. The two researchers concluded that seeing political ads causes people, especially more educated people, to dislike commercial advertising. They said their results substantiated what advertising executives had been saying—that "dirty" political ads harmed public reception to their "clean" commercial advertisements.[3]

In her book, *Barbershops, Bibles, and BET*, Melissa Harris-Lacewell conducted two experiments with college students. One of these experiments included ninety-eight male and female African American students discussing two events organized by and for men—the 1995 Million Man March, which was almost entirely black, and a 1997 Promise Keepers Rally, which was mostly white. Both events had been criticized by women's groups as being misogynist and patriarchal. In the experiment, the ninety-eight participants completed pretest questionnaires and then were randomly placed into six test groups and one control group; at the end, all the students completed posttest questionnaires. Students in all the test groups read articles on the two events. Students in one test group then completed the final questionnaire. In the other five test groups, students discussed the articles for twenty minutes before completing the questionnaire. All discussions were audiotaped. Students in the second group discussed the articles among themselves. Students in the final four groups participated in discussions with one of two black facilitators—a man, introduced as a minister, or a woman, introduced as a professor. Each facilitator posed as a feminist in one group and as a conservative in another group.

Results of the experiment revealed, in the words of Harris-Lacewell, "two big stories." First, students in both groups with the "feminist" facilitators became more feminist themselves, but those in the male-led "feminist" group became the most feminist. Harris-Lacewell hypothesized that a male feminist would be more of a novelty and might force the students to "sit up and take notice." In addition, a male feminist might be perceived as more credible because he would not be arguing from a self-serving position.[4] The second "big story" was that students with the "conservative" facilitators became less conservative. In these two groups, the students resisted conservative arguments about black pathology and blamed negative black images on media bias and racism. They also rejected conservative individualism as self-serving rather than being interested in black advancement.[5] Harris-Lacewell used both quantitative analysis of the pre- and posttest questionnaires and qualitative analysis of the twenty-minute discussions. She uncovered many other findings from this experiment and a later similar one. These two findings are included here as examples of experimental research.

Analysis of Mail

In *Mobilizing Public Opinion*,[6] Taeku Lee makes a convincing argument that public opinion can be read by studying letters written to politicians. He studied letters about racial issues that individuals had written to U.S. presidents from 1948 to 1965. He showed how the letters reflected the changes in public perceptions about race over those seventeen years. According to Lee, the problem with using survey data to study momentous change is that questionnaire writers are often behind the times; they cannot, and should not be expected to, anticipate great changes in the political agenda. Letters to politicians, on the other hand, often anticipate agenda changes and can react very quickly to changing issues. Lee pointed out how letters changed quickly both in number and content in reaction to political events. He explained how the letters reflected the opinions and the writers' frames of reference. His data showed how often the most common themes occurred in the letters. The following table contains his data concerning letters written to presidents from 1960 through 1965 from African Americans, antimovement white Southerners, and pro-integration (usually non-Southern) whites. The differences in their perspectives are clear. While the African American and racially liberal white

TABLE 3.1. Most Common Individual Frames, 1960–1965.

Frames	Type of Correspondent		
	African Americans	Southern Whites	Racially Liberal Whites
Universal rights	34%	–	36%
Justice and equality	24	–	13
Democratic principles	11	–	–
Black identity, interests	15	–	–
Religious morality	12	8%	–
World opinion	12	–	19
Political symbols	11	–	–
Communism, cold war	–	24	–
States' rights	–	18	–
Civil rights activists as communists	–	17	–
Whites', taxpayers' rights	–	17	–
Movement leaders, organizations	–	13	–
Religious essentialism*	–	6	–
Police brutality	–	–	19
Equal protection under the law	–	–	15
Number of letters	*459*	*892*	*722*

*"Religious essentialism" refers to the claim that the Bible says that whites and blacks are essentially different.

Source: This table is abridged from three tables on pages 158,163, and 169 of *Mobilizing Public Opinion*.

letter writers emphasize universal rights more than any other subject, the Southern antimovement whites mention communism and states' rights, and they claim that the movement activists are communists.

He also claimed that analysis of the letters gave more information than answers to survey questions. He wrote, "These individual letters . . . revealed not only the views of correspondents about civil rights and racial integration but also the choices they made concerning the wording and framing of those views. These choices showed the powerful rhetorical force of dearly held values and the resounding influence of group-based interests, conflicts, and animosity."[7]

Lee did not claim that letters accurately capture the opinions of the entire public. Letter writers are not representative of all adults; they tend to be better educated and more interested in the issues—especially the issue they write about—than most people are. However, Lee says that letter writers are a reasonable measure of the opinions of the interested mobilized public, a layer of people between the elites and the mass public.

QUALITATIVE METHODS

Surveys, most experiments, and Lee's mail analysis are quantitative; that is, they involve the use of quantitative, or numerical, data. But some research methods are qualitative; they involve the use of nonnumerical data such as people's ideas, observations, or opinions stated in their own words. The purpose of **qualitative research** is to uncover the *quality* of opinion. Although quantitative analysis is very useful in determining *how many* people have a specific opinion, it is not very good, except superficially, in determining *how* people think and *why* they think the way they do. Qualitative research has the opposite strengths and weaknesses; it is useless in determining how many people have a specific opinion, but it is very useful for uncovering how people think and why they think the way they do. There are many types of qualitative research, but the most important ones for political research are in-depth interviews and focus groups.

In-Depth Interviews

In conducting **in-depth interviews**, researchers talk with people, usually face to face, for much longer amounts of time than they would in survey research—often several hours, which may be divided between days. The main purpose of in-depth interviews is to uncover the outlooks and perspectives of the people who are interviewed. Instead of asking a respondent to place herself in an answer category on abortion (e.g., "A woman should always be able to obtain an abortion"), a respondent in an in-depth interview might be asked simply how she feels about abortion. She would then give her opinion and her perspective on the issue. Instead of labeling herself by one specific answer, she would explain what she thinks when she thinks about abortion. There are many possible perspectives from which to view the abortion issue. With qualitative research, one can find out which of these perspectives a person uses. Here are some possible perspectives:

- When does life begin? Is a fetus a baby? What rights, if any, should it have?
- Should there be some laws for early pregnancy and others for late pregnancy? What should they be?
- Should abortion be legal for some circumstances, such as rape, but not for others? Why?
- Should some types of abortion be legal and others illegal? Which ones?
- Should laws distinguish between surgical and nonsurgical abortions? How?
- Would more women obtain unsafe illegal abortions if there were no legal abortions? How many? What would happen to the women?
- If abortion were illegal, should doctors be arrested and imprisoned for performing them? Should women be arrested and imprisoned for consenting to them? What effects would these arrests and incarcerations have on the United States?

Although it is possible to ask all these questions in a quantitative survey, it would probably be a tedious interview. And, with a quantitative survey, a researcher would only know how the respondent answered the specific questions asked. The researcher would not know which questions were most important to the respondent or how the respondent connected them in her mind. If a researcher did not ask a specific question, the respondent certainly would not answer it, even if it were on a subject important to the respondent. But an in-depth interview is designed to find out what each respondent thinks and how she connects her thoughts. It is also designed to uncover questions the researcher did not think to ask. A respondent in an in-depth interview might talk for thirty minutes on one subject if she really cares about it—or for less than a minute if she does not. In in-depth research, the respondent has a major role in determining the agenda of the interview.

The data obtained from in-depth interviews can be very nuanced and subtle. One can learn the context of respondents' opinions and how they structure the world in their minds. A researcher can learn how somebody really thinks about abortion rather than which answer category she places herself in. Of course, one cannot conduct enough in-depth interviews in one research project for statistical reliability; a typical number of respondents is fifteen to thirty. Therefore, the findings of in-depth research studies are not projectable to the entire population under investigation. In in-depth research, as in qualitative research in general, there is a trade-off of statistical reliability for more textured and contextual data.

Jonathan Schell, a journalist, interviewed members of one family and their neighbors repeatedly over the course of the 1984 election. He summarized the advantages of his method in this way:

I knew that on the basis of my talks with these people I could not make political generalizations of the kind that political polls allow, but I wanted to find out things that a poll could not reveal. Instead of finding out a little about a lot of votes, I wanted to find out everything I could about a handful of votes. After all, I thought it was here—in the minds of individual voters—that an election, in the last analysis, took place.[8]

Probably the most famous study of this type is *Political Ideology* by Robert E. Lane.[9] In this study, published in 1962, Lane talked with fifteen "average" American men from one neighborhood in an Eastern seaboard American city (that he calls "Eastport"). All the men were white married fathers. Lane talked with these fifteen men over several evenings for several months in 1957 and 1958. In the end, he compiled approximately 3,750 pages of verbatim transcripts. Lane principally sought to uncover the men's latent ideologies, the sources of those ideologies, and how they supported or weakened the institutions of democracy.

With his extremely textured and detailed data, Lane examined the ideas and ideologies of the fifteen men from several perspectives. In Chapter 9, for example, Lane explored the views of the fifteen men on the role of government and found a lack of cynical opinions. Lane found that the men felt that public officials served their own—the men's—interests by serving the public welfare. Because the men believed that public officials tried to serve the interests of the people, they thought that the people were sovereign—and that individuals, including the men, were important. Lane concluded that the men believed, although they did not explicitly say so, that the people "run things by having their welfare serve as the criterion of policy."[10] The men felt that government officials cared about ordinary people, which is what mattered to the men themselves.

In a 1980 book, *We Shall Not Overcome: Populism and Southern Blue-Collar Workers*,[11] Robert Emil Botsch interviewed fifteen textile workers in a Southern city. All the workers were aged between eighteen and thirty-three years old and had similar blue collar jobs in two textile mills. Ten were white and five were black. Botsch questioned them about politics, with particular emphasis on economic and racial issues. His methodology was consciously modeled on Lane's, even to the extent of interviewing fifteen men.

In a chapter on economic issues, Botsch showed how qualitative research can enhance, explain, and further develop quantitative findings. When asked, fourteen of the fifteen men said they favored to some extent the government providing jobs for people who wanted to work but were unable to find jobs. But, he noted, the men's opinions on this issue were very complex. For example, one of the men first said "sure" when asked if the government should provide jobs for those who wanted to work. "But when asked whether he minds having his tax money spent for this sort of thing, he quickly began to back away."[12] Botch pointed out that an analyst would have to examine the details of the men's opinions to really understand their opinions on the government providing jobs. He then summarized their opinions in a more nuanced manner:

A summary of their opinions on this issue would be close to the following proposition: The government should provide jobs if (1) merit is proved by the potential employee's willingness to take jobs like those that these men have been willing to accept in their lives; (2) jobs such as these are not available (most of the men believe they are available) and there is nowhere else to turn. A majority of these men, both black and white, also believe that government-provided jobs should not be of higher quality than those they endure. Enthusiasm is notably lacking for increasing taxes to finance the creation of such jobs.[13]

Jennifer L. Hochschild[14] conducted an in-depth study of twenty-eight adults, both men and women, poor and wealthy. Her sample consisted of eight poor women, eight poor men, six wealthy women, and six wealthy men. She investigated the people's views toward distributive justice, especially why poor

---

BOX 3.1

The Diversity of Opinion in a Demographically Homogeneous Group

When analysts look at public opinion data, they compare demographic groups and classify people by their groups. Analysts write things like, "Group X is more negative toward 'A' than Group Y is." Although we know that *not every single member* of Group X is negative toward "A," it is easy to get into the habit of thinking of members of Group X as being anti-A. For example, we might find from a survey that young working-class white men were generally opposed to busing for racial reasons. We could think, "Well, of course. Young working-class white men are very susceptible to feelings of racial prejudice."

When looking only at survey data, it can be easy to fall into this type of classification. But qualitative data shows the individual differences of unique human beings. Robert Emil Botsch shows the uniqueness of the fifteen men in his book, *We Shall Not Overcome*. Conducting interviews during the winter of 1976–1977, he asked the men a series of questions about racial integration. Their answers are shown on the following page. Keep in mind that the only major demographic difference between the men was race; they were all aged eighteen to thirty-three, all had high school educations or less, and all worked in blue-collar jobs in furniture factories in the same town. Yet, they gave a wide variety of opinions about race. The following table includes the names he gave them in his book (presumably not their real names). In order to facilitate reading the table, it lists all the white respondents first.

Note that only Melvin opposed all five measures dealing with racial integration, and he had to have Botsch explain the racial implications of busing. Dave opposed four of the measures and did not perceive busing as having a racial component. Of all the men, black or white, only Paul supported all five measures; none of the other men supported interracial marriage.

Note also the pattern of answers is much more complex than if the men had said only that they support or oppose each measure; note especially the need for footnotes. In fact, this table simplifies the men's answers; it is the nature of qualitative research not to be confined to tables like this very easily.

Opinions of 15 Men of Furntex on Racial Issues.

			Issue		
Name	School Integration	Racial Busing	Integrated Churches	Integrated Housing	Interracial Marriage
White Men					
Dave	Oppose	Not racial[*]	Oppose	Oppose	Oppose
Eddie	Ambivalent	Oppose	Favor, with reservations	Ambivalent	Acceptance[†]
Jim	Ambivalent	Oppose	Support	Support	Acceptance[†]
Junior	Ambivalent	Not racial[*]	Support	Oppose	Oppose
Kevin	Ambivalent	Acceptance[#]	Support	Favor with reservations	Acceptance[†]
Mark	Support	Support	Support	Support	Acceptance[†]
Melvin	Oppose	Oppose[‡]	Oppose	Oppose	Oppose
Paul	Support	Support	Support	Support	Support
Roy	Support	Oppose	Favor, with reservations	Support	Acceptance[†]
Terry	Support	Acceptance[#]	Support	Support	Acceptance[†]
Black Men					
Albert	Support	Oppose	Support	Oppose	Oppose
Brent	Support	Support	Support	Support	Acceptance[†]
John	Support	Support	Support	Support	Acceptance[†]
Lewis	Support	Oppose	Support	Support	Oppose
Rick	Support	Support	Support	Support	Acceptance[†]

[*] Dave and Junior did not perceive busing as a racial issue and did not answer the question.

[#] Kevin and Terry did not particularly like busing but accepted it as being necessary for school integration.

[‡] Melvin did not perceive busing as a racial issue but opposed it after Botsch explained it to him.

[†] Nine of the men accepted interracial marriage as a reality, although they did not like it.

Source: Botsch, *We Shall Not Overcome*, pp. 127–150.

people did not object more strenuously to unequal distribution of wealth in the United States. She found that people tend to have different perspectives on different domains in their lives. Most of her respondents thought that people's personal lives, family and friends, should be viewed from a perspective of equality; most also thought that the equality perspective was appropriate for the political domain. But most respondents had a competitive view of the economic domain in which individuals should differentiate themselves from each other through education and hard work. She concluded that most of the respondents in her sample simply did not believe that the standard political perspectives commonly accepted by Americans ("All people are created equal." "One person, one vote.") are relevant to the economic world.

Focus Groups

Businesses use **focus groups** in marketing research nearly every day. They are also used by political candidates on a regular basis. In the past ten years or so, they have been increasingly used by academic researchers.

A **focus group** involves a small group of people, generally about eight to twelve, and a moderator. The moderator asks questions, almost always open-ended. A typical question might be, "What do you think about the president's

Photo 3.1. Focus groups are moderated small-group discussions that try to simulate "real world" dialogue and opinion formation. © *Spencer Grant/PhotoEdit.*

policies?" The main purpose of focus group research, similar to in-depth interview research, is to find out what people think about important issues and how they think about them. That is, what perspectives do they use when thinking about issues? How do they frame the issues? What issues do they think are important? John R. Hibbing and Elizabeth Theiss-Morse explained the advantage of focus groups:

> Although focus groups lack the systematic qualities of traditional surveys, they do permit participants to express themselves with greater flexibility and in a more nuanced and interactive fashion than is possible in surveys, particularly on topics that are not constantly on their minds, such as attitudes toward political institutions.[15]

Hibbing and Theiss-Morse conducted eight focus groups in conjunction with a national random sample of American adults to study the public's views of congressional power. In their report on the research, they quoted some focus group participants about the power of Congress. One person they cited said, "The Congress. They're the ones that the president and everybody else has to go to to get them to approve things." Another said, "I think the presidency is kind of a figurehead position limited in power by the Congress. And no matter how much you like an individual, he can probably put a little bit of pressure on, but it's owned and regulated and operated by our Congress."[16] From the focus groups, Hibbing and Theiss-Morse concluded:

> Most often, focus group discussion of power pitted Congress against the president, and Congress nearly always won, but not by being active. According to several participants, the president desperately tries to get things done, but Congress often gets in the way.[17]

Hibbing and Theiss-Morse later conducted another national study on people's beliefs about how government should work. They combined eight focus groups in Nebraska, Maine, California, and Georgia with a telephone survey of 1,266 respondents conducted by the Gallup Organization. One of their main findings concerned explanations for low political participation in the United States. They concluded:

> Participation in politics is low because people do not like politics even in the best of circumstances; in other words, they simply do not like the process of openly arriving at a decision in the face of diverse opinions. They do not like politics when they view it from afar and they certainly do not like politics when they participate in it themselves. . . . These preferences, properly understood, suggest that the ultimate danger for the American polity is not, after all is said and done, that a populace bent on collecting power in its own hands will destroy any opportunity for Burkean and Madisonian sensibilities to be displayed by suitably detached elected officials. Rather, the deeper danger is that people will seize the first opportunity to tune out of politics in favor of government by autopilot. . . .[18]

In another study, Pamela Johnston Conover, Ivor M. Crewe, and Donald D. Searing conducted eight focus group discussions, four in the United States and four in Britain, to investigate people's perspectives toward citizenship. They used qualitative research because they wanted to see not only *what* people thought about citizenship but also *how* they viewed it. They said, "An essential part of understanding *what* citizens think about their rights, duties, and identities is understanding *how* they think about these matters."[19]

One of the concepts they studied was political rights. Some of the questions they asked were:

> It is often said that *citizens* have certain *rights*. What do you think these rights are? Any others? What would you say are the most important rights? Which are the least important? Where do rights come from? That is, when people say they have rights as citizens on what grounds do they base their claims?[20]

They found that American and British citizens perceived the concept of rights very differently. Participants in all four of the American groups viewed rights as civil rights, such as freedom of speech or religion. British participants, on the other hand, viewed rights as social rights, such as the rights of people to have "a roof over their heads, food in their bellies, clothes on their backs, and an education for their children."[21] Whereas American focus group members tended to view rights as individual rights, British participants referred to rights of groups or categories of people. [22]

Conover and colleagues found several important differences in the ways American and British citizens thought of rights. It would have been extremely difficult to find these differences through quantitative research because these contrasts were revealed in the way the focus group members constructed their thoughts and worded their explanations. A quantitative questionnaire would simply have asked the respondents to answer questions the researchers had constructed. Of course, Conover and colleagues did not claim that all Americans, or any specific proportion of Americans, viewed rights the same way the focus group members did, but the research did reveal how some Americans view rights. The research provided insights into how people construct the idea of citizenship and how American and British citizens do so differently.

Advantages and Disadvantages of Qualitative Research

The principal advantage of qualitative research is that it can uncover the perspectives and thought patterns of ordinary people. Researchers can not only find out what people's opinions are but also how they think of those issues and why they have the opinions they do. In qualitative research, people explain their own ideas in their own words rather than responding to researchers' questions in predetermined categories.

Focus groups, but not in-depth interviews, have an additional advantage of being more like real political life because they require people to discuss their opinions with others, just as people tend to do in the real political world. Of course, this can also be considered a disadvantage because people can be temporarily influenced by other participants who are especially persuasive. In addition, some focus group members may be shy or intimidated by more aggressive members and may say less. A researcher needs to be careful not to informally "weight" focus group results by giving more credence to people who talk more.

Qualitative research can also shed much light on *why* people have the opinions they do. Whereas in quantitative research, the number of people with an opinion is important, the reasons for those opinions are secondary. For example, if a researcher finds that 36 percent of the respondents to a survey support a woman's right to an abortion, that researcher is unlikely to find out why each of the respondents has the opinion he or she does. The proportion is the important thing. A survey researcher will probably not find that Respondent #135 supports the right to abortion because she sees it as a "right to privacy" issue, while Respondent #257 supports the right to abortion because he feels it is important to obey the current law, Respondent #445 actually opposes abortion but answered that she favors it because she sees the difficulty of trying to enforce an antiabortion law, and Respondent #543 really had not thought about the issue before but says he favors it because he does not want to appear uninformed and has to say *something*. In most quantitative research, the numbers are compiled and whether respondents have good reasons for their opinions is not considered.

However, in qualitative research, study participants are asked to explain their opinions. In focus groups, participants can disagree with each other. The reasons for opinions are examined, and a researcher can gain a fuller understanding of the people's viewpoints and opinions. In the case of abortion, the participants can explain their positions, and researchers can find out who supports abortion from a right to privacy perspective and who supports it from an enforcement, or other, perspective.

In qualitative research, a respondent can explain the relationships between opinions, whereas in survey research the researcher needs to figure out the relationships through statistical techniques like cross-tabulations and correlation analysis. Jennifer Hochschild pointed out this advantage of qualitative research in the context of in-depth interviewing:

> In opinion polling, the *researcher infers* the links between variables; in intensive interviewing, the researcher induces the *respondent* to *create* the links between the variables as he or she sees them. [emphasis in original][23]

Another advantage of qualitative research is that researchers can investigate the quality or depth of people's opinions. Because the researcher can probe opinions intensively, holes in a respondent's knowledge or inconsistencies in opinions can be revealed. In focus group discussions, participants can disagree and uncover each other's problems in information or logic.

Qualitative research can also find out how firmly people hold their opinions. Especially in focus group arguments, participants can change their minds. While it is possible to examine in a survey how people's minds change as they encounter new evidence,[24] it is infrequently done. Such investigation is done much more easily, and often, in qualitative research.

Another important advantage of qualitative methodologies is that researchers can find the answers to questions they did not think to ask. In both in-depth interviews and focus group discussions, respondents often stray into areas the researcher had not intended to cover. In fact, one of the main purposes of qualitative research is to allow the respondents to approach the questions from their own perspectives and bring up issues that the researchers had not anticipated. In a quantitative survey, it is common to receive answers that one did not expect, but it is practically impossible for a researcher to ask a question on a topic that he or she had not thought about. It is even more difficult for a respondent to answer a question that is not asked.

The principal disadvantage of qualitative research is that results are not projectable. Qualitative results are not generalizable for two reasons. First, the subjects are seldom selected randomly; people who fit the requirements of the study are chosen without any effort to make sure that everybody in the population has an equal chance to be selected. Even if the subjects are selected randomly, the sample sizes are too small to use quantitatively (the 95 percent confidence range for a random sample of fifteen respondents is ± 26 percentage points, which is much too large to be useful). Because of the lack of generalizability in qualitative research, if six of ten participants in a focus group have an opinion, we cannot responsibly say that 60 percent of people in the population have that opinion. We cannot say that between 50 percent and 70 percent have that opinion. In fact, we cannot say *any* percent of people have that opinion. The correct percent may be 4 percent or 97 percent; we do not know. We can find out what people think and why they think the way they do, but we cannot learn how many think that way from qualitative research.

At the end of *What's Fair?* Jennifer Hochschild correctly notes that her findings are not projectable and cannot be used to estimate how many Americans hold what views of economic equality. She calls for a survey as a next step in her research to determine the extent of opinions in the United States. By doing so, of course, she acknowledges both the differences between qualitative and quantitative research and reveals the high level of credibility that survey research enjoys:

> The next task for social scientists is to determine how many and what kinds of people endorse, acquiesce, are differentiating opponents, indifferent, or egalitarian opponents. A survey would need to distinguish among kinds and degrees of non-support for redistribution of wealth. It should examine distributive beliefs in other domains of life besides the economic. It would also need to query distributive norms, ambivalence, and emotional reactions. Only after such a study is completed can we definitively pronounce on American beliefs about distributive justice.[25]

INFORMAL WAYS TO MEASURE PUBLIC OPINION

So far, we have discussed formal research methodologies that political scientists use to study public opinion. Practicing politicians also use these methods, especially surveys and focus groups. These methods, particularly survey

BOX 3.2

Hard *Numbers: The Hazards of Interpreting Quantitative Data*

Some advocates of quantitative research dismiss qualitative research; they say that by using quantitative methods they are dealing with hard numbers rather than touchy-feely qualitative findings. However, we encourage you to be aware of the ambiguities in quantitative data and be skeptical of how hard the numbers are.

Here is an example. During the 1980s and 1990s, many electric and natural gas utilities were required by law to develop programs promoting energy conservation. They were also required to evaluate the effectiveness of their programs. One such evaluation involved a survey of appliance store owners and managers about their sales of energy-efficient appliances. In that study, twenty appliance store owners and managers were asked several questions about the program and how they conducted their businesses. One question concerned the recommendations that appliance distributors give to store owners and managers. The owners and managers in the survey were asked how important the recommendations were. They were given five responses to choose from: (1) Very Important; (2) Somewhat Important; (3) Neither Important nor Unimportant; (4) Somewhat Unimportant; and (5) Very Unimportant. The next question was an open-ended follow-up; it asked, "Why do you feel that way?" In the first question, nine of the twenty respondents said the recommendations were "(2) Somewhat Important."

The answers of those nine respondents to the follow-up question ("Why do you feel that way?") were:

- "They [the distributors] go according to inventory. We do not have confidence in their suggestions. We go with the models that do the job in our area."
- "Will actually seek recommendations but take it with a grain of salt. Our past experience counts more."
- "I don't always take their recommendations."
- "They are able to guide us. Show us the sales trend."
- "They have knowledge of factory support of product. They know the benefits of product, and that is a great value in purchasing."
- "Certain products sell better in certain areas. Distributors sell in varied markets. I know what is good in our area."
- "They try to give you models they think are the best buys and available."
- "They have better knowledge of popularity of product compared to other products."
- "Depends on their knowledge in the marketing area."

Do you see much consistency between the open-ended answers? We don't. Although all nine of these respondents answered "(2) Somewhat Important" for the distributors' recommendations, their explanations for their answers range from "They are able to guide us" to "Depends on their knowledge" to "We do not have confidence in their suggestions." From the strictly quantitative point of view, they all gave the same hard answer of "2," but they meant very different things by it. The "2" appeared to be a hard number, but in fact nine people used it to mean nine very different, often conflicting, things.

research, tend to be used extensively by political scientists nearly to the exclusion of other methods. There are some additional methods of studying public opinion that political scientists typically do not use when studying public opinion—but that practicing politicians are very likely to use. These methods are often very important in how politicians understand public opinion and how opinion gets converted into policy. In the end, public opinion is important not because political scientists study it; it is important because politicians—elected and appointed officials—study it.

Elections

The most common way for a democratic government to learn about public opinion is through elections. Elections are built into the system. They are important because they determine who staffs the government, and they are also one way for the public to express its feelings about politics. But they are not a particularly precise method for ascertaining public opinion.

Politicians and researchers may try to figure out why one person won an election rather than another, but usually there are so many factors that it is impossible to single out one or even a few determining reasons. A candidate may have won because he or she is in touch with the voters and understands their needs better than any other candidate. But, on the other hand, a candidate may have won because he or she is a better speaker or because of more or better television advertisements. Even if a candidate won on "the issues," it may be difficult to determine which issues were most important. Some voters may have decided on the basis of economic issues, while others decided on the basis of a candidate's stand on abortion or gun control. In the end, all that elections tell us about "what the public wants" is that they preferred one candidate over another—not why.

Elections are also imperfect measures of public opinion because they reflect only the opinions of those who voted. Certainly, in societies in which all adults have the right to vote, elections can reflect the various views of all the people. But in practice, not everyone votes—especially in the United States, where only about half the eligible voters participate in presidential elections, and even fewer do so in other elections. Therefore, elections tend to reflect the views of those who vote, who are not necessarily representative of the public. As we shall see later in this book, elections tend to reflect the viewpoints of more educated, wealthier citizens.

While elections are a blunt measure of public opinion, they are the most effective means by which public opinion can control the government and public policy. Elected politicians, who are future candidates, will avoid taking especially unpopular positions on issues because they know that voters might notice and could show their displeasure at the polls. If voters do not notice a candidate's position on their own, opposing candidates will be happy to point it out. In this way, elections serve to hold politicians accountable to voters' opinions—even latent opinions that the voters may not consciously hold. Politicians' perceptions of public opinion, then, may be as important as the actual public opinion itself. A state legislator may refrain from voting for an obscure but unpopular bill because she is afraid that constituents would be offended and vote for her opponent in the next election—even if, in fact, they would never know.

Interest Groups and Lobbying

It may seem unlikely that interest groups would be valid measures of public opinion. They are remarkably unrepresentative of the public as a whole. The wealthy and the educated members of society are much more likely to be organized into interest groups and employ lobbyists. The poor and uneducated are much less able to speak to the government through interest groups. Nevertheless, legislators, staffers, and other government personnel do pay attention to what interest groups say. They have good reason to do so. Good lobbyists tend to be well informed about issues concerning their employers; they have access to facts necessary to write laws; they understand the political process; and they are present when necessary to answer questions.

In a study of committee staffers in the Illinois state legislature, Susan Herbst[26] found that the staffers did pay a great deal of attention to lobbyists and, in fact, considered what they said to be public opinion. Herbst was very clear that some of the staffers did not merely consider their views to be surrogates for public opinion; they considered them to *be* public opinion. The staffers relied on lobbyists to be their conduit to understanding public opinion partly because they perceived them to be in touch with the people of Illinois and to honestly relay the people's opinions. The staffers felt that the lobbyists were honest because their credibility would be ruined if they were caught lying. Another reason the staffers relied on the lobbyists to understand public opinion was that the lobbyists were always there and were knowledgeable about the issues and the bills being considered in the legislature. While the public might be "for" lowering a tax, ordinary people would not understand how a tax could be lowered or how much it could be lowered. The lobbyists could. The staffers, according to Herbst, saw ordinary citizens as lazy and uninterested in politics.

The Media

Many government officials, and many regular citizens, look to the media to understand the views of the public. In Herbst's study, she found that legislative staffers also considered the media to accurately present public opinion. The media are important in understanding people's opinions, and we will devote an entire chapter to the media later in this book.

Media, such as television, newspapers, and magazines, are important because of the news they choose and how they portray the issues. In other terms, they are important in determining the political agenda (what people in the government are thinking about) and in framing the issues (how the issues are being considered).

The print media are also important as conduits of opinions from editorialists, columnists, and ordinary people who write letters to the editor. Most large newspapers print the opinions of their editors and run the articles of liberal and conservative columnists. Most also print letters to the editor that allow ordinary people the power to express practically any sort of opinion. Some magazines, such as *Time* and *Newsweek*, cover politics in an essentially nonpartisan way, but there are many more magazines that represent practically any political point of view in the American political spectrum. Conservative magazines such as *National Review* express views right of political center, while liberal magazines such as *The New Republic* tend to explain politics from a more left-leaning point of view. These ideological magazines are useful for explaining their perspectives to their readers and to government officials. Conservative, or liberal, elected officials often look to conservative, or liberal, magazines for support and justification of their opinions.

Feedback from Constituents

People use letters and telephone calls to express their opinions to their elected representatives. While many of these letters and calls are about specific personal problems, such as lost Social Security checks, many of them are about contentious political issues. Politicians notice when their constituents write. A few letters from constituents may represent the opinions of thousands of other voters.

Letters and calls often spontaneously arise from interested ordinary people. But sometimes interest groups organize their members to write or call their representatives in state legislatures or in Congress. The interest groups understand how elected officials pay attention to contact from their constituents and use those constituents to "lobby" lawmakers. This is known as "grassroots" lobbying. In two examples from President Clinton's administration: (1) interest groups in the student loan industry (the people who may have handled your loan) urged their members to contact their representatives and senators to fight against a bill that would reform the student loan procedures;[27] and (2) interest groups in the health care industry, such as HMOs and hospitals, rallied their members to contact their representatives and senators to oppose Clinton's national health insurance plan.[28] While "grassroots" lobbying is not always successful, it was effective in these two examples; neither the student loan industry nor the health care industry was reorganized by Congress.

Again, letters are not a "fair" way to assess public opinion. Letter writers tend to be better educated and wealthier than average citizens. So the voices lawmakers hear in the calls and letters they receive from constituents tend to speak with higher-class accents than most citizens.

But politicians do not passively wait for people to contact them. They frequently conduct meetings to hear from their constituents. In one newsletter sent to the constituents of a Midwestern congressman, sixteen constituent "town hall meetings" with the congressman are listed for a two-month period. That same newsletter contains a fifteen-question questionnaire, with answers to be put on the back of an attached postcard already addressed to the congressman's Washington office.[29]

It is unlikely that town hall meetings or responses to newsletter questionnaires yield accurate information about the opinions of constituents as a whole. The most vocal or most aggrieved constituents are usually the most likely to speak at the meetings or return the questionnaires. They may not be the most thoughtful constituents and are extremely unlikely to represent a random sample of citizens. Nevertheless, these meetings and questionnaires may be useful to the elected representatives. They give the politicians insight into what some constituents are thinking and may reveal important issues or foretell impending problems.

CONCLUSION: MEASURING AND UNDERSTANDING OPINIONS

Now that we have examined five "formal" research methodologies (surveys, experiments, mail analysis, in-depth interviews, and focus groups) and four informal techniques (elections, lobbying, media coverage, and feedback from constituents), we should ask not only if government officials should use research to guide their actions, but which research, if any, they should use. The only advantage of survey research is its ability to be projected to the entire population. That is only one advantage, but it is a massive one. The overwhelming majority of public opinion research is conducted through surveys. Taeku Lee counted the articles on race in *Public Opinion Quarterly* for sixty years, from its beginning in 1937 through 1996; he found that while 14 percent of the articles in the first decade (1937–1946) used survey research, 91 percent of the articles did in the decade 1987–1996.[30] In fact, survey research is the method we use most in this book.

But remember that there are other methods that achieve different kinds of results. When we discuss later in this book how governmental officials attempt to learn about public opinion, we will see that they put great stock in focus groups. If you want to know *how many* people have a certain opinion, there is no substitute for survey research. But if you want to know *why* they feel the way they do, or how they configure the political world in their heads, other types of research may be better.

Suggested Readings

Botsch, Robert Emil. *We Shall Not Overcome: Populism and Southern Blue-Collar Workers*. Chapel Hill: University of North Carolina Press, 1980.

Conover, Pamela Johnston, Ivor M. Crewe, and Donald D. Searing. "The Nature of Citizenship in the United States and Great Britain: Empirical Comments on Theoretical Themes." *Journal of Politics* 53 (1991): 800–832.

Harris-Lacewell, Melissa Victoria. *Barbershops, Bibles, and BET: Everyday Talk and Black Political Thought*. Princeton: Princeton University Press, 2004.

Herbst, Susan. *Reading Public Opinion: How Political Actors View the Democratic Process*. Chicago: University of Chicago Press, 1998.

Hochschild, Jennifer. *What's Fair: American Beliefs About Distributive Justice*. Cambridge, MA: Harvard University Press, 1986.

Lane, Robert E. *Political Ideology: Why the American Common Man Believes What He Does*. New York: The Free Press, 1967.

Lee, Taeku. *Mobilizing Public Opinion: Black Insurgency and Racial Attitudes in the Civil Rights Era*. Chicago: University of Chicago Press, 2002.

Milburn, Michael A. *Persuasion and Politics: The Social Psychology of Public Opinion*. Pacific Grove, CA: Brooks/Cole Publishing Company, 1991.

 **Interactive Learning Exercise:**

Analysis of Community Opinion

This exercise requires you to analyze real-world data and make recommendations to a city government that is contemplating closing a main street to accommodate a university. You will examine various types of qualitative and quantitative data to determine the opinions of people who live in the university's neighborhood. An important aspect of this exercise is integrating the results of different kinds of research into a coherent analysis.

Notes

1. This quotation from Winston Churchill was taken from ThinkExist.com. The Web address is: http://en.thinkexist.com/search/ searchquotation.asp?search=five+minutes.

2. Shanato Iyengar and Markus Prior, "Giving Advertising a Bad Name: The Effect of Political Ads on Commercial Advertising," in Barbara Norrander and Clyde Wilcox, eds., *Understanding Public Opinion*, 2nd ed. (Washington, DC: CQ Press, 2002), pp. 43–60.

3. Ibid., p. 59.

4. Melissa Victoria Harris-Lacewell, *Barbershops, Bibles, and BET: Everyday Talk and Black Political Thought* (Princeton: Princeton University Press, 2004), p. 122.

5. Ibid., pp. 135–140.

6. Taeku Lee, *Mobilizing Public Opinion: Black Insurgency and Racial Attitudes in the Civil Rights Era* (Chicago: University of Chicago Press, 2002). See also Taeku Lee, "The Sovereign Status of Survey Data," in Jeff Manza, Fay Lomax Cook, and Benjamin I. Page, eds., *Navigating Public Opinion: Polls, Policy, and the Future of American Democracy* (Oxford: Oxford University Press, 2002), pp. 290–312.

7. Ibid., p. 193.

8. Jonathan Schell, *History in Sherman Park* (New York: Alfred A. Knopf, 1987), p. 4.

9. Robert E. Lane, *Political Ideology: Why the American Common Man Believes What He Does* (New York: The Free Press, 1967).

10. Ibid., p. 160.

11. Robert Emil Botsch, *We Shall Not Overcome: Populism and Southern Blue-Collar Workers* (Chapel Hill: University of North Carolina Press, 1980).

12. Ibid., p. 62.

13. Ibid., p. 63.

14. Jennifer Hochschild, *What's Fair: American Beliefs About Distributive Justice* (Cambridge, MA: Harvard University Press, 1981).

15. John R. Hibbing and Elizabeth Theiss-Morse, "Too Much of a Good Thing: More Representation Is Not Necessarily Better," *PS: Political Science and Politics* 31 (1988): 28–31, 253.

16. Ibid., p. 257.

17. Ibid., p. 258.

18. John R. Hibbing and Elizabeth Theiss-Morse, *Stealth Democracy: Americans' Beliefs about How Government Should Work* (Cambridge: Cambridge University Press, 2002), pp. 3, 10.

19. Pamela Johnston Conover, Ivor M. Crewe, and Donald D. Scaring, "The Nature of Citizenship in the United States and Great Britain: Empirical Comments on Theoretical Themes," *The Journal of Politics* 53 (1991): 800–832, 804.

20. Ibid., p. 828.

21. Ibid., p. 807.

22. Ibid., p. 809.

23. Hochschild, p. 24.

24. For example, see Robert Weissberg, *Polling, Policy, and Public Opinion: The Case Against Heeding the "Voice of the People"* (New York: Palgrave Macmillan, 2002). He demonstrates that if an interviewer informs respondents of how much government programs will cost, support for those programs decreases.

25. Hochschild, p. 279.

26. Susan Herbst, *Reading Public Opinion: How Political Actors View the Democratic Process* (Chicago: The University of Chicago Press, 1998).

27. Steven Waldman, *The Bill: How Legislation* Really *Becomes Law: A Case Study of the National Service Bill* (New York: Penguin Books, 1995), Chapter 10.

28. Lawrence R. Jacobs and Robert Y. Shapiro, *Politicians Don't Pander: Political Manipulation and the Loss of Democratic Responsiveness* (Chicago: University of Chicago Press, 2000).

29. Jim Sensenbrenner. *Keeping In Touch* 52 (April 2004).

30. Lee, p. 293.

PART

II

The Context of Public Opinion

Organizing Public Opinion

Liberals feel unworthy of their possessions.
Conservatives feel they deserve everything they've
stolen.

— Mort Sahl[1]

Questions to Think About

Many people make sense of the political world by using an organizational scheme. In this chapter and the next, we examine two such schemes, party identification and ideology. As you read this chapter, ask yourself:

- Are you a Republican, Democrat, independent, or something else? Why? How did you come to have the party identification that you have?
- We use the terms liberal and conservative to describe political opinions. What do these terms really mean in actual politics? Why are opinions on two dissimilar issues, such as being in favor of exploring for oil in the Arctic National Wildlife Refuge and being opposed to abortion, both described as conservative? What makes some positions liberal and others conservative?
- Are you a liberal, moderate, or conservative? Are you liberal on some issues and conservative on others? Why? How do you decide your opinions about issues?
- When you arrive at a position on a political issue, how often do you consider the concepts of liberalism or conservatism as guides to help you decide?

THE POLITICAL world is a complicated place. At any given time, there are a myriad of national, state, and local issues—many of which are complex, with many aspects. Furthermore, new issues are constantly arising and old ones receding in importance. On most election days in the United States, there are different sets of candidates running for many offices. Only a few serious political junkies could possibly know about all of them. Most people simply cannot understand the entire political world in all its confusing complexity. Indeed, it would be irrational to put in the amount of time necessary to understand all the issues and to become familiar with all the candidates.[2] Therefore, people need help in organizing their thoughts. In the United States, and in most democracies, there are many different ways to classify political opinions. We will emphasize two classification systems, which we think are the most important for Americans: political party identification and ideology. Understanding how people organize their political opinions is vital to understanding the *democratic dialogue*. The main dynamic in the democratic dialogue is communication. When the people communicate with governmental decision makers, they must do so in language that people in the government can understand. If people's ideas are disorganized, citizens will find it difficult to communicate with the government coherently. Even if individual people organize their opinions coherently but do so idiosyncratically—that is, each person uses a unique organizational scheme—communication will be difficult between people and the government. If people organize their opinions differently from the way those in the government do, communication will be even more difficult. But if both the government and the governed use the same basic methods to organize their thoughts, they will be better able to communicate easily and effectively.

To govern themselves competently in practice, people need to be able to understand the political world. On the one hand, organizational frameworks may make people better able to handle the responsibilities of citizenship. On the other hand, if people cannot think about politics coherently or deal effectively with political complexity, then the quality of public opinion will be poor: People will make rash or even contradictory decisions. Thus, how people think about politics and organize their thoughts is also important for the *democratic dilemma*.

PARTY IDENTIFICATION

Perhaps the most important way people in the United States make sense of the political world is through their party identification. Party identification is a sense of psychological attachment to or affiliation with a particular political party. Political parties are important sources for structuring political attitudes because parties run candidates in elections, organize government officials, and take issue positions.

As Angus Campbell and colleagues argued over forty years ago (1960) in *The American Voter*, "In the competition of voices reaching the individual, the political party is an opinion-forming agency of great importance."[3] Campbell and his colleagues further explained the significance of party identification:

[P]arty has a profound influence across the full range of political objects to which the individual voter responds. The strength of relationship between party identification and the dimensions of partisan attitude suggest that responses to each element of national politics are deeply affected by the individual's enduring party attachment.[4]

Other researchers have also found that party identification appears to affect a number of different aspects of political attitudes and behavior, such as how people vote; how involved they are in politics; and how they respond to political candidates, groups, and issues.[5] Partisan identification acts as a socialization vehicle, with Democrats seeing the world differently from Republicans—simply because they are Democrats. For example, if people consider themselves to be strong Democrats, they are not only more likely to vote for candidates of the Democratic Party, but they are more likely to agree with policies in the Democratic Party platform and to view policies promoted by Democratic officials more favorably than ones promoted by Republicans or others.

Probably one of the best illustrations of the power of party identification in shaping opinions concerns the sudden changes in popular assessment of General (and eventual President) Dwight D. Eisenhower in 1952. Eisenhower was one of the country's most popular figures, essentially a nonpartisan hero of World War Two, prior to his public announcement he was a Republican in January of that year, leading up to his presidential run. According to one set of researchers, there was no reason to believe his popularity had been influenced in any way by political or social cleavages, yet practically overnight, public opinion of Eisenhower became heavily colored by partisan affiliation. The more loyal a Republican one was, the more likely one was to hold a favorable opinion of Eisenhower, and conversely, the stronger people's attachment to the Democratic Party, the more negatively they thought of him. We have every reason to believe that if Eisenhower had instead declared himself to be a Democrat, a similar result in the opposite direction would have occurred.[6]

Thirty-six years after *The American Voter*, Warren E. Miller (one of the authors of *The American Voter*) and J. Merrill Shanks argued that party identification was, in fact, a long-term, stable disposition of the American electorate. Party identification not only directly guides people's voting, but also shapes people's perceptions about politics and political attitudes that indirectly affect their votes:

Where the importance of party identification was once assessed largely in terms of its simple correlation with vote choice, well-specified credit is now given for its many indirect contributions as well. These occur as party identifications shape perceptions and transmit values to the attitudes and beliefs that, in turn, lead to the individual's vote choice.[7]

Thus, identification with a political party helps an individual navigate the political world in many different ways. People use their partisanship to filter, interpret, and put into context new political information, even if in some ways this partisanship may actually distort reality.[8]

A person's party identification is generally classified into one of three categories, based on the major parties in the United States: Democrats, Republicans, and independents (those with no party affiliation). This classification is further refined by considering strength of association (Strong Democrat, Weak Democrat, etc.). On many surveys, including the National Election Study, the question on party identification is asked in two stages; first, respondents are asked, "Generally speaking, do you think of yourself as a Republican, a Democrat, an Independent, or what?" If respondents say they are Republicans or Democrats, they are asked if they are "strong" or "not very strong" in their loyalty. If they say they are independents, they are asked if they considered themselves closer to the Republican or Democratic party. A respondent may, of course, identify with a minor political party such as the Socialist Workers, America First, or Greens, although in many survey analyses, those people are classified as independents.

Party identification is also significant because it is relatively widespread. Approximately three-fifths of the electorate voluntarily identifies with one of the two major parties today. Figure 4.1 shows the distribution of Americans into seven party categories. One can see that there are many people in each of the categories, but there are more people on the Democratic side of the scale.

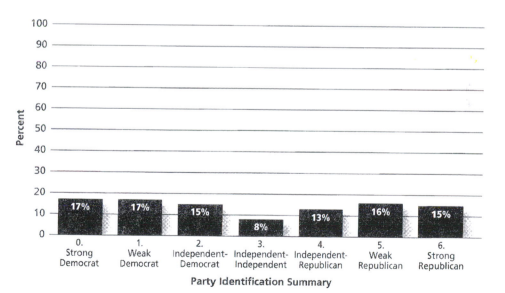

Party Identification Summary

FIGURE 4.1. Distribution of Party Identification.

Source: 2002 National Election Survey.

However, the Democratic advantage is hardly overwhelming. The "weak" versions of each party tend to have a few more people than the other categories.

If we look at the National Election Studies' biennial surveys since 1988, we see that between 34 percent and 39 percent of the respondents have said they were Democrats, and between 24 percent and 30 percent have said they were Republicans. These figures, however, are not as high as they once were, especially for the Democrats: in the NES surveys 1952–1964, between 44 percent and 52 percent said they were Democrats, and between 27 percent and 30 percent said they were Republicans. During the 1960s and 1970s, the number of independents increased, and the number of strong partisans decreased. Figure 4.2 below shows the changes in party identification during presidential election years from 1952 through 2000, with the addition of 2002.

To explain the drop in levels of party identification, observers have noted that citizens now rely on the media more than on parties for political information than they did in the past. Observers have also noted greater education and issue orientation as opposed to simple party guides among voters. In addition, candidates have made their campaigns more focused on themselves and less party-centered.[9]

Some argue the decline in party identification is misleading. They note that many of the new independents are leaners toward one of the two major parties, who behave rather like weak partisans and tend to vote for that party's candidates and support their positions; these leaners simply do not say publicly that

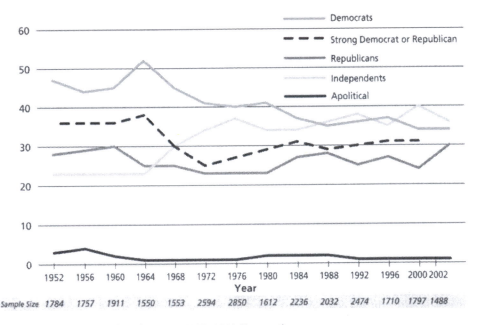

FIGURE 4.2. Party Identification, 1952–2000 (Percent).

Source: National Election Survey Web Page: http://www.umich.edu/~nes/nesguide/toptable/tab2a_1.htm.

they are affiliated with that party. If they are counted as partisans rather than as independents, the number of party supporters, in fact, hasn't changed that much since the 1950s.[10] Also, the number of strong partisans rebounded in the 1980s and 1990s, perhaps as a result of the resurgence of partisanship in the government and election campaigns, as seen in the bitter conflicts between Democrats and Republicans during the Clinton and George W. Bush administrations.[11]

It is probably true that party identification is not as powerful a psychological cue and political anchor as it once was—at least not for as many people. Yet it remains a strong force in opinion formation, as well as a key concept for understanding American public opinion. Evidence for this conclusion can be seen in the 2004 presidential election: 93 percent of Republicans voted for President Bush, while 89 percent of Democrats voted for Senator Kerry.[12]

IDEOLOGY

As we use the term in this book, an ideology is a set of interrelated beliefs and attitudes that hang together in a coherent structure. This belief system helps people organize the political facts, events, institutions, and individuals that make up the political world. Using an ideology, people can understand the context of political events. Robert E. Lane described the value of an organizing system:

> [O]ne of the features of what is sometimes called "understanding" is to grasp the context of an event, that is, temporally to know what went before and what is likely to follow, spatially to know the terrain, in human terms to see the play of the many motives involved. To understand an event in this way is to *contextualize* it; not to do this is to *morselize* it, to see it isolated from the surrounding features that give it additional "meanings."[13]

There are several types of political ideologies and ways of classifying them, but the most common model used in analyzing politics—the main one we use in this book—is a linear left–right scale. In the American version of this model, the liberal position is left of center, the conservative one right of center, and moderates are in the middle, with more extreme far left and far right at the ends. One's ideology places one at a point along the scale; according to surveys, the vast majority of Americans fall between the two extremes. (See Fig. 4.3.)

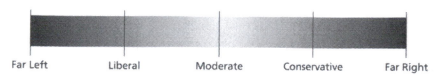

Far Left   Liberal   Moderate   Conservative   Far Right

FIGURE 4.3. The Political Spectrum.

Common sense suggests that it would be impossible to array all, or even most, opinions on *one* continuum. There are too many opinions on too many disparate subjects. In the 2004 election, for example, a large number of different, if not unrelated, issues were important, including abortion, the definition of marriage, taxation, health care, Social Security, affirmative action, the environment, the war in Iraq, the war on terrorism, civil liberties, President Bush's and Senator Kerry's Vietnam War records, and more. In addition, there are many long-term values that Americans cherish, including equality, democracy, individualism, belief in God, faith in education, the free-enterprise system, and others. Yet, for most practical political purposes, there is a common understanding among Americans active in politics that issues can be understood along one common dimension. In the words of John Zaller:

> [A]lthough there are numerous "value dimensions" between which there is no obvious logical connection, many people nonetheless respond to different value dimensions *as if* they were organized by a common left-right dimension. There is, in other words, a tendency for people to be fairly consistently "left" or "right" or "centrist" on such disparate value dimensions as economic individualism, opinions toward communists, tolerance of nonconformists, racial issues, sexual freedom, and religious authority. The correlations among these different value dimensions are never so strong as to suggest that there is one and only one basic value dimension, but they are always at least moderately strong, and among highly aware persons, the correlations are sometimes quite strong. And, of course, there are also moderately strong correlations between people's self-descriptions as liberal or conservative and their scores on the various values measures [emphasis in original].[14]

In addition, the massive number of separate issues can be boiled down to a few issue dimensions or domains. In this book, we isolate four dimensions: economic or social welfare issues, racial issues, social issues, and foreign policy. We have chosen these four issue domains because they are commonly used when discussing politics. We do not mean to imply that they are the only or the best domains, or that there are precisely four domains. We also acknowledge that some issues, such as financial assistance to ethnic minorities, fit into more than one domain. However, we and other political scientists have found it useful to categorize issues when discussing them.

Economic and Social Welfare Issues

Include such programs as Social Security, taxes, welfare, health care, school vouchers, and government regulations. Liberals tend to emphasize social programs, especially those that help the middle class and the poor, while conservatives emphasize free enterprise, the benefits of a smaller government, and lower taxes. In terms of the issues, liberals favor the government's attempting to ensure that everyone has a job and good standard of living, while conservatives feel the government should let people get ahead on their own. Liberals have favored larger welfare payments to the poor, while conservatives have argued for smaller welfare programs, often arguing that welfare programs foster dependence on the government and hurt poor people in the long run. In terms of government health care insurance, liberals have favored more government involvement, including government programs, while conservatives have favored individuals' and private insurance companies' taking care of medical costs.

When it comes to taxes, liberals tend to favor graduated income taxes that place more of the burden on wealthier taxpayers, while conservatives favor less progressive taxes and lower taxes on investors. In labor-management disputes in private companies, liberals tend to favor labor, while conservatives tend to favor management.

On the issue of school vouchers, conservatives tend to favor those that allow poor children and children in poor schools to go private schools. Liberals tend to oppose the vouchers and ask for more support for public schools.

Racial Issues

Include antidiscrimination laws, provision of services and financial assistance to ethnic minorities, and race-based programs like affirmative action. Liberals tend to point to great disparities between white Americans and other Americans, especially African Americans and Latinos. Reflecting their opinions on economic issues, liberals tend to favor government programs aimed at providing services, such as training, to the poor, who disproportionately belong to minority groups. Liberals are also more likely to support programs aimed at fighting ethnic discrimination. Liberals are also more supportive of race-based programs such as affirmative action. Conservatives tend to oppose government programs designed to achieve racial parity, considering them wasteful and ineffective. They also tend to oppose affirmative action as a form of discrimination against the most qualified job or school applicants.[15]

Social Issues

Include lifestyle issues, such as abortion, women's rights, rights of homosexuals, same-sex marriage, dealing with drug abuse, and religious issues. For the last thirty years or so, the clearest dividing line between conservatives and liberals has been defined by the abortion issue. Conservatives tend to be pro-life, opposing abortion, while liberals favor the pro-choice position of letting each woman decide on her own if she wants an abortion.

Liberals tend to favor more equality in men's and women's roles, treatment for nonviolent drug offenders, and a more strict separation between church and state. Conservatives tend to emphasize traditional gender roles (although very few oppose equal rights for women), stress interdiction to stop drug traffic and punishment for drug offenses, and less strict church-state separation (favoring, for example, prayer in public schools and more widespread use of faith-based initiatives in tax-supported social welfare programs).

Homosexuality is another important social issue. The conservative position favors preventing gays and lesbians from joining the military or adopting children, and opposes same-sex marriages. The liberal position tends to favor allowing gay and lesbian individuals to serve in the military and permitting same-sex couples to marry and adopt children.

Foreign Policy

Issues include the size of the defense budget, alliances, foreign commitments, and military actions and wars. Liberals favor lower spending for defense, more emphasis on using the United Nations in international negotiations, more multinational cooperation in general, more economic aid and less military aid to poor countries, and less use of military force. Conservatives favor more spending for defense, less emphasis on international treaties and using the United Nations, more assertion of U.S. power abroad, and more willingness to use military force in the advancement of American interests.

SELF-PLACEMENT ON THE LIBERAL-CONSERVATIVE CONTINUUM

It is important to understand that the collection of issue positions that we call liberalism or conservatism are not necessarily related logically. For example, the liberal position favors more government programs to help the poor, more research for alternative energy sources, affirmative action for women and minorities, and the right of a woman to choose an abortion. There is no necessary logical reason that fostering alternative energy sources is the same as, or consistent with, the right to choose an abortion. Yet we would say that somebody who favors more federal spending to develop wind power has a liberal position, just as we would say that somebody who favors a woman's right to choose an abortion also has a liberal position. What we call liberalism and conservatism are cultural constructs, but politically aware people know what they mean and understand how various issues fit together.

A word on terminology is appropriate here. Typically, liberals and conservatives in the United States do not think of themselves as left or right, even if political scientists do. Politicians and political activists tend to use these terms pejoratively, saying the *other side* is left or right. For example, when Bill and Hillary Clinton said there was a "vast right-wing conspiracy" against them, they meant the term right-wing to be interpreted in a negative way. In other democracies, left and right are more descriptive terms; for example, when politicians in France, which has several important political parties, speak of "parties of the left" or "parties of the right," they are simply describing the parties, not criticizing them. In part, this dislike of left or right labels is because

BOX 4.1

Third Parties

In the United States, there are a few people to the left of the liberals and a few to the right of the conservatives. Sometimes, they work with the Democratic and Republican parties, but sometimes they form separate political parties, which tend to be centered around individual interests or ideologies. Historically, some ideological parties have included the American Party before the Civil War (usually known as the Know-Nothing Party), centered on anti-immigration and anti-Catholicism; the Prohibition Party after the Civil War, centered around the prohibition of alcohol; and the American Independent Party of the 1960s and 1970s, centered around support for the Vietnam War and opposition to racial integration. Today, two ideological parties are the Green Party on the left, centered around environmentalism (http://www.gp.org), and the America First Party on the right, centered around limiting international alliances and immigration (http://www.americafirstparty.org). Ideological parties tend to be small and be more interested in advancing their policy ideas, such as environmentalism or opposition to immigration, than in winning elections. They would *like* to win elections, but electoral victory is not their main goal. Organizers of ideological third parties are typically not discouraged by repeatedly losing elections. In fact, many parties continue to exist for many decades without hope of winning an election. For example, both the Prohibition and American Independent parties still exist today.

One convenient guide to political parties is found on the Web at http://www.politics1.com/parties.htm. This Web site lists the Democratic and Republican parties as well as thirty-six third parties ranging, alphabetically, from the America First Party to the Workers World Party. In addition, it lists seventeen other parties that exist but have not nominated candidates for office.

One political philosophy, libertarianism, and its accompanying political party, the Libertarian Party, merit special note. Libertarians are neither left nor right. Instead, they believe in individual freedom and as small a government as possible. They support some positions that are on the liberal side and others that are on the conservative side. For example, they are liberal on social issues, in that they oppose laws to restrict abortion, for example, but are conservative on economic issues, in that they are very much in favor of the free market.

The party itself says it "is committed to America's heritage of freedom: individual liberty and personal responsibility; a free-market economy of abundance and prosperity; and a foreign policy of nonintervention, peace, and free trade."[*]

According to a quiz on the party's Web site, a libertarian agrees with the following statements:

- Government should not censor speech, press, media or Internet.
- Military service should be voluntary. There should be no draft.
- There should be no laws regarding sex for consenting adults.
- Repeal laws prohibiting adult possession and use of drugs.
- There should be no National ID card.
- End "corporate welfare." No government handouts to business.
- End government barriers to international free trade.
- Let people control their own retirement; privatize Social Security.
- Replace government welfare with private charity.
- Cut taxes and government spending by 50% or more.

Continued

BOX 4.1—Cont'd

You can see that liberals would oppose (and favor) some of those ideas, while conservatives would oppose (and favor) others. If you want to see where you stand according to the libertarian framework, you can answer a series of questions at http://www.theadvocates.org/quiz.html. After you answer the questions, you will be classified using two criteria: (1) a "personal issues score" (the first five statements); and (2) an "economic issues score" (the last five statements). You can be classified as a libertarian, a centrist, a conservative, a statist (favoring big government), or a liberal.

*http://www.lp.org.

Americans for the most part are pragmatic people, and to be seen as an extremist is negative, putting one outside the mainstream. This is one reason why political actors attempt to label their opponents in this way.

In measuring the number of people at different locations on the liberal-conservative continuum, American political scientists have often used a survey question with seven points: (1) extremely liberal; (2) liberal; (3) moderately liberal; (4) moderate; (5) moderately conservative; (6) conservative; and (7) extremely conservative. Figure 4.4 shows the distribution of Americans immediately before the 2002 election.

You will notice that there are more people on the conservative side. But, like the Democratic advantage in Figure 4.1, the conservative advantage here is not

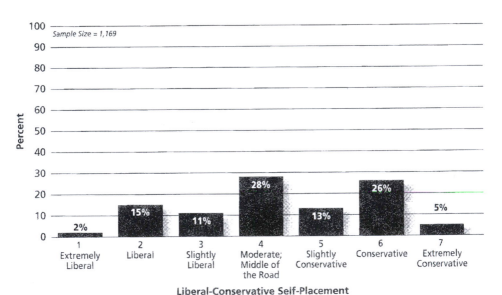

FIGURE 4.4. Distribution Along the Liberal-Conservative Continuum.
Source: 2002 National Election Survey.

overwhelming. The predominance of conservatives is not a new phenomenon. The liberal-conservative question has been asked in the National Election Studies since 1972. Table 4.1 shows the distributions of liberals, moderates, and conservatives in presidential election years since then.

The results to the question tend to be very stable from year to year. There have always been more conservatives than liberals; the proportion of conservatives varies from 25 percent to 33 percent, while the proportion of liberals varies from 16 percent to 20 percent. In addition, there have always been many people who said they did not know or had not thought about where they would place themselves on the continuum. In fact, the proportion of those who said they did not know was often about the same size as the conservatives and always greater than the liberals.

However, one clear change we do notice is the proportion of people who answered with one of the two most extreme answers on either the liberal or conservative ends of the continuum (1, 2, 6, or 7) has been creeping up through the years. From about 20 percent in the first few surveys, the proportion increased to more than one-fourth and finally reached 39 percent in 2002. Although it is hard to know what to make of this trend, it may reflect the fact that political elites (politicians, party leaders, political commentators, and the like) appear to have become more polarized in recent years, possibly providing cues to some members of the public.[16]

Consistency of Issue Opinions and Ideology

When we say that people are liberal or conservative, we do not mean that they are liberal or conservative on all issues. Many people are liberal on some issues and conservative on others. Since the issues are linked culturally

TABLE 4.1. Liberal-Conservative Positions: 1972–2002 (Percent)*.

	1972	1976	1980	1984	1988	1992	1996	2000	2002
Liberals (1–3)	18	16	17	18	17	20	18	20	23
Moderates (4)	27	25	20	23	22	23	24	23	22
Conservatives (5–7)	26	25	28	29	32	31	33	30	35
Don't know/ Haven't thought about it	28	33	36	30	30	27	25	27	22
"Extreme" answers (1–2 or 6–7)	19	21	23	24	25	26	26	29	39
Sample Size =	2,155	2,839	1,565	2,229	2,035	2,483	1,712	849	1,490

Source: NES Web page, http://www.umich.edu/~nes/nesguide/toptable/tab3_1.htm.

instead of logically, a person could very reasonably have, say, a liberal economic position of favoring higher welfare payments for poor mothers and have a conservative social position of opposition to abortion. Some people are liberal on some issues and conservative on other issues within the same issue domain—such as a person who favors more generous welfare payments (a liberal position) and school vouchers (a conservative position). In fact, there are several issues that cause individuals to be conflicted themselves and to have different opinions on the same issue. Such conflicted opinions are most likely where dearly held values conflict with each other. For example, in the abortion issue, the value of life conflicts with the value of individual choice. In the issue of affirmative action, the value of egalitarianism conflicts with the value of individualism. Paul M. Kellstedt described the contemporary conflictual nature of affirmative action for Americans who believe in equality and in individualism:

> Before, America was divided into two groups of people, some of whom thought blacks deserved the full benefits of American citizenship, others of whom thought blacks were inherently inferior beings. Today, the fault lines are not between individuals but within them. One part of most Americans cries out for compensatory justice, that our society must atone for its sins, right the wrongs of the past; therefore, government must be involved. But another part objects . . . maintaining that, once the legal barriers have been eliminated, government ought to stay out of the picture and let individuals of any color compete for society's riches. America now has trouble making up its mind on what to do about race largely because most *individuals* have difficulty making up their minds on what to do about race [emphasis in original].[17]

We illustrate people's inconsistent opinions in Table 4.2A. We examine people's position on two very different issues—an economic issue and a social issue—and we see that many people are not consistently liberal or conserva-

TABLE 4.2A. Positions on an Economic Issue and a Social Issue: Spending on Services and Same-Sex Adoption as Percent of Total Table.

Position on Same-Sex Adoption	Position on Government Spending for Social Services		
	Reduce Spending (conservative)	Middle Position	Increase Spending (liberal)
Should be permitted (liberal)	5%	19%	21%
Should not be permitted (conservative)	13%	22%	20%

Total Sample Size = 1,358
Source: 2000 National Election Survey.

tive. The economic issue is a respondent's position on a seven-point scale concerning government spending on services; at one end of the scale are those who want to reduce spending, and at the other end are those who want to increase spending on services. The respondents who answered the two most conservative responses (1 and 2) are grouped together, as are those who answered the two most liberal responses (6 and 7), and those who answered in the three middle points (3–5) are together. The social issue is whether homosexual couples should be legally permitted to adopt children. We chose those two issues because in a series of issues in the 2000 National Election Study, they had the highest correlations with the seven-point Liberal-Conservative scale.* The table shows that 21 percent of the respondents who answered both questions gave consistently liberal responses, and 13 percent gave consistently conservative responses. But 25 percent gave inconsistent answers—one liberal and one conservative.

We can see that one-fourth of all the survey respondents were inconsistent in their answers. However, research has shown that those people who are more aware of politics, and more educated, tend to be more consistent. If we look at the same information comparing only the most educated and least educated respondents (see Table 4.2B), we see that more educated respondents are ideologically consistent in their issue positions.

So, when we discuss liberals and conservatives, keep in mind that many people have both liberal and conservative opinions. When we say that a person is a conservative, we mean that the person is generally conservative on most issues. Although more college graduates tend to be consistent in this example, a large proportion of them (18 percent) are not. However, we do not typically see as much inconsistency when looking at political activists and politicians; they are much more likely to have consistently liberal or conservative opinions. Some researchers have found that political elites have become more polarized ideologically over the past few decades, although the public has not.*

Similarly, one should take measures of ideological self-classification with a grain of salt. For instance, some people who identify themselves as liberals have what researchers consider to be conservative opinions on some or even many

TABLE 4.2B. Percent Consistent and Inconsistent by Education.

Educational Level	Percent Consistent	Percent Inconsistent
College graduate	39	18
Total Sample	34	25
High School Grade or less	32	31

Source: 2000 National Election Survey.

* The correlation of the liberal-conservative scale with the spending scale is .31; the correlation with the adoption question is .38.

political issues. In other words, people's own description of their overall ideological position may be quite different from where their actual issue positions would place them on the ideological scale. This phenomenon may be due to people's over generalizing, or because they are forced to choose some position in a survey, or simply because of confusion over what the terms liberal, conservative, and moderate mean.

The Significance of Ideology for Political Thinking

Ideology can be a very useful tool for understanding politics. With a ready-made framework, one can fit new issues and new ideas into a comprehensible whole. Ideology is also very useful for communicating; someone can say, "She's a moderate Democrat," or "He's a liberal Republican," and people will understand. But an important question that political scientists have asked for almost fifty years is: How many people actually use the liberal-conservative continuum in their understanding of politics? At first glance, it seems that many people do. Table 4.1 shows that about 75 percent can place themselves somewhere along the scale, and about half say they are either liberals or conservatives. But upon further investigation, beginning in the 1950s, political scientists have questioned whether people really understand what the terms liberal and conservative mean in a political context and whether they actually use those concepts to understand politics and guide them in voting. Some analysts have found that most people do not use the concepts of liberalism and conservatism to structure their thinking. Indeed, the general lack of consistency between people's own ideological self-classification and their actual issue positions mentioned above strengthens this conclusion. Since ideology is so useful in understanding politics, this question of using the liberal-conservative continuum has, over the years, merged into a question of how competent Americans are in terms of holding opinions and understanding politics.

Some political scientists have linked use of ideology with political competence and have sometimes drawn discouraging conclusions.[18] Others, however, question the link between ideology and competence, arguing that individuals have other ways to organize their political opinions.[19] We more fully address the issue of the connection between ideological consistency, political sophistication, and the quality of public opinion—that is, the democratic dilemma of whether people are capable of governing themselves—in Chapter Eleven.

Different Ideologies for Different People?

Still, even if we do not consider idiosyncratic belief systems, it is possible that some subgroups in the American population use different types of ideologies to structure their opinions. Other bodies of research challenge the notion that political beliefs are structured along a single left-right dimension.

"Next question: I believe that life is a constant striving for balance, requiring frequent tradeoffs between morality and necessity, within a cyclic pattern of joy and sadness, forging a trail of bittersweet memories until one slips, inevitably, into the jaws of death. Agree or disagree?"

Borrowing from social psychology and the study of cognition (how people think), some researchers have instead focused on individual thought processes and how people deal with new information. The most relevant idea from this work is people's use of **schemas** as a processing device, otherwise known as *schematic thinking*. Although there is no universally agreed-upon definition, a schema may be defined as a "cognitive structure consisting of organized knowledge about situations and individuals abstracted from previous experience."[20] In essence, schemas are networks of beliefs arranged in long-term and short-term memory, connected by mental links to themselves and each other. A schema is generally not as broad or all-encompassing as an ideology, but is not as narrow as attitudes toward specific issues. When someone absorbs incoming information, specific schemas filter, select, encode, and integrate it into new or existing patterns.

Robert Entman provides the example of a possible schema surrounding the September 11 terrorist attacks.[21] The symbol "9/11" itself would constitute the node or center, with corresponding links to other associated objects, which might include the World Trade Center, airplane hijackers, Osama Bin Laden, the New York Fire Department, or New York Mayor Rudolph Giuliani, among others. Each idea has an emotional and directional association—presumably, for Americans, positive feelings about the WTC, the New York Fire Department, and Giuliani, but negative for hijackers, Osama Bin Laden, and terrorists generally.

When evoked, as in a news story showing clips of the latest Osama Bin Laden video or even a "George W. Bush for President" ad showing him with firefighters at Ground Zero, such a schema might be activated. Thus, a person with liberal values on certain dimensions might in turn have positive feelings toward President Bush (a conservative) as a leader in the fight against terrorism. People's 9/11 schema might thus provide a coherent organizational framework for opinions on a variety of issues, such as homeland security, immigration policy, civil liberties, foreign policy toward Arab countries, and so forth.

The schema might be linked to earlier preexisting attitudes and associations. In the previous example, the fact Rudolph Giuliani is a Republican might link him further to preexisting knowledge networks, attitudes, and so on, about Republicans and the Republican Party. Although Entman doesn't discuss this possibility directly, presumably a Democratic-leaning person (with positive feelings toward Democrats and the Democratic Party) using this 9/11 schema might have positive associations with Giuliani in the context of connections with 9/11, his views on a Ground Zero Memorial, and so forth, but have negative ones at other times, such as when he is mentioned in the context of his speech at the 2004 Republican National Convention.

Conover and Feldman, for example, developed several political schemata relevant to individuals' political thinking in different issue areas: the amount of power government should have in general, and government's responsibility in solving social problems, poverty, and racial problems, respectively. They found that opinions on issues in these areas or schemata were not highly related to one another: In other words, a person who was liberal on one schematic dimension would not necessarily be liberal on another.[22] In another study, Lau discovered four different political schemata used by respondents in the University of Michigan's National Election Study: issues, groups, personality, and party. People appeared to use the same schemas when evaluating political objects, and the schemata were also predictive of their voting behavior.[23]

The schema approach also moves beyond the notion that use of the left-right framework is a measure of political sophistication or the only way to conceptualize politics. It "does not assume that there is one overarching dimension called ideological (or political) sophistication along which all members of society must be judged; rather it clearly postulates that there are a number of different schemata available for making sense of the world of politics. Because a citizen cannot use one framework (e.g., ideology) does not necessarily imply that the individual has no 'judgmental yardstick' for handling political events and should therefore be relegated to the ranks of the uninformed."[24]

Therefore, even people who do not view politics from the perspective of having a completely consistent or even explicit ideology nevertheless interpret political issues and events from the perspective of these preexisting belief systems. Schemas give a more fluid and changing approach to how people organize their political thinking.[25]

Issue Publics

If we take a different view and look at population subgroups as coherent entities in themselves, we might see that subgroups use different structuring mechanisms from other people. Various groups of people are often called issue publics. These are citizens who care passionately about a particular issue, think more often and in depth about it, and whose attitudes about that issue tend to be very resistant to change as well as very influential in their political behavior.[26] For many voters, a candidate's stand on gun control is the most important issue, and for some voters, it is the *only* important issue. After the 2004 presidential election, many analyses stressed the importance of voters who were concerned about moral values (meaning, in 2004, issues such as abortion, same-sex marriages, and stem cell research). The majority of the issue public who were concerned about moral values voted for George W. Bush and were instrumental in his victory.

Using issue publics does not argue against the use of the liberal-conservative scale because it is not difficult to array these people's opinions along one scale. Individuals who oppose gun control and same-sex marriage have conservative opinions, and those who favor them have liberal opinions. However, various issue publics may arrange their opinions differently; for example, people who are concerned about moral values may think of opposition to homosexuality and support for national health insurance as consistent although one view is, by contemporary definitions, conservative while the other is liberal. Or perhaps the same person might feel strongly and positively about gun control (a liberal position) as a member of one issue public, and equally strongly and negatively about gay marriage (a conservative position) as a member of another.

Krosnick found that indeed, much of the public appears to fall into many small issue publics, the particular ones being determined by each individual's unique self-interests, social and group identifications, and cherished values. Because citizens have different individual interests, identifications, and values of importance to them, these differences lead to different sets of issue publics, so that a policy option of vital concern to one is of trivial or no importance to another. Thus, "a large segment of the nation may have personally important attitudes addressing questions of public policy, but in a patchwork quilt fashion. At most, each citizen probably has a small, idiosyncratic handful of such attitudes."[27]

Demographic Groups

We might also see that specific demographic groups may view issues differently and develop their own ideologies. For example, Paula D. McClain and Joseph Stewart, Jr. reviewed the literature on ethnic minorities and ideology and found that:

> those who study black and Latino political attitudes argue that it is inappropriate to use the standard political ideology labels of liberal, moderate, and conservative, which were developed from national studies that contained few nonwhites, and apply them to the black and Latino population.[28]

Melissa Victoria Harris-Lacewell studied black thought and found that African American political ideology is structured around four basic ideologies:

- *Black nationalism*: Contemporary black nationalists believe in some form of cultural, social, economic, and political independence for blacks. They believe in black self-reliance through the creation of separate institutions. They tend to honor race over other identities, such as gender and class.
- *Liberal integrationism*: Liberal integrationists want a society in which black people enjoy the same political, economic, and social freedoms and rights as other people. They perceive the government as a good tool for achieving their goals.
- *Black conservatism*: Black conservatives locate the source of black inequality in the behavior or attitudinal pathologies of African Americans themselves. They tend to stress the significance of moral and personal characteristics, rather than race, to explain unequal life circumstances. They stress self-reliance and shun government assistance. Most argue that the external factors of black inequality have been largely addressed.
- *Black feminism*: Black feminism is rooted in the recognition of the intersection of race, class, and gender. Black feminists portray themselves as self-defined, self-reliant individuals confronting race, gender, and class oppression.[29]

Clearly, these four ideologies do not describe a liberal-conservative continuum. They could be very useful to African Americans and, in modified form, to other ethnic minorities in structuring their political opinions, even if they would not be of much use to most white Americans. This type of organization—specific to one or a few subgroups—may be widespread. Any effort to discover a subgroup's unique ideology would be extremely difficult, using surveys of a cross-section of Americans. The fact that cross-sectional studies have not found subgroup-specific belief systems is no indication that they do not exist.

The Resilience of the Traditional View of Ideology

Despite these concerns, the traditional left-right conception of ideology remains a powerful characterization of the public's political thought. As noted by John Zaller earlier in the chapter, while not everyone's opinions fit neatly into such a framework, at the same time it is the rare individual who is extremely liberal in one issue area and extremely conservative in another, so that there is at least a tendency for people to stake out roughly comparable positions on a number of issues.[30]

Furthermore, the left-right, unidimensional scale is the model used in the language of actual day-to-day politics in the United States. You won't hear "an economic freedom schema," or "black feminism" mentioned on the news. Even if other ways of characterizing ideology or the public's organizational frameworks about politics might be more accurate, politically aware people discuss, and therefore often think about, politics in terms of a liberal-moderate-conservative spectrum. That alone makes this model of ideology important.

THE RELATIONSHIP BETWEEN PARTY IDENTIFICATION AND IDEOLOGY

Ideology and party identification are separate, distinct ways of organizing political thought, although there is some connection between the two. In general, Democrats are more liberal, and Republicans more conservative, than the general population, but that doesn't mean that all Republicans are conservative—or that all conservatives are Republican. In other words, one can be a conservative Democrat, a moderate Republican, a liberal independent, or whatever. The two major parties in the United States want, above all else, to win elections, so they try to appeal to a wide range of voters and, consequently, strain toward the center of the political spectrum.

There are generally clear ideological differences, however, between the people who call themselves Democrats and Republicans. In Figures 4.5A–4.5C, we show what percentage of Democrats, independents, and Republicans are liberal, moderate, or conservative. Figure 4.5A shows the percentage of Democrats who fall into each of the seven classifications along the liberal-conservative continuum, while Figure 4.5B shows the same thing for independents, and Figure 4.5C for Republicans.

Figures 4.5A–4.5C show that there is a clear relationship between party identification and political ideology. The distribution of Democrats is clearly centered slightly to the left of center; the highest bar is the "moderate" bar but the next two highest are the "liberal" and "slightly liberal" bars. Democrats are more liberal than the population as a whole, but not much more so. The distribution of the independents is much more centered. The middle, "moderate" bar is nearly twice as tall as the second tallest, and there are practically no people in the "extremely" liberal or conservative positions.

With the Republicans, we see a shift to the right that is even more pronounced than the Democratic shift to the left. The highest bar is the "conservative" bar, and there are hardly any Republicans on the liberal side of the center. The Republicans are much more ideologically homogeneous than the Democrats.

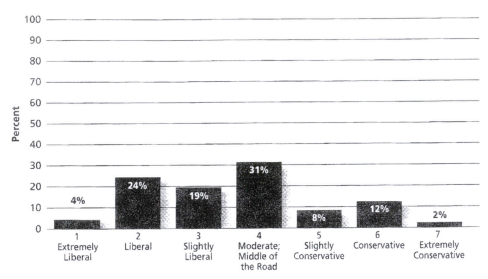

FIGURE 4.5A. Distribution Along the Liberal-Conservative Continuum (Democrats Only).

Source: 2002 National Election Survey.

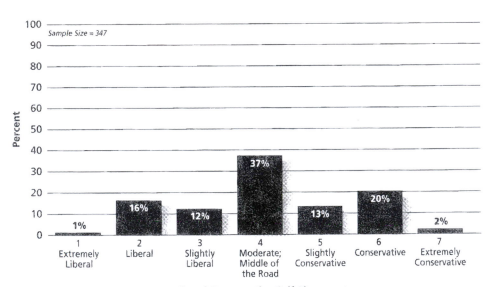

FIGURE 4.5B. Distribution Along the Liberal-Conservative Continuum (Independents Only).

Source: 2002 National Election Survey.

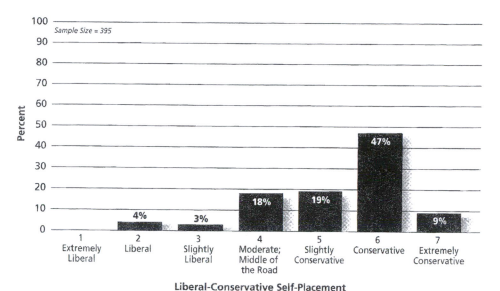

FIGURE 4.5C. Distribution Along the Liberal-Conservative Continuum (Republicans Only).

Source: 2002 National Election Survey.

In fact, there is some evidence that the two main parties, at least at the elite level of activists and elected officials, are becoming more ideologically coherent. Despite these connections, however, there is a great deal of ideological variation within grassroots members of both parties (not to mention those who claim to be independents). This makes it very dangerous to make blanket generalizations about Democrats being liberal or Republicans being conservative. Indeed, some researchers argue that party identification is as much a social group association as a psychological or belief one, making it something more akin to religious affiliation.[31] No one makes that claim about ideology. Therefore, for all of these reasons, it makes sense to treat these two concepts as distinct, if not entirely independent, variables.

CONCLUSION

Since matters of politics and government are complicated, people may understandably rely on organizational frameworks to structure their attitudes and opinions. Whether and how they organize their thinking, then, is important. Party identification refers to a psychological attachment to a political party. Ideology is a rough summation of a person's general political issue positions and is usually measured on an abstract left-right scale. In the United States, unlike most democracies, the left-right scale is called a liberal-conservative scale. Although this model is not, as we discussed, the *only* way to classify opinions, it is extremely useful because its ideological labels are commonly used by ordinary people, and it is the model primarily used by political scientists, media analysts, and politicians.

How the public thinks about politics and puts issues into perspective affects how well public opinion is translated into public policy. Again, to use our democratic dialogue metaphor, we see organizational frameworks as affecting what the public eventually says about politics. If the public utilizes a different type of framework for organizing or thinking about politics, this could make successful communication between leaders and led more difficult. Furthermore, it appears that political elites, especially politicians, as well as the more active and informed segments of the population, appear to have more consistent, extreme ideological views than many members of the mass public do. Thus, leaders may be more ideological than their constituents. If officials choose to follow their own views or those of their activist allies, this disparity in turn could lead to a disconnect between what the people want and what the government does. We take up these matters in Chapter 12.

How individuals organize their thinking and process political information also has implications for the democratic dilemma—the issue of how much government should follow the wishes of its citizens. Yet the research exploring this process doesn't directly solve this dilemma; it deepens the problem. Is party identification a superficial, knee-jerk substitution for deeply understanding political issues, or is it a useful cue built upon a core set of values over one's lifetime? Is the use of schemata proof of people's lack of sophistication? Or are they instead a reasonable, low-information way of dealing with a complicated political environment? Much of the answers to such questions depends upon the standards one uses to judge the quality of public opinion. In Chapter 11 we more fully explore these issues.

Suggested Reading

Campbell, Angus, Philip E. Converse, Warren E. Miller, and Donald E. Stokes. *The American Voter*. Chicago: The University of Chicago Press, 1960.

Harris-Lacewell, Melissa Victoria. *Barbershops, Bibles, and BET: Everyday Talk and Black Political Thought*. Princeton: Princeton University Press, 2004.

Kellstedt, Paul M. *The Mass Media and the Dynamics of American Racial Attitudes*. Cambridge: Cambridge University Press, 2003.

Lau, Richard R., and David O. Sears, eds. *Political Cognition*. Hillsdale, NJ: Erlbaum, 1986.

Miller, Warren E., and J. Merrill Shanks. *The New American Voter*. Cambridge, MA: Harvard University Press, 1996.

www ▶▶▶ Interactive Learning Exercise:

Classifying Students Along the Liberal-Conservative Continuum

In this exercise, you will answer twelve issue questions on this book's Web site. Using multiple regression based on the 2004 National Election Study, students are classified along the liberal-conservative continuum. They are classified on four scales: (1) overall; (2) economic and social welfare issues; (3) racial issues; and (4) social issues.

Notes

1. See Mark Groubert, "Survival Humor," www.lacitybeat.com/article.php?id=177& IssueNum=10. Accessed May 25, 2005.

2. Anthony Downs, *An Economic Theory of Democracy* (New York: Addison Wesley, 1958 [1997]).

3. Angus Campbell, Phillip E. Converse, Warren E. Miller, and Donald E. Stokes, *The American Voter* (New York: Wiley, 1960), p. 128.

4. Ibid.

5. Paul R. Abramson, *Political Attitudes in America* (San Francisco: Freeman Publishing, 1983), pp. 72–84.

6. Philip E. Converse and George Dupeux, "DeGaulle and Eisenhower: The Public Image of the Victorious General," in Angus Campbell, Philip E. Converse, Warren E. Miller, and Donald E. Stokes, *Elections and the Political Order* (New York: Wiley, 1966), pp. 324–325, cited in George C. Edwards, *The Public Presidency* (New York: St. Martin's Press, 1983), p. 213.

7. Warren E. Miller and J. Merrill Shanks, *The New American Voter* (Cambridge, MA: Harvard University Press, 1996), p. 133.

8. William H. Flanigan and Nancy H. Zingale, *Political Behavior of the American Electorate*, 9th ed. (Washington, DC: CQ Press, 1998), p. 54.

9. See, for example, Norman Nie, Sidney Verba, and John Petrocik, *The Changing American Voter* (Cambridge, MA: Harvard University Press, 1976).

10. Marjorie Randon Hershey, *Party Politics in America*, 11th ed. (New York: Longman, 2004), pp. 104–105. On the specific issue of independents, see Bruce Keith, David B. Magleby, Candice J. Nelson, Elizabeth Orr, Mark C. Westlye, and Raymond Wolfinger, *The Myth of the Independent Voter* (Berkeley: University of California Press, 1992).

11. Hershey, *Party Politics in America*, pp. 105–106.

12. These are the exit poll numbers from the 2004 National Election Poll: http://www.cnn.com/ELECTION/2004/pages/results/states/US/P/00/epolls.0.html.

13. Robert E. Lane, *Political Ideology: Why the American Common Man Believes What He Does* (New York: The Free Press, 1967), p. 350.

14. John R. Zaller, *The Nature and Origins of Mass Opinion* (Cambridge: Cambridge University Press, 1992), p. 26.

15. Paul M. Sniderman and Thomas Piazza, *The Scar of Race* (Cambridge, MA: The Belknap Press of the Harvard University Press, 1993), p. 9, argues that there are three types of racial issues today: discrimination prevention, provision of services and financial assistance to ethnic minorities, and race-based programs like affirmative action. This description of the liberal and conservative views reflects that three-way classification.

16. This explanation seems plausible, based on the conception of ideology and its connection to "elite cues" by the masses enunciated in Zaller, *Nature and Origins*, pp. 327–328.

17. Paul M. Kellstedt, *The Mass Media and the Dynamics of American Racial Attitudes* (Cambridge: Cambridge University Press, 2003), pp. 135–136.

18. Philip E. Converse, "The Nature of Belief Systems in Mass Publics," in David E. Apter, ed., *Ideology and Discontent* (New York: Free Press, 1964); Philip E. Converse, "Attitudes and Non-Attitudes: Continuation of a Dialogue," in Edward R. Tufte, ed., *The Quantitative Analysis of Social Problems* (Reading, MA: Addison-Wesley, 1970). See also Benjamin I. Page and Robert Y. Shapiro, *The Rational Public: Fifty Years of Trends in Americans' Policy Preferences* (Chicago: University of Chicago Press, 1992), pp. 5–6.

19. Robert E. Lane, "Patterns of Political Belief," in Jeanne N. Knutson, ed., *Handbook of Political Psychology* (San Francisco: Jossey-Bass, 1973); Jennifer L. Hochschild, *What's Fair: American Beliefs About Distributive Justice* (Cambridge, MA: Harvard University Press, 1981).

20. Doris Graber, *Processing the News: How People Tame the Information Tide* (New York: Longman, 1984), p. 23.

21. Robert M. Entman, *Projections of Power: Framing News, Public Opinion, and U.S. Foreign Policy* (Chicago: University of Chicago Press, 2004), pp. 7–9.

22. Pamela Johnston Conover and Stanley Feldman, "Belief System Organization in the American Electorate: An Alternative Approach," in John C. Pierce and John L. Sullivan, eds., *The Electorate Reconsidered* (Beverly Hills, CA: Sage, 1980), pp. 49–68.

23. Richard R. Lau, "Political Schemata, Candidate Evaluations, and Voting Behavior," in Richard R. Lau and David O. Sears, eds., *Political Cognition* (Hillsdale, NJ: Erlbaum, 1986), pp. 95–126.

24. Ruth Hamill and Milton Lodge, "Cognitive Consequences of Political Sophistication," in Lau and Sears, ed., *Political Cognition,* p. 92.

25. Michael A. Milburn, *Persuasion and Politics: The Social Psychology of Public Opinion* (Pacific Grove, CA: Brooks/Cole, 1991), pp. 72–82.

26. John A. Krosnick, "Government Policy and Citizen Passion: A Study of Issue Publics in Contemporary America," *Political Behavior* 12 No. 1 (March 1990): 59–92; for a specific case-study example of an "issue public" in action, see Jon Krosnick and Shibley Telhami, "Public Attitudes Toward Israel: A Study of the Attentive and Issue Publics," *International Studies Quarterly* 39 No. 4 (December 1995): 535–554.

27. Krosnick, "Government Policy," p. 75.

28. Paula D. McClain and Joseph Stewart, Jr., *Can We All Get Along? Racial and Ethnic Minorities in American Politics*, 3rd ed. (Boulder, CO: Westview Press, 2002), p. 66.

29. Melissa V. Harris-Lacewell, *Barbershops, Bibles, and BET: Everyday Talk and Black Political Thought* (Princeton: Princeton University Press. 2004), chapter 1.

30. Zaller, *The Nature and Origins of Mass Opinion*, p. 27.

31. Donald Green, Bradley Palmquist, and Eric Schickler, *Partisan Hearts and Minds: Political Parties and the Social Identities of Voters* (New Haven: Yale University Press, 2002).

5 Sources of Public Opinion: Political Socialization

In the end, then, we are only doing some sophisticated guessing when we try to assemble aggregate explanatory chains of influence from one generation to the next, and to develop systematic explanations for the nature of political socialization. But, still, we do try.

Michael Kahan[1]

Questions to Think About

Before public opinion can be expressed, it must come from somewhere. We now turn to the topic of where the public gets its voice or where people's opinions come from. This chapter addresses questions such as

- What is political socialization, and why is it important?
- What are the forces that influence people as they grow up, and what effects do these forces have on the opinions people express as adults?
- How do people's opinions develop during adulthood, and how malleable are they?
- What are the effects of the socialization process on the democratic dilemma and the democratic dialogue?

H UMANS MAY be political animals, but they aren't born that way. They instead develop their values, predispositions, and opinions through interactions with other people and institutions—that is, they are socialized. **Political socialization** is the process by which people learn the political norms of their society and their political behavior: It's how members of the public become aware of politics, learn political facts, and form their political opinions.

THE SIGNIFICANCE OF POLITICAL SOCIALIZATION

Political socialization is thought to be important for two main reasons. First, at the individual level, it is thought that to understand adult public opinion, it is necessary to understand where opinions come from, namely political development in childhood. Second, political socialization is important for the maintenance and functioning of the political system itself.[2]

What and how one learns about politics form the basis of the opinions people eventually express. Political learning takes place throughout life, so in a sense the process of socialization is never finished. However, most research in political socialization places strong emphasis on early learning. Two important tenets flowing from this belief are the **primacy principle** and the **structuring principle.**

The primacy principle posits that "what is learned first, is learned best." In related fashion, the structuring principle takes for granted that early learning structures later learning.[3] Therefore, the belief is that early learning—primarily in childhood—is crucial in influencing adult opinions and that, presumably, the time when a political value or piece of information is first encountered and absorbed will have important ramifications for later opinions about related matters.

Given the variety of political events, situations, and messages over the course of one's life, these two principles may not always be operative in practice. But it is perfectly reasonable to think that what one learns growing up has an important effect on what one thinks later on. In fact, research shows that although the need to cope with information about new events and changing conditions requires some readjustment and new learning, for the most part one's basic value system remains intact, even if specific attitudes are modified. For example, how much of what you think and believe now is attributable to what you learned earlier?

How well the socialization system imparts the norms and values of a society is also an important question for the political system. Political systems cannot function if they do not have the basic support and legitimacy of their populations, who at a minimum accept the government's authority, obey the laws, and pay taxes. An additional requirement for democratic political systems is the creation of a citizenry that is supportive of democratic values and interested and engaged in politics.

These two dimensions of socialization have implications for the democratic dialogue and the democratic dilemma. Understanding how individuals develop their political values, orientations, and opinions helps to explain where the people get their voice, and this in turn influences how well the government listens. At the same time, analyzing socialization from the system level helps to evaluate how well and to what extent the citizenry as a whole lives up to its democratic responsibilities. Thus, how much the government should listen to the people may depend in part upon how well the people are prepared for and involved in democratic government.

THE SOCIALIZATION PROCESS

Socialization can occur through direct (overt) and indirect (covert) means. Direct political socialization occurs when political values are explicitly taught, such as in a high school civics class or when parents tell their children why abortion, the death penalty, and so forth are good or bad. Indirect political socialization occurs more subtly, when the development of ostensibly nonpolitical attitudes shapes the later development of political attitudes. For example, media portrayals of police and politicians in entertainment programs might influence how one later views politicians and law enforcement officials; or general attitudes about human nature—such as whether people are basically lazy or whether hard work is rewarded—might later impact how people view certain political issues, such as welfare or job training programs.

For socialization to occur at all, it must have the proper context. Three necessary prerequisites are exposure, communication, and receptivity. First, a person must be exposed to the value or attitude in question. Second, its meaning must be communicated clearly (and usually frequently). Third, people must be receptive to the message. Usually, this means that they find the source of the message to be credible. The more these factors are at work, the stronger the influence.

AGENTS OF SOCIALIZATION

Socialization is conducted by several different agents. These are forces that influence and contribute to our learning. They include (in rough order of their appearance in our lives) family, schools, peers, and mass media.

The discussion of each of these agents will be divided into two sections: the mechanism by which the agent or force attempts, either directly or indirectly, to influence our opinions, and the effects of that process on future attitudes and behavior. Agents may affect opinion in four main areas: political knowledge; political orientations (alignments like ideology and party identification); attitudes toward the system (citizenship, participation, trust); and attitudes on specific issues. One must recognize at the outset, however, that most of the research on political socialization occurred during the 1960s and 1970s, after which scholars lost interest in the subject. It is only recently that new work—much of it spurred by the apparent declining civic engagement of young people today—has come along.

The Family

Families, especially parents, obviously play a crucial initial role in the creation and development of our attitudes and opinions. Parents are potentially strong forces of political socialization because of their dominant position in teaching and raising children. Exposure, communication, and receptivity are likely to be high in parent-child relationships, at least in the early years.

Children learn about politics from their parents, both directly and indirectly. First, parents may share or teach children their political preferences directly, and children may simply adopt them as their own. Second, children may imitate or otherwise assimilate views from their parents indirectly. They may overhear their father's derogatory comments about the president, and decide they don't like the president either. This may be one way political party affiliation is learned. Third, children may generalize or transfer opinions learned from their parents to other objects. For example, if they have a negative relationship with their parents, they may carry this over to having a negative attitude toward all authority figures, such as the police or the president.

As far as the lasting effects of parenting or what adult children learn from their parents, most researchers have concluded that parents have the greatest effect on general predispositions and orientations toward politics, rather than on specific issues, despite their efforts at teaching values in the early years. For example, one of the main things people learn from their parents is their party identification. Even here, the effect varies: If both parents are of the same political party affiliation, their child is more likely to identify with that party than if only one, or neither of them, identifies with a party.[4] However, as party identification has weakened over time, so too has this relationship, with more parents and offspring declaring themselves independents.

Family background also plays an important role in civic development. The political knowledge level of high school students is directly related to the educational level of their parents. Even when included in studies controlling for other factors, research shows that the amount of education one's parents have is still a significant predictor of student political knowledge.[5] Parental educational level is also related to youths' attitudes and behavior toward community and political participation. Parental participation likewise seems to have a parallel effect on child behavior regarding community volunteerism.[6] A more recent comparative survey of high school students found close parent-child connections

"Yes, son, we're Republicans."

on political knowledge, interest in politics, and attention to political news, as well as some attitudes toward political behavior. In other words, students with high political knowledge scores had parents with high knowledge scores; students with parents who read the news regularly tend to do likewise, and so forth.[7]

Could these early orientations shape later behavior? It seems plausible. For example, one of the authors came from a family whose mother was very politically active, including once being president of the state chapter of the League of Women Voters, a frequent delegate to state Democratic party conventions, and the like. Furthermore, both parents attained higher education, with his father pursuing a graduate degree. Couldn't these influences explain why one of their children became a political science professor?

Also, the family determines the socioeconomic environment in which children grow up, putting them in a particular network of relationships with others, which may influence how they view the world. Children raised in affluent households in upper-class urban neighborhoods will likely view the world differently than those raised in poor, rural areas, for example, regardless of their future social standing. Studies show that poor and minority children generally have more negative views and impressions about the political system and leaders than middle-class whites, and while not solely due to the influence of family, these differences are likely related to that environment.[8]

Yet, in other respects, the opinion connection between parents and their children about politics is not very strong. Studies comparing parents and offspring on measures of **political efficacy** (whether one can make a difference in politics, personal empowerment, and so on), have found only weak relationships.[9]

When it comes to more specific political issues—such as taxes, abortion, education, and so forth—teenage, not to mention adult, offspring are far less likely to share the same views as their parents. Again, however, it depends on the issue. In a comparative study of high school seniors and their parents in 1965, researchers found moderate correlations between parent-student opinions on the issues of school racial integration and prayer in school, but a much weaker (almost no) relationship on the issues of whether they would allow an elected Communist to hold office or a person to make a public speech against religion. Clearly, the racial and religious questions were more likely to be visible and of concern to both parents and children, whereas the civil liberties questions were more abstract, and less likely to have been the kinds of issues or value questions discussed at home. Nevertheless, in no case were the correlations between student and parent opinions on any political issue as high as on party identification.[10] Direct parental influence on issue opinions is likely strongest when children clearly perceive the parents' preferences and when such matters are important to the parents.

Therefore, parents appear to have only a "meager" effect on political opinions later in life, save for party identification and general political orientations.[11] As children mature, the influence of other agents in shaping opinion increases. Furthermore, since the number of single-parent households and homes where both parents work has increased in the United States in the last few decades, parents may no longer be as dominant in a child's preschool and pre-adult years as they once were, perhaps limiting the impact of the family all the more. The family does, however, impart general predispositions toward the political system, and basic values, along with some political attitudes.

The socializing role of the family plays an ambiguous role in preparing young people for adult citizenship. Some parents seem to do it well (usually, if they themselves are educated or interested in politics); some do it poorly. It is therefore unclear whether familial socialization contributes to the democratic dilemma. Perhaps the fact that children appear not to adopt many of the direct opinions of their parents indicates the population can think for itself and adapt to new circumstances, but on the other hand it is by no means certain that this is the case.

Because of differences between families in their education, their interest in politics, their political behavior, and even their political views, these attitudes may be transferred to their offspring. This is one reason for diversity of opinions within the adult population. These differences, however, in turn have implications for the democratic dialogue. Since parental education and to a lesser extent interest and participation in politics do have lingering effects on their grown children, it may lead to some people being more willing to speak out or comfortable speaking out than others, and in turn government may listen to or hear those voices more often. However, because people's education, job, social status, etc., as well as their life experiences, may be different than that of their parents, their opinions may be also, thereby limiting the influence of the family in the end.

Primary and Secondary Schools

Schools have long been thought to be powerful agents of socialization. Indeed, in totalitarian societies like Nazi Germany, the Soviet Union, and Communist China, education has been seen as a crucial part of building support for the regime and making enthusiastic citizens. The importance of schools in educating students for responsible citizenship has also been emphasized in the United States—although in theory, at least, more along the lines of democratic values.

In terms of direct socialization, in American schools the key values and symbols of the polity are explicitly taught. Schools promote patriotic rituals (such as the Pledge of Allegiance) and include other patriotic themes, songs, and sayings in the program of study. One of the authors still fondly remembers his role in his fifth-grade musical play, "Tall Tom Jefferson," where he played Jefferson's political rival, Alexander Hamilton.

In lower grades, children are exposed to the basic symbols and ideas of the United States, such as learning about national holidays and the history associated with them (Thanksgiving, Presidents' Day, Martin Luther King, Jr. Day, and other holidays). This builds pride in country and respect for the polity. Young children generally absorb simple, idealistic images, such as that the president is strong and good. In the upper grades, school elections, mock political conventions, debate teams, and the like introduce students to the ideas of how their government works. Clubs operate along democratic lines and reinforce ideas such as majority rule and participation. These all provide indirect forms of socialization.

In high school, students may take civics or social studies courses, which are in varying degrees directly related to learning about the political system. It is here that education is thought to be most connected to adult citizenship and attitudes.

School textbooks also have a socializing bent. According to scholarly analyses, textbooks often encourage loyalty to the nation and government and acceptance of the status quo. The ones used in elementary school have underlying themes of compliance, the need to be a good citizen, and respect for authority. Even the more sophisticated ones used in advanced grades idealize and oversimplify the way government works and exaggerate the power of individual citizens. Ironically, they are less likely to emphasize the importance of participation or to provide an understanding of democratic values. In similar fashion, they fail to help students understand that conflict and differences of opinion are a necessary part of healthy democratic society.[12]

The effects of schooling on knowledge, democratic values, and opinions are mixed. Schools do seem to promote loyalty and attachment to country, compliance with laws, authority, the legitimacy of the system, and abstract support for democratic principles.[13] However, while democratic principles are taught and conveyed in school, they are more symbolic slogans than practically applied.[14]

Furthermore, direct attempts by schools to foster democratic citizenship seem to have limited impact, if not being outright failures. The long-held consensus of political science was that taking a civics or social studies course doesn't produce more political interest or knowledge[15]—though for some groups, such as the upper-middle class or blacks—there were modest positive effects.[16]

Recently, this disappointing and surprising conclusion has been challenged. Some research suggests schools and individual coursework, especially the amount and recentness of civics classes, do pay off in terms of increased political knowledge.[17]

Even these more positive findings point to the school curriculum's being more successful at increasing political knowledge than at fostering democratic attitudes. Social studies instruction has been found to have few direct effects, mostly imparting simple factual knowledge rather than participatory attitudes or skills.[18]

Still, some argue that new and different civics instruction might be more successful. The renewal of specific efforts at civic education and their possible effects are discussed more fully in Box 5.1.

The amount of education one receives clearly does have an indirect effect on measures of civic literacy and engagement. As years of schooling increase, so does engagement. People with higher levels of education are generally more knowledgeable about and interested in politics, are more likely to participate in political affairs, and so on. For example, sheer amount of education is the strongest and most consistent demographic factor related to political knowledge among individuals.[19] Niemi and Chapman's comprehensive study of ninth- through twelfth-graders in 1996 found that students in higher grades were more knowledgeable about politics, paid greater attention to political news, were more politically efficacious, and more tolerant of diversity than those in lower grades.[20] Similarly, level of educational attainment is the strongest predictor of whether someone will vote. All of these results appear to be an offshoot of education, in that the skills and resources education provides carry over into the political realm.

Yet despite these seemingly positive effects, schools overall may still fall short. Critics charge that while relative levels of knowledge do increase with education, actual levels, even following years of school, are still disturbingly low.[21] For example, only 8 percent of high school students were able to correctly answer all five political knowledge questions in Niemi and Chapman's recent study.[22]

Also, while tolerance and support for democratic values seem to increase with education, educated Americans are no less likely than others to view political institutions favorably[23] or to understand that politics requires debate and compromise. As Hibbing and Theiss-Morse put it, "education may help with knowledge, interest, involvement, and support for constitutional arrangements, but there is no evidence it helps foster an appreciation for the nitty gritty of democratic politics."[24] Nor does more education appear to significantly affect political alienation. Data from the American National Election Studies provide a case in point. From 1958 to 2000, on average 36 percent of people with grade school through high school educations said they "trust[ed] the federal government to do what's right" most of the time. The average comparable figure for those with at least some college education through graduate degrees was 39 percent—basically no different.[25]

The failure of schools to foster interest and involvement in politics, and support for basic values of democracy, may be due not to what is taught in classes but instead to how schools are run. Some argue there is a hidden curriculum, by pointing out that schools themselves as institutions are not democratically organized and don't encourage students to participate in any meaningful way. Given an environment in which schools don't practice what they preach, preaching such values may not have much meaning.[26]

However, involvement in school extracurricular activities such as clubs or student government has been found to aid participatory attitudes and skills.[27] In particular, students who participate in student government tend to be more knowledgeable about politics, confident in their participation skills, and more tolerant of controversial books and materials in their schools.[28] In some ways, though, this finding should not be surprising. The kinds of students who would who get involved in these activities may already be the sorts of people who want to be involved in the system and are likely to be interested and engaged to begin with. Still, this does suggest that practicing democratic involvement in school might transfer to the political realm later in life.

The major impact of schooling (K–12) thus appears to be in helping create good citizens only in certain respects—that is, in getting them to accept political authority, support established political institutions, and channel their energies into legitimate outlets. One reason why the United States may be such a patriotic country, and why Americans believe it to be the best country in the world, may be due to the nature of primary and secondary education.

At the same time, however, schooling fails to give Americans a realistic image of politics in a democratic society, and the idealistic and simplistic visions of the political system it perpetuates may in turn foster cynicism toward practical politics and politicians later in life. And, while generally increasing knowledge and interest in politics, in the end schooling does not produce a large corps of active, engaged, and knowledgeable citizens. In this way, schools contribute to rather than solve the democratic dilemma.

College and Beyond

College usually comes as an important transition stage into full adulthood and has long been thought to be a transforming experience, even for older adults. Is higher education any different from primary and secondary school in terms of its impact on political engagement and opinions?

Effects of Higher Education on Knowledge, Interest, and Engagement

The answer appears to be, for the most part, no, although there are some notable exceptions. Higher education in general simply continues the general trend toward greater political knowledge, interest in politics, and political participation found at lower levels of education. (We explore educational effects on political participation more fully in Chapter 9.) But on many of these measures, the differences between the higher and lower educated are not huge; in other words, higher education brings greater civic skills, which allow for greater civic engagement, but the improvements come in a continuing, gradual fashion rather than in a quantum leap.

In an exhaustive and very recent study, Stephen and Linda Bennett analyzed survey results from two sets of young people (ages eighteen to twenty-nine)—those with higher education (with at least some college education, on up through a graduate degree) and those in the same age-cohort without higher education. The participants were compared on a number of different dimensions of civic engagement.[29] The ones with higher education had higher levels of engagement on several measures, including interest in political affairs, claiming to have voted in the last election, campaign and local activism, talking about politics, exposure to print and electronic national news, and, especially, political knowledge. This group was also more tolerant of dissent on such issues as allowing someone to give a public speech against religion and allowing a controversial book to be kept in the public library.

But only on measures of political knowledge, political interest, reported voting turnout, and local participation were these differences statistically significant, meaning that the differences were mathematically unlikely to be due to error or chance. And the less-educated group actually scored higher in other areas such as attention to entertainment news and to early and late local news broadcasts, although only the latter was statistically significant.

The researchers also found that those who had had some exposure to college were also slightly more cynical than those who had no exposure. The better-educated group was a bit more likely to believe government will listen to the public, and slightly less likely to think government will listen to people like them, but in fact there was little difference between the groups. The Bennetts also echoed the points other researchers have made about K–12 education, by noting that, with the exception of political knowledge and possibly voting, young people with college exposure did not perform very well in terms of political interest, attention to news, and political activism.[30] In other words, although their scores on these dimensions were higher, they were not very high in any event.

Overall, it appears that young Americans with some college education are really not much more politically engaged than their same-age peers who have no college experience. Although political knowledge was clearly greater, those with some college experience did not seem to take advantage of that greater knowledge to become more involved, interested, and active. In the end, the

Bennetts in part blame the faculty for failing to engage students and teach them responsible citizenship: "[A]s faculty, our own political cynicism and ambivalence about the goal of civic education, even how to define what citizenship means, contributes to the civic ignorance of our students."[31] The concern over the future of youth and democracy in America, coupled with a re-commitment to civic education in recent years, is explored in Box 5.1.

BOX 5.1

New Civic Education for Today's Apolitical Youth

In recent years, apparent declines in civic engagement and increases in apathy, if not cynicism, among the young have led to widespread concern that we may be raising a lost generation when it comes to politics. The fear is that once young people are socialized in this way, they may continue to disengage from politics for the rest of their lives.

A survey of college freshmen in 1998 found that only 26 percent thought "keeping up with politics and public affairs" was very important, less than half the 1966 level of 58 percent, and only 14 percent reported discussing politics in the past year, half the level of those who discussed religion.[1] This measure did increase in two consecutive years, being "very important" for 31 percent of freshmen in 2001, and for 33 percent in 2002, undoubtedly due to the influence of the controversial 2000 election and the September 11, 2001, terrorist attacks.[2] Nevertheless, even these increasing levels are not high, compared with previous generations.

Voting is also a source of concern. Although younger Americans have always voted at lower rates than most other groups, even fewer are voting today than in the past. Voting among those between the ages of eighteen and twenty-four declined from 49.6 percent in 1972 (the first presidential election in which people under 21 could vote) to 32.4 percent in 1996.[3] Bennett and Bennett, utilizing National Election Study surveys, found that the portion of young respondents (ages eighteen to twenty-nine) with more than a high school diploma claiming to have voted in the last election dipped from 83 percent in 1972 to 70 percent in 2000. Among those with high school educations or less, it fell from 53 percent to 36 percent.[4] And these later numbers came from young populations with generally greater education, something that is supposed to increase political participation.

These trends have led some in the educational community, along with nonprofit, business, and even political leaders, to call for greater civic education as a remedy for the situation. At the same time, academics in education and political science have renewed emphasis on research into civic education and on finding ways to promote it.

In addition to programs focusing explicitly on civic education, some of these efforts have been linked to or even combined with another educational trend, known as service learning. Service learning attempts to incorporate community service and other forms of experiential learning into the curriculum. The belief is that the skills and values learned through service will carry over into the political realm, making participants more interested in others and in their community, and, hence, in the political system as well.

As a result, several organizations and efforts have been created. Among these at the K–12 level are Kids Voting USA, and We, the People. Kids Voting USA is a biennial program linked with national and state elections. It incorporates the current electoral process into the school curriculum. In election years, students participate like adults, by following political news, learning about candidates, participating in debates, and actually casting a mock vote in a class election, among other activities. We, the People, sponsored by the Center for Civic Education, is an instructional program at the middle school and high school levels. The program for middle school students is Project Citizen, an educational program designed to develop interest in public policymaking and participation in state and local government through simulations, reports, and the like. The high school program, We the People: The Citizen and the Constitution, focuses on American history and the content and practice of the American Constitution, including classroom simulations of the U.S. Congress, in addition to traditional academic content.[5] Service learning has also been incorporated into a number of schools' curricula.

At the university level, two of the largest efforts are Campus Compact and the American Democracy Project. Campus Compact is a national coalition of more than 900 college and university presidents committed to the civic purposes of higher education. It promotes community service initiatives on college campuses, both in and out of the classroom, to develop students' citizenship skills. It also supports campus-community partnerships and teaching and research on community service.[6] In essence, it promotes a variety of individual service learning efforts at campuses across the country.

The American Democracy Project is a national, multicampus initiative that seeks to create an intellectual and experiential understanding of civic engagement for undergraduates enrolled at institutions that are members of the American Association of State Colleges and Universities (AASCU). The goal of the project is "to produce graduates who understand and are committed to engaging in meaningful actions as citizens in a democracy."[7] It was only launched in 2002 and is mainly dedicated to getting institutions of higher education to engage in conversations about how to best promote civic engagement and how to develop and implement changes in curriculum, administration, and even university structure to achieve that goal.

There are numerous other efforts. Perhaps your high school or college has been involved in such a program.

Proponents claim that through service learning and civic engagement projects in coursework, students can be energized and taught to be fuller, more involved citizens. These advocates believe that increases in political knowledge, as well as political interest and participation, will flow from such efforts.

Many of these programs are too new to have been fully evaluated, and in any event results are mixed. Service learning programs have been found to have little direct effect on political knowledge, and results examining indirect effects on the political efficacy of participants have varied.[8] Similarly, service learning efforts may increase students' interests in their communities, but not to become better analysts of democracy nor to become more directly involved in public policy.[9]

On the other hand, more explicitly political and civic education programs appear to have greater effects. Studies of the We, the People program have shown that it increased students' knowledge of American government significantly. The program also tended to reduce students' cynicism about government and politics, and to make them more likely to vote,

Continued

BOX 5.1—Cont'd

participate in politics, and work for a political campaign.[10] A follow-up study of its alumni found that the effects lasted years after the program.[11] An analysis of the Kids Voting program in San Jose, California, found similar results. The curriculum had positive effects on students' participation (in the mock elections), their personal political efficacy and trust in the system, and their knowledge, interest, and attention to political news.[12]

But critics argue that by their very nature, the goals, design, and implementation of many of these programs make them less successful at creating *politically* better citizens. Professor J. Jackson Barlow, in a review of service learning and citizenship, argues that service learning itself may not increase civic engagement. In part, this is because the underlying focus of these efforts is on altruism and charitable concern for one's fellow citizens, but these efforts do not necessarily translate into political engagement, which may actually be very self-interested. This failure of service learning to directly impact political attitudes may be because many programs encourage students to think of service as an alternative to politics, and a morally superior one at that. Therefore, it is likely that students could engage in an altruism-oriented program of service learning and fail to discern a connection between service and the political process. He notes how civic education programs like We, the People have found direct effects on knowledge and engagement, as mentioned above, whereas simple service learning programs like Learn and Serve America showed almost no difference between participants and nonparticipants.[13]

This is not to say that service learning has no salutary effects. One intensive study found students associated with service learning programs had a greater sense of social responsibility, commitment to social justice, increased tolerance, support for volunteering, and greater connectedness to community.[14] It is more that service learning, at least based on early research results, has not had the spillover effect on civic engagement some proponents had expected. As one of these advocates puts it, "what research suggests, and what my own experience confirms, is that civic learning does not *automatically* happen from a community service experience. . . . [S]ervice-learning [can be] an effective vehicle in producing a more engaged and knowledgeable citizenry, but only when specific course characteristics are considered."[15]

Political scientist Russ Brown makes the more fundamental point that the goals of even the most specific civic education efforts are misguided, and so they are likely to have little real effect in changing the American political system. He argues that proponents of these programs often fail to distinguish between *procedural* democracy and *substantive* democracy. Procedural democracy means that the mechanisms of the system operate through democratic means: There are elections, rights like free speech are protected, and so on. Substantive democracy means that the outcomes of the system are democratic: fair, equal, and just. For Brown, the United States is obviously substantively undemocratic, given the power of wealthy elites, special interest groups, the role of money in politics, and so forth. Simply increasing the number of people voting or those interested and engaged in politics won't necessarily make the system more substantively democratic—indeed, the only result is that more people will be interested and involved in an undemocratic system! He also notes that political disengagement may be a rational response by the youth to a political system that is viciously negative, appears to be corrupt, and is inherently oligarchic.[16]

Brown asks if we want the end result of civic education to be merely "participation for participation's sake" (or knowledge for knowledge's sake), or instead whether we want to create critical, analytical, and independent-thinking citizens who will change the system for the better, making it more substantively democratic. This loftier goal is clearly more difficult, and has not been directly addressed by civic education programs as currently envisioned.

If past is prologue in socialization research, the results of all of these programs are likely to be minor, although, as noted, the traditional research finding that civics had little effect is under review. In any event, whether successful or not, their actual socializing effects on today's youth won't be seen for many years to come.

Notes

1. Sheilah Mann, "What the Survey of American College Freshmen Tells Us about Their Interest in Politics and Political Science," *PS: Political Science and Politics* 32 No. 2 (June 1999): 263–268.
2. UCLA Higher Education Research Institute press release, January 2003, accessed at http://www.gseis.ucla.edu/heri/heri.html.
3. http://www.fairvote.org/turnout/youth_voters.htm.
4. Stephen Earl Bennett and Linda L. M. Bennett, "Reconsidering the Effects of Education on Civic Virtue Among the Young." Paper presented at the International Conference for Civic Education Research, New Orleans, November 15–18, 2003.
5. See Center for Civic Education, http://www.civiced.org.
6. See http://www.campuscompact.org.
7. See the discussion at Indiana University, http://www.americandemocracy.iu.edu.
8. Rahima C. Wade and David Warren Saxbe, "Community Service Learning in the Social Studies: Historical Roots, Empirical Evidence, Critical Issues," *Theory and Research in Social Education* (Fall 1996): 331–359.
9. Mary A. Hepburn, Richard G. Niemi, and Chris Chapman, "Service Learning in College Political Science: Queries and Commentary," *PS: Political Science and Politics* 33 (September 2000): 617–622; Susan Hunter and Richard A. Brisbin, Jr., "The Impact of Service Learning on Democratic and Civic Values," *PS: Political Science and Politics* 33 (September 2000): 623–626.
10. Suzanne Soule, "We the People. . . The Citizen and the Constitution: Knowledge of and Support for Democratic Institutions and Processes by Participating Students [in the] National Finals 2000" (Center for Civic Education, 2000); Kenneth W. Tolo, "An Assessment of 'We the People . . . Project Citizen': Promoting Citizenship in Classrooms and Communities" (Lyndon B. Johnson School of Public Affairs, University of Texas and Center for Civic Education, 2000). (Both are available at http://www. civiced.org.)
11. Suzanne Soule, "Voting and Political Participation of 'We the People . . . the Citizen and the Constitution' Alumni: Survey Results 2001" (Center for Civic Education, 2001). (This report is also available at http://www.civiced.org.)
12. Jack M. McLeod, William P. Eveland, Jr., and Edward M. Horowitz, "Going Beyond Adults and Voter Turnout: Evaluating a Socialization Program Involving Schools, Family, and Media," in Thomas J. Johnson, Carol E. Hays, and Scott P. Hays, eds., *Engaging the Public: How Government and the Media Can Reinvigorate American Democracy* (Lanham, MD: Rowman and Littlefield, 1998).

Continued

BOX 5.1—Cont'd

13. J. Jackson Barlow, "Service Learning and Citizenship: Creating Habits of the Heart?" delivered to a conference "Active Participation or Retreat into Privacy," cosponsored by the Center for Civic Education and the German Federal Center for Political Education, Potsdam, Germany, October 2001; accessed at http://www.bpb.de/veranstaltungen/XGJUMO,0,0,Service_Learning_and_Citizenship%3A_Creating_Habits_of_the_Heart.html.

14. Janet Eyler and Dwight E. Giles, Jr., *Where's the Learning in Service-Learning?* (San Francisco: Jossey-Bass, 1999), pp. 29–34, quoted in Rick Battistoni, *Civic Engagement Across the Curriculum* (Providence, RI: Campus Compact, 2002), p. 6.

15. Battistoni, *Civic Engagement*, pp. 7–8.

16. Russ Brown, "Civic Education: For What? More Participation or Real Democracy?" Paper delivered at the International Conference on Civic Education Research, New Orleans, November 15–18, 2003.

Effects of Higher Education on Specific Value Orientations

There are some indications that college education does impact people's views and perspectives on politics. The most significant finding is that, in some ways at least, college appears to make people more liberal. College students are more liberal than the general population, and the longer they are in college, the more liberal they become. This generalization is true for both ideological self-identification and issue positions, although this is more evident in views on social issues than economic ones (where the generally higher incomes of the higher educated appear to push them more toward conservatism). College graduates remain more liberal than the rest of the population throughout life.

Three main explanations have been offered for this phenomenon. One argues that college professors indoctrinate their students—and that since professors tend to be liberal, their students become liberal too. Despite the stereotype of the knee-jerk liberal college professor, in fact there is some variation among college faculty. Faculty in the humanities and social sciences are more liberal than the general population, but those in business and the natural sciences are relatively more conservative, and similar to other Americans.[32] Although it is true that the people teaching subjects most relevant to politics are more likely to be liberal, students' exposure to professors from other fields and exposure to other points of view more generally would seemingly limit a faculty effect.

The view that teachers indoctrinate their students also assumes that college professors both make concerted attempts to influence their students and that they are highly successful in doing so. As any professor can tell you, both of these assumptions are flawed: Not all professors try to indoctrinate their students, nor are students so easy to persuade. Also, while faculty political orientations have changed little over the past twenty-five years, among students there has been a slight increase in the number who identify themselves as conservatives, and a much larger increase in self-proclaimed moderates, over the same time period.[33] This is not a record of great success for any would-be indoctrinators. Furthermore, as with high school civics, it is unlikely that college courses even have much effect on students' knowledge and attitudes toward the political system (though there is some dispute about this, as we discuss later). If such direct socialization efforts fail to do much about these types of political attitudes, why would they greatly impact students' ideology and views on specific political issues?

Another school of thought suggests a self-selection bias: Perhaps the kinds of people who go to college are more liberal to begin with. Although entering students in the 1960s–1970s were more liberal than the general population, those in the 1980s through mid-1990s were not, with most labeling themselves moderates. In 1998, for example, only 23 percent of freshmen identified themselves as liberal, the lowest percentage in fourteen years, and 20 percent were conservative or far right, both slightly lower than the general population.[34] Although the number of self-proclaimed liberals increased to roughly 30 percent in 2001, it dipped to 28 percent in 2002, and moderates still outnumbered ideologues (see Fig. 5.1).

But even this liberal trend isn't uniform when examining issue positions: In 2002, students were more conservative on some economic issues and in supporting greater military spending (clearly due to the impact of 9/11), but they expressed far more liberal opinions on social issues such as gay rights and legalizing marijuana.[35] In any event, despite these notable differences, students are not radically different from the population as a whole.

The third explanation, the enlightenment hypothesis, argues that exposure to the wide range of views and greater educational understanding people receive in college in turn leads them to be more liberal and open-minded. This view provides a plausible explanation for such things as the fact that college-educated people are more tolerant of people with extreme views than are people with less education. But this view also seems an oversimplification—especially since the college educated are only more liberal on social issues, which may be in part related to a reduction in stereotypes and an ability to think that comes with education.

Obviously, none of these explanations is perfect. Perhaps the college experience itself and the people one meets in college alter one's life views. Indeed, one of the most famous research works, the Bennington College study, supports such a conclusion. The Bennington students studied were upper-class women from conservative Republican families, women who initially differed little in their political orientations from their parents. However, after four years at Bennington, exposed to liberal professors, new ideas and perspectives, and more importantly, new peers and life experiences during the height of the Great Depression, they emerged more liberal and more Democratic.

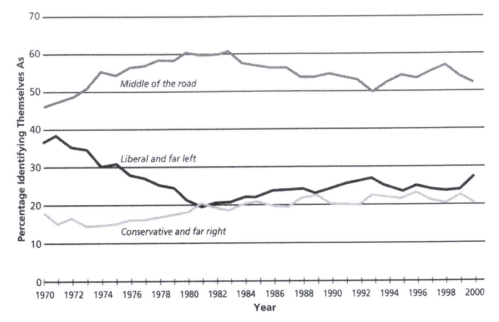

FIGURE 5.1. Changing Political Attitudes of College Students.

Source: Alexander W. Astin, et al., *The American Freshman: Thirty Year Trends, 1966–1995* (Los Angeles: Higher Education Research Institute, Graduate School of Education, University of California, 1997); Alexander W. Astin, et al., *The American Freshman: Norms for 2000* (Los Angeles: Higher Education Research Institute, Graduate School of Education University of California, 2001).

They maintained many of these orientations throughout their lives.[36] But given that liberal self-identification and value orientations on some political issues are simply *greater* with the higher educated, rather than an absolute majority, all one can say for certain is that liberalism is more prevalent among the higher educated.

Peers

Peer groups are people one associates with regularly outside of the family. In childhood and adolescence, peers consist of friends and classmates, while in adulthood, they include friends, neighbors, and coworkers, although spouses also fit into this category. Peers can impact opinions and behavior, as the very phrase "peer pressure" suggests. They do this through simple day-to-day interaction, via assimilation or the adoption of views. They may have both a direct and indirect influence on political opinions, depending upon the nature of the group.

In many instances, however, peers may simply reinforce opinions developed by family or school. Furthermore, peer groups may have a larger effect on nonpolitical issues that are more important to young people, like music or hair styles. Likewise, studies show that peers have more influence than parents and family on issues important to members of the peer group. In one study, high school students were more like their friends than parents on the issue of giving eighteen-year-olds the right to vote, but were closer to their parents than peers on party identification and some other issues.[37]

Peers also are more influential on opinions in adulthood. As we mentioned, the women in the Bennington study appeared to be influenced by their peer groups in college, and these groups continued to play an important role later in life. Among those Bennington women who changed views during their life, the most important factor appeared to be having a spouse and friends with opposing views. Those who chose to be among people with similar views kept the same attitudes they had in college.[38]

The actual influence of peers on opinion has been difficult to determine in practice. One problem with sorting out peer effects is that one might choose associates whose political views are already similar, rather than changing one's views to fit those of one's peers. So, similarities between peers may be due to this self-selection bias. Furthermore, few people are willing to admit publicly that they change their views to conform to those of others. This tendency makes survey research in this area somewhat unreliable. Finally, while peers are often seen as being important influences on opinion, little research has been done in this area.[39]

Peer influence is perhaps most evident in group political attitudes. Relying on friends, coworkers, spouses, etc., as a basis for opinions does not necessarily mean that people are duped or ignorant about politics, although for some that may be the case. For example, suppose your peers are all ardent Bush-haters. You might blindly adopt their perspective and dislike President Bush's latest policy proposal, even though it might be something you would otherwise agree with. On the other hand, if your values drove you to select those peers in the first place, using them as a cue for developing your own opinions makes some sense. Therefore, peer influence also plays an ambiguous role in this aspect of the democratic dilemma. More importantly, because peers may be politically homogeneous—you tend to agree with them, whether because you chose them for that reason, or you adopt their opinions to be part of the group—the influence of peers may encourage narrow thinking or prevent exposure to alternative views that might change or better educate the public.

Peer influence impacts the democratic dialogue, as peer groups become subsets of public opinion or publics (although such subsets may also develop due to media, family, or even educational effects). We discuss differences in certain group opinions in Chapter 8. Nevertheless, given the diversity between peer groups and the scarcity of research on this agent, it is difficult to tell whether they increase governmental responsiveness to public opinion overall, or whether they limit it, since some peer groups are more politically involved than others.

Mass Media

The mass media have become a powerful agent of socialization, now influencing people from a relatively early age rather than merely later in life. In some ways, the media have become the new babysitter, as children are exposed to hours of television every day. Some children may even have more interaction with the media than with their parents or teachers. In fact, when asked about their information sources for their attitudes on issues like the economy and race relations, high school students mention the mass media more often than they mention friends, families, teachers, or even personal experience. Furthermore, even information they get from nonmedia sources, like parents and teachers, probably came from the media originally or was in some way influenced by it. Children who are heavy media users also know more about public affairs than their peers.[40]

Given their smaller amount of life experience, children may be more susceptible to media influence than adults. However, some direct impact of media portrayals is likely muted by the fact that some children aren't sophisticated enough (either in mental development or personal experience) to get some media messages, and most children are not exposed to much political information in the media at all, unless their parents are political junkies. Therefore, media effects may interact with other socializing agents.

Some argue that images from popular media greatly influence children's perceptions. For example, stereotypes of women, racial and ethnic minorities, and homosexuals may be developed or reinforced through media content, although changing portrayals recently might have reversed these trends.[41] It's also possible that the more negative depictions of police, politicians, and other authority figures in recent years may account for the decline in respect for institutions and the political cynicism of today's youth. In the 1950s, for example, police and politicians were more likely to be portrayed as noble public servants, whereas today they are more often seen as selfish, corrupt, or ridiculous.[42] Lastly, many point to the large amounts of violence Americans witness on television, especially in entertainment shows but also on the news. Such violence may negatively impact peoples' opinions—making them either more fearful or more tolerant of violence. All of these effects, however, are difficult to prove with certainty.

The long-term impact of media socialization on civic engagement is a matter of dispute. Some blame the increasingly negative, critical, and analytical coverage of politics by the press—especially since the Vietnam-Watergate era of the 1970s—for increasing alienation and cynicism, while likewise decreasing trust in government and voter turnout. These scholars see a "spiral of cynicism" in which negative media portrayals reinforce a jaded public.[43] Others, however, note the strong correlations between political knowledge, interest, and participation on the one hand, and media use on the other. These observers conclude that media usage can be a positive force for citizenship. For them, a "virtuous circle" exists in which attention to news media gradually reinforces civic engagement, just as civic engagement prompts attention to news.[44] Of course, given such interrelationships, it is hard to separate out causes and effects of the media from other factors, and it is possible that both perspectives may be correct, in that media may have both positive and negative effects on different types of people.

Mass media also play a more important role as one ages, making the media a key element of adult socialization, and potentially a powerful force on attitudes and opinions about politics. The next chapter examines the specific effects of the mass media on public opinion in more detail.

Although the role of the media in the democratic dilemma and the democratic dialogue will also be explored more fully in the next chapter, a few words about the impact of its role as a socializing agent are in order here. Clearly, if the media increase political engagement (knowledge, interest, and participation in politics), as the relationship between the two suggests, then the media are strengthening the case that the government should listen to the people, as well as making it more likely it will actually do so. If, on the other hand, the media have made the public more cynical about politics and politicians, and have contributed to a lack of political trust among the populace, the media have had a negative impact on both the civic capacity of the public (the democratic dilemma) and political interest and involvement, thereby weakening the government's ability to reflect the wishes of the people accurately (the democratic dialogue).

ADULT SOCIALIZATION

Over the course of one's life, it is thought that the influences of some agents wane, while others become stronger. In particular, the influence of the family and schools declines, while that of peers and mass media increases, since that is what people are exposed to as adults. (See Figure 5.2.)

The assumptions and even historical findings of research are that after the impressionistic phase of adolescence and early adulthood, people's basic political patterns are set and change only marginally, if at all. This perspective dominated the research agenda in political socialization and was one reason for the strong emphasis on early learning.

Recently, however, new evidence has emerged, which challenges the old assumptions that little learning takes place in adulthood and that parents are the dominant forces of socialization in the family. Michael McDivitt and Stephen Chaffee argue that, in fact, parents can learn about politics and be stimulated to become more involved, through a process they term "trickle up" socialization, as opposed to the usual notion of "top-down," parent-to-child influence. They examined Kids Voting USA, a civic education program targeted at school children in poor areas during the 1994 election. It incorporated media exposure,

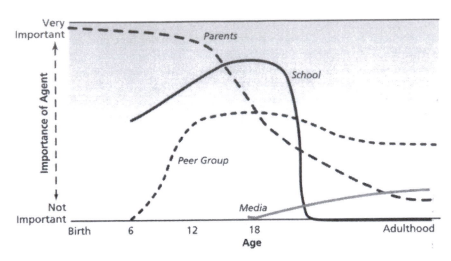

FIGURE 5.2. The Importance of Different Agents of Socialization Through the Life Cycle.

From *American Electorate,* 1st Edition by Bruce A. Campbell. Copyright © 1979. Reprinted by permission of Wadsworth, a division of Thomson Learning: www.thomsonlearning.com.

mock political activities, and other efforts directly into the school curriculum. The program not only increased civic literacy among the participants, but it also increased voting and political engagement among the *parents* of involved children, through discussions and interactions within the family. The researchers concluded that "for parents who were not adequately socialized into politics in their youth, their children's participation in a civics curriculum can provide a second chance at citizenship."[45]

As notable as this finding is, it also suggests that there may be limits to adult socialization. Although it might be possible for someone's attitudes about political interest and involvement to undergo change in adulthood, it seems far less likely that one's basic values and political opinions (as opposed to views about the political system) would do so.

Indeed, there is evidence to support such an interpretation. An analysis of the so-called Terman study, one of the only long-term panel studies of political attitudes, reveals more stability than change over adult life. This study measured the party identification and ideological attitudes of the same 1272 adults in California four times from 1940 to 1977 (1940, 1950, 1960, and 1977), from roughly age thirty to retirement age. Party identification was rather stable, with 65 percent keeping the same position in 1977 as in 1940, and ideology less so, with 54 percent doing so. Although these results did show some change across time, in the interim the most common pattern for both attitudes was to hold the same position at all three subsequent time points. Fifty-nine percent of the respondents kept the same party identification at every point, and an additional 6 percent returned to their original position in the end. With ideology, 42 percent remained stable across all three time periods, with an additional 12 percent who defected eventually returning. Relatively few actually changed political sides over the period of the study: 19 percent changed parties, and 13 percent changed ideological sides.[46] This is only one study, and the researchers themselves cautioned that the sample was a relatively well-educated one, making it difficult to generalize to the whole population. Nevertheless, the study points to the general crystallization rather than transformation of opinion across time.

CONCLUSION

Before people can express themselves about political matters, they must first learn about the political world and develop their opinions. This development comes from the process of political socialization. People get their views, values, and opinions from their parents and family, their schools and education, their peers, and the mass media. These factors interact throughout one's life, although the influence of parents and schools wanes as we grow older and move farther away in time from these influences. The influence of peers and the media, by contrast, increases as we grow older.

It appears that the family has the biggest effect on general political orientations, such as allegiances to a political party or attitudes about politics and the political system. Schools can affect one's attitudes toward the political system, as well as degree of tolerance, but generally they have a modest impact, although new efforts at instruction may change that. Peers seem to have a reinforcing effect on attitudes and opinions, but are more powerful in adulthood, although it is hard to measure whether people choose their peers because they already have similar opinions or whether the desire to please friends or to value their opinions leads people to change their original opinions. Lastly, the mass media can increase political knowledge, but the effect on civic engagement is unclear, since the media may encourage some people but turn off others.

The American socialization system, therefore, affects the nature of the people's voice and its quality, as part of the democratic dilemma. How effective is the system at creating good citizens? It appears greatly successful at inculcating loyalty, feelings of patriotism, and general support for the polity in the abstract, which undoubtedly helps account for the stability, longevity, and legitimacy of the American political system. Apparently, however, it isn't nearly as successful in shaping a population that knows or cares a lot about politics. Some blame parents, some blame the schools, some blame the media, and others blame the victim—the citizens themselves. Regardless of who may be to blame, differences in people's interest and knowledge in politics, along with their political opinions, which are rooted in the socialization system, impact the democratic dialogue.

Suggested Reading

Center for Civic Education: http://www.civiced.org

Gimpel, James G. J., Celeste Lay, and Jason E. Schuknecht, *Cultivating Democracy: Civic Environments and Political Socialization in America*. Washington, DC: Brookings Press, 2003.

Jennings, M. Kent, and Richard G. Niemi, *The Political Character of Adolescence*. Princeton, NJ: Princeton University Press, 1974.

Reeher, Grant, and Joseph Cammarano, eds., *Education for Citizenship: Ideas and Innovations in Political Learning*. Latham, MD: Rowman and Littlefield, 1997.

Notes

1. Michael Kahan, *Media as Politics: Theory, Behavior, and Change in America* (Upper Saddle River, NJ: Prentice-Hall, 1999), p. 170.

2. Michael Corbett, *American Public Opinion: Trends, Processes, and Patterns* (New York: Longman, 1991), pp. 204–205.

3. Steven A. Peterson, *Political Behavior: Patterns in Everyday Life* (Newbury Park, CA: Sage, 1990), pp. 28–29.

4. M. Kent Jennings and Richard G. Niemi, *The Political Character of Adolescence* (Princeton, NJ: Princeton University Press, 1974); L. Kent Tedin, "The Influence of Parents on the Political Attitudes of Adolescents," *American Political Science Review* 68 (1974): 1579–1592.

5. Sidney Verba, Kay Lehman Schlozman, and Henry E. Brady, *Voice and Equality: Civic Volunteerism in American Politics* (Cambridge, MA: Harvard University Press, 1995); Richard Niemi and Jane Junn, *Civic Education: What Makes Students Learn* (New Haven: Yale University Press, 1998).

6. Sidney Verba, Kay Lehman Schlozman, and Henry E. Brady, *Voice and Equality: Civic Volunteerism in American Politics* (Cambridge, MA: Harvard University Press, 1995); M. Nolin, M. Collins, N. Vaden-Kernan, and E. Davies, *Comparison of Estimates in the 1996 Household Education Survey*, NCES Working Paper 97-28 (Washington, DC: U.S. Department of Education, National Center for Education Statistics).

7. Richard Niemi and Chris Chapman, *The Civic Development of 9th-through-12th Grade Students in the United States: 1996* (Washington, DC: U.S. Department of Education, National Center for Education Statistics, 1998).

8. Dean Jaros, Herbert Hirsch, and Frederick Fleron, Jr., "The Malevolent Leader," *American Political Science Review* (June, 1968): 564–575.

9. Paul R. Abramson, *Political Attitudes in America* (San Francisco: Freeman Press, 1983).

10. Jennings and Niemi, *The Political Character of Adolescence*, pp. 77–78.

11. Paul Allen Beck, "The Role of Agents in Political Socialization," in Stanley A. Renshon, ed., *Handbook of Political Socialization* (New York: Free Press, 1977), pp. 122–27.

12. John Hibbing and Elizabeth Theiss-Morse, "Civics Is Not Enough: Teaching Barbarics in K–12," *PS: Political Science & Politics* 29 No. 1 (March 1996): 57–62.

13. Richard E. Dawson andKenneth Prewett, *Political Socialization: An Analytic Approach* (Boston: Little, Brown, 1969), p. 155.

14. Robert D. Hess, "Political Socialization in the Schools," *Harvard Educational Review* 38 No. 4 (1968): 528–536; Gail L. Zellman and David O. Sears, "Childhood Origins of Tolerance and Dissent," *Journal of Social Issues* 27 (1971): 109–136.

15. Beck, "Role of Agents," p. 129.

16. Kenneth P. Langton and M. Kent Jennings, "Political Socialization and the High School Civics Curriculum in the United States," *American Political Science Review* 62 No. 4 (1968): 862–867.

17. David C. Berliner and Bruce J. Biddle, *The Manufactured Crisis: Myths, Flaws, and the Attack on America's Public Schools* (Reading, MA: Addison-Wesley, 1995); Niemi and Junn, *Civic Education: What Makes Students Learn.*

18. Paul Ferguson, "Impacts on Social and Political Participation," in James P. Shaver, ed., *Handbook of Research on Social Studies Teaching and Learning* (New York: Macmillan, 1991).

19. Herbert Hyman, Charles Wright, and John Reed, *The Enduring Effects of Education* (Chicago: University of Chicago Press, 1975); Michael X. Delli Carpini and Scott Keeter, *What Americans Know About Politics* (New Haven: Yale University Press, 1996); Norman H. Nie, Jane Junn, and Kenneth Stehlik-Barry, *Education and Democratic Citizenship: Creating Enlightened Political Autonomy* (Chicago: University of Chicago Press, 1996).

20. Richard Niemi and Chris Chapman, *The Civic Development of 9th-through-12th Grade Students in the United States: 1996* (Washington, DC: U.S. Department of Education, National Center for Education Statistics, 1998).

21. John J. Patrick, "Political Socialization and Political Education in the Schools," in Stanley A. Renshon, ed., *Handbook of Political Socialization* (New York: Free Press, 1977).

22. Niemi and Chapman, *The Civic Development of Ninth-through-Twelfth Grade Students,* p. iii.

23. John R. Hibbing and Elizabeth Theiss-Morse, *Congress as Public Enemy* (New York: Cambridge University Press, 1995), pp. 108–112.

24. Hibbing and Theiss-Morse, "Civics is Not Enough," p. 60.

25. Derived from National Election Studies data, accessed at http://www.umich.edu/~nes.

26. Richard Merelman, "Democratic Politics and the Culture of American Education," *American Political Science Review* 74 (June 1980): 319–332.

27. Paul A. Beck and M. Kent Jennings, "Pathways to Participation," *American Political Science Review* 76 No. 2 (1982): 94–108; Verba, Schlozman, and Brady, *Voice and Equality: Civic Volunteerism in American Politics,* pp. 422–425.

28. Niemi and Chapman, *The Civic Development of Ninth-through-Twelfth Grade Students,* p. v.

29. Stephen Earl Bennett and Linda L. M. Bennett, "Reconsidering the Effects of Education on Civic Virtue Among the Young." Paper presented at the International Conference for Civic Education Research, New Orleans, November 15–18, 2003.

30. Ibid., pp. 13–14.

31. Ibid., p. 24.

32. A Carnegie Commission survey found that 64% of social science faculty in the nation's colleges and universities classified themselves as liberal, and only 20% as conservative. However, faculty in other fields were less so, with only 30% classifying themselves as liberal, only slightly more than the general population. See, for example, Everett Carl Ladd and Seymour Martin Lipset, *The Divided Academy* (New York: McGraw-Hill, 1975).

33. UCLA Higher Education Research Institute press release, January 2003, accessed at http://www.gseis.ucla.edu/heri/heri.html.

34. Sheilah Mann, "What the Survey of American College Freshmen Tells Us about Their Interest in Politics and Political Science," *PS: Political Science and Politics* 32 No. 2 (June 1999): 263–268.

35. UCLA Higher Education Research Institute press release, op.cit.

36. Theodore Newcomb, *Persistence and Change: Bennington College and Its Students After Twenty-Five Years* (New York: John Wiley & Sons, 1967).

37. Jennings and Niemi, *The Political Character of Adolescence,* pp. 246–247.

38. Duane F. Alwin, Ronald L. Cohen, Theodore M. Newcomb, *Political Attitudes Over the Life Span: The Bennington Women after 50 Years* (Madison: University of Wisconsin Press, 1991).

39. Beck, "The Role of Agents in Political Socialization"; Sara L. Silbiger, "Peers and Political Socialization," in Stanley Renshon, ed., *Handbook of Political Socialization* (New York: Free Press, 1977), pp. 172–189.

40. Doris Graber, *Mass Media and American Politics,* 6th ed. (Washington, DC: CQ Press, 2002), pp. 198–199.

41. David L. Paletz, *The Media in American Politics,* 2nd ed. (New York: Longman), pp. 130–148.

42. S. Robert Lichter, Linda S. Lichter, and Daniel Amundson, "Government Goes Down the Tube: Images of Government in TV Entertainment, 1955–1998," *Press/Politics* 5, No. 2 (Spring, 2000): 96–103.

43. Joseph N. Cappella and Kathleen Hall Jamieson, *Spiral of Cynicism: The Press and the Public Good* (New York: Oxford University Press, 1997); Thomas Patterson, *Out of Order* (New York: Vintage, 1993); James Fallows, *Breaking the News: How the Press Undermines American Democracy* (New York: Vintage, 1996).

44. Pippa Norris, *Virtuous Circle: Political Communications in Post-Industrial Societies* (Cambridge: Cambridge University Press, 2000).

45. Michael McDivitt and Stephen Chaffee, "From Top-Down to Trickle-up Influence: Revising Assumptions About the Family in Political Socialization," *Political Communication* 19 No. 3 (July–September 2002): 281–301.

46. David O. Sears and Carolyn L. Funk, "Evidence of the Long-Term Persistence of Adults' Political Predispositions," *The Journal of Politics* 61 No. 1. (February 1999): 1–28.

6

The Mass Media and Public Opinion

Scholars have usually attempted to find evidence that the media are persuaders, deliberate causes of public thinking. It may be more realistic to think of the media as contributing to—but not controlling—the structure of publicly-available information that shapes the way people can and do think politically.

Robert Entman[1]

Questions to Think About

This chapter examines the relationship between the mass media and public opinion. As the term suggests, the media are an information conduit between the public and government, and are another potential source of the people's voice. Ponder the following as you read the chapter:

- How much influence do the media have on what the public thinks? How autonomous and independent is the media audience? How have researchers attempted to answer these questions, and what have they found?
- How do the media cover and portray public opinion to the people and the government? What effects might this have both on public opinion itself and on politics in general?
- How well do the media perform their democratic jobs of informing the public about politics and providing a wide range of views so that the public can make up its mind? What role do the media play in the democratic dilemma?

I N THE United States, few things have grown faster than the variety and number of mass media outlets and the public's use of them. At the beginning of the twenty-first century, America truly is a mediated society, not just the TV nation it was in the 1960s–1980s. Every day, Americans are bombarded by a variety of messages from various media sources, including newspapers, magazines, radio, television, and the Internet.

In addition to the growth of mass media outlets resulting from technological changes, societal changes have spurred a similar growth in the public's reliance on the media as their major source of information. More and more, Americans depend upon mediated sources as opposed to personal ones. And even if people get their information from family and friends, it's likely that information originally came from some media source, since few of us have direct experience with leaders, events, or issues.

For example, studies show that outside of work, Americans spend much of their time watching television.[2] Since the 1970s, Americans have come to rely on television more than any other source for their news, although many still report regularly reading a newspaper or magazine. The rise of computer usage and the Internet, along with twenty-four-hour cable TV channels, now allows people to receive information almost all the time, any time they want, although television remains the medium of choice.[3]

Given this dependence on media content, the power of the media to influence what the people think is potentially very great. But just how much do the mass media affect public opinion? Even though we are exposed to media information, we don't necessarily take it as gospel. Is the public a slave to what appears in the media, or are most people independent-thinking news consumers?

The answer, it seems, as with everything else dealing with public opinion, isn't simple. Nevertheless, it does appear that, under some circumstances at least, the media can indeed affect our opinions. This chapter will review and synthesize the research on the effects of media on public opinion and then will go on to examine another important role of the media in the opinion process: the way it portrays public opinion to both policymakers and the public itself. We will also evaluate the role of the media in the democratic dilemma—how well the media perform their democratic functions. Please note that by the mass media, we mean primarily the news media, which explicitly focus on public affairs. This is not to say that popular media don't necessarily affect public opinion, but our focus, as with most research, is on news outlets.

THE IMPORTANCE OF THE MEDIA TO THE PUBLIC AND DEMOCRACY

In theory, the media should play a key role in democracy and in the public opinion process. Among other things, they should help educate the public by providing high quality information, so that people can make good decisions in the voting booth and more generally; the media should also investigate government actions and report on government performance, playing a watchdog function so as to help the public hold government accountable; and lastly, they should provide a wide range of viewpoints—a so-called "marketplace of ideas"—so that the public can be exposed to a variety of views and issues, and thereby deliberate effectively before coming to an informed opinion.[4]

All of these functions are interrelated, although sometimes contradictory. While we will briefly examine these roles later in the chapter, for a more thorough discussion the interested student should consult relevant works on media and politics.[5]

MEDIA IMPACT ON PUBLIC OPINION: HOW GREAT?

Given the media's importance as the public's main source of information, debate over the power of media to influence the public has been around for some time. Scholars have gone from viewing the media as very powerful, to rather weak—and back again. The current consensus view is somewhere in the middle—that media can affect how and what people think about politics, under certain circumstances.

The Research Tradition: From Powerful to Minimal Effects

Scholars in the early part of the twentieth century took the approach that the media were inherently powerful persuaders, seeing the public as a passive audience that absorbed media content much as patients absorbed medicine from a hypodermic needle. This perspective presumed strong media effects, based primarily on anecdotal evidence stemming from government propaganda campaigns in World War One and Nazi Germany, the rise of Hollywood films, and the like. Although it undoubtedly overestimated media power, this view dominated until after World War Two.

Subsequent research, attempting to document the influence of media messages on people's opinions more directly, led instead to a revision in the opposite direction. For example, voting studies conducted in the 1940s and 1950s found that people's social groups and acquaintances were more influential than media use in determining their voting decisions.[6] Scholars saw the public as resistant to media influence, for two main reasons. The first was the two-step flow of communication: Many people received information indirectly from the media through opinion leaders—other people they trusted, who in turn interpreted the news in ways consistent with the views of their social group. The second was selective exposure: People largely controlled which messages they were exposed to, and usually chose media outlets whose messages they already agreed with. Republicans, for example, would choose to read a Republican newspaper, and so its support for Republican candidates already fit within their established views. Given these pre-built barriers to persuasion, the mass media were seen as agents of attitude reinforcement, rather than change.[7]

The problem with the minimal-effects perspective was that it perhaps unrealistically expected the media to demonstrate the power that the earlier view had largely assumed. Despite their shortcomings, both the hypodermic and the minimal effects traditions contributed something to the future understanding of media effects. The hypodermic perspective at least pointed out that mediated communication mattered, even if one had to be far more precise about documenting how it operated. The minimal-effects research rightly noted that changing people's minds about long-standing issues or strongly-held views is likely to be difficult.

The Current View: Multiple, Contingency Effects

Since the late 1960s, new research methods, along with new developments in politics, news coverage, and American society, have led to revisions of the minimal-effects perspective. Declining party identification and decreased reliance on social groups for political cues, coupled with increased media use among the populace, led scholars to suspect that media sources had a bigger impact on public opinion. Researchers also developed better means to detect media effects. These included *experimental studies*—in which people were put into separate groups of treatment and control subjects, exposed to different media content, and then compared in their opinions—and *passive correlational studies*—in which measures of media content were statistically related to the results of public opinion polls taken afterward. Research utilizing these techniques uncovered evidence suggesting the media could in fact impact public opinion.

The current perspective answers the question of how much power the media have over public opinion by saying, "it depends." Thus, it does appear that the media can have powerful effects on the public, but these effects are dependent, or contingent, on a number of factors that determine the degree and scope of influence.

In fact, scholars have found a variety of ways in which the media can impact public opinion. One can divide these influences into four main types:

- *Educational or informational effects*: Simply by transmitting information, the media inform or educate the public about leaders, issues, and policies.
- *Agenda-setting effects*: The media can influence what issues the public (and, by extension, the government) finds important.
- *Framing effects*: These include subtle features of presentation and context that lead the public to look at issues (or leaders, etc.) in a particular way,

thereby influencing the definition of the situation, the solutions, or even the attribution of responsibility for the problem.

- *Persuasion:* The media influences what people think about politics, and hence, their policy preferences, either directly or indirectly.

We examine each of these in detail below. These effects constitute a rough sequence, so that normally the latter types of effects are dependent upon the previous ones.[8]

Informational or Educational Effects

Along with schools and other sources, the mass media are a major source of information and learning about politics. The media act as information conduits, transmitting facts and other information about politics to the public (or at least, their audience). As noted earlier, the public is heavily dependent on the media for information. It's likely that one learns about a war breaking out in some foreign land, who one's member of Congress is, or which party favors cutting taxes, from attention to current political news. At this level of influence, then, the media don't tell us what to think about these things, but merely make us aware of them.

Oddly, given the theoretical importance of the media as public educator, there has been little research on the direct effectiveness of the media in increasing learning about politics. Indeed, Americans are apparently about as well (or ill) informed about political events, leaders, issues, etc., as they were fifty years ago, when the media weren't so prevalent.[9]

Much more work has been done comparing the educational value of different types of media. This has led some to argue television is largely to blame for Americans' lack of knowledge.[10] Various studies have demonstrated that heavy television watchers apparently learn less and are able to recall fewer facts and stories than those who rely on newspapers or multiple sources for their information.[11] Others dispute this finding, arguing that television can teach just as effectively, although perhaps in different ways. Though the length of most television news stories delivers far less textual content than a newspaper article, some believe the visual information and attention-grabbing nature of TV may compensate.[12]

Like many areas of research, however, intervening factors raise their ugly head, making it difficult to tell. Education levels and interest in seeking out political news also affect political learning. For example, Table 6.1 shows the interrelationship between education and media use in the 1996 election. People who are already interested in politics, such as the better-educated, are also more likely to use the media for information. Prior knowledge about politics also aids in absorbing and understanding information, so that those with more knowledge gain more information. As one set of researchers concluded, "knowledge leads to learning, just as learning leads to knowledge in a spiraling process."[13]

TABLE 6.1. Education and Print Media Usage in the 1996 Election.

Education Level	Frequency of Use: Percent of Respondents Who Said They					
	Didn't Read	Read, Not Campaign	Read Some	Read Daily	Read Daily Paper & Magazine	Total
Not H.S. Graduate	34.8	38.7	10.0	12.6	3.9	100% of 230
H.S. Graduate	27.7	35.4	14.6	14.1	8.2	100% of 548
Some College	24.6	32.4	22.5	12.5	8.0	100% of 463
College Degree / Higher	17.7	22.6	27.2	11.9	20.6	100% of 470

Source: Calculated from 1996 National Election Study data, accessed via Houghton Mifflin *Crosstabs* Web site, http://college.hmco.com/xtabs/templates/FR_XTabs.html

Despite the difficulty of telling how much media content alone leads to information gains, evidence strongly points to it doing so. Research shows heavy media exposure increases political knowledge in children, leading to the supposition that it does the same with adults.[14] Furthermore, media use itself can have positive impacts on knowledge about politics. A good example comes from the results of a cross-national study of the role of the media on citizens' knowledge of foreign affairs (a subject that requires reliance on mass media since it deals with events in other countries). Utilizing a poll on media use and political views in the United States, Canada, France, Great Britain, and Germany, researchers found that attention to foreign news, along with regular book reading and newspaper and radio usage, were all significantly related to success on the same five-question factual knowledge test. These findings held even after controlling for important related factors, such as education, income, and age. Interestingly enough, television news usage only increased knowledge in Canada and Great Britain.[15] Thus, it seems obvious that one impact of media use is obtaining political information. The quality of that information is another question—many argue that the media do a poor job in covering real issues of importance, and instead emphasize infotainment, such as sensationalism, scandals, and coverage of personalities rather than larger social concerns and the like. (We return to the issue of the quality of media information in a subsequent section.) Still, the media do disseminate information about politics, which is picked up by the public, especially the more aware.

Agenda-Setting

The media can also play an agenda-setting role. In other words, the media can influence the relative importance of issues in the public mind (and by extension, the government as well). The usual way of describing agenda-setting is, "the media may not tell us what to think, but they are very successful at telling us what to think about."[16]

The media set the agenda by the amount and emphasis of coverage they place on certain issues. Studies have shown that what the public sees as important problems is closely related to the amount of media coverage devoted to those issues in the news.[17] For example, people's fear of crime is better explained by the amount of crime news to which they are exposed rather than by the actual crime rate. In other words, heavy media coverage of crime leads people to be more fearful of it, even though in actuality—based on declining crime rates, say—they may be safer![18] Furthermore, experimental studies using manipulated news stories (some emphasizing one particular issue more than any other) also found people rated the researchers' highlighted issues as more important to them than did others in the control group who weren't exposed to such messages.[19]

With this type of effect, then, the media aren't influencing our position on crime, or what to do about it, but rather they are merely encouraging us to think more about the issue of crime (or taxes, or North Korea's nuclear arsenal, or whatever), rather than other issues. While not directly brainwashing us, agenda setting nevertheless can have important political effects. The rise and fall of the issue of illegal drugs as the main problem in 1990 illustrates many of these ramifications (see Box 6.1: "The Gulf War Replaces the Drug War in the Nation's Consciousness"). For one thing, the public has only a limited appetite for issues on their agenda menu, and those issues on the agenda will likely at least receive some treatment from policymakers, while those off it are more easily ignored. Likewise, as any policy advocate can tell you, you must first get attention focused on your problem or issue before you can actually promote a favored solution to fix it.

Framing

Journalists have many options as to how they portray events or the issues they cover. How the media present issues can in turn lead people to think about them in certain ways. Framing is the selecting, highlighting, and associating of certain elements of reality to tell a coherent story.[20] In effect, frames are the context within which the media place an issue, event, or person.

Studies have shown that media framing does affect public opinion. This happens when the media frame influences how the public views a particular issue, problem, person, and so forth, although not necessarily in the way the media outlet intended.[21] There are several different dimensions of framing effects.

BOX 6.1

The Gulf War Replaces the "Drug War" in the Nation's Consciousness

One of the most dramatic instances of media agenda-setting concerns the rise and fall of the issue of illegal drugs as the nation's "most important problem" in mid-1989 to late 1990. In a period of less than a year and a half, it rose from competing with several issues for the leading spot, to a dominant, overwhelming position in the public's mind, and then went back down again, when a new issue began to take off: crisis, and then war, in the Persian Gulf.[1]

A good way to see the dynamics of agenda-setting is by examining open-ended (free response) surveys on the question, "What do you think is the most important problem facing the nation today?" In the summer of 1989, drugs became a hot issue, moving in a few weeks from around 10 percent (along with several other issues) to 27, already a relatively large number. (See graph, Fig. 6.1.)

In mid-August, the White House announced that President George H. W. Bush would address the issue in a speech on prime-time television. Soon after Bush delivered his "War on Drugs" speech in September, calling drugs "the gravest threat facing the nation today," the topic shot up to an astounding 63 percent in the survey, virtually crowding out all other issues on the public agenda.

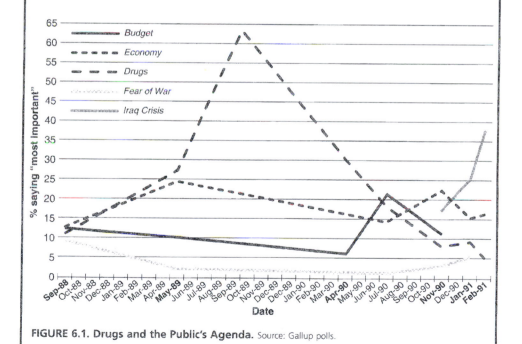

FIGURE 6.1. Drugs and the Public's Agenda. Source: Gallup polls.

Continued

BOX 6.1—*Cont'd*

Then, according to Gallup, only a few weeks later the issue slid from this lofty height to 38 percent. Although it remained in the top spot through the spring of 1990, new issue concerns, such as the budget deficit and the economy, once again became equal competitors for the nation's attention. The next summer and fall, with a budget battle raging between President Bush and the Democrats in Congress, and the invasion of Kuwait by Iraqi forces under Saddam Hussein, the issue of drugs dropped back to single digits. By the end of January 1991, with a U.S.-led military counter-offensive in full swing, the Gulf War became the nation's dominant problem at 37 percent. Drugs garnered a mere 6 percent—slightly below where the issue was over two years before.

Why did the drug issue suddenly skyrocket to rivet the nation's attention, and then, almost as quickly, fade away? The answer doesn't have to do with reality: no one could argue the war on drugs was won or that the drug problem had gone away. In fact, as measured by real usage, drug levels apparently had already leveled off well before Bush gave his speech, and were even somewhat on the decline. The attractiveness of the issue for the media and the resulting amounts of coverage it received—followed by its becoming old news and other issues coming to the fore—better explains these patterns. As Michael Oreskes of the *New York Times* put it, "a review of the entire episode teaches a great deal about the alliance of Presidents and news directors, as well as the pitfalls of policy by polling public opinion."[2]

Drugs became a pressing issue in the public's mind because of a convergence of factors. First, there was elite attention to the issue, as dramatized by a presidential speech, which signaled to the media (and thus the public) "this is important." The advance billing of Bush's speech encouraged the media to play up the issue—for example, the major TV networks increased their stories on drugs from less than one a day to three a day in the two weeks leading up to it. After Bush's speech, the media responded even more fervently, with the networks upping the number of stories to around four a day for several weeks after. (Undoubtedly, other media outlets did likewise.)[3]

Second, in related fashion, was the attraction of the issue for the media itself: the newsworthiness of drugs and excitement surrounding it. The drug war was an interesting story—one filled with illicit behavior, violence, good guys versus bad guys, law and order, etc., and was an issue the whole country could rally behind. Lastly, and perhaps a key factor, was the lack of other issues in the news at the time. For example, summer is normally a slow news time, when most of the public is on vacation, and so to some extent is the government. Also, the country was at peace (the Cold War had recently ended), and the economy was relatively sound—factors that were to change over the course of the cycle.

As the months went by, the drug crisis lost its luster, and new, dramatic, and therefore newsworthy issues such as the budget conflict arose to attract media (and thus public) attention. Finally, the prospect of a real shooting war in the Persian Gulf as opposed to a symbolic one against drugs at home, coupled with all the saturation media coverage that accompanied it, pushed the drug issue out of sight, out of mind for both the media and the American people.

This story doesn't just illustrate the power of the media to set the public's agenda; it also highlights some important implications of that process. The public clearly has a limited menu for issues, and thus can only focus on a few at a time, those foremost in their mind. They also apparently have a limited attention span. Presidents, and, rarely, some other political actors (although they have a harder time attracting the spotlight), can influence the public agenda, as Bush did here, or sometimes even lead it—although it seems Bush was following public opinion, or at least jumping on a bandwagon that was already moving. However, while politicians may be able to affect the agenda, they only can do so if the media follow suit, and in any event they will have difficulty sustaining that level of attention. This case also tells us something about the news media themselves, and their thirst for new topics. Media coverage of issues, as Walter Lippmann described it, is like "the beam of a searchlight that moves restlessly about, bringing one episode and then another out of darkness and into vision."[4] One likely effect of the media's agenda-setting function is increased volatility in policymaking, as America seems to lurch from one crisis to another. Not all issues are like this, but still the moral of the story is that issues in the public mind may be here today, gone tomorrow, due in large part to the media's coverage of them.

Sources: Gallup Poll for data; Michael Oreskes, "Drug War Underlines Fickleness of the Public," New York Times (p. A22), Sept. 6, 1990, p. A22; Hoyt Purvis, Media, Politics, and Government (Orlando, FL: Harcourt Publishers, 2001), p. 63–64); Graber MM in Amer. Politics has Lippmann quote.

Notes

1. Michael Oreskes, "Drug War Underlines Fickleness of the Public," *New York Times*, September 6, 1990, p. A22.

2. Oreskes, "Drug War."

3. See Thomas R. Dye, Harmon Ziegler, and S. Robert Lichter, *American Politics in the Media Age*, 4th ed. (Pacific Grove, CA: Brooks/Cole, 1992), pp. 103–104.

4. Walter Lippmann, *Public Opinion* (New York: Free Press, 1965 reissue of 1922 ed.), p. 229.

One framing effect is influencing how people attribute responsibility for the problems or issues they are thinking about. Psychologists have noted that people instinctively seek out causes or reasons, wishing to allocate responsibility for events—blame in the case of bad things or failures, credit in the case of positive events or successes. Through experiments, Iyengar found that the ways in which the media framed issues did impact how and where people attributed responsibility for them. He argues the media frame stories in two major ways: either episodically or thematically. *Episodic* frames or stories present issues in isolation, as an event or situation in a concrete instance. *Thematic* frames or stories instead present issues with background information, in context, and provide abstract or interpretive analysis. In television news, episodic reports are often visually appealing, whereas thematic reports are more text-centered and likely to be given by talking heads. Although most news stories have both thematic and episodic elements rather than being solely one or the other, one type of frame usually dominates. The episodic/thematic distinction in turn has important consequences for the public's placement of blame or credit for issues and events. Episodic frames tend to cause people to blame individuals in stories or isolated events rather than other factors, namely larger social forces, institutions, and actors, like the government or political leaders. Which type of frame is emphasized in the media may lead people to interpret the issue in completely different ways. For example, episodic framing of the issue of unemployment—depicting individuals out of work due to laziness, unfortunate circumstances, lack of skills, etc.—encourages viewers to look at joblessness as an individual problem, and to place the blame on the unemployed themselves. On the other hand, thematic framing of unemployment, which depicts it as a national trend, the consequence of an economic downturn, international trade policies, technological or other changes, and so on, leads people to place the blame on political leaders, government policies, business, or other institutions, and to think about different kinds of alternatives. Since news (especially on TV) tends to be more episodic than thematic, it may limit the public's understanding of problems and lead them to focus on individual rather than societal solutions.[22]

By placing issues, people, or events in a particular context, media frames can also have broader political implications for how people understand and think about them. Frames may activate particular *schemas* (cognitive frameworks or attitude networks that people use to process new information) in people's minds, influencing how they process the information and consequently how they see the situation. For example, framing Iraqi leader Saddam Hussein as "another Hitler" invokes for most Americans a number of stored impressions, identifying him as an agent of evil, a madman, a threat to American interests, and one who must be resisted by force and not negotiated with.[23]

Framing may indirectly influence opinions about policy alternatives for dealing with a particular issue. A comparative study of two similar events, which received very different framing by the media, illustrates this point. In 1983, a Soviet military plane shot down a Korean passenger airliner, killing all 269 on board; in 1988, the U.S. Navy ship *Vincennes* shot down an Iranian airliner in the Persian Gulf, killing 290 passengers. Both militaries officially claimed their actions were errors. Political scientist Robert Entman examined U.S. television and magazine coverage of both events, and found that the Soviet/Korean case was portrayed as an intentional, bloodthirsty, and morally repugnant act, while the U.S./Iranian one was seen an accident based on technological failure (a mistake). Stories on the downing of the Korean airliner emphasized words like "murder" and "attack," such as the *Time* magazine headline, "Shooting to Kill," which directly indicted the Soviets. On the other hand, rather than U.S. culpability, textual themes in the coverage of the Iran Air incident emphasized words such as "tragedy," "error," and the like, such as *Newsweek*'s "Tragedy in the Gulf: Why It Happened."[24]

The Korean airliner case apparently heightened anti-Soviet attitudes among the public and Congress, which may have adversely affected support for more dovish policies like a freeze on the American production of nuclear weapons.

In the Iran Air case, depicting the event as an accidental tragedy likely led Americans to continue to support, and not to question, U.S. military involvement in the Persian Gulf region. Different perceptions of such a policy might have occurred with alternative or negative frames. The point here isn't whether one depiction was true or not, nor whether the two events were actually different and thus deserved different framing, just that different framing encouraged different ways of looking at similar events, resulting in different types of opinions in each case.

Lastly, in related fashion, framing may influence people's definition of an issue and which type of values they bring to bear on it when expressing their opinion. In an experimental study on the issue of gay rights, Paul Brewer simulated exposure to different value frames in media coverage, giving different groups of people media information that framed the issue either in terms of equality (such as equal rights for gays) or morality (gay behavior as threatening traditional morality). When asked to explain their opinions afterward, participants who received an equality frame were more likely to explain their own views on gay rights in terms of equality, while those receiving the morality frame were more likely to cast their opinions in the language of morality.[25] Like gay rights issues, framing also may affect racial issues in similar ways, as the example of coverage of affirmative action in higher education shows (see Box 6.2: "Framing University Admission").

Demonstrating the point that people can show some independence when presented with frames, Brewer also found that exposure to the frames encouraged participants to use value language not only in ways suggested by the media frames, but also in ways that challenged them. Other research shows that people are more likely to question dominant frames when they know more about the issue to begin with.[26] These findings also illustrate that the media are more powerful at influencing opinion on new issues or on ones about which people have little alternative information. The point nevertheless is that framing effects are not cases of the media telling the public exactly what to think, but media portrayals in a sense do affect *how* people think about the issue in question.

Persuasion

Persuasion is the most powerful media effect—namely, influencing people's preferences about policies, politicians, ideas, or events. Persuasion can happen either directly or indirectly.

Indirect persuasion is the sum total of information, agenda setting, and framing effects, otherwise known as priming. Through the combination of each of the previous levels of influence, the public can then be influenced, or primed, to change its mind. How does this work? First, the media disseminates new information, making the public aware of an issue or event. Then, through agenda setting, increased media attention increases the relative importance of that issue to the public. If the issue is framed in a consistent way by the media,

BOX 6.2

Media Framing of University Admission

One of the media's greatest powers is their ability to frame political issues. Media use *frames* as "ways of organizing a story in order to direct and focus the way their audience thinks about and understands events and conditions."[1] In 2003, the way that the media framed the affirmative action story was very influential in affecting the way the American public perceived it.

In 2003, the U.S. Supreme Court was asked to decide two cases in which the University of Michigan gave preference to applicants of minority ethnic groups in its admission process to its undergraduate school (*Gratz* v. *Bollinger*) and its law school (*Grutter* v. *Bollinger*). The media portrayed the issue as one of special considerations for members of minority ethnic groups being admitted, although white applicants might be better qualified by such criteria as high school grade point averages or SAT or ACT scores. The main reason given for Michigan's affirmative action policy was to develop a diverse student population.

In a Gallup survey taken before the Supreme Court decided the case, Americans favored "affirmative action programs for racial minorities" by a small margin of 49 percent in favor and 43 percent opposed. (Among whites, 44 percent were in favor and 49 percent were opposed.) However, when asked specifically about college and university admission, 69 percent of the respondents said college applicants "should be admitted solely on the basis of merit, even if that results in few minority students being admitted" and 27 percent said "an applicant's racial and ethnic background should be considered to help promote diversity on college campuses." Among white respondents, 75 percent said admissions should be based solely on merit, and 22 percent said ethnicity should be considered. Seeing the issue differently, 44 percent of black respondents said colleges and universities should look only at merit, and 49 percent said ethnicity should be considered. Among Hispanic respondents, the percentages were 59 percent and 36 percent.

Throughout the controversy, the frame of the story was race or ethnicity—of less qualified black, Hispanic, or other minority applicants being admitted over more qualified white applicants. With this frame, it is not surprising that people of different ethnic groups would see the issue so differently. Particularly controversial was the fact that the University of Michigan gave bonus points to undergraduate applicants in minority ethnic groups.

But what most of the media sources did not discuss is that the University of Michigan gave bonus points to many types of applicant, not just those in racial or ethnic minority groups. The following table shows some of the ways that applicants could earn bonus points.

Very few media stories referred to those other bonus point opportunities; instead, they focused only on the ethnic or racial aspect of Michigan's admission criteria.

What most media sources also did not point out is that it is common for many universities, especially elite universities, to use nonacademic criteria when admitting students in order to develop diverse student populations. Universities want students with high GPAs and SATs, but they also want poets, students who can play a cello or throw a football, and BWRKs—bright well-rounded kids.[2] In order to get diverse entering classes, universities often admit applicants with lower GPAs and SATs than some they reject. In fact, some universities deny admission to some students with perfect 1,600 SAT scores. According to Louis Menand, Harvard rejects one-fourth of its 1,600 SAT applicants.[3]

Admission Criteria
Partial List of "Bonus Points" Awarded

Criterion	Bonus Points
Michigan resident	10
Underrepresented Michigan county	6
Legacy: parents or step parents attended the University of Michigan	4
Men majoring in Nursing	5
Socio-economic disadvantage	20
Underrepresented racial-ethnic minority	20
Scholarship athlete	20
Provost's discretion	20

Source: http://www.cnn.com/2003/ALLPOLITICS/01/15/bush.affirmativeaction

By ignoring these facts and framing the admissions issue as solely one of race, the media led the public to have one kind of opinion. We suspect that public opinion of the University of Michigan's admission policy would be different if racial preferences were framed as only one part of an overall, and widespread, policy of developing diverse student bodies.

References

Jacobs, Lawrence R., and Robert Y. Shapiro. *Politicians Don't Pander: Political Manipulation and the Loss of Democratic Responsiveness.* Chicago: University of Chicago Press, 2000.

CNN News. "Bush Criticizes University 'Quota System,'" at www.cnn.com/2003/ALL POLITICS/01/15/bush.affirmativeaction.

Menand, Louis. "The thin envelope: Why college admissions has become unpredictable." *The New Yorker*, April 7, 2003, pp. 88–92.

Moore, David W. "Public: Only merit should count in college admissions." *The Gallup Organization*, June 24, 2003.

Notes

1. Lawrence R. Jacobs and Robert Y. Shapiro, *Politicians Don't Pander: Political Manipulation and the Loss of Democratic Responsiveness* (Chicago: University of Chicago Press, 2000), p. 177.

2. Louis Menand, "The thin envelope: Why college admissions has become unpredictable," *The New Yorker*, April 7, 2003, pp. 88–92.

3. Ibid., p. 92.

it then interacts with agenda setting, changing the public's standards of evaluation for leaders or policies—in essence priming the public to weigh that issue more heavily in forming their opinions.[27]

The change in President George W. Bush's job approval ratings (measures of how many Americans approve of the job the president is doing) in the few months before and after the terrorist attacks of September 11, 2001, is an illustration of this process. Before that event, Bush's approval ratings hovered in the mid-50 percent range, historically somewhat low for a president so early in his term. After September 11, they jumped dramatically, eventually reaching the record level of 90–92 percent, depending upon the poll. They continued to stay quite high for months afterward (see Fig. 6.2). One can argue that the media had much to do with this shift in opinion. In the months prior to September 11, terrorism and foreign affairs in general were not on the minds of most Americans, nor were they on the news. Instead, the focus was squarely on domestic issues. Furthermore, the news was not good for Bush: Early administration actions, such as withdrawing from the Kyoto Treaty on global warming, overruling Clinton administration actions regulating the amount of arsenic in drinking

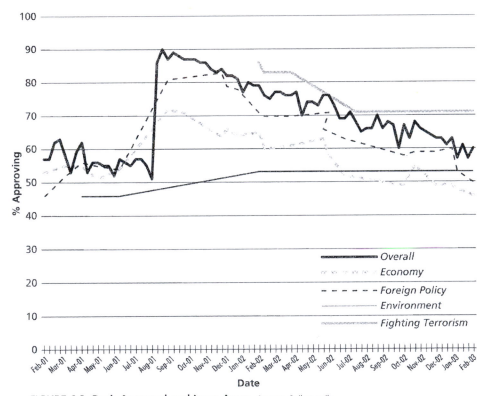

FIGURE 6.2. Bush Approval and Issue Areas. Source: Gallup polls.

water, his compromise on the embryonic stem-cell issue, and other topics, brought criticism from media commentators and other political figures at home and abroad. Also, by the summer of 2001, an economic recession was in full bloom, with media coverage suggesting Bush needed to do more to fix it.

Therefore, information was being provided to the public, some of whom paid attention; the news focused on these particular issues, which were controversial and not favorably framed for the president. This coverage in turn persuaded a number of Americans to disapprove of the job Bush was doing, or at the very least maintained a split in public opinion about his performance.

Then the terrorist attacks of September 11 occurred, and everything changed: New information was suddenly transmitted to the public, information of relevance to their assessment of President Bush's handling of his job. Next, came agenda setting: In the months that followed, on the heels of widespread media coverage of the attacks, the anthrax scare weeks later, and various antiterrorist actions, the issues of terrorism and national security flooded the media and suddenly took top priority over other domestic concerns like the economy and the environment. With new public support behind him, Bush (and Congress) quickly took action through domestic security measures like the USA PATRIOT Act, and by pursuing international terrorism abroad through the war in Afghanistan, which was portrayed as quick and relatively successful. Therefore, terrorism and other related issues were favorably framed for Bush—he was not blamed for the terrorist attacks and was praised by news commentators and other politicians for his responses to the new threat. This focus then primed people to highlight these aspects of his job in forming their assessment of his *overall* job rating. Despite the fact that the economy remained sluggish and was even worsened by the attacks, and that the national debt (due to new spending to fight terrorism and the bad economy) would now once again increase dramatically, the public did not rely on this information much in their assessment of Bush, or else didn't hold him responsible. Such a perspective was directly influenced by the focus of the media during that time.

In other words, people now saw Bush's job as primarily fighting terrorism, rather than fixing the ailing economy or the environment, and the image they saw was of him doing it well. As a result, his approval rating soared and stayed high thereafter, until such time as media coverage of new events and issues, with altered framing, came along to change it. (Chapter 13 addresses the topic of presidential approval ratings, and whether they are influenced by events or media coverage of those events, in more detail).

At other times, media can directly influence the public. Direct persuasion occurs when sources in the news impart political information directly to the public, and some segments of the populace absorb it, adopting it as their position. One notable study by Page, Shapiro, and Dempsey found that changes in public opinion on issue positions could be predicted rather accurately by what stories appeared on television news between one survey and the next. Positions espoused by media commentators, experts, and popular presidents had the strongest effects, respectively, while those from other politicians, officials, foreign sources, and so forth had no effect, and interest groups actually had negative effects.[28]

The key to persuasion, as we noted with individual information processing, is the interaction of source and audience. The audience must be aware of and receptive to the message, and must find the source credible, or they will not accept it. Note that the most influential sources listed above were the ones most likely to be credible: Journalists and media commentators are seen as more trustworthy than government sources, as are politically neutral experts like scientists, professors and the like. Presidents are influential only when popular—when the public presumably supports them. All other sources are viewed with suspicion or seen by the public as biased, thus limiting their persuasive power.

Persuasion of either kind isn't easy. Selective exposure, inattention, and people's preconceived ideas and opinions all serve to limit media influence, which is why the media probably have the strongest impact on new, emerging issues or on people without strong opinions. So the media apparently can tell us what to think, but such occurrences are greatly dependent, or contingent, on a number of different factors coming together.

MEDIA IN THE DEMOCRATIC DIALOGUE: COVERING PUBLIC OPINION

One important democratic role for the media is not only informing the public, but also in communicating public wishes to both the people and policymakers—thereby telling the public what it thinks, and telling the government too, so that policymakers can heed the public will when making decisions. How can the public know if the government is listening to it, if the public doesn't know what it wants? Furthermore, how the media cover public opinion may have an important effect on public opinion itself, and how policymakers interpret it. In this section, we examine media coverage of various types of opinion.

Polls in the News

News coverage of polls and the use of poll results in stories are the most notable and common ways in which public opinion is portrayed in the media. In fact, polls are often big news, and appear to be getting bigger. Asher found that polls played a role in about one-third of all cover stories in the big three newsmagazines *Time, Newsweek,* and *U.S. News and World Report* from 1995 to 2000.[29] Another study using a sample of major newspapers from large urban areas in 1989 found that nearly 40 percent sponsored or conducted polls.[30]

Polls are most abundant during presidential election years, and their appearance in the media has increased over time. For example, network television news devoted over two total hours to polls in their coverage of the 1996 election, as opposed to only 40 minutes in 1968.[31] News organizations use polls to query voters about issues, but more often ask their opinions about candidates and candidate standing (who they will vote for). Most infamous and ubiquitous are the exit polls of voters, used to predict outcomes on Election Day. Problems with exit polls in the close 2000 presidential election between Al Gore and George W. Bush led to a re-examination of their use, but other than some greater caution in relying on them to forecast election results, media organizations have continued to feature them in their coverage. In fact, in the two days following the 2004 election, the three major television networks (ABC, CBS, and NBC) aired a total of twenty-one stories about or including exit polls, while major newspapers the *New York Times* ran twelve, and *USA Today* a whopping thirty-two, respectively.[32]

Poll Reporting and Its Effects

A crucial question concerning news reports of poll results is whether they are accurate and representative. Professional polling associations have developed formal reporting standards for polls to protect the public, insure full disclosure, and maintain the integrity of the polling process. The two main codes for reporting poll results are those put out by the American Association for Public Opinion Research (AAPOR) and the National Council on Public Polls (NCPP). While slightly different, they both emphasize revealing important technical information about how the poll was conducted, such as who sponsored it, when and how it was conducted, the sample size, question wording, and any alterations that were made such as weighting, results that are based on a subset of the sample, and so forth.

However, these standards, while important, really only apply to the *polling organization* that conducted the survey and how it disseminates its results (in a press release, public document, etc.) *not* to media organizations that cover the poll. As pollster Hadley Cantril noted, "Even as pollsters work toward consensus on criteria by which to assess each other's work, they have little clout when it comes to the performance of newspapers and broadcasters who conduct or report polls."[33] And in a sense, both codes implicitly assume that by having this information, news consumers of poll data can in turn critique the validity of the poll and draw their own conclusions, something that most of the public is clearly ill-equipped to do.

Studies on the reporting of surveying procedures in poll stories have found mixed results. The media appear to report some aspects of how polls are done better than others. Most have found the media have done the best job in terms of consistently reporting such aspects as the sponsoring organization, the sample size, and the date, and have done much worse with such important details as margin of error, question wording, or whether certain questions were asked of a subset of the sample (such as reporting the results for blacks in an all-race survey). Again, there is variation: Not surprisingly, given their greater space capability, newspapers do a better job than television reports, and media of all types do a much better job with in-house polls (ones they or their partners conduct) than ones done by outside organizations.[34]

Sometimes, the media insist on reporting polls that are unscientific and non-random, and thus entirely unreliable. These include 1-900 call-in surveys, Internet polls, and the like. They usually fail to explain to the news consumer the fact that these polls are biased and unrepresentative, and therefore likely to be wrong. But many times these polls are inherently newsworthy due to their interest or excitement. The liberal Internet organization MOVEON.ORG held an online "e-primary" for Democratic Presidential hopefuls on June 25, 2003, promising to publicly endorse whoever received the most votes. Given its unusual nature and early-bird status, the event received a fair amount of news attention as if its results were significant, even though it was clearly unscientific and unrepresentative of Democrats as a whole. If you remember from the discussion of straw polls and other informal methods in Chapter 2, online votes and polls not only suffer from a self-selection bias (people choose to take part in them), but also people who use computers to participate in political events are more motivated and usually better educated, etc., than those who do not.

The accuracy and substantive content of the poll results reported in the media are even more important than the providing of the methodological details. For the most part, studies have shown the media report the numbers accurately, but may draw mistaken conclusions or read into polls things that aren't exactly there. For example, the media consistently report presidential trial-heat polls of prospective Democratic and Republican party candidates long before the party nomination contest even starts. At that point, voters likely are not paying attention, some candidates may not have even announced, and others may even drop out, so the whole exercise is essentially meaningless. In May 2001, some media outlets reported the results of a nationwide survey on whom they wanted to see as the Democratic candidate in 2004, almost three years before the nomination process was to begin, and less than six months after George W. Bush had taken office. The poll showed Al Gore ahead of Hillary Clinton, 44 percent to 22 percent, with Joe Lieberman, Joe Biden, and John Kerry following in single digits in that order. Clearly, what the poll was really measuring was familiarity with major Democrats in general, since many politicians had not yet declared their intentions, and most Americans weren't even thinking about the next election yet. (Indeed, both Gore and Clinton later chose not to run!)[35]

Or, if the media do report the methodological details of polls, they may in turn ignore them. A case in point was an NBC reporter in Paletz and colleagues' study who, after noting a Gallup Poll showing then-Governor Ronald Reagan ahead of incumbent President Gerald Ford by 40 percent to 32 percent among Republicans and Independents for the Republican presidential nomination in 1976, said, "Statistically, there is an eight percent error factor in these figures, but that does not diminish their political importance." Of course, if one just does the math, one knows that the eight percent margin of error could tip the results either way.[36]

All things considered, then, based on the research, the media do a far from perfect job. Still, incidences of intentionally misleading the public about poll results are probably low.

Horse Race Journalism

The most widely recognized effect of media polls is in aiding and abetting so-called **horse race journalism** in campaigns. This refers to the media framing elections as a game or contest, much like a horse race—who's ahead, who's behind, what their strategy and tactics are for winning the election, and so on. The media's heavy and increased reliance on polls assessing candidate standing drives campaign news to the point where the polls may drown out coverage of other important election information, such as issue stands and candidate character.[37]

Explanations for this horse race emphasis generally point to news organizations' gathering and production routines. Horse race aspects more readily fit news values. This is because they are predictable, concrete events, which at the same time change and develop over time, thus remaining fresh and new. Also they are both easy to report and explain to the news audience, and since the campaign and struggle between politicians provide a coherent backdrop, they fit easily within the dramatic, narrative plot lines of a story. Journalists, moreover, can make more concrete evaluations of such matters without appearing to be biased, since they're "just covering what the polls say." Policy issues, on the other hand, provide none of these advantages. Instead, they are rarely dramatic, are often complicated to explain, and are seldom new (candidates don't often change their positions). Critics argue that this emphasis doesn't serve the public well, since average voters are more concerned with policy issues and where candidates stand on them.[38]

Some counter that media attention to polls and to horse race strategy and tactics can have some positive effects. Two separate studies examining the connection between the amount of horse race or polling coverage, issue coverage, and voter knowledge found no directly negative effects of the strategy emphasis. One even found a positive correlation between attention to poll coverage and attention to issue coverage, which were likewise connected to greater knowledge about candidates and issues. It argued that instead of turning off or confusing voters, poll exposure may lead to increased exposure to issue content, which leads to better understanding of where candidates stand on issues.[39] Regardless of its effects, however, there is no question that polling has contributed to the increased horse race emphasis in election coverage.

Bandwagon and Spiral of Silence Effects

Another possible impact of publicizing poll results is that they themselves may influence public opinion. Psychologically, the need to be popular or support the winner might induce some people to change their opinion to the majority side: for example, jumping on the bandwagon of a candidate shown to be leading in pre-election polls. Thus, the very publication of poll results should increase the margin of the leading candidate.

Studies have failed to find any sizable bandwagon effect, although research on this subject is difficult to conduct, and so results are uncertain.[40] Pollster Albert Cantril has found that voters' assessments of candidates, especially in primary elections where they have little information, are correlated with their assessments of the candidates' chance of winning, thus suggesting poll results could influence them. But he concludes that even then, "bandwagon effects early in the cycle tend to dissipate as the election approaches, because there are more important cues for voters to take into account in making up their minds."[41] However, rarely do candidates hold and even increase their lead as Election Day nears (if anything, races usually tighten), and surveys have shown that undecided voters late in the election don't disproportionately go for the candidate ahead in the polls, weakening the case that the bandwagon effect is significant in the real world.

A related, and more powerful concept is what Noelle-Neumann calls the "Spiral of Silence."[42] In this process, people who perceive that their position is in the minority are less likely to speak out, for fear of public ridicule, and so remain silent. Others with similar opinions do likewise, causing dissent to decrease in a spiraling fashion, even though in reality the position may be a sizable one among members of the public. When applied to polls, the key idea here is that news coverage of poll results—even if inaccurate—may discourage those on the minority side in the poll from expressing their opinions in the future. The spiral of silence was first discovered in studies of German small-group behavior, and its relationship to media polls remains unclear. Although researchers have debated the validity of the spiral of silence theory in practice, it remains an important idea in understanding how public opinion develops.[43] It may help explain, for example, the rising support for President Bush's actions following the Sept. 11, 2001, terror attacks. Even though some Americans may have had misgivings about how he was fighting terrorism, they may have been afraid to speak out in the rising tide of patriotism and pro-Bush sentiment that was sweeping the country. This theory, then, may be more important for understanding the effects of *perceived* public opinion on political behavior.

Underdog Effects

Some have claimed that dissemination of polls in the media may have the opposite effect: namely, increasing support for the candidate or issue position found to be on the losing side. This so-called underdog effect posits that sympathetic or independent-minded voters will rally to the side of the minority, perhaps because they don't want the media or some pollster telling them whom to support. Although there is some limited experimental evidence to support this possibility, like the bandwagon effect the underdog effect depends heavily on the public's awareness of polls, and is probably small in any event.[44]

Misreading or Inventing the Public Will

The most common criticism of media reporting of polls is that it distorts public opinion itself. Media errors in method or interpretation, discussed above, amplify their bad effects by making them known by the public and policymakers. Similarly, others argue the media reporting of polls *creates* news and opinions, rather than reporting them. In other words, the poll itself becomes the event, which wouldn't have been reported or wouldn't exist otherwise.[45] Polls are thus a type of pseudo event, which exists solely for the media, and not apart from it. This development is seen as a problem because it allows journalists to control the news agenda even more than they already do, taking it away from public officials or actual events. In a campaign setting, for example, the candidate's standing in the polls might become the story rather than the candidate's speaking event or position on issues.

Some of these criticisms, of course, have to do with polls themselves as much as the media. But they do raise the issue of whether media polls should be taken seriously.

Making Public Opinion more Prevalent and Relevant

Clearly, however, one effect of widespread coverage of polls is to legitimize the idea that the public has and should have a voice on the affairs of the day. Since polls on almost every conceivable subject are reported, media polls have increased the visibility of polling, making what the public wants more important. The reporting of polls has also made journalists more aware of majority sentiment, at least as expressed through the polls (or what Entman and Herbst call "mass opinion"). As CBS News pollster Kathleen Frankovic puts it, "the reporting of opinion polls clearly makes the case that the people's opinions matter."[46]

Precision and Public Journalism

Others have argued that polls, if used properly, can have a positive effect on journalism and media coverage of politics. Philip Meyer advocates a precision journalism in which reporters, properly trained in survey research methods, utilize polls in their stories to provide deeper context to the issues of the day. Like George Gallup before him, Meyer believes polling can thus be used to present a more accurate and objective accounting of what the people think than that provided by politicians or interest groups.[47]

In the 1990s, another journalistic convention, public journalism pushed for better uses of polling. Reacting to the perceived negative effects of horse race journalism and the domination of campaign agendas by candidates and their media advisers, adherents of this school believe journalists should engage the citizenry in elections, giving them relevant information and encouraging them to participate. Polls, rather than being used as horse race indicators of who's up and who's down, should instead help journalists identify the key issues voters care about and then drive reporters to hold the candidates accountable for addressing them.[48] Public journalism has led to some limited applications, such as an experiment in Charlotte, North Carolina, during the 1996 election. The *Charlotte Observer* utilized issue polls to set the issue agenda for its coverage and also tried to be more issue-oriented in its campaign stories.[49] While both precision and public journalism have worthy goals, and have had some influence over certain reporters and news organizations, neither has been widely adopted.

Media Coverage of Other Expressions of Opinion

Polls aren't the only form of expression of public opinion portrayed in the media. The media also cover other public voices such as interest groups, protests, and election results. As with polls, by presenting these other expressions, the media may in turn influence the public and policymakers.

Interest Groups and Their Activities

Although a fair amount of research has been done on the efforts of interest groups to use the mass media, little is known about how interest groups themselves are portrayed by the media to the public. Based on what evidence exists, one can conclude that the picture is not a flattering one. Although some groups receive a favorable hearing for their views, many appear as one-sided purveyors of information in policy debates.[50] Since journalists are self-appointed defenders of the public interest, they tend to portray interest groups, as does the general American political culture, as selfish and wanting special advantages for themselves at the expense of the public. Also, when interest groups attempt to influence the political process, which after all is their prime function and is protected under the First Amendment, their lobbying activities are often portrayed as unsavory techniques of powerful arm twisting, bending the process for their benefit. Although it is true some interest group activity can be unseemly, controversial, or even illegal, such as campaign donations or bribes, this certainly isn't the norm.[51] All of these elements may explain why their impact on public opinion was actually negative in the study by Page and colleagues referred to earlier in the chapter.

Interest groups who are identified with a certain issue area and become accepted as a legitimate, expert voice on that topic—especially where official government sources or outside experts are lacking—can receive favorable media treatment. Examples in this mold might include the good government group Common Cause on issues of campaign finance or election reform; the American Civil Liberties Union on issues of civil liberties; the U.S. Chamber of Commerce on matters relating to small business; or the Children's Defense Fund on child welfare.[52] But for the most part, media coverage of interest group activity tends to be negative.

Mass Social and Protest Movements

The media are even more important to social and protest movements, which are generally groups of political outsiders without much direct influence on the government. Given this position, they must take to the streets to make their issues heard. Media coverage is therefore crucial to their success, since they must first get the public's, and government's, attention, and then convince them to support their policy positions.

Most research on media coverage of social movements has determined that the nature, conduct, and legitimacy of the movements themselves influence, and in turn are influenced by, the kind of coverage they receive. The civil rights movement of the late 1950s–early 1960s succeeded in gaining sympathetic media coverage because it was a peaceful movement dedicated to winning blacks rights that other Americans already enjoyed, which were goals and tactics well within mainstream American values. On the other hand, the anti–Vietnam War and anti–nuclear weapons movements failed to do so, in part because the media focused on their counter-cultural sides and their emotional, unpatriotic opposition to American national security.[53] During the buildup to the 2003 Iraq War, for example, the Bush administration was able to marginalize the opposition movement simply by ignoring it. President Nixon tried to do the same thing in Vietnam with his claims of a Silent Majority in favor of the war versus the vocal minority against it.

Violent protest activity or rioting is almost always covered negatively. Violence, at least when instigated by protesters themselves and not the government, is universally condemned and generally portrayed in a dim light. The Los Angeles riots of 1992, for example, while heightening awareness of racial tension and black poverty, nevertheless did not receive favorable treatment by the press. Similarly, acts of violence committed by a small minority in a movement, because of their newsworthiness, may dominate news attention and give the public a misleading representation of what the protest is all about. During the demonstrations against the World Trade Organization (WTO) at its 1999 meeting in Seattle, vandalism and looting by a small anarchist faction set off violent clashes between police and a wide variety of groups; this focus drowned out the legitimate concerns about the WTO expressed by environmental, labor, and peace groups not involved in the violence.[54]

Elections and Voting

Another way the media cover public opinion is by portraying the people speaking at the ballot box. The literature on media coverage of elections is too voluminous and multifaceted to summarize. Here, we are mainly concerned with how the media cover what the election means, not how they treat candidates, issues, or parties.

One role the media play in portraying what the people want is journalists' interpretation of actual election results, in part based upon evidence of the public's voting decision gathered through exit polls. Voting may be one way to express public opinion, but one of its major difficulties as a gauging device is the fact that it doesn't say much. Who knows why one candidate got more votes than another, or what the people were saying in the election? It's all a matter of interpretation, and the media are the prime forum where the meaning and mandate of elections is decided. Jon F. Hale argues that the media focus heavily on the debate between competing inside Washington sources,

Photo 6.1. Violent protest activity receives heavy and usually negative treatment by the media, as coverage of the 1999 protests of the World Trade Organization meeting in Seattle, WA, suggest. © AP/Wide World Photos.

each with its own political agenda riding on a particular interpretation, until ultimately a conventional wisdom on the meaning of the election emerges. The winning interpretation of the election may not be the only plausible one, but instead is the one most vigorously and successfully promoted by its side. In his study of the post-election process in 1988, Hale found the dominant message was that President-Elect George H. W. Bush had no mandate with Congress, and that the Democratic Party lost because its message was too liberal. Whether that was true or not, of course, was debatable, but he thinks it did have an effect on the post-election political climate.[55]

The key implication of Hale's study is that the public's act of voting and electing officials is in turn read by the fortunetellers and seers in the mass media, which may have an important effect on how politicians *perceive* what the people were expressing through their votes, and thus what they want done. For example, Ronald Reagan's landslide victory over Jimmy Carter in 1980 was widely interpreted as an endorsement of Reagan's more conservative views and policy stands. Indeed, this perception likely helped Reagan advance his more conservative policy agenda in Congress during his first year in office. In fact, according to polls, the public was no more conservative (or liberal for that matter) than in earlier years.[56] The public was probably voicing its dissatisfaction with Carter rather than agreeing with Reagan—in other words, it's more likely most people were voting against Carter rather than for Reagan.

The 2004 election provides other examples of media interpretation. One widely touted explanation for the results was a deep religious divide in the electorate, with regular churchgoers supporting George W. Bush and non-attendees backing John Kerry. When combined with increased turnout by Bush's Christian conservative base and an emphasis on cultural issues like gay marriage and abortion, this factor was supposedly responsible for putting Bush over the top.[57] A number of exit polls suggested as much, but a post-election poll by Zogby International, sponsored by some mainstream religious groups, painted a different picture. It found that, in fact, most religious voters are moderate-to-progressive on domestic and national security issues, are more concerned about social-justice issues like poverty and corporate greed, and want a president who is "faithful, but non-intrusive" in the affairs of others who may disagree with him.[58] Another common media theme, building on the controversial and divisive 2000 election, was of a polarized America split between conservative Republican red states and liberal Democratic blue ones, neither seeing eye to eye politically. Again, while there is some evidence for this interpretation, political scientist Morris Fiorina argues (echoing the point about the 1980 election above) that in fact public opinion polls show most Americans are moderate and not deeply divided over cultural and religious issues; instead, it is the parties and political elites who are.[59] Yet perspectives like Fiorina's received far less media attention than the more exciting divided America theme.

The point is not that one picture of reality or message of the election is necessarily more accurate than another. But, as with framing, media emphasis gives more attention and wider acceptance to certain divinations of what the people were saying through the election.

THE DEMOCRATIC DILEMMA AND THE RELATIONSHIP BETWEEN THE MEDIA AND THE PUBLIC

Earlier in the chapter, it was noted that the media are very important in the processes of public opinion formation and transmission. Unlike small groups, large publics need more organized, mass mediated means of exchanging ideas.[60] Indeed, in today's complex, technological society, the public must rely on professional communicators and mediated information to make up their minds and, to some extent, to communicate their preferences to policymakers. The media, as their name suggests, thus play a crucial mediating role between leaders and led.

The Quality of Media Information

One of the media's most important roles is to effectively inform the citizenry about political issues, officials, and events. This educational function must be performed well, or else the citizenry will not be able to make good decisions or hold its leaders accountable. Similarly, if the public is misled or given bad information, it may then form opinions that are not in its best interests, or ones that it would not have embraced if it were fully and accurately informed. Therefore, the media's ability to educate and inform the public is key to assessing the quality and effectiveness of public opinion itself.

How well the media do at informing the public depends of course on one's standards, and since almost everyone has their own definition of good news, it's almost impossible to definitively answer such a question. While recognizing these difficulties, given the importance of evaluating media quality, we will nevertheless attempt to make some generalizations about the political information system in the United States.

Amount and Content of Information

On the surface at least, there are a vast number of media outlets. As of early 2004, there were over 1,700 licensed television stations and 13,000 radio stations in the United States; over 1,400 daily newspapers; and countless numbers of magazines.[61]

However, these figures give a misleading impression, since the bulk of these outlets are concerned with entertainment, not politics and government.[62] The amount of airtime major television networks give over to news programs each day (around two hours) is far less than the amount devoted to daytime soap operas and game shows, and prime time sitcoms, reality programs, and talk shows, which take up the rest. The number of cable television channels devoted to news and politics is dwarfed by the large number of ones on sports, religion, home shopping, movies, re-runs of old television shows, and so on.

Still, on the positive side, it is clear that the media nevertheless present a good deal of political information. For example, the *New York Times* alone presents loads of relevant political information each day. Thanks to advertising, newspapers, magazines, and television news provide information free or at little cost to the public. Computers and the Internet allow people to easily find information and explore it in depth if they wish.

And the American mass media are quite free to provide whatever information they please to their audiences. The First Amendment to the Constitution insures that the media are free from government interference, ownership, or allegiance, meaning that they are not censored or directly controlled, as in authoritarian societies. They are thus able to criticize the government and to provide information it would rather keep secret, and they are also capable of highlighting new or emerging issues—things most citizens would not have time to do on their own.

Yet the quality of information the media present may leave much to be desired. To some observers, the news is primarily trivialized, sensationalized infotainment[63] that teaches the public little. Others argue people can learn from the media, especially if they engage in a discussion of its contents with others.[64] Even soft news sources such as tabloid newspapers like the *National Enquirer* or television shows like *Entertainment Tonight* may promote learning among the less-informed.[65] Still, one is left with the fact that the studies show people retain very little from the news, and, as noted earlier, political knowledge has not notably increased in the last fifty years, despite increases in education levels and the availability of information provided by the rise of mass media.

Questions of Bias

Another contentious issue in evaluating media quality is the issue of **bias.** As communications scholar Vincent Price notes, "Reliance on mass media for public debate introduces communication biases that are not present in small groups. . . . The news media are selective in determining what kinds of messages are relayed. Beyond their facilitative role in gathering and exchanging ideas, mass communicators also assume a much more directive role in trying to shape and mold opinion. Media elites are not merely passive conveyors of public information and debate, but active participants as well."[66]

Developed in part to combat these problems, objectivity has been a long-standing norm of the journalistic profession. According to this canon, reporters should be passive observers who neutrally convey what's happening to the audience.[67]

However, some claim that rather than presenting just the facts, as objective journalism proscribes, the media intentionally bias or slant their stories in a particular direction. Charges that the media are *politically* or *ideologically* biased are the most common of these complaints.

One set of critics believes the media are liberally biased, and thus color the news in favor of liberal viewpoints, issues, and politicians.[68] This perspective grows out of the discovery that journalists on the whole are more liberal than the general public, based on surveys comparing the opinions of the two groups, and that by extension, this ideological identification influences media content. Some people within this school of thought go so far as to argue that journalists inherently slant the news to the left in their portrayals, simply because they naturally see the world that way, completely oblivious to their own biases.[69] More direct research purports to find evidence of liberal bias in the content and framing of particular news stories.[70]

Another group charges the media are actually biased in a conservative direction. They point to the media's capitalist ownership, in particular its dominance by large corporations, as leading to media content that bolsters support for the status quo, and generally favors freer markets and less government involvement in the economy.[71] Besides, even if the reporters are liberal, their bosses are conservative, and they call the shots. One often-mentioned piece of data in support of this proposition is that newspaper editorial endorsements have heavily favored the Republican candidate in almost every presidential election since 1952.[72] They also note there are a number of outwardly conservative media outlets, like Rupert Murdoch's Fox Network and fundamentalist televangelist Pat Robertson's Christian Broadcasting Network.[73]

Who's right? The inherent difficulty of documenting bias is that one would need an agreed-upon standard that constitutes objective reality in order to measure deviance from it, and that is very hard to do. In essence, the root of the problem is that bias is often in the eye of the beholder: Liberals tend to see the media as conservatively biased, and conservatives see the media as liberally biased, since they both have biased images of what constitutes objectivity!

David Niven attempted to overcome this inherent problem by comparing news coverage of politicians of different parties under similar circumstances (e.g., Democratic and Republican presidents when unemployment was at 5 percent; Democratic and Republican members of Congress involved in the House banking scandal, etc.). Using this methodology, his study found no systematic bias toward either Democrats or Republicans.[74] Of course, for hardcore advocates on both sides of this debate, this finding hardly settles the matter.

Structural Biases in the News Itself

But some people argue that ideological or political bias in the news, even if it could be measured accurately, isn't such a problem. According to this line of thinking—rooted in the ideas of selective exposure mentioned earlier—people can identify and resist political messages that conflict with their preconceived views. Liberals listening to a conservative talk radio show are unlikely to have their views changed very much, for example.

Instead, these critics argue that the quality of media information is poor because of the nature of what is defined as news and how the media present it. The drive to make news interesting to the audience and fit the narrative conventions of a story creates news that is heavily personalized (focused on people and celebrities rather than on larger forces), oversimplified, fragmented (stories that are not connected to one another, or across time), and dramatic (showing conflict, controversy, "tune in tomorrow" uncertainty, etc.).[75] These *structural biases* within the news itself thus hamper the public's ability to effectively learn about politics.

Finally, the media may be limited in their educational role by the very desires of the public itself. Most people don't appear to want much meaty political news, at least judging from their low levels of interest in politics, preferring entertainment instead. Since the media are first and foremost businesses, needing to make a profit in order to survive, ironically competition in the economic marketplace leads them to emphasize what the people want. Media organizations thus can't really afford to supply the high-quality political journalism the public needs to be good citizens.[76]

The Media as a Forum for Deliberation

Presenting reasoned debate on the issues of the day is an offshoot of the media's educational role. The public cannot possibly be expected to know all angles and sides of an issue, or the merits of every policy proposal. How well do the media do at providing a marketplace of ideas so that the public can be exposed to a wide range of views, and come to a considered opinion?

A Wide Variety of Outlets and Idea Dissemination

Although the bulk of media outlets are not politically oriented, nevertheless there still is a wide range of them out there if people look. In addition to large mainstream, generally more middle-of-the road outlets like network news, major news magazines, and newspapers, there are small and/or more specialized ones, such as journals of opinion, talk radio shows, e-zines, and the like, which put out information and ideas from across the political spectrum.

It is true, however, that much high-quality political information is located in outlets with small distribution, making it difficult to find. Still, as Benjamin Page notes, as long as good information is available somewhere, the public may eventually be able to find it.[77]

In a large, complex society like the United States, deliberation must be mediated, and is in fact done through a division of labor between policy experts, the media, and the public. The key is for there to be competition and diversity among ideas among specialists and experts, and for these to be eventually publicized by mainstream media commentators and politicians. The public can then take cues from these helpful opinion leaders and form sensible and reasonable opinions based on the best available evidence. A citizen does not have to be a medical expert, for example, to take advantage of publicized expert opinion about the health risks of smoking and thus come to a reasonable decision about tobacco policy.

Provided these factors are at work, the public can resist poor or misleading information, sometimes quite rapidly. In the case of the aftermath of the 1992 Los Angeles riots, Page found that claims by the incumbent George H. W. Bush administration that social welfare policies of the 1960s were the root cause of the riots, and not the racial anger stirred by the acquittal of a white policeman who had beaten a black man, were quickly dismissed and attacked as ridiculous by opposition Democrats and independent media commentators. Even some notable Republicans backtracked from the administration position. A consensus among elite voices in the media emerged that such a charge was politically motivated and incorrect in any event. Within days, the public followed suit and also rejected such an explanation, instead placing more blame on the Bush administration for not doing enough to help the inner city.[78]

With the huge increase in information outlets, especially the Internet, and even small, obscure journals of opinion, even crackpot ideas may find their way into the marketplace, and someday be accepted.[79] Thus, Page believes, the process of mediated deliberation generally works well.

Limitations on the Range of Ideas

One problem with this interpretation, however, is that much of the public may not be exposed to this information, even second-hand. Few people actually behave as educated consumers should in the ideal marketplace of ideas, seeking out a number of different outlets and perspectives. They are instead exposed to only a limited range of voices.

Journalistic practices and the processes by which news is produced also tend to narrow the range of ideas in the news. Even within political media sources, once again the demands of the economic marketplace limit the marketplace of ideas. First, news media in the United States rely heavily on official sources—government officials and other elite newsmakers—for their information. This practice is in part due to cost concerns by media organizations: News must be produced, so it is cheapest and easiest to get it from government sources, or around arranged beats like the White House, courthouse, fire and police departments, etc., where news is likely to take place. Journalists' definition of what constitutes news is also based on widely held criteria, leading to something of a consensus on what issues, events, and people should be included in the day's stories. These factors in combination mean that in the end, most major, mainstream news organizations end up producing information that is not much different from each other's.[80]

Second, and in part related to the first, reporters and news organizations appear to index the range of opinions they present to the ones expressed in official debates, especially regarding foreign policy issues.[81] Again, because of their reliance on elite sources, news coverage tends to mirror the debate taking place among political officials. If most officials in Washington D.C., for example, are arguing about whether to go to war with Iraq or instead to impose economic sanctions, those will be the only options relayed to the public, and not others such as negotiating a settlement or doing nothing altogether.[82] This reporting norm or practice has the practical effect of reducing the range of opinions heard in the mainstream mass media.

This process is further bolstered by the two-party political system in the United States, which encourages the idea that there are only two (or both) sides of issues to be presented, a Democratic and Republican perspective, or sometimes an American and a foreign one, rather than many different viewpoints.[83] Ironically, one could argue that in some ways, the objectivity standard itself encourages such a position: Showing what recognized, legitimate sources say, and usually in a pro/con, Democratic/Republican, or conservative/liberal format, promotes balance and deters journalists from placing their own values into the news. However, critics ask: What about issues with more than two sides or in cases where the Democrats and Republicans are in agreement?[84]

Yet another potential threat to a wide range of ideas is the consolidation and monopolization of media ownership. Diversity in ownership of media outlets has decreased dramatically in the last several decades, to the point where a few large conglomerates (often subsidiaries of other companies) now dominate the information industry.[85] Fewer and fewer cities have more than one daily newspaper, and many newspapers are owned by large chains. In radio, Clear Channel Communications went from owning 40 stations in the mid-1990s to 1,225 in 2003, and dominates audience share in 100 of 112 major media markets.[86] Some of this consolidation even represents cross-media ownership, where due to mergers, one mega-corporation has holdings across several types of media, such as AOL-Time-Warner (owners of *Time* magazine, Warner Brothers film studios, the cable television news network CNN, and the Internet service provider America Online). Some argue that this threatens the diversity of perspectives presented to the public, since media outlets want to save money by consolidating messages and prevent competition with themselves. Others retort that independence of editorial content and audience remain. At the very least, however, a narrower range of ownership does suggest by implication a narrower range of perspectives.

CONCLUSION

The media are important to the public opinion process because the public (and the government) rely on them, in whole or in part, for their political information. We have seen that the media can and do influence people's opinions about politics, through educating, agenda setting, framing, and persuading them with the information that the media provide. How the media measure, interpret, and portray public opinion itself may also affect how political leaders, activists and even the public understand what the people want on a given topic. Furthermore, as the primary provider of facts, interpretations, and views about politics, how well the media perform their democratic roles in turn affects how well the people perform theirs.

Thus, through their educational and watchdog functions, the media both contribute, and respond, to the democratic dilemma. Their fundamental roles as information mediators, as well as reporters of expressions of public opinion, thus also make them a crucial part of the democratic dialogue. Given their effect on what the people think, the extent to which the media succeed or fail in living up to their ideal democratic roles likewise affects the practical role of public opinion in twenty-first century America.

Suggested Reading

Graber, Doris. *Processing the News: How People Tame the Information Tide*, 2nd ed. White Plains, NY: Longman, 1988.

Iyengar, Shanto. *Is Anyone Responsible? How Television Frames Political Issues.* Chicago: University of Chicago Press, 1991.

————, and Donald R. Kinder. *News That Matters.* Chicago: University of Chicago Press, 1987.

Jamieson, Kathleen Hall, and Paul Waldman. *The Press Effect: Politicians, Journalists, and the Stories That Shape the Political World.* New York: Oxford University Press, 2003.

Leighley, Jan E. *Mass Media and Politics: A Social Science Perspective.* Boston: Houghton Mifflin, 2004.

Page, Benjamin I. *Who Deliberates? Mass Media and Modern Democracy.* Chicago: University of Chicago Press, 1996.

Protess, David, and Maxwell McCombs. *Agenda Setting: Readings on Media, Public Opinion, and Policymaking.* Hillsdale, NJ: Lawrence Erlbaum Associates, 1991.

Notes

1. Robert M. Entman, *Democracy Without Citizens: Media and the Decay of American Politics* (New York: Oxford University Press, 1989), p. 84.

2. For some statistics, see Gary Woodward, *Perspectives on American Political Media* (Needham Heights, MA: Allyn and Bacon, 1997), pp. 3–4.

3. For example, see the Pew Center for the People and the Press report, "Cable and Internet Loom Large in Fragmented Political News Universe," January 11, 2004, accessed at http://people-press.org/reports/display.php3?ReportID=200.

4. Stephen Ansolabehere, Roy Behr, and Shanto Iyengar, *The Media Game* (New York: Macmillan, 1993); J. Herbert Altschull, *Agents of Power*, 2nd ed. (New York: Longman, 1995); Benjamin I. Page, *Who Deliberates? Mass Media in Modern Democracy* (Chicago: University of Chicago Press, 1996).

5. See, for example, W. Lance Bennett, *News: The Politics of Illusion*, 4th ed. (New York: Longman, 2001); Doris Graber, *The Mass Media and American Politics*, 6th ed. (Washington DC: CQ Press, 2002); Jan Leighley, *Mass Media and Politics: A Social Science Perspective* (Boston: Houghton Mifflin, 2004); David Paletz, *The Media in American Politics: Contents and Consequences*, 2nd ed. (New York: Longman, 2002).

6. Paul Lazerfeld, Bernard Berelson, and Helen Gaudet, *The People's Choice* (New York: Columbia University Press, 1948).

7. Joseph Klapper, *The Effects of Mass Communication* (Glencoe, IL: The Free Press, 1960).

8. This entire section draws heavily upon Ansolabehere, Behr, and Iyengar, *The Media Game*, pp. 139–140, in format and classification, though not in content.

9. Robert M. Entman, *Democracy without Citizens*, p. 4; Michael X. DelliCarpini and Scott Keeter, *What Americans Know About Politics and Why It Matters* (New Haven: Yale University Press, 1996), pp. 105–106.

10. Joshua Meyorwitz, *No Sense of Place: The Impact of Electronic Media on Social Behavior* (New York: Oxford University Press, 1985); Neil Postman, *Amusing Ourselves to Death* (New York: Viking, 1985).

11. John Robinson and Mark Levy, *The Main Source* (Beverly Hills, CA: Sage, 1986); W. Russell Neuman, Marion R. Just, and Ann N. Crigler, *Common Knowledge: News and the Construction of Political Meaning* (Chicago: University of Chicago Press, 1992), p. 10.

12. See the discussion and research cited in Graber, op.cit., pp. 196–198.

13. Neumann, Just, and Crigler, *Common Knowledge*, p. 101.

14. Dan Drew and Byron Reeves, "Children and Television News," *Journalism Quarterly* 57 (1980): 45–54.

15. Stephen Earl Bennett, Richard S. Flickinger, John R. Baker, Staci L. Rhine, and Linda L. M. Bennett, "Citizens' Knowledge of Foreign Affairs," *Press/Politics* 1 No. 2 (Spring 1996): 10–29.

16. Adapted from Bernard Cohen, *The Press and Foreign Policy* (Princeton, NJ: Princeton University Press, 1963), p. 13.

17. Maxwell E. McCombs, "The Agenda-Setting Function of the Mass Media," *Public Opinion Quarterly* 36 (1972): 176–187.

18. See, for example, Richard Morin, "An Airwave of Crime: While TV News Coverage of Murders Has Soared—Feeding Public Fears—Crime Is Actually Down," *Washington Post National Weekly Edition,* August 18, 1997, p. 34; Dennis T. Lowry, Tarn Ching Josephine Nio, and Dennis W. Leitner, "Setting the Public Fear Agenda: A Longitudinal Analysis of Network TV Crime Reporting, Public Perceptions of Crime, and FBI Crime Statistics," *Journal of Communication* 53 No. 1 (March 1, 2003): 61–73; and Daniel Romer, Kathleen Hall Jamieson, and Sean Aday, "Television News and the Cultivation of Fear of Crime," *Journal of Communication* 53 No. 1 (March 1, 2003): 88–104. Also, studies show heavy TV viewers are more afraid in general; see George Gerbner, Larry Gross, Marilyn Jackson Beeck, Suzanne Jeffries Fox, and Nancy Signorielli, "Cultural Indicators: Violence Profile No. 9," *Journal of Communication* 28 (Summer 1978).

19. Shanto Iyengar and Donald Kinder, *News That Matters: Television and American Opinion* (Chicago: University of Chicago Press, 1987).

20. See Robert M. Entman, "Declarations of Independence: The Growth of Media Power After the Cold War," in Brigitte L. Nacos, Robert Y. Shapiro, and Pierangelo Isernia, eds., *Decisionmaking in a Glass House* (New York: Rowman and Littlefield, 2000), p. 12.

21. Robert M. Entman, "Framing: Toward Clarification of a Fractured Paradigm," *Journal of Communication* 43 (1993): 52.

22. Shanto Iyengar, *Is Anyone Responsible? How TV Frames Political Issues* (Chicago: University of Chicago Press, 1991).

23. Entman, in Nacos et al., *Glass House*, p. 12.

24. Robert M. Entman, "Framing U.S. Coverage of International News: Contrasts in Narratives of the KAL and Iran Air Incidents," *Journal of Communication* 41 No. 4 (Autumn 1991): 6–27.

25. Paul Brewer, "Framing, Value Words, and Citizens' Explanations of their Issue Opinions," *Political Communication* 19 No. 3 (July–September 2002): 303–316.

26. William A. Gamson, *Talking Politics* (New York: Cambridge University Press, 1992).

27. Iyengar and Kinder, *News That Matters*; and Jon A. Krosnick and Donald R. Kinder, "Altering the Foundations of Public Support for the President through Priming," *American Political Science Review* 84 No. 2 (June 1990): 497–512.

28. Benjamin I. Page, Robert Y. Shapiro, and Glenn Dempsey, "What Moves Public Opinion?" *American Political Science Review* 81 (1987): 23–43; Donald Jordan found similar but slightly different findings using the *New York Times* (Donald Jordan, "Newspaper Effects on Policy Preferences," *Public Opinion Quarterly* 57 No. 2 [Summer 1993]: 191–204).

29. Herbert Asher, *Polling and the Public*, 5th ed. (Washington, DC: CQ Press, 2001), p. 3.

30. Jack Holley, "The Press and Political Polling," in Paul Lavrakas and Jack Holley, eds., *Polling and Presidential Election Coverage* (Newbury Park, CA: Sage, 1991), pp. 215–237. Holley's survey of 129 daily newspapers of various sizes found that 40 percent conducted polls.

31. Jerry Yeric, *Mass Media and the Politics of Change* (Itasca, IL: FE Peacock, 2001), pp. 162–163.

32. Calculated by the authors from lists of election stories containing the term "exit poll(s)" from each media outlet retrieved from the *Lexis-Nexis* database for November 3–4, 2004.

33. Albert H. Cantril, *The Opinion Connection: Polling, Politics and the Press* (Washington, DC: CQ Press, 1991), p. 173.

34. See Asher, *Polling and the Public*, pp. 100–101.

35. Bill Hutchinson, "Hil Second to Gore in Prez Poll," *New York Daily News*, May 28, 2001, p. 13.

36. Cited in Paletz, *Mass Media in American Politics*, p. 165.

37. The literature on this topic is voluminous, but probably the best source is Thomas Patterson, *Out of Order* (New York: Vintage, 1993).

38. Patterson, *Out of Order*; Kathleen Hall Jamieson, *Dirty Politics: Deception, Distraction, and Democracy* (New York: Oxford University Press, 1992); James Fallows, *Breaking the News: How the Media Undermine Democracy* (New York: Vintage, 1996), pp. 60–65.

39. Xinshu Zhao and Glen L. Bleske, "Horse Race Polls and Audience Issue Learning," *Press/Politics* 3 No. 4 (Fall 1998): 13–34; and Philip Meyer and Deborah Potter, "Preelection Polls and Issue Knowledge in the 1996 U.S. Presidential Election," *Press/Politics* 3 No. 4 (Fall 1998): 35–43.

40. Sam Tuchman and Thomas E. Coffman, "The Influence of Election Night Television Broadcasts in a Close Election," *Public Opinion Quarterly* 35 (1971):

315–326; Robert Navazio, "An Experimental Approach to Bandwagon Research," *Public Opinion Quarterly* 41, 2 (1977): 217–225.

41. Cantril, *The Opinion Connection*, p. 216.

42. Elisabeth Noelle-Neumann, *The Spiral of Silence: Public Opinion—Our Social Skin* (Chicago: University of Chicago Press, 1984).

43. Carroll Glynn, Susan Herbst, Garrett O'Keefe, and Robert Y. Shapiro, *Public Opinion* (Boulder, CO: Westview Press, 1999), pp. 204–205.

44. Asher, *Polling and the Public*, pp. 148–149.

45. Kathleen Frankovic, "Public Opinion and Polling," in Doris Graber, Denis McQuail, and Pippa Norris, eds., *The Politics of News, the News of Politics* (Washington, DC: CQ Press, 1998), especially p. 166.

46. Frankovic, "Public Opinion and Polling," p. 167.

47. Philip Meyer, *Precision Journalism: A Reporter's Introduction to Social Science Methods* (Bloomington: Indiana University Press, 1973).

48. Michael Schudson, "The Public Journalism Movement and Its Problems," in Graber, McQuail, and Norris, eds., *The Politics of News*, pp. 132–134.

49. For a discussion of this experiment, see Schudson, "The Public Journalism Movement," and Philip Meyer and Deborah Potter, "Hidden Value: Polls and Public Journalism," in Paul J. Lavrakas and Michael W. Traugott, eds., *Election Polls, the News Media, and Democracy* (New York: Seven Bridges Press, 2000), pp. 113–141.

50. Lucig Danielian, "Interest Groups in the News," in J. David Kennamer, ed., *Public Opinion, the Press, and Public Policy* (Westport, CT: Praeger, 1992), pp. 63–79.

51. Anthony J. Nownes, *Pressure and Power: Organized Interests in American Politics* (Boston: Houghton Mifflin, 2001), pp. 4–7 and 220–221.

52. David L. Paletz, *Mass Media in American Politics* (New York: Longman, 2001), pp. 197–202.

53. Todd Gitlin, *The Whole World is Watching* (Berkeley: University of California Press, 1989); Robert M. Entman and Andrew Rojecki, "Freezing Out the Public," *Political Communication* 10 No. 2 (April–June 1993): 155–174; and Andrew Rojecki, *Silencing the Opposition: Antinuclear Movements and the Media in the Cold War* (Champaign: University of Illinois Press, 2000).

54. Nancy B. Burgoyne and Timothy M. Cole, "Showdown in Seattle: Media Representation of the World Trade Organization Protests," paper delivered at the Western Political Science Association Annual Meeting, March 15–17, 2001, Las Vegas, NV; for further discussion of how violent "anarcho-terrorists" garnered the bulk of media attention at the expense of peaceful protesters, see Brigitte L. Nacos, *Mass-Mediated Terrorism* (Lanham, MD: Rowman and Littlefield, 2002), pp. 70–74.

55. Jon F. Hale, "Shaping the Conventional Wisdom," *Political Communication* 10 No. 3 (July–September 1993): 285–302.

56. Thomas Ferguson and Joel Rogers, *Right Turn: The Decline of the Democrats and the Future of American Politics* (New York: Hill and Wang, 1986).

57. Richard N. Ostling, "Election Affirms Religious Divide," *Ellensburg Daily Record*, November 5, 2004, p. A1.

58. John Podesta and John Halpin, "A New Silent Majority has Formed," *Ellensburg Daily Record*, November 12, 2004, p. A4.

59. Morris P. Fiorina, *Culture War? The Myth of a Polarized America* (New York: Pearson-Longman, 2005).

60. Vincent Price, *Public Opinion* (Newbury Park, CA: Sage Publications, 1992), p. 77.

61. The numbers for television and radio come from a quarterly report of the Federal Communications Commission, released in late March, 2004, accessed at www.fcc.gov/mb/audio/totals/index.html. Officially, there were 13,476 licensed AM and FM radio stations, and 1,744 licensed UHF and VHF television stations. The newspapers data comes from *The Statistical Abstract of the United States, 2003* (Washington, DC: Government Printing Office, 2003), which listed the number of daily newspapers at 1,457 in 2002. Given their great diversity, it is hard to estimate the number of magazines, which number in the thousands.

62. Again, it is true that some mainly "entertainment" outlets do have political content, such as the news-spoof program *The Daily Show* on the cable channel Comedy Central. But the point is that most entertainment media sources are devoid of serious political discussion.

63. For example, see Michael X. Delli Carpini and Bruce A. Williams, "Let Us Infotain You: Politics in the New Media Environment," in W. Lance Bennett and Robert M. Entman, eds., *Mediated Politics: Communication in the Future of Democracy* (New York: Cambridge University Press, 2001), pp. 160–181.

64. Doris Graber, *Processing the News* (Lanham, MD: University Press of America, 1993); John P. Robinson and Michael R. Levy, "Interpersonal Communication and News Comprehension," *Public Opinion Quarterly* 50 (1986): 160–175; William P. Eveland, Jr., "The Effect of Political Discussion in Producing Informed Citizens: The Roles of Information, Motivation, and Elaboration," *Political Communication* 21 No. 2 (April 2004): 177–194.

65. Matthew A. Baum, "Sex, Lies, and War: How Soft News Brings Foreign Policy to the Inattentive Public," *American Political Science Review* 96 No. 1 (March 2002): 91–110.

66. Vincent Price, *Public Opinion*, pp. 77–78.

67. See the discussion in W. Lance Bennett, *News: The Politics of Illusion,* 4th ed. (New York: Longman Publishing, 2001), pp. 181–208.

68. Pat Buchanan, *The New Majority* (Philadelphia: Girard Bank, 1971); Edith Efron, *The News Twisters* (Los Angeles: Nash Publishing, 1971); Joseph Keely, *The Left-Leaning Antenna* (Rochelle, NY: Arlington House, 1971); Robert Lichter, Stanley Rothman, and Linda S. Lichter, *The Media Elite* (Bethesda, MD: Alder and Alder Publishing, 1986).

69. Bernard Goldberg, *Bias: A CBS Insider Exposes How the Media Distort the News* (New York: Perennial, 2003); Reginald Estoque Ecarma, *Beyond Ideology: A Case of Egalitarian Bias in the News?* (Lanham, MD: University Press of America, 2003).

70. Jim A. Kuypers, *Press Bias and Politics: How the Media Frame Controversial Issues* (Westport, CT: Praeger, 2002).

71. Edward S. Herman and Noam Chomsky, *Manufacturing Consent: The Political Economy of the Mass Media* (New York: Pantheon Books, 1988); Mark Hertsgaard, *On Bended Knee* (New York: Schocken Books, 1989); Michael Parenti, *Inventing Reality: The Politics of the News Media*, 2nd ed. (New York: St. Martin's Press, 1993); Eric Alterman, *What Liberal Media?* (New York: Basic Books, 2003).

72. See various election-year editions of *Editor and Publisher;* exceptions where the Democrat received more endorsements were 1964 and 1992. In 2000, twice as many newspapers endorsed Republican George W. Bush as Democrat Al Gore, accounting for more than half the circulation (*Editor and Publisher,* November 6, 2000, p. 24). The magazine also reported a poll of 193 editors and publishers, which showed more of them planned to vote for Bush themselves.

73. Alterman, *What Liberal Media?*; Al Franken, *Lies and the Lying Liars Who Tell Them* (New York: Dutton, 2003), p. 3.

74. David Niven, *Tilt? The Search for Media Bias* (Westport, CT: Praeger, 2003). Of course, as was noted in Chapter 4, Republicans are not uniformly conservative, nor are all Democrats liberal, so it is possible that an ideological bias might still have been in operation; however, since most Democratic elected officials are more liberal than the population, and Republican ones more conservative, his use of party to measure political bias is less of a problem.

75. Bennett, *News,* pp. 33–70.

76. Entman, *Democracy Without Citizens,* pp. 17–20.

77. Page, *Who Deliberates?,* p. 123.

78. Ibid., pp. 43–76.

79. Page, *Who Deliberates?*; John R. Zaller, *The Nature and Origins of Mass Opinion,* pp. 328–331.

80. Bennett, *News,* pp. 99–100 and 169–170; Entman, *Democracy Without Citizens,* pp. 98–99.

81. W. Lance Bennett, "Toward a Theory of Press-State Relations in the United States," *Journal of Communication* 40 (1990): 103–125; John Zaller and Dennis Chiu, "Government's Little Helper: U.S. Press Coverage of Foreign Policy Crises, 1946–1990," in Nacos, Shapiro, and Iserina, eds., *Decisionmaking in a Glass House,* pp. 61–84.

82. On the case of Iraq in the first Gulf War, see Robert M. Entman and Benjamin I. Page, "The News Before the Storm: The Iraq War Debate and the Limits of Media Independence," in W. Lance Bennett and David L. Paletz, eds., *Taken by Storm: The Media, Public Opinion, and U.S. Foreign Policy in the Gulf War* (Chicago: University of Chicago Press, 1994), pp. 82–103.

83. Page, *Who Deliberates?,* p. 10.

84. Bennett, *News,* pp. 182–185.

85. Ben Bagdikian, *The Media Monopoly,* 6th ed. (Boston: Beacon Press, 2000).

86. See Peter Phillips and Project Censored, *Censored 2004: The Top 25 Censored Stories* (New York: Seven Stories Press, 2003), p. 87.

Voices of the People: Public Opinions on Political Matters

Historical Development of Political Issues

When I was governor, the laws said the races should be separated. But now the law is different, customs are different, public opinion has changed, and it's an entirely different situation.

Senator J. Strom Thurmond (R-SC), 1978[1]

Questions to Think About

Nothing comes from nothing. All political issues have histories. In this chapter, we look at the development of American political issue opinions since modern scientific polling began. We will see the backgrounds of many of the issues that are important in politics today, so that we can better understand their current context. As you read this chapter, ask yourself:

- How does change in the political system change the issues that are important? How does political change lead to opinion change, and vice versa?
- What has really fundamentally changed, and what has changed only on the surface? For example, what has been the nature of the change concerning illegal drugs—from alcohol in the 1920s to cocaine today?
- How important do you think political correctness or socially acceptable answers have been, particularly in women's rights and racial issues? How often do people say what they really think, and how often do they say what they think is socially acceptable?
- How would you have answered the questions if you had been born earlier? For example, how would you have answered questions on civil liberties in the 1950s or about black rights in the 1960s?

IN ORDER to understand public opinion today, we need to understand public opinion yesterday. Issues have histories. People's opinions this year are related to their opinions last year—and ten years ago and one hundred years ago. Even if people do not remember, or have never heard of, issues from fifty or a hundred years earlier, those issues have influenced the modern political scene and have shaped contemporary public opinion. The issues have changed over the years—the specific issues that were important in 1906 are not the same ones that were important in 2006—but the types of issues are remarkably similar. The issues that grip a political system change constantly, but they change within a framework of continuity. For example, the issue of drugs has been with us for a long time; in 1906, the drug in the political spotlight was alcohol and its prohibition, while today it is marijuana and cocaine and other drugs and their eradication. Women's issues have also shown great consistency, although the specific issues have changed from women's suffrage, to the Equal Rights Amendment, to women's proper place in society (home, business, government), gender discrimination, and sexual harassment. In addition, the question of African American rights has remained over the centuries, although the specific issues have changed. Foreign policy issues have changed, but the basic issues of war and peace have remained stable. In this chapter, we will look at how the issues have changed within this framework of consistency. We will examine opinions since modern polling began in the 1930s.

We will find that public opinion on some issues has changed dramatically, while it has remained essentially stable on others. At the end of this chapter, we will examine theories of why public opinion changes on some important issues and why it does not on others.

We include a fair amount of history in this chapter. Because we know that some of your classmates will not be up on twentieth-century American history, we include a short timeline with some of the historical events we mention in this chapter.

Timeline of Events.

Year	Political Events	Survey Research Events
1933–1945	Franklin Roosevelt is president. His administration is called the New Deal.	
1935		Gallup Organization begins.
1936	*Literary Review* predicts Alf Landon to win presidential election (the perfect bad example of polling). Gallup correctly predicts that Franklin Roosevelt will win.	
1941		National Opinion Research Center begins.
1941–1945	United States is in World War Two.	

Continued

Timeline of Events—*Cont'd*

Year	Political Events	Survey Research Events
1948	Polls predict Thomas Dewey to win presidential election (end of quota sampling).	National Election Studies begin.
1950–1953	Korean War	
1960		*The American Voter* is published.
1960–1965	Civil rights movement	
1963–1969	Lyndon Johnson is president; his administration is called the Great Society. It includes an expansion of the New Deal.	
1962–1973	Height of U.S. involvement in Vietnam War	
1972	Equal Rights Amendment passes Congress (is never ratified by states).	General Social Survey begins.
1981–1989	Ronald Reagan is president.	
1991	First Gulf War	
2001	Terrorist attacks on September 11	
2003–2004	War in Iraq	
	Same-sex marriage is legalized in Massachusetts; voters in several other states vote to ban it in their own states.	

THE FOUR ISSUE DOMAINS

In studying the history of issues in the American political system, it is useful to use some sort of organizational scheme. Here, we classify issues into four over-lapping issue domains: (1) economics and social welfare; (2) race; (3) social issues; and (4) foreign policy. These are the main issue domains typically used by political scientists and historians. Classifying issues is not necessarily easy or neat. Some issues belong in two or more domains, and some are hard to classify in any domain. You may disagree with how we have classified the issues. However, classifying issues into these four domains will help us understand the historical context of today's issues and will enable us to more easily understand the relationships of the issues in the current century.

As we examine the issues in each domain, we will show data about public opinion on those issues. We will use primarily three sources. The first major resource is the National Election Study (NES), conducted by the Center for Political Studies, located at the University of Michigan. The NES was first conducted in 1948, 1952, 1956, and every two years since (as well as limited pilot studies in odd-numbered years). The second is NORC, located at the University of Chicago. Also known as the National Opinion Research Center, NORC has conducted thousands of studies since the 1940s. The one continuing study that we will use most here is the General Social Survey (GSS); this survey has been conducted almost annually since 1972—twenty-five times through 2004, nineteen times from 1972 through 1993 and biennially since 1994. The third source is data from the American Institute of Public Opinion (AIPO), or the Gallup Organization.

Although we will examine data since the advent of polling in the 1930s, we will tend to look at more recent data, especially since the 1960s. Although the AIPO was established in 1935, NORC in 1941, and the NES started in 1948, there are not a lot of data that are comparable to more recent numbers. In an effort to keep this chapter relevant to modern readers (you), we will emphasize issues that continue to be important in the twenty-first century. Occasionally, we will show data from the 1940s, and even the 1930s, but most of our data will come from the past forty years. Because the General Social Survey began in 1972, a great deal of our data will begin then.

We will see that sometimes people's opinions change markedly, and sometimes they remain rather stable. We will emphasize questions that have been asked in the same ways over several years or decades, although we will sometimes look at data for shorter periods of time. If question wordings change slightly, we will note that.[2]

In reviewing the data in the following tables and figures, you should keep two thoughts in mind. First, as political issues change over the decades, so too do questions change. You will notice some questions in which the wording was changed to fit new political circumstances. When question wordings change, comparison becomes more difficult. We have tried to find questions in which the wordings do not change very much. Second, even when wordings do not change, the meanings of the words may change. One example is the word "equality" in a question on racial policies. In the 1960s, "equality" would unambiguously mean black and white equality. Today, however, it could indicate opposition to affirmative action, such as "equality" instead of "preferential treatment."

Economics and Social Welfare

The economic and social welfare domain has included a wide variety of issues, from British taxes on the American colonists in the 1760s and 1770s to President Bush's tax cuts in the twenty-first century. Issues in this domain involve taxes, government expenditures and programs, and government regulation. In the first approximately 140 years of the Republic's existence (1789–1932), the economic domain included taxes and tax breaks, the National Bank, tariffs, public works to develop the West, subsidies to railroads and other industries, the gold standard, coinage of silver, and government suppression of labor unions.

Since 1932 and Franklin Roosevelt's New Deal, the main economic issues of taxes and tax breaks remain, as well as government regulation of business, government relations with businesses and labor unions, government provision

Photo 7.1. President Franklin D. Roosevelt, along with his New Deal social programs, reshaped the American party system and helped to define modern liberalism. © Bettmann/CORBIS.

of services such as electrical power, Social Security, welfare, health care, and education, and actions against inflation and unemployment.

Survey Data

Economically, the New Deal and its offspring, the Great Society, still dominate American politics. Liberals want to expand their programs, while conservatives want to reduce the role of government in the American economy. Tables 7.1 and 7.2 show people's opinions about two important New Deal/Great Society priorities: ensuring that all Americans have jobs and good standards of living. Since 1972, the National Election Studies have asked respondents whether "the government in Washington should see to it that every person has a job and good standard of living." The question is asked on a "1 to 7" scale in which "1" means that the government should see to it and "7" means that "the government should just let each person get ahead on his/their own." To make the table easier to read, we have collapsed answers 1–3 into the liberal "see to it" category and answers 5–7 into the conservative "let each person get ahead on their own" category. We have classified answers of 4 as "neutral."

TABLE 7.1. Should the government in Washington see to it that every person has a job and a good standard of living, or should the government just let each person get ahead on [his/her] own? (Percent).

	All Respondents							
	1972	1976	1980	1984	1988	1992	1996	2000
Government see to it (liberal 1–3)	28	24	26	28	24	26	24	22
Neutral (4)	20	17	18	20	18	20	19	17
Each person on own (conservative 5–7)	40	39	41	38	43	41	46	49
DK, Haven't thought about it	13	20	16	14	15	13	10	11

Source: National Election Studies.

In Table 7.1, we see overall stability over the course of twenty-eight years and eight presidential elections. Consistently, more people favor letting each person get ahead on his own rather than having government see to it that every person has a job and good standard of living. However, the percentage of those favoring people getting ahead on their own seems to be increasing incrementally, while the proportion thinking the government should see to it that everybody has a good standard of living has been slowly declining. In the first few years, the conservative margin is about 10 to 15 percentage points,

TABLE 7.2. Should there be a government medical insurance plan or should medical expenses be paid by individuals and through private insurance? (Percent).

	All Respondents							
	1972	1976	1980*	1984	1988	1992	1996	2000
Government plan (liberal 1–3)	37	35	**	31	35	44	35	40
Neutral (4)	12	10	**	17	16	18	19	19
Individual/private (conservative 5–7)	33	35	**	35	32	24	35	32
DK, Haven't thought about it	18	21	**	18	16	14	12	9

*Not asked in 1980.

Source: National Election Studies.

but beginning in 1988, the gap expands until by 2000, the margin is 27 percentage points—a 49 percent to 22 percent tilt to the conservative side. Although many analysts have pointed out that Ronald Reagan's elections were not accompanied by a massive shift to conservatism in the electorate[3], we see something like creeping conservatism on this issue ever since the 1980s.

The second question concerns governmental health insurance. This question in the NES has also been asked on a 1 to 7 scale in which 1 means the respondent favors a government insurance plan, and 7 means the respondent thinks that medical expenses should be paid by individuals and through private insurance. As we did with the first question, we have collapsed answers 1–3 into the liberal "see to it" category and answers 5–7 into the conservative "let each person get ahead on their own" category. We have classified answers of 4 as "neutral."

Government health insurance was proposed by President Truman and has been on the political agenda ever since. Medicare, for the elderly, and Medicaid, for the poor, were enacted in the 1960s as part of President Johnson's Great Society. President Clinton placed a great deal of emphasis on a national health care plan in 1993 and 1994 but ultimately lost in Congress. The public shows remarkable stability on this question. The distribution of answers in 2000 is practically the same as it was in 1972. The proportion of respondents favoring a government plan is consistently a little higher than the proportion favoring individual and private insurance paying medical expenses. The only serious change in opinions came in 1992, when the liberal opinion reached its high point and the conservative opinion reached its low point. This was the year that Bill Clinton ran for the presidency the first time, emphasizing health insurance in his campaign.

Figure 7.1 shows people's opinions on whether the government should reduce the income difference between the rich and the poor. Again, we see very little change from 1978 to 2002. The percentage that said "yes" (1–3 on a 1–7, liberal-conservative scale) varied only from 42 percent to 50 percent, while those giving conservative answers varied from 26 percent to 38 percent. There is no pattern of either liberal or conservative answers increasing. Looking at economic opinions three ways, we have not seen evidence of important opinion change over thirty years, throughout the administrations of Richard Nixon, Jimmy Carter, Ronald Reagan, George H. W. Bush, Bill Clinton, and George W. Bush.

Racial Issues

The issue of race has been important in the United States, from the establishment of slavery in Florida in the 1570s and Virginia in 1619. Until the Civil War, the most important racial issues were the slave trade, slavery, and its expansion in new states and territories. In the decades after the Civil War, the issue involved mostly the maintenance of a segregated system in both the North and the South, with the southern system turning into a straightjacket of

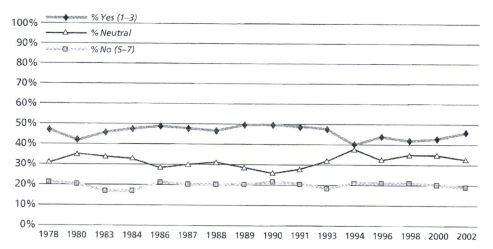

FIGURE 7.1. Should the government reduce the income difference between the rich and the poor? (1–7 scale).

Source: National Opinion Research Center General Social Survey: 1978–2002.

racial apartheid. Before the 1930s, race was barely an issue on the American political agenda because most of the people with power, white people, simply did not care about it or even think about it very often.

Since then, the racial issue domain has evolved very rapidly. In the 1930s, it included the issue of whether lynching should be tolerated. Since the 1950s, it has included fairness in hiring, open housing, segregation and integration, the Ku Klux Klan, public access, civil rights, voting, and school busing. Probably the most contentious racial issue today is affirmative action.

Survey Data

In this section, as we examine data from surveys of racial opinions, we will look at the answers of the white and black respondents separately. We do this because almost all the racial questions in the surveys have been concerned principally with African Americans. As you will note from the tables below, whites and blacks tend to answer racially oriented questions much differently. Including the answers of all ethnicities together would hide the opinions, and the opinion changes, of both the white and black respondents.

We can see the changes in the racial issues by looking first at what questions were asked and then at how Americans answered them. In Table 7.3, we see, beginning in the 1940s, the opposite of an affirmative action question—should whites have the first chance in getting jobs? In 1944, a majority of white respondents (52 percent) thought that whites should get the first chance. By 1972, the last time the question was asked, only 3 percent felt that way, while 96 percent thought that blacks should have as good a chance.[4]

TABLE 7.3. Do you think Negroes/blacks should have as good a chance as white people to get any kind of job, or do you think white people should have the first chance at any kind of job? (Percent).

	White Respondents Only				
	1944	1946	1963	1966	1972
Negroes/blacks should have as good a chance.	42%	48%	83%	87%	96%
White people should have the first chance.	52	49	15	10	3
Don't know	7	3	2	3	1

Source: NORC, p. 366 in Mayer.

A question, which would be considered insulting if asked today, inquired about the intelligence of African Americans compared to that of whites. In Table 7.4, we see that in 1942, only about four in ten white respondents (42 percent) thought African Americans were as intelligent as whites. By the 1960s, that percentage had increased, but only to a high of 79 percent. When black respondents were asked the question, 92 percent in 1946 and 98 percent in 1964 said "yes."

Before the 1960s, most white Americans accepted racial segregation as a normal part of life. With the advent of the civil rights movement, segregation became very controversial, prompting the Center for Political Studies to include several questions about it in its National Election Study. The simplest one is on the following page—whether one is in favor of desegregation, segregation, or something in between. By the time of the survey in 1964, the civil rights movement had been in high gear for well over four years, so all Americans had had ample opportunity to notice and think about segregation.

TABLE 7.4. In general, do you think Negroes are as intelligent as white people—that is, can they learn things just as well if they are given the same education and training? (Percent).

	White Respondents Only							
	1942	1944	1946	1956*	1963*	1964	1966	1968
Yes	42	44	53	77	75	79	78	73
No	48	47	40	20	20	18	19	22
Don't know	10	8	6	3	4	3	3	5

* The entries for 1956 and 1963 are the averages of two surveys in each year.

Source: NORC, p. 365 in Mayer.

TABLE 7.5. Are you in favor of desegregation, segregation, or something in between? (Percent).

	1964	1968	1972	1976
Whites only				
Desegregation	27	32	37	35
Something in between	47	50	46	53
Segregation	25	17	14	10
Blacks only				
Desegregation	72	74	68	71
Something in between	20	20	30	24
Segregation	6	5	2	1

Source: National Election Studies.

The data show us that in 1964 whites were almost equally split between desegregation and segregation, with about half saying they favored "something in between." By 1976, only 10 percent favored segregation, but only about one-third favored desegregation; half still favored "something in between."

Among black respondents, segregation had practically no appeal. However, 24 percent in 1976 did say they favored "something in between."

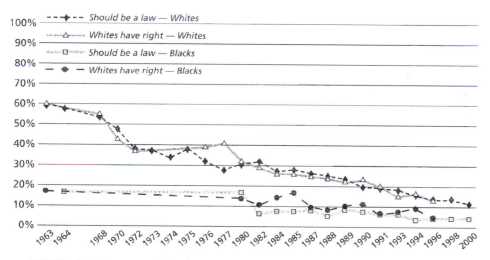

FIGURE 7.2. Do you think there should be a law against marriage between Negroes/blacks and whites? Do white people have a right to keep Negroes/blacks out of their neighborhoods if they want to, and Negroes/blacks should respect that right?

Source: National Opinion Research Center General Social Survey: 1972–2000 in William G. Mayer (*The Changing Mind: How and Why American Public Opinion Changed Between 1960 and 1988*. Ann Arbor, MI: The University of Michigan Press, 1993), pp. 370–371.

This question was not used in the NES after 1978. The most probable reason is that racial segregation no longer had enough appeal to any segment of the American population to make asking about it worthwhile.

White opinions have changed considerably over the years concerning laws against interracial marriage and whites' right to keep African Americans out of their neighborhoods. Figure 7.2 shows us that in 1963, 60 percent of white respondents said there should be laws against interracial marriage and that whites had a right to keep blacks out of their neighborhoods and that blacks should respect that right. By the 1990s, less than 20 percent of whites expressed those opinions. Black agreement has also dropped over the years, although not as much because the levels of agreement were never very high. While 17 percent of black respondents agreed in the 1960s that there should be laws against interracial marriages and that whites had the right to keep them out of white neighborhoods, only 5 percent favored bans on interracial marriage in 2002, and only 4 percent thought in 1996 that whites should be able to keep African Americans out of their neighborhoods.

One of the most important civil rights issues since the 1950s has been school integration. We see in Figure 7.3 that while both white and black opinion neared

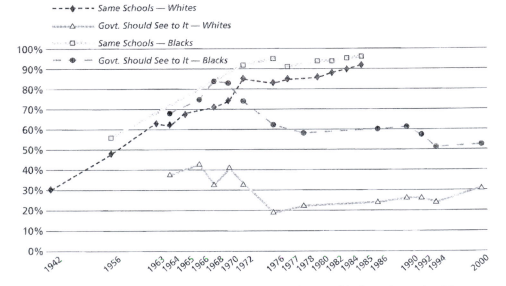

FIGURE 7.3. Do you think that white students and Negro/black students should go to the same schools? (NORC) Do you think that the government in Washington should see to it that white and black children go to the same schools or do you think this is not the government's business? (NES*).

*From 1964 to 1970, the NES question read, "are allowed to go to the same schools."

Source: National Opinion Research Center General Social Survey: 1972–1985 in William G. Mayer (*The Changing Mind: How and Why American Public Opinion Changed Between 1960 and 1988.* Ann Arbor, MI: The University of Michigan Press, 1993), p. 369.

unanimity that white and black students should go to the same schools, we see nothing near unanimity when it comes to the federal government ensuring that they do so. While over half of the black respondents said the government should see to it that the children go to the same schools, the percentage of whites agreeing is much lower, never rising higher than 33 percent after 1970. Figure 7.3 also shows us that we should examine question wording closely. Both black and white respondents have higher levels of agreement for the government seeing to school integration from 1964 through 1970; the drop in 1972 and later is probably due to the fact that the focus of the question was changed from the government's seeing to it that white and black children "be allowed to go to the same schools" to the government's seeing to it that they "go" to the same schools. The focus changed from permission to requirement. In addition, many respondents said they did not know if the government should see to integration or that they did not care; in 2000, 38 percent of whites and 37 percent of blacks said they did not know or did not care. However, even with these caveats, Figure 7.3 shows that people are much more likely to favor racial integration in schools, and increasingly so over the years, than they are to favor government intervention to make it happen.

People's reluctance to favor government intervention is shown even more clearly in reference to preferential hiring and promotion of blacks. Table 7.6 shows that white respondents are clearly opposed to it, while black respondents are divided. At their highest levels of support ("strongly" and "not strongly" combined), only 13 percent of whites and 52 percent of blacks support preferences for blacks.

TABLE 7.6. Some people say that because of past discrimination, blacks should be given preference in hiring and promotion. Others say that such preference in hiring and promotion of blacks is wrong because it discriminates against whites. What about your opinion—are you for or against preferential hiring and promotion of blacks? (Percent).

	1994	1996	1998	2000	2002
Whites only					
Strongly support preference	4	5	5	7	4
Not strongly support preference	6	6	5	6	6
Not strongly oppose preference	25	26	23	27	28
Strongly oppose preference	60	59	60	55	61
Don't know	5	5	7	5	2
Blacks only					
Strongly support preference	41	35	21	29	34
Not strongly support preference	11	12	13	10	9
Not strongly oppose preference	19	20	21	20	28
Strongly oppose preference	21	27	32	30	28
Don't know	9	7	12	10	1

Source: NORC GSS.

Social or "Lifestyle" Issues

The social domain has included a variety of issues that are more related to each other culturally than in any objective sense. These are issues that involve personal or cultural expression and usually, with some exceptions, do not involve money. Some important social issues in the past have included immigration, religion, alcohol and its prohibition, women's voting, Sunday closing laws, birth control, and use of foreign languages in the United States. Today, some important issues include abortion, the relationship between religion and government, the role of women, sexual orientation, immigration, and crime.

In 1973, the Supreme Court ruled in *Roe* v. *Wade* that abortion was a constitutionally protected right. Since then, the abortion dispute has been one of the most important social issues in the United States. That dispute remains today and shows no sign of going away. Since 1973, pro-life forces have fought to have the ruling overturned. On the state and local levels, they have worked to make abortion more restricted and more inconvenient. The pro-choice forces have fought to maintain the decision and to make abortion more accessible to more women. This is probably the most emotional issue of the age.

Another social issue is the proper relationship between religion and government. A loosely organized group of people, fundamentalist Christians, rose to political prominence with the election of Reagan in 1980 and remain important politically today. Fundamentalist Christians existed long before Reagan's election, but they have assumed a new national political importance. In the 1980s, the most prominent fundamentalist Christian organization was the Moral Majority; today, it is the Christian Coalition.

Another important social issue is the proper place of women in American society. The Equal Rights Amendment was defeated in 1982, but as more and more women join the workforce and get jobs in previously all-male positions, women are assuming more influential positions both inside and outside the political arena. But issues remain over the treatment of women, including gender discrimination, especially in jobs traditionally held by men, sexual harassment, and comparable worth, or paying men and women the same for comparable jobs. Affirmative action, which has been very controversial when applied to racial minorities, has been applied to women with less rancor.

The place of homosexual Americans assumed new prominence in the 2004 elections. Before that, beginning in the 1970s, homosexuals had become more assertive about their rights. In 1992 and 1993, a major issue was whether gays could serve in the U.S. military. A compromise of sorts was reached in which gays could serve as long as they did not identify themselves as being homosexual. By the end of the 1990s, gay activists demanded the right to marry legally and to have their unions receive all the rights of any married couples. In 2003, Canada legalized same-sex marriages, which led activists in the United States to intensify their efforts. They succeeded in May 2004 in Massachusetts. Later that year, President Bush declared his support for a Constitutional amendment that would define marriage as a union between one man and one woman. Several analysts later credited his antigay marriage stand as an important factor in his electoral victory in November 2004. During that same election, voters in eleven states outlawed same-sex marriages in their states.

Another issue involves immigration. There has been opposition to immigration since at least the 1840s; now, most of the immigrants come from Latin America and Asia. There are periodic efforts to reduce immigration and to crack down on illegal immigration. One manifestation of the anti-immigration sentiment is an effort to make English the official language of the United States and not to print government documents in other languages; however, this issue has not advanced very far. Since September 11, 2001, many Americans have seen the prevention of immigration of potential terrorists as a national security issue.

The last social issue has been fear of crime. Crime was an important issue in the late 1960s, especially in 1968 when both Richard Nixon and George Wallace ran on law and order platforms. At that time, the term "law and order" included white fear of African Americans and dislike of antiwar protesters as well as fear of crime. But ordinary crime has been a concern; throughout much of the mid-twentieth century, crime rates increased. Even in the 1990s, when crime rates were actually declining, many people perceived crime as increasing. Illegal drug issues have been intertwined with the crime issue for decades, including the appropriate penalties for drug use and efforts to legalize marijuana. Today, an important drug issue is the relative emphasis government should place on punishment and treatment.

Survey Data

We will first look at women's rights and opinions of women's proper place in society. The proper role of women has been an important issue in the United States for more than two hundred years, but it entered the American political agenda in the 1960s with greater urgency. By the time the question about an equal role for women was included in the NES in 1972, the issue of women's rights was a familiar one.

Figure 7.4 shows the answers to the question of whether women should have an equal role with men in running business, industry, and government. The question has been asked using a 1 to 7 scale in which 1 meant that women should have an equal role with men in running business, industry and government and 7 meant women's place is in the home. Figure 7.4 also shows the percentage of respondents who approve of a woman working even if she has a husband capable of supporting her. The data show impressive changes. Over the last three decades, we have seen a steady increase in the equal role answers. The proportion of people saying women should have an equal role increased from 47 percent to 77 percent in twenty-eight years. The equal role of women

FIGURE 7.4. Some people feel that women should have an equal role with men in running business, industry, and government. Others feel that women's place is in the home. (Respondent asked to place self on a 1–7 scale in which "1" means "equal role.") (NES) Do you approve or disapprove of a married woman earning money in business or industry if she has a husband capable of supporting her? (AIPO*, NORC).

*The AIPO question began, "Do you approve of a married woman..." It was limited to registered voters.

Source: NES: 1972–2000; AIPO: 1938–1970, p. 393 in Mayer; NORC GSS: 1972–1998.

is, at least according to survey answers, no longer a very divisive issue. The proportion approving of women working increased dramatically from 21 percent in 1938, long before the modern women's movement emerged, to 55 percent in 1969, to 80 percent or more in the 1990s. The issue of women working seems also to have been resolved in the arena of public opinion.

Figure 7.5 shows the same movement in attitudes but from an explicitly political perspective. Using Gallup and NORC data from 1937, we see that the proportion of Americans saying they would vote for a qualified woman of their party increased from 33 percent to 90 percent.

An important part of the women's movement was the Equal Rights Amendment, passed in Congress but not ratified by three-fourths of the states (38 of 50). Its time ran out in 1982. A question asked about in the ERA in 1977 and 1982 showed that two-thirds of the respondents favored it (see Table 7.7).

Abortion has probably been the most divisive issue in American politics for the last thirty or so years—ever since the Supreme Court's *Roe* v. *Wade* decision in January 1973. The Center for Political Studies had the foresight (or good fortune) to include a question on abortion several months before the *Roe* v. *Wade* decision.

Table 7.8, on abortion, shows two things. First, it shows great stability over the decades as the abortion battles have been fought. Second, it shows how changing question wording can change answers. Questions about abor-

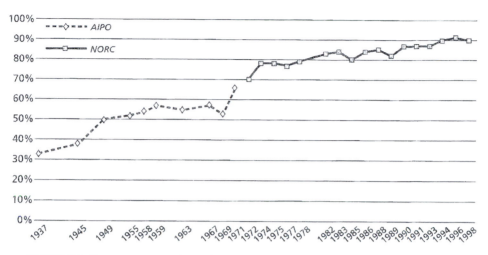

FIGURE 7.5. If your party nominated a woman for president, would you vote for her if she were qualified for the job? (Percent saying "yes").

Source: AIPO: 1937–1971, p. 394 in Mayer; NORC GSS: 1972–1998.

tion have been asked with two different, though similar, wordings, each with four answer options.[5] The first version was asked from 1972 to 1980, and the second has been asked since 1980; both versions were asked in 1980. The "extreme" options (the first and fourth answer categories) remained roughly the same in both versions—abortion should never be permitted or should always be permitted. But the two "intermediate" options changed. For the first option, the first version of the questionnaire included an option for allowing abortion if the life and health of the woman was in danger; the second version kept "life" of the mother but took out "health" and added cases of rape or incest to this option. For the third answer option, the first version of the

TABLE 7.7. The Equal Rights Amendment will amend the United States Constitution to provide equal rights for men and women. Do you strongly favor, somewhat favor, somewhat oppose, or strongly oppose this amendment? (Percent).

	1977	1982
Strongly favor	21	26
Somewhat favor	46	44
Somewhat oppose	15	16
Strongly oppose	9	8
No opinion	8	5

Source: NORC GSS.

questionnaire included an option for abortion if "the woman would have difficulty in caring for the child." The second version removed that answer and substituted the words, "only after the need for the abortion has been clearly established."

From 1972 to 1980, about one-tenth of the public said abortion should never be permitted, while about one-fourth said it should never be forbidden. Almost half said it should be permitted when the life and health of the woman was in danger. Since the second version has been used, about one-third or more said a woman should always be able to obtain an abortion, and between 10 percent and 13 percent said abortion should never be permitted.

Since 1980, we have seen remarkable stability. The percentage completely opposing abortion has remained between 10 percent and 13 percent, and, except for 1992, the percent completely supporting a woman's right to abortion has remained between 35 percent and 40 percent.

Two other social issues have been important in American political history through the centuries—drugs and religion. For the first 150 years of the na-

TABLE 7.8. Views on Abortion (Percent).

	All Respondents								
	1972	1976	1980	1980	1984	1988	1992	1996	2000
Should never be permitted	11	11	10	11	13	12	10	13	12
Permitted when life and health of woman is in danger* / rape or incest, or life of woman **	46	44	44	32	29	33	28	30	31
Difficulty caring for child* / need clearly established**	17	16	18	18	19	18	14	16	15
Should never be forbidden* / a woman should always be able to obtain an abortion**	24	26	27	35	35	35	46	40	39
Don't know, other	3	4	3	4	3	1	2	2	2

*First version of the questionnaire: 1972–1980.
**Second version of the questionnaire: 1980–2000.

Source: National Election Studies.

tion's existence, the drug in question was alcohol. The issue of prohibiting alcohol on a national scale was not finally settled until 1933, when the Prohibition Amendment (Eighteenth) was repealed by the Twenty-First Amendment. Since the 1960s, other drugs have taken the center of attention; these drugs include marijuana, heroin, cocaine, and a host of others. All these drugs are officially illegal. Although there has not been an important move to legalize "hard" drugs such as heroin or cocaine, the issue of legalizing marijuana continues. If you are a college student reading this book, you may have an opinion on this issue.

The issue of religion also has a long history in the United States. Although the First Amendment seems to rule religion out of politics, religious disagreements have always been with us. Since the 1980s and the rise to political importance of fundamentalist Christians, the conservative viewpoint has received widespread attention. In addition to abortion, which has a strong religious component, especially among its opponents, some religious issues have included teaching evolution and public display of the Ten Commandments in courtrooms. One important issue, which dates to the 1962 U.S. Supreme Court decision *Engel* v. *Vitale,* is required prayer or Bible reading in public schools. That decision declared required prayer in public schools to be unconstitutional. Although there are significant exceptions,[6] conservative Christian organizations typically want required prayer to be returned to public schools.

We have placed these two dissimilar social issues in Figure 7.6 to show the very slight movement in public opinion on each issue. The position of legalizing marijuana has never enjoyed majority support, but over thirty years has increased in popularity from 18 percent in 1973 to 34 percent in 2002. However, that increase has not been steady or consistent—the lowest levels of support were 16 percent in 1989 and 1990.

On the other hand, the position favoring required readings of the Lord's Prayer and Bible verses—or, at least opposition to the Supreme Court's decision on the subject—has enjoyed majority support every year the question has been asked. But we do see a slight decrease in disapproval of the Court's decision; in the 1970s and in 1982, over 60 percent disapproved of the decision, but since 1990, the disapproval rate has been in the high 50 percent range.

Another social issue, one that has emerged in the past few years, is same-sex marriage. Both civil and religious authorities have dealt with the issue of homosexuality since the 1990s. While we do not have longitudinal data on same-sex marriages going back very far, we do have twenty-nine years of data on homosexuality. We see in Figure 7.7 that homosexuality is increasingly considered to be acceptable behavior. The proportion of respondents saying sexual relations between two adults of the same sex is "always wrong" declined from 70 percent in 1973 to 53 percent in 2002, while the percentage saying it is "not wrong at all" increased from 11 percent to 32 percent. So, while a

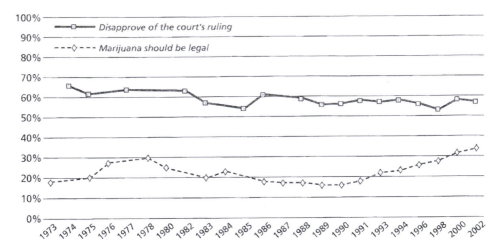

FIGURE 7.6. Do you think the use of marijuana should be made legal or not? (NORC) The United States Supreme Court has ruled that no state or local government may require the reading of the Lord's Prayer or Bible verses in public schools. What are your views on this—do you approve or disapprove of the court's ruling?* (NORC)

*Disapprove of court's ruling indicates the respondent *approves* of required prayer or Bible reading in public schools.

Source: National Opinion Research Center General Social Survey: 1973–2002.

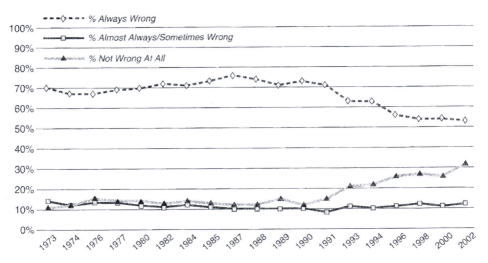

FIGURE 7.7. What [is your opinion] about sexual relations between two adults of the same sex?

Source: National Opinion Research Center General Social Survey: 1973–2002.

majority of Americans still disapprove of homosexual relations, that majority has shrunk considerably over the years.

Foreign Policy Issues

Between the War of 1812 and the U.S. entry into World War One, foreign policy was usually not a large part of American politics, although it was important at times. The domain included the avoidance of entangling alliances, the Monroe Doctrine's discouragement of European colonization of the Western hemisphere, involvement in Latin America, and a war with Spain. After its participation in World War One, the United States tried to slip back into isolation but joined World War Two after the Japanese attack on Pearl Harbor.

Since World War Two, the United States has been very active in world politics and is now at the top of a "unipolar" world in which no other nation is comparable to the United States, either economically or militarily. Since World War Two, the foreign policy issue domain has included a large military budget, the Cold War, and a series of smaller wars, including the Korean War, the Vietnam War, and two Persian Gulf wars. The United States, with its great power, now acts intermittently as the world's policeman. American troops have been sent to several countries, including Somalia, Bosnia, Haiti, and Liberia, on humanitarian missions.

American foreign policy has been focused on the Middle East since Iraq's invasion of Kuwait in 1990 and the short war to expel Iraq in 1991, and especially after the terrorist attacks on September 11, 2001. After those attacks, the second Bush administration invaded Afghanistan, the home of Al Qaeda, the terrorist organization responsible for the attacks. In 2003, the United States led a war to overthrow Saddam Hussein in Iraq and soon found itself fighting a guerilla war that critics found reminiscent of Vietnam.

Survey Data

Figure 7.8 shows the increasing opposition to American intervention in the Vietnam War from 1965 to 1973. We can see that opposition grew almost monthly. This figure shows the results of twenty-four polls taken from September 1965 to January 1973. We include this figure about a war that was probably over before you were born to show how surveys can be used to chart public opinions about fast-changing government policies.[7] The figure shows the percentage of Americans who, at the time, considered sending troops to Vietnam to be a mistake. The percentage begins very low, with only about one-fourth of the respondents considering intervention to have been a mistake, but it increases to 36 percent in May 1966 and stayed in the 31 percent to 37 percent range until July 1967. The percentage who thought intervention was a mistake rose to 47 percent in October 1967. These sagging polls convinced

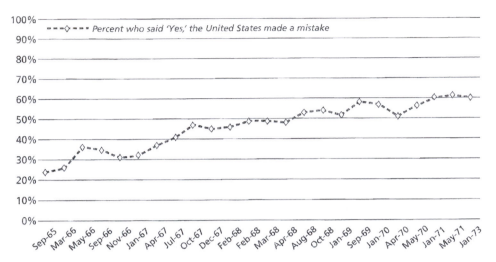

FIGURE 7.8. In view of the developments since we entered the fighting in Vietnam, do you think the United States made a mistake sending troops to fight in Vietnam? (Percent saying "yes").

Source: National Opinion Research Center General Social Survey: 1965–1973 in William G. Mayer (*The Changing Mind: How and Why American Public Opinion Changed Between 1960 and 1988*. Ann Arbor, MI: The University of Michigan Press, 1993), p. 432.

President Johnson that he needed to reassure the American people that the war was going well, and he brought the commanding general, General William Westmoreland, back to the United States to conduct a morale-building speaking tour. We see no evidence from these numbers that Westmoreland was successful; in any event, in late January 1968, the South Vietnamese Communists, called the Viet Cong, staged a very aggressive military offensive, the Tet Offensive. Militarily, the Tet Offensive was a disaster for the Viet Cong and a resounding success for the United States. However, the media stressed the unexpectedness and ferocity of the offensive rather than any eventual American triumph, and American disfavor with the war continued to increase.

By August, 53 percent of the people thought that intervention had been a mistake. By 1973, when almost the last Americans were withdrawn, 60 percent of Americans thought it had been a mistake.

Military spending has been a significant issue since the American buildup began for World War Two in 1940. Table 7.9 shows how Americans have varied in their opinions on this subject over thirty years. Respondents were asked in 1972 and 1976 whether they thought "military spending should be cut" or "should it continue at least at the present level?" Since 1980, respondents were asked to place themselves on a 1 to 7 scale in which 1 meant that "we should spend much less money for defense" and 7 meant "defense spending should be greatly increased." Because the pro-spending responses were so different in 1973–1976 and 1980–2000 ("continue at least at the present level" and "increased"), we have shown those responses on different lines of the table.

TABLE 7.9. Should defense spending be decreased or increased? (Percent).

	All Respondents							
	1972	1976	1980	1984	1988	1992	1996	2000
Cut military spending*/ Spend less money for defense (liberal 1–3)**	35	18	10	28	29	40	26	13
Neutral (4)	NA	NA	15	28	29	29	28	22
Continue at present level*	57	76	—	—	—	—	—	—
Defense spending should be increased (conservative 5–7)**	—	—	61	32	29	17	32	45
DK/Other/Haven't thought	8	6	15	13	14	14	15	20

*First version of the questionnaire.
**Second version of the questionnaire.

Source: National Election Studies.

The table shows wildly varying percentages of the public favoring cutting or increasing defense spending. In 1972, during the American participation in the Vietnam War, 35 percent of the people wanted to cut military spending; this declined to 18 percent after the war ended. From 1980, the year when Ronald Reagan was first elected, to 1992, the year of Clinton's first election, the proportion wanting to spend less money for defense rose from 10 percent to 40 percent. In fact, 1992 was the only year in which more people wanted to cut defense spending than increase it. It is clear that opinions of defense spending increase and decrease in reaction to outside influences. William G. Mayer[8] has noted that opinions change in reaction to events, such as the Vietnam War or the seizing of American hostages in Iran in 1979, or government policy changes (or proposed changes, such as candidate Reagan's campaigning on a platform to increase defense spending).

We are fortunate to have a long history of American opinion about U.S. isolationism and internationalism since the end of World War Two. Gallup asked questions about the United States taking an active part in world affairs beginning in 1945, NORC began in 1947, and the National Election Studies began in 1956. This remarkable continuity allows us to compare opinions over more than fifty years.

In contrast to the opinion on defense spending, views on the United States taking an active part in world affairs seem to be very steady (see Figure 7.9). Since the 1940s, the distribution of opinion has barely changed at all. So, while people change on how much they want the government to spend on defense, around two-thirds to three-fourths of Americans consistently say that the United States should be actively involved in world affairs.

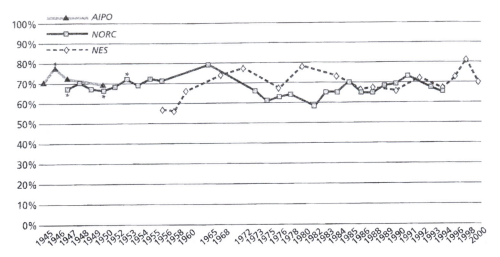

FIGURE 7.9. Should the United States take an active part in world affairs? (Percent who said "yes").

*Average of two or three surveys combined in one year.

Source: AIPO: 1945–1950, p. 424 in Mayer. Question: Do you think it would be best for the future of this country if we take an active part in world affairs, or if we stay out of world affairs?; NORC: 1947–1965, p. 424 in Mayer; NORC GSS: 1973–1994. Question: Do you think it would be best for the future of this country if we take an active part in world affairs, or if we stay out of world affairs?; NES: 1956–2000. Question: This country would be better off if we just stayed home and did not concern ourselves with problems in other parts of the world. (Agree/Disagree: "Disagree" is in the figure.)

WHY OPINIONS CHANGE

We have seen some impressive changes in public opinion, especially in the areas of racial and social issues. For example, we have seen the percentage of white respondents who thought that whites should have the first chance at getting jobs go down from 52 percent in 1944 to only 3 percent in 1972. We have also seen the proportion of respondents who would vote for a qualified woman in their party for president go from 33 percent in 1937 to 90 percent in 1998. But we have also seen great stability in some areas. For example, the proportion of Americans who feel the United States should be actively engaged in world affairs barely changed from 1945 (70 percent) to 2000 (70 percent).

Why do mass opinions change? Or why don't they? There are several reasons.

Reality Changes

The main reason is that reality changes.[9] Events and processes happen that change reality, so opinion changes to reflect it. This reality change may be of different types or the result of different causes. First, long-term demographic or social changes lead to new realities, and people adjust their opinions to fit what they see. Examples are increased numbers of women working, blacks moving to the North after World War One, more babies born outside marriage and more single mothers, more elderly citizens, and other demographic changes.

A second way that reality can change is that the people themselves change. Although this is very similar to demographic change, the shift goes beyond demographics. For example, as more women entered the workforce, more of them went to college. As they gained more education, they saw the world, and themselves, differently. Similarly, as African Americans gained more education, participated in politics, and were elected to public office, they saw themselves differently and began to have different expectations from the political system.[10] Page and Shapiro point out, "As average education levels increased further after the 1950s, higher proportions of Americans expressed tolerance for allowing dissenters—Communists, Socialists, atheists—to give public speeches, have their books in public libraries, and teach in schools."[11]

Third, sometimes events change reality. Certainly, the Civil War, the Great Depression, and World War II changed American politics. For example, the advent of World War Two ended the option of American isolationism as a realistic political alternative. Senator Arthur Vandenberg wrote in his diary at the end of the day December 7, 1941:

> In my own mind, my convictions regarding international cooperation and collective security for peace took form on the afternoon of the Pearl Harbor attack. That day ended isolationism for any realist.[12]

The terrorist attacks on September 11, 2001, have already had a significant impact on American public opinion that is still unfolding today.

Fourth, reality can change because of mass movements—people intentionally set out to change reality. Black advancement was helped by migrations to the North and increasing levels of education, but it was the civil rights movement of the 1960s that put black rights at the forefront of the political agenda and ended the Jim Crow laws of the South. Before the civil rights movement, it would have been absurd to think of a Negro secretary of state; since 2001, there have been two African-American secretaries of state. The women's movement and the gay rights movement also benefited their members by insisting on, and achieving, changes that altered reality.

A fifth way that reality can change occurs when intentional government policy forces it to change. For example, Roosevelt's New Deal changes have affected American politics—and practically every other aspect of American life—ever since they were created. Just the increase in the size and power of the federal government has changed which issues are discussed and which public policies are enacted. One deliberate policy that has had wide-ranging effects is the GI Bill of Rights. Because of that legislation, millions of veterans have been able to buy houses and further their education (including one of your authors—Thanks Uncle Sam!). The expanded educational base in the United States has made American technological change much more prevalent.

These changes in reality are often described as period effects or generational effects. Period effects are caused by events that affect young and old people roughly the same, such as the end of the Cold War or globalization today. Generational effects are those that affect one age group (or political generation) more than other people. As a general rule, those people who are just becoming aware of the political world and are being socialized into politics—in their late teens and early twenties—are more impressionable and are affected more than others when there is a change in the political system. For example, Americans who came of age during the Great Depression, and during the New Deal, tended to be more Democratic than earlier and later generations. Likewise, those who were socialized into politics during the Vietnam War and Watergate tend to have more anti-party and anti-establishment attitudes.

We have yet to see what effects the September 11 terrorist attacks or the current war on terrorism will have in the long run. It is probable that those Americans just being socialized into the political system will be more affected than older people.

Perception of Reality Changes

Another way that reality can change is that *reality* does not change, but the *perception* of reality changes. John Zaller has two examples of academic and professional change that later affected public opinion. The first involves alleged black inferiority to whites. For most of recorded history, practically all white people believed in their superiority to blacks and other races as common sense. As Zaller points out, in the first part of the twentieth century, "Virtually all white elites accepted some notion of the inferiority of other racial groups."[13] But because of mounting evidence, during the 1920s and 1930s, elite opinion began to shift, and by the end of World War Two, there was practically no informed elite opinion that held that whites had any innate superiority over other racial groups.[14]

Another of Zaller's examples is the changed opinion toward homosexuality. Sixty years ago, homosexuality was classified by psychiatric authorities as a disorder. However, in several studies beginning in the 1940s and early 1950s, researchers failed to find evidence to support that classification. Zaller points out that psychiatrists were faced with the conflict between their own prejudiced beliefs and the results of psychiatric research that that they valued highly. In the end, they had to choose between their prejudice and an important justification for their status and income. As Zaller puts it:

> Either psychiatrists could remove homosexuality from the list of mental disorders on the grounds that the standard assessment techniques had failed to uncover evidence of psychic problems among homosexuals, or they could devalue the standard

assessment techniques—the basis for psychiatry's authority in other domains—on the grounds that they had failed to uncover the pathology inherent in homosexuality. This must, in the end, have been an easy choice.[15]

It may not seem that *public* opinion was affected, simply because some elites became less racist or because the American Psychiatric Association removed homosexuality from its list of afflictions. But elite opinion is very important in influencing mass opinion. (Zaller insists that it is nearly dominant.) Ordinary people may not immediately change their minds when experts change theirs, but other elites do. When professional beliefs change, curricula in school change; when a prejudice is assaulted, there are not as many people to defend it. For example, the U.S. Supreme Court rejected Jim Crow laws concerning voting and school segregation in the 1940s and 1950s; without the change in elite opinion, we think it is unlikely the Court would have reacted as it did. When the civil rights movement erupted in the South, there were virtually no elites outside the South who supported Jim Crow laws. The civil rights workers were able to mobilize a sympathetic white opinion outside the South to support desegregation and antidiscrimination laws largely because the elites had abandoned any respectable racist opinion to support Jim Crow.

Generational Replacement

Over the long run, generational effects turn into generational replacement. As new, mostly young, people enter the public and old ones leave, the public changes. Young people are different from older ones. Warren E. Miller and J. Merrill Shanks[16] have pointed out that declining levels of voter turnout in the second half of the twentieth century were due largely to intergenerational replacement of older citizens with younger ones. The new, younger citizens were less likely to vote than the older ones had been when they were young. Converse and Shanks attribute the lower incidence of voting among young citizens to the fact that they came of age during the 1960s and 1970s, around the time of the Vietnam War and Watergate, so that:

> their politically formative years coincided with political events in a period that could have socialized them into anti-party, anti-establishment predispositions that militate against orthodox political engagement.[17]

Kristi Andersen[18] has shown that most of the change from a Republican-dominated party system in the 1920s to a Democratic-dominated party system in the 1930s was due to the fact that millions of new voters, often immigrants or the children of immigrants, entered the political system in the 1930s. Since Franklin Roosevelt and the Democratic Party were ascendant at that time, they entered the political system as Democrats. While most Republicans who had voted for Roosevelt eventually returned to the

Republican fold, these new voters stayed Democratic. The distribution of opinion on issues, like voting behavior and party identification, can change without anybody changing.

Intergenerational change often interacts with important events. If fact, it almost always does. Younger people tend to be "particularly vulnerable to influence by historical events in their political environment."[19] While everybody may be influenced by the Great Depression, the Vietnam War, or September 11, those people who are just becoming politically aware at the time are likely to be the most affected and are likely to carry the seeds of change from those events into the political system.

Lifecycle Effects

The fourth cause of changing public opinion comes under the label "lifecycle effects." As people grow older, their perspectives change—often in very predictable ways. For example, as teenagers go into their twenties and thirties, they acquire an interest in the quality of public education. As they become older, they have more reason to object to property taxes and income taxes. As they proceed into their sixties and seventies, they have an ever-increasing interest in Medicare and government assistance with medical bills and buying prescription drugs. In the first decade of the twenty-first century, as the oldest baby boomers move from age fifty-four to age sixty-four, the cost of prescription drugs has become an important issue in Congress.

Manipulation by Elites

Elites, either in government or outside, can manipulate public opinion. On some issues, elites have very limited ability to sway opinion. We say that some social and economic trends are "autonomous." That is, they are "largely independent of, and resistant to, distortion by the media or special interests."[20] Examples would be inflation and unemployment; nobody needs to tell the people that there is inflation, and the media do not need to tell people that they are unemployed. But other issues, especially those in foreign affairs, are brought to people's awareness through the media, and these issues are subject to distortion by the media, interest groups, or politicians. Page and Shapiro said that opinion manipulation is not just a short-term phenomenon. They said that elite interests can institutionalize their opinions:

> It would be a mistake . . . to conclude that organized groups are not major factors affecting opinion in the long run. The messages of protests and demonstrations may sink in over time. Our findings are also quite consistent with the idea that organized groups—especially those with a lot of talent and money, like business corporations—are able to encourage and publicize the work of chosen experts and quite possibly influence news commentators as well, which in turn

affect the opinions of the general public. By these indirect methods, and by other means including institutional advertising and influence upon school textbooks and curricula, interest groups may have an extremely important impact on public opinion.[21]

CONCLUSION

We have looked at public opinion in its historical context and have examined how it has changed, or not changed, during the time that sample surveys have been conducted. It is important to look at the historical context of modern issues. The historical context is important for understanding the *democratic dialogue*. In some issues, we have seen little change over the decades. But for some issues in the racial and social issue domains, we have seen large changes, especially in regard to the proper roles of African Americans and of women. The increasing acceptance of equal roles for these two groups in American society contributes to the increasing democratization of the United States.

The increasing acceptance of homosexuals seems to be a part of this trend. These trends may seem puzzling in light of the 2004 election results, in which opposition to homosexuality was seen as a contributing factor to President Bush's election and during which the voters of eleven states declared opposition to same-sex marriages. Time will tell us if November 2, 2004, was part of a reversing trend or, as we suspect, an aberration on what appears to be a continuing opening up of American politics.

However, on the very important issue of abortion there has been little change since 1980, when the current question wording was adopted for the National Election Studies. This one issue seems to be an example of an issue that the political system simply cannot resolve. Neither the pro-life nor the pro-choice advocates can change public opinion very much, and neither side has enough electoral influence to settle the issue once and for all. At the state level, we are likely to see the abortion issue played out in skirmishes aimed at making abortion more or less accessible and convenient. At the national level, we are likely to see abortion played out in presidential elections and in appointing Supreme Court justices. Since neither side can prevail, the courts will continue to decide the law.

From the perspective of this book, it is ironic that one of the most important issues in American politics cannot be settled through the political process. Unelected judges will, for the foreseeable future, decide public policy on abortion. This issue could be seen as an example of the *democratic dilemma*. When competing sides of a highly contentious issue cannot compromise and neither can win, the judicial branch is forced to decide, and public opinion is taken out of the public policy process.

We have examined the backgrounds of some issues that are important today. In the next chapter we will see the most pressing issue domains today.

Suggested Reading

Andersen, Kristi. *The Creation of a Democratic Majority 1928–1936.* Chicago: University of Chicago Press, 1979.

Kellstedt, Paul M. *The Mass Media and the Dynamics of American Racial Attitudes.* Cambridge: Cambridge University Press, 2003.

Mayer, William G. *The Changing American Mind: How and Why American Public Opinion Changed Between 1960 and 1988.* Ann Arbor: University of Michigan Press, 1993.

Miller, Warren E., and J. Merrill Shanks. *The New American Voter.* Cambridge: Harvard University Press, 1996.

Page, Benjamin I., and Robert Y. Shapiro. *The Rational Public: Fifty Years of Trends in Americans' Policy Preferences.* Chicago: University of Chicago Press, 1992.

Stimson, James A. *Public Opinion in America: Moods, Cycles and Swings,* 2nd ed. Boulder, CO: Westview Press, 1999.

Notes

1. Quoted in Nadine Cohodas, *Strom Thurmond and Politics of Southern Change* (New York: Simon and Schuster, 1993); also quoted in Paul M. Kellstedt, *The Mass Media and the Dynamics of American Racial Attitudes* (Cambridge: Cambridge University Press, 2003), p. 1.

2. We will show survey data for each of the four issue domains. We are indebted to William G. Mayer (*The Changing American Mind: How and Why American Public Opinion Changed Between 1960 and 1988* [Ann Arbor: University of Michigan Press, 1993]) for compiling historical data for several of the issues we use here. We use his data from the Gallup Poll and NORC. On each figure that includes data from his book, we cite the page number on which the data can be found. However, for any General Social Survey data, we use the data supplied directly by NORC.

3. Ibid., and Benjamin I. Page and Robert Y. Shapiro, *The Rational Public: Fifty Years of Trends in Americans' Policy Preferences* (Chicago: University of Chicago Press, 1992), chapter 4 and p. 280.

4. We have repeated the questions, using the words used at the time. Until the late 1960s, the proper, politically correct, term for Americans of African descent was "Negro" or "colored." From the late 1960s, the term "black" was preferable. The term "African American" was first used in the late 1980s. For a history of terms from the late nineteenth century, see Tom W. Smith, "Changing Racial Labels: From "Colored" to "Negro" to "Black" to "African American," *The Public Opinion Quarterly* 56 (1992): 496–514.

5. The four answer categories for the 1972–1980 version were (1) Abortion should never be permitted; (2) Abortion should be permitted only if the life and health

of the woman is in danger; (3) Abortion should be permitted if, due to personal reasons, the woman would have difficulty in caring for the child; and (4) Abortion should never be forbidden, since one should not require a woman to have a child she doesn't want. The answer categories for the 1980–2000 version were (1) By law, abortion should never be permitted; (2) The law should permit abortion only in case of rape, incest, or when the woman's life is in danger; (3) The law should permit abortion for reasons other than rape, incest, or danger to the woman's life, but only after the need has been clearly established; and (4) By law, a woman should always be able to obtain an abortion as a matter of personal choice.

6. For example, the leaders of Bob Jones University, a very conservative Christian university, oppose required prayer in public school (www.bju.edu).

7. For your background, the United States intervened in the Vietnamese conflict first during President Truman's administration, providing funds to pay for the post–World War Two French effort to re-establish its colonial empire in Southeast Asia. In the late 1950s, after the French had been expelled from Vietnam and the country had been divided into North Vietnam and South Vietnam, the Eisenhower administration sent in military advisors to help pro-American South Vietnam fight the Communist North Vietnam. President Kennedy continued and expanded Eisenhower's policy of sending advisors.

In 1965, President Johnson began sending American combat troops to fight the Communist forces directly. The war did not go well for the American side, and in 1969, President Nixon began withdrawing American troops, and by 1973, virtually all Americans were withdrawn from Vietnam. In 1975, North Vietnamese troops defeated the South Vietnamese army, and the country was reunited under Communist rule. By the end of the war, more than 58,000 Americans had been killed. In retrospect, the American intervention in the war was not advantageous to the United States, and most Americans today would consider it to have been a mistake.

8. Mayer, *The Changing American Mind*, Chapter 9.

9. Ibid.; and Page and Shapiro, *The Rational Public*, Chapter 10.

10. During World War Two, when Congress was voting on the GI Bill of Rights, John Rankin, a representative from Mississippi, was opposed to the legislation because he was afraid that black Mississippi veterans would go to college and would then no longer accept Jim Crow restrictions. As things turned out, he was correct.

11. Page and Shapiro, *The Rational Public*, pp. 326–327.

12. Arthur H. Vandenberg Jr., ed., *The Private Papers of Senator Vandenberg* (Boston: Houghton Mifflin, 1952), p. 1, quoted in Ole. R. Holst, *Public Opinion and American Foreign Policy* (Ann Arbor: University of Michigan Press, 1996), p. 16.

13. John R. Zaller, *The Nature and Origins of Mass Opinion* (Cambridge: Cambridge University Press, 1992), p. 9.

14. Ibid., pp. 9–14.

15. Ibid., pp. 324–325.

16. Warren E. Miller and J. Merrill Shanks, *The New American Voter* (Cambridge, MA: Harvard University Press, 1996), chapter 3.

17. Ibid., p. 43.

18. Kristi Andersen, *The Creation of a Democratic Majority 1928–1936* (Chicago: University of Chicago Press, 1979), chapter 1.

19. Miller and Shanks, *The New American Voter*, p. 43.

20. Page and Shapiro, *The Rational Public*, p. 330.

21. Ibid., p. 353.

Public Opinion Today

Politics generally comes down, over the long run, to a conflict between those who have and those who have less. . . .

V. O. Key, Jr.[1]

Questions to Think About

In the last chapter, we examined the historical development of today's issues by looking at four issue domains. In this chapter, we will look at important issues today in those same domains. We will change our focus somewhat by looking at subgroups in the population, classified according to income, gender, and race. In the end, we will review political scientists' evaluations of the relative importance of each of the issue domains in shaping Americans' political opinions and behaviors. As you read this chapter, ask yourself:

- How important are your demographic categories in shaping your opinions? What **social class** are you in? Are you a man or a woman? What is your ethnicity? What other characteristics are important as you develop your political opinions?
- As you look around, which issue domains seem most important in the American political system? Which were most important in the recent presidential election? Which helped George W. Bush? Which helped John F. Kerry?
- How do modern issues compare with issues in the past? Perhaps you do not have much memory of issues in the 1960s or 1980s, but from your knowledge of history, how would you politically compare those two decades with the present time?

W E ARE now going to look at public opinion at the beginning of the twenty-first century. We will examine the issue domains through the eyes of Americans, classified three ways—by income, gender, and race. These are three of the most common and important ways to classify the American people and their opinions. We will see Americans' opinions on the four issue domains and see how they have continued the development of opinions that we reviewed in the previous chapter. But we will go beyond issue positions. Keeping with the quotation that begins this chapter, we will examine views of those who "have" and those who "have less." We will see Americans' views of inequality (class, gender, and racial inequalities) and their explanations for inequality. We will also look at people's spending priorities.

We will see that although there are clear and important differences between Americans with varying levels of income and between men and women, the largest differences are grounded in race. The greatest divide between Americans is between whites and blacks. There is a great deal of literature documenting racial differences. In a way, the great differences between white and black Americans seem logical; race has been a major division since before the American Revolution. But on the other hand, it also seems logical that the importance of race in modern politics may have decreased, since, as we saw in the previous chapter, whites' level of racial prejudice has decreased and white opinions have changed to be much more accepting, or at least tolerant, of black interests.

In the fourth part of this chapter, we will review some literature that claims that the New Deal party system, the basis of the current division between Democrats and Republicans, has moved away from the economic and social welfare issues that originally defined it to a combination of racial issues and social issues. We will also look at theories about the relative importance of the issue domains in modern American politics. Just as the previous chapter used issue domains to cover the history of public opinion to the present, this chapter uses the domains to cover the state of public opinion today and will conclude with some thoughts about the issue domains and about the future of American politics. We will not attempt to foretell the future, but we will identify some theories and evidence that can give you some basis to predict it.

INCOME: ECONOMIC AND SOCIAL WELFARE ISSUES

Social class was the foundation of the New Deal coalition that developed during the Great Depression, and it is still an essential component of competitive politics today. There are several ways to define social class;[2] here, since we are mainly interested in Americans' views of government spending, especially social welfare spending, and their views of the fairness of the economic system, we have chosen to use family income. Income is clearly the typical way that class is measured when dealing with views of social welfare. As Martin Gilens said:

family income has been shown to be the best objective measure of economic condition for the purpose of assessing welfare views and is virtually the only such measure used in previous studies of this topic.[3]

In this analysis, we use data from the 2000, 2002, and 2004 National Election Studies. We will divide the samples into three roughly equally-sized income groups. For the 2000 and 2002 samples, the groups will be: less than $35,000 per year, $35,000–$64,999, and $65,000 or more per year. The 2004 data are coded in the dataset a little differently, so the top of the middle category, and the bottom of the highest, will be $70,000 instead of $65,000. Since social class has served as the basis of the modern party system, and the keystone of the liberal-conservative continuum, we should expect that people with lower incomes should be more Democratic than those with higher incomes. This is generally what we see in Table 8.1. Although the differences are not dramatic, they are clear. Those with household incomes under $35,000 are 11 percentage points more likely to be Democrats and those in the highest income grouping are 16 percentage points more likely to be Republicans.

Views on Economic Inequality

People's perceptions of the political environment are vital in determining their opinions on political issues and the political system itself. People's perceptions determine, for them, what is real. Here we will look at Americans' perceptions of economic inequality. Has America become more unequal economically? Approximately three-fourths of Americans surveyed in 2002 thought so (see Table 8.2). Surprisingly, people from all three levels of income tended to perceive economic realities pretty much the same. We see a consensus across all three income groupings—about three-fourths in each group—who said that

TABLE 8.1. Party Identification by Income.

	Total Sample	Household Income		
		$35,000	$35,000–$69,999	$70,000 +
Party Identification				
Democrat	32%	38%	29%	27%
Independent	33	34	35	30
Republican	29	21	30	37
Other/None	7	8	6	5
Sample Size	*1,212*	*368*	*321*	*366*

Source: 2004 National Election Study.

TABLE 8.2. Perceptions of Change in Income Inequality by Household Income.

	Total Sample	Income		
		Under $35,000	$35,000–$64,999	$65,000 or more
Change in income inequality in last 20 years				
Much larger	43%	43%	41%	47%
Somewhat larger	33	33	35	28
About the same	16	17	15	16
Somewhat smaller	6	4	8	7
Much smaller	2	3	1	1
Sample Size	*1,482*	*464*	*454*	*488*
Is the change in inequality a good thing or a bad thing (among those who said inequality was larger)?				
Good thing	14%	14%	15%	14%
Bad thing	86	86	85	86
Sample Size	*758**	*226*	*227*	*275*

*Note that the number of respondents was reduced. Nearly 38% of the respondents said they did not know or "hadn't thought" about the issue.

Source: 2002 National Election Study.

income inequality had increased in the previous twenty years. Of those who said that inequality had increased and had thought about the implications of growing inequality, almost all said that the increase was a bad thing—86 percent, with only miniscule differences between the three groups. (However, there was a large proportion of respondents—38%—who said they had not thought about the growing inequality enough to say if it was good or bad.) Clearly, among those who have thought about it, growing inequality is widely perceived by the American public to be a negative development.

Why are people unequal? It is clear to almost everybody that some people have better jobs and higher incomes than other people. Why is that? Respondents to the 2002 NES were asked if each of seven reasons was "very important," "somewhat important," or "not important at all." Table 8.3 shows the percents who said each reason is "very important." The table breaks the reasons in two types: ones that reflect negatively on the individual person (his or her industriousness, abilities, or choices), and others that reflect on societal forces (reasons that cannot be attributed to an individual's own qualities). One might expect that the rich would attribute poverty to personal failings of the poor people, while the poor themselves would attribute their own poverty to flaws in the economic system.[4] However, we do not see that. The reason most often cited is the lack of access to good education. It is the only reason that a majority of each

TABLE 8.3. Reasons why some people have better jobs and higher incomes and Why some people have worse jobs and lower incomes (Percent Saying Each Reason is "Very Important").

		Income		
Issue	Total Sample	Under $35,000	$35,000–$64,999	$65,000 or more
Personal Reasons				
Some people just don't work as hard*	48%	49%	44%	50%
Some people have more in-born ability to learn	37	48	34	25
God made people different from one another	25	32	22	14
Some people just choose low-paying jobs	22	30	17	17
Societal Reasons				
Some people don't get a chance to get a good education	60%	67%	54%	59%
Government policies have helped higher-income workers more	30	44	23	20
Discrimination holds some people back	27	43	24	15

* Note: Each reason was given to respondents in two ways. A randomly selected half of the respondents were asked for the reasons that some people have better jobs and higher incomes, while the other half were asked why some people have worse jobs and lower incomes. There was not much difference between the two versions, and they are combined in this table.

Source: 2002 National Election Study.

income group said was "very important." Next in order was that some people simply do not work as hard; about half of each group said this reason is "very important." Except for these two reasons, the main difference between the groupings of respondents is that those with low incomes are much more likely than other respondents to say that each reason is "very important." Even for a reason that is very uncomplimentary to poor people—that "some people have more in-born ability to learn"—more low income people said it was "very important." We do not know why low-income people would be more critical of poor people than high-income people are. Perhaps those with lower incomes are harsher in evaluating themselves, or perhaps those with low incomes are more familiar with the causes of and know of more reasons for their situation.

People's views of taxation are important in influencing their perceptions of economic inequality. When asked about other Americans and the taxes they pay, a majority of respondents—even those with high incomes—thought the rich were paying less than they should pay (see Table 8.4). At the same time,

TABLE 8.4. Perceptions of Other People's Taxes by Household Income.

	Total Sample	Income		
		Under $35,000	$35,000– $64,999	$65,000 or more
Do the rich pay the right amount in taxes?				
More than they should pay	15%	12%	16%	18%
About right	30	30	29	30
Less than they should pay	54	57	55	52
Sample Size	*1,484*	*473*	*449*	*487*
Do the poor pay the right amount in taxes?				
More than they should pay	46%	53%	46%	42%
About right	44	37	46	49
Less than they should pay	9	9	8	8
They don't pay at all	1	1	1	1
Sample Size	*1,483*	*469*	*443*	*487*

Source: 2002 National Election Study.

almost half (46 percent) thought the poor were paying too much. There were differences in the three income groups, in that the respondents with higher incomes tended to be more sympathetic to rich people and those with lower incomes tended to be more sympathetic to the poor—but those differences were not large.

The overall lessons of these data on inequality are that Americans at all economic levels tend to see economic inequality in the same light—increasing and bad. They also see inequities in the present tax system. The implications of this point of view could be significant; perhaps some day there will be a popular majority willing to reverse the current trend and impose higher taxes on the wealthiest Americans.

Spending Priorities

Which government programs are most important to poor people? To middle-class people? To rich people? People's priorities may indicate both their objective conditions and their belief systems. While people typically want lower taxes, they also want more government services. Which services they want—that is, how they want their tax money spent—may be a sign of their desire for more government benefits for themselves, or it may reflect a principled commitment to spending on other deserving people. Government spending

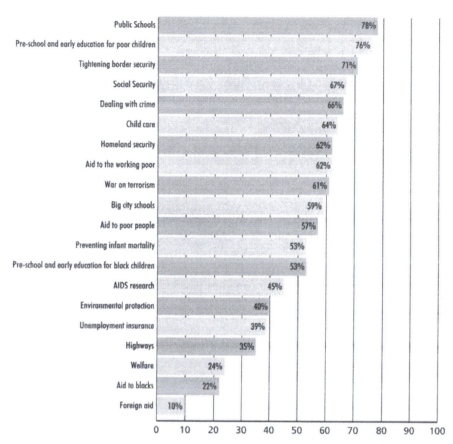

FIGURE 8.1. Federal Spending Priorities (Percent Wishing to Increase Spending).

Source: 2002 National Election Survey.

can be seen as a scorecard by which observers can tell who is winning and who is losing the political struggle; it has been described as the most sincere indication of the government's values. We continue the quotation from V. O. Key, Jr., that begins this chapter. Although he was writing about state governments, his point is valid for governments at all levels. Key continued his paragraph:

> In state politics the crucial issues tend to turn around taxation and expenditures. What level of public education and what levels of other public services shall be maintained? . . . [I]f there is a single grand issue it is that of public expenditure.[5]

NES respondents were asked in 2002 whether spending on each of twenty types of programs should be increased, decreased, or kept about the same. Figure 8.1 shows the percentage who said each type of program should have its spending increased. Education is prominently at the top of people's spending priorities. Over three-fourths favored spending more on public schools and on preschool and early education for poor children. This emphasis on education reinforces people's consistent belief that lack of education was the chief explanation for poor jobs and low incomes, as we saw earlier in Table 8.3.

Overall, we see clear evidence that Americans support government programs, including social welfare programs. Robert Y. Shapiro and John T. Young cited research on American public opinion and government social welfare programs; their findings showed "the American public has accepted and even expected an active government role as the last economic resort.[6] In addition to public schools and aid to early education for poor children, most respondents supported increasing spending on the following social welfare programs: Social Security, child care, aid to the working poor, aid to big city schools, aid to poor people, preventing infant mortality, and on preschool and early education for black children.

But if most Americans favor social welfare programs, they do not favor *welfare*. At the bottom of the figure, only 24 percent support increasing spending on welfare. The only less-popular programs are aid to blacks (22 percent) and foreign aid (10 percent). There is a vast literature on Americans' dislike of welfare and support for welfare programs. Americans are opposed to the concept of welfare, not actual programs that could be classified as welfare. Americans are most likely to support social welfare programs that involve helping vulnerable segments of the population, such as children, senior citizens, and even poor people, particularly the working poor—as long as they are not called welfare and are not classified as welfare programs.[7] Looking at studies on support for social welfare programs, Martin Gilens found:

> Education, health care, and benefits for the elderly receive nearly unanimous support among the U.S. public, as do programs that are seen as enhancing self-sufficiency. But support often turns to ambivalence or opposition when benefits are limited to the poor and provide direct cash or in-kind transfers. Programs such as Aid to Families with Dependent Children (AFDC), General Assistance, and Food Stamps, all of which offer assistance directly to poor families and individuals, are the least popular components of the U.S. welfare state.[8]

If we look at the thirteen popular programs that garnered majority support, we see that six of them involve children (and four of those concern educating children), and two include aid to poor people, while one includes aid to senior citizens (Social Security). Of the four other programs, three involve terrorism, and one is about dealing with crime.

In the next figure, which shows support of increased spending for the twenty programs for each of the three income groups, we can see very high support from all three income groups for two programs: public school and early education for poor children. About three-fourths of the respondents favored more spending on these two programs. After these programs, however, we see there is a general, though not universal, tendency for lower-income respondents to favor

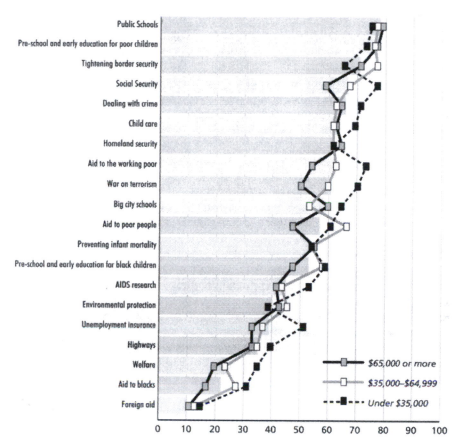

FIGURE 8.2. Federal Spending Priorities (Percent Wishing to Increase Spending by Income).

Source: 2002 National Election Survey.

more spending and higher-income ones to be less supportive. However, there is more similarity than difference. The wealthiest respondents hardly show overwhelming opposition to increased spending; for fifteen of the twenty programs; at least 40 percent of those with incomes of $65,000 or more support increasing spending. In addition, while lower-income respondents are more likely than the other two groups to support increased spending on welfare; only one-third of even that group are in favor of spending more money.

Issue Positions

Issue positions can be seen as the heart of public opinion. In many analyses, people's opinions are summarized by their opinions on the important issues of the day. In addition, many studies linking public opinion to public policy compare people's issue opinions with later government policies. Looking at the issues in Table 8.5, including a new category of environmental issues but not racial issues (which we save for Table 8.6), we see that overall there are moderate differences between Americans with different levels of income. The differences we do see are those we should expect. Lower-income people tend to be more liberal on economic issues, while higher-income respondents are more liberal on social issues. For example, on all three economic issues, those with lower incomes are somewhat more liberal. In the social issues, higher-income people are more liberal on four of the six issues: abortion, same-sex marriage, homosexuals adopting children, and a woman's place in society. But there was no consistent pattern on gun control, and those with higher incomes were less likely to oppose the death penalty. On foreign policy, the higher-income respondents were more likely to be interventionist rather than isolationist but were less likely to want to reduce defense spending. There were hardly any differences in the one environmental issue.

When we look at issues in the racial domain in Table 8.6, we separate white and black respondents, as we have done previously. There are clear and massive differences between respondents in the two races, but there are only moderate, or no, differences within each race. White respondents were overall very moderate, with about half giving liberal answers to questions. Among the African American respondents, overwhelming majorities gave liberal answers. The only exception concerned government aid to blacks, for which respondents in both racial groups were less likely to give the two most liberal answers of 1 or 2 on a 1 to 7 scale.

Social Class Summary

We have examined differences between people of three levels of income, but, by and large, we have not seen many large differences. True, there have been some variations in the answers, but they have typically been overshadowed by the similarities. Those with lower incomes are more likely to be Democrats, and those with higher incomes are more likely to be Republicans, but the differences are not large. Respondents in all three income levels tended to see income inequality in the same light. Even their views of taxes tended to be more similar than different.

In a sense, opposing economic interests seem to be a natural dividing line in democratic politics. As we have earlier noted, "Politics generally comes down, over the long run, to a conflict between those who have and those who have less."[9] The largest differences are about support for social welfare programs; except for educational programs, which everybody supports, lower-income Americans tend to support more programs than those with higher incomes do. Concerning most issues, lower-income respondents tended to be more liberal on economic issues and more conservative on social issues, but the differences

TABLE 8.5. Issue Positions: Liberal Positions by Income.

	Income			
Budget Item	Total Sample	Under $35,000	$35,000–$69,999	$70,000 or More
Economic or Social Welfare Issues				
The government should guarantee a job and good standard of living (1–2 on a 1–7 scale)	22%	29	22	13
The government should provide health insurance (1–2 on a 1–7 scale)	34	45	34	23
Pro-service on a "cut spending v. more services" scale (6–7 on a 1–7 scale)	28	38	28	18
Social Issues				
Abortion should always be obtainable	36	28	36	47
Allow homosexual couples to marry	33	31	31	38
Allow homosexual couples to adopt children	48	43	48	55
Men and women should have equal roles	75	74	71	79
Government should make it harder to buy a gun	57	61	51	58
Oppose death penalty	29	34	28	26
Foreign Policy Issues				
Reduce defense spending	9	14	10	7
Try to solve world's problems (not isolation)	79	70	80	88
Environmental Issue				
Pro-environment on an environment v. jobs scale (1–2 on a 1–7 scale)	26	25	28	25

Source: 2004 National Election Study.

TABLE 8.6. Racial Issue Positions: Liberal Positions by Income.

	Total Sample	Income		
		Under $35,000	$35,000–$64,999	$65,000 or more
Racial Issues (Whites Only)				
Government should aid blacks (1–2 on a 1–7 scale)	15	21	12	14
The U.S. should have affirmative action	48	51	46	51
Government should see to school integration	47	57	38	43
Government should see to it blacks get fair treatment in jobs	48	49	43	51
Racial Issues (Blacks Only)				
Government should aid blacks (1–2 on a 1–7 scale)	45	38	48	*
The U.S. should have affirmative action	83	82	91	*
Government should see to school integration	78	84	74	*
Government should see to it blacks get fair treatment in jobs	91	93	97	*

*Sample size < 30.

Source: 2000 National Election Study (We use racial issues from the 2000 National Election Study because the 2004 survey did not include the issues of school integration or generic affirmative action, which we consider important. We do use one racial issue from the 2004 survey, preference for blacks in hiring and promotion, at the end of this chapter.).

were not striking. On racial issues, there are massive differences between blacks and whites, but not many differences between income groups within each race.

Overall, we see definite class-based difference, but they are not especially large. The greatest differences are between black and white respondents. Where we have examined them, racial differences dwarf economic differences.

GENDER AND THE GENDER GAP

Gender as a fault line in American politics has existed since before the Nineteenth Amendment gave women the power to vote. Men and women have always had some differences in their interests and opinions. However, in the last twenty-five to thirty years those differences have seemed to grow and have been manifested clearly in the vote. This difference, which has been widely noticed since Ronald Reagan's election in 1980, is typically called the gender gap.

Voting and Party Identification

Figure 8.3, which displays the Republican percentage of the two-party presidential vote since 1948, plainly shows why the gender gap was first noticed in the Reagan administration. From 1948, when the National Election Study began, to 1976, men's and women's votes were about equally Republican. From 1948 through 1960, women voted slightly more Republican than men, and from 1964 through 1972, men voted a little more Republican than women. In 1976, 49 percent of both men and women voted Republican. But beginning in 1980, the year Ronald Reagan was first elected president, men have voted more Republican in each election, with the smallest gap (6 percent) in 1988 and the largest difference (14 percent) in 1996. In the 2004 election, George W. Bush received 54 percent of the men's two-party vote but only 47 percent of the women's vote.

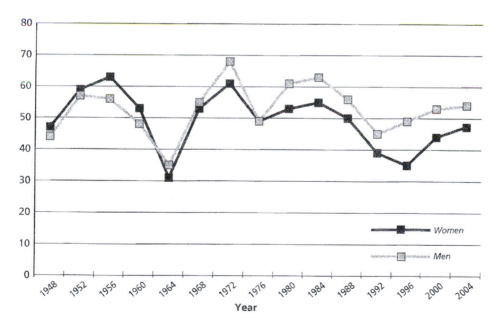

FIGURE 8.3. Republican Percent of Two-Party Vote, 1948–2004 (Percent).

Source: 1948–2004: National Election Survey.

Although the voting differences became apparent in the 1980s, data on the party identifications of men and women show the gender gap began to appear much earlier.

Figures 8.4A and 8.4B show that the gap between men's and women's partisan loyalties began in the 1960s. The figures also show that the gap was created principally because men began leaving the Democratic Party. As Karen M. Kaufmann and John R. Petrocik wrote:

> *The continuous growth in the gender gap is largely a product of the changing politics of men.* Men have become increasingly Republican in their party identification and voting behavior since the mid-sixties while the partisanship and voting behavior of women has remained essentially constant [emphasis in original].[10]

The data on the gender gap for voting and partisan identification are clear. The questions we need to address are why the gap developed and how opinion differences between men and women led to differences in their partisan loyalties and their voting. We will approach this question—as we did the question of social class in the previous section of this chapter—by look-

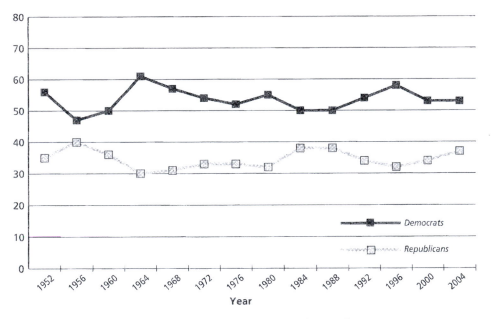

FIGURE 8.4A. Party Identification, 1952–2004: Women (Percent).

Party identifiers include "leaners," those respondents who originally said they were independents but, when asked, said they thought of themselves as "closer" to the Republican or Democratic Party.

Source: 1952–2004 National Election Study.

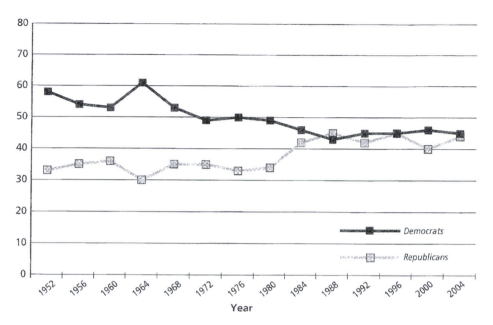

FIGURE 8.4B. Party Identification, 1952–2000, Men (Percent).

Party identifiers include "leaners," those respondents who originally said they were independents but, when asked, said they thought of themselves as "closer" to the Republican or Democratic Party.

Source: 1952–2004 National Election Study.

ing at men's and women's views of inequality, their spending priorities, and issue positions.

Gender Inequality

It is not a secret that men tend to have better jobs and higher incomes. Women's income compared to men's income is continually tracked. In 2003, for example, one organization calculated that women's median weekly earnings were 79 percent of men's.[11] Many analysts have pointed to gender discrimination in jobs. The term glass ceiling is still used to describe invisible limitations on women's career advancement.

In the 2002 NES respondents were asked for reasons that men have better jobs and higher incomes. Table 8.7 shows that both men and women place more emphasis on societal reasons rather than on personal reasons. The most often cited reason, in fact, is discrimination, and the least-often cited is men's alleged greater in-born ability to learn. The table also shows that men and women tend to give nearly identical answers; both men and women perceive the reasons in about the same ways.

TABLE 8.7. Reasons for Gender Inequality: Why Men Have Better Jobs and Higher Incomes (Percent Saying Each Reason is "Very Important" or "Somewhat Important").

	Gender		Difference
Issue	Women	Men	(W–M)
Personal Reasons			
Men have more in-born ability to learn*	19%	22%	−3
Women just don't work as hard	21	22	−1
Women just choose low-paying jobs	37	38	−1
God made people different from one another	38	30	8
Societal Reasons			
Women don't get a chance to get a good education	48	43	5
Discrimination holds women back	84	79	5
Government policies have helped men more	61	55	6

* Each reason was given to respondents in two ways. A randomly selected half the respondents were asked for the reasons that men have better jobs and higher incomes, while the other half were asked why women have worse jobs and lower incomes. There was not much difference between the two versions, and they are combined in this table.

Source: 2002 National Election Study.

Spending Priorities

Just as we looked at opinions on federal spending for different income groups, we will look at spending priorities for men and women. We can see from Table 8.8 that there is very little difference between men and women in terms of their priorities for the federal budget. Generally, about the same proportions of women and men want to see federal spending increased for each of the twenty budget items. There are only four programs on which women and men differ by ten percentage points or more, and there is no clear pattern in those differences. For example more women want to see spending increased for big city schools (64 percent versus 53 percent) but more men want to see spending increased for preschool and early education for black children (59 percent versus 49 percent).

Overall, in spite of the fact that many critics have pointed to serious disparities between the political and economic situations of men and women, there are not large or consistent differences between men and women in their opinions of gender inequality and their spending priorities.

TABLE 8.8. Federal Spending Priorities by Gender.

Budget Item		Gender		Diff. (W–M)
		Women	Men	
1	Public schools	80	76	4
2	Preschool and early education for poor children	73	78	−5
3	Tightening border security	71	71	0
4	Social Security	67	66	1
5	Dealing with crime	70	60	10
6	Child care	67	61	6
7	Homeland security	60	64	−4
8	Aid to the working poor	59	66	−7
9	War on terrorism	62	59	3
10	Big city schools	64	53	11
11	Aid to poor people	54	60	−6
12	Preventing infant mortality	53	53	0
13	Preschool and early education for black children	49	59	−10
14	AIDS research	43	48	−5
15	Environmental protection	40	39	1
16	Unemployment insurance	42	36	6
17	Highways	30	41	−11
18	Welfare	25	22	3
19	Aid to blacks	21	24	−3
20	Foreign aid	8	12	−4

Source: 2002 National Election Study.

The Gender Gap

Much of the literature on the gender gap centers on women's and men's opinion differences on a variety of kinds of issues. Because the term gender gap did not enter political language until the 1980 election, some have supposed that Reagan's conservative stand on issues important to women was a catalyst to the development of the gender gap. In the 1980 election, Ronald Reagan "ran a campaign dominated by his opposition to the Equal Rights Amendment and to abortion and his support of 'traditional family values,' which many interpreted as a return to traditional roles for women." Because of the temporal proximity of Reagan's appeal to traditional family values and the apparent emergence of the gender gap, one might think that the gender gap is centered around family issues or, from a different perspective, around feminist or women's issues. However, the gender gap is in fact not centered around family, feminist, or women's issues. The issues that most clearly differentiate men's

opinions from women's opinions have not been on the issues that affect the
two genders differently.[12]

Verba and colleagues summarized this phenomenon:

> There is no unanimity of opinion among women on policy issues—even those issues
> such as abortion or the Equal Rights Amendment that affect them differently.
> Instead, women's attitudes are divided along more or less the same lines as men's.
> Indeed, to the extent that there are opinion differences between the sexes, they tend
> to be more pronounced on issues like war and the use of violence than on what are
> often referred to as 'women's issues.'"[13]

In the 1980s, Robert Shapiro and Harpreet Mahajan[14] reviewed surveys
from the General Social Survey, Gallup, and other sources, and found consistent, although not always large, differences between women and men. Looking
at seven types of issues in Table 8.9, we see they found the largest average differences on issues of force; women oppose using force, both domestically and
internationally. The area of smallest difference is in the area of women's equality, where, ironically, men were more supportive of women's rights than
women were. The main reason for this apparent aberration is that men were
more likely than women to be pro-choice.

Morris Fiorina and his associates[15] compiled results of surveys conducted
in 1994, 1996, and 2000 and found clear differences between men and
women on issues of the government's role in society and force and violence
issues. Table 8.10 shows their data and demonstrates how clear the differences are. Men were more likely to say they were conservative and that the
government should provide fewer services. Women were more likely to favor
affirmative action for blacks and other minority groups. For all five items
involving force, men were more likely to choose the option involving force
than women were. Four of the five items have double-digit differences

TABLE 8.9. Differences Between Women and Men (Percent Women—Percent Men).

Issues	Difference*
Opposition to force—domestic	9.0
Opposition to force—foreign	6.2
Support for regulation and protection	5.8
Support for compassion	3.3
Support for traditional values	2.3
Support for women's equality, including abortion	−2.2
Other issues	4.6

* Differences are average differences in surveys conducted by the General Social Survey, Gallup polls, and other surveys.

Source: Robert Y. Shapiro and Harpreet Mahajan, 1986 "Gender Differences in Policy Preferences: A Summary of Trends from the 1960s to the 1980s," *Public Opinion Quarterly* 50: 42–61.

TABLE 8.10. Differences Between Women's and Men's Opinions.

	Gender		
	Women	Men	Diff. (W–M)
Role of Government			
Consider self conservative	29%	43%	−14
Government should provide fewer services	30	45	−15
Poverty and homelessness are among the country's most important problems	63	44	19
Favor affirmative action program for blacks and other minority groups	69	58	11
Force/Violence			
American bombers should attack all military targets in Iraq, including those in heavily populated areas	37	61	−24
Handguns should be illegal except for use by police and other authorized persons	48	28	20
Favor death penalty	76	82	−6
Approve of caning the teenager in Singapore who committed acts of vandalism	39	61	−22
Approve of the way the Justice Department took Elian Gonzalez from his Miami relatives	35	52	−17

Source: From *Culture War? The Myth of a Polarized America* by Fiorina Morris, p. 50. Copyright © 2005. Reprinted by permission of Pearson Education, Inc.

between women and men; the only difference in single digits was favoring the death penalty; both men and women favor it by large margins, but the men favor it just a little more.

The largest difference concerned bombing Iraq, years before the 2003 invasion. The next largest difference was about the caning of an eighteen-year-old American, Michael Fay, for vandalism in Singapore. Fay pled guilty to four counts of vandalism and retaining stolen property and was whipped four times with a rattan cane, a very painful punishment. Most American men approved of his caning, while most women did not.

Many other studies have been undertaken to identify and explain the differences in opinions between women and men.[16] These researchers have found that the largest gender differences were found on the following types of issues:

- *Policies concerning domestic force and violence:* Women tend to choose the less violent alternatives. They are more likely to support crime prevention measures such as gun control, and they are more likely than men to oppose harsh criminal penalties such as capital punishment (although most women do support capital punishment). They are less likely to support corporal punishment of children in school. Women are more likely to see violent behavior as seriously criminal and are less accepting of violence on television. They are less likely to choose force in response to public disturbances. However, women are more favorable to inflicting harsh penalties on rapists and domestic abusers. They are also more likely than men to favor life in prison for criminals convicted of selling drugs to children.

- *Policies concerning international military intervention:* Women are less likely than men to support involvement in foreign wars and are less accepting of wartime casualties. They are also less supportive of military spending.
- *Compassion issues:* Women tend to have greater sympathy for the disadvantaged and are usually more likely to favor aid to the poor, the unemployed, or others in need. Women typically are more likely than men to favor protecting the well-being of people in general. They are more likely than men to support rehabilitation for drug offenders. They are more likely to favor reducing poverty, rather than cracking down on criminals as a way to reduce crime.
- *Social welfare issues:* Women are more likely to support government intervention in the economy to provide jobs and a good standard of living, and to help those in financial need, as well as to reduce income differences. They are more likely to support government services in general, including support for social welfare programs, education, and health care.
- *Regulation and protection of people:* Women are more likely than men to support environmental and nuclear power regulations and consumer protection proposals. They are also more likely to favor low speed limits, laws against drunk drivers, and laws requiring seat belts.
- *Women's issues:* Women have not been more supportive of issues typically labeled women's issues. For example, men and women have tended to have similar views on the Equal Rights Amendment and abortion.

Many scholars have questioned why this gender gap arose. What is it about women and men that has led to different opinions on so many issues? Researchers have posed five possible explanations for the gender gap.[17] First, it may be that women are more compassionate. Either through heredity or socialization, women are more cooperative, caring, and nurturing, while men are more rule-bound and likely to emphasize justice over compassion.[18] Second, women may be more liberal on social welfare issues because they tend to have lower incomes and to be further down the socioeconomic scale than men. Liberalism then, for the women, is in their rational economic interests. A third possible explanation is that women are more likely to be in positions where they encounter government programs and to see the negative effects of cuts in funding. For example, they may be grade school teachers, social workers, or welfare case workers; they can see what happens to people who lose government support.

Fourth, the rise of the modern feminist movement has made women more aware of inequities in the system and has motivated them to favor policies to make public policy more supportive of women's interests.

The fifth reason is that because of changes in the society, some women have become more autonomous from men. Women with more education and higher-status occupations can form their opinions outside men's influence. At the same time, unmarried women, who may be in any social class, also live their lives separate from men's authority. Autonomous women have developed political opinions and voting patterns different from men's.[19]

Why did the gender gap arise when it did? Several variables may be responsible for the timing of the gender gap.[20] The rise of the women's movement and feminism in the 1960s and 1970s fostered women's independent political thought. At the same time, the rise in government programs gave many women jobs in the social service sector where they saw the results of the programs. Meanwhile, two contrasting economic trends developed in the 1970s. The first trend was economic stagnation for many Americans that began in the mid-1970s and was coupled with growing economic inequality—a trend that hit women harder than men. These women became poorer economically and supported more extensive government programs aimed at alleviating poverty. At the same time, other women experienced greater levels of education and social position, which led them to develop their own beliefs and political loyalties. Some of these women encountered new types of discrimination in their higher-level jobs (the glass ceiling). These women reacted by advocating greater government action to reduce antiwomen bias.

When Ronald Reagan ran for president in 1980 and promised more conservative social polities, especially opposition to abortion, and a rollback in social welfare programs, women reacted less positively than men. As we have already seen in this chapter, women did not "turn left" as much as men "turned right." Men were more moved by the Reagan message than women were.

Issue Positions

If we look at data from the 2004 National Election Study (Table 8.11), we see that the differences between men and women are not always dramatic, but they are clear. Overall, previous findings on the gender gap are supported. Women tend to have more liberal opinions than men. The largest differences concern women's greater support for gun control (20 percentage points more liberal than men) and allowing homosexuals to adopt children (10 points more liberal). Women were also 8 percentage points more likely to favor government spending over saving money and oppose the death penalty than men were. On two gender-specific issues, equal roles for men and women and abortion, women were only slightly more liberal. There were small and inconsistent differences between men and women on foreign policy and the environmental issue.

TABLE 8.11. Issue Positions: Liberal Positions by Gender.

Issue Position	Gender		
	Women	Men	Diff. (W–M)
Economic or social welfare issues			
The government should guarantee a job and good standard of living (1–2 on a 1–7 scale)	23%	20%	3%
The government should provide health insurance (1–2 on a 1–7 scale)	35	32	3
Pro-service on a "cut spending v. more services" scale (6–7 on a 1–7 scale)	32	24	8
Social Issues			
Abortion should always be obtainable	37	35	2
Allow homosexual couples to marry	34	32	2
Allow homosexual couples to adopt children	53	43	10
Men and women should have equal roles	77	72	5
Government should make it harder to buy a gun	66	46	20
Oppose death penalty	33	25	8
Foreign Policy Issues			
Reduce defense spending	10	8	2
Try to solve world's problems (not isolation)	78	81	–3
Environmental Issue			
Pro-environment on an environment v. jobs scale (1–2 on a 1–7 scale)	24	29	–5

Source: 2004 National Election Study.

As another way to inquire about abortion, an important gender-related issue, respondents to the 2002 General Social Survey were asked if abortion should be permitted under each of six conditions and then if a woman should be able to obtain an abortion "for any reason." Table 8.12 shows that there is very little difference between men and women in terms of allowing abortions. To the extent there is any difference, men are slightly more likely to permit abortions.

In the following Tables 8.13A and 8.13B, we examine racial issues and separate men and women by race. We see that any differences between white women and white men or between black women and black men are dwarfed by the differences between the races. While all the gender differences except one are in single digits, the differences between the races range from 26 to 45 percentage points.

There have always been differences in the political interests of men and women. Since the 1960s, and even more since the 1980s, we have seen consistent,

TABLE 8.12. Should it be possible for a woman to obtain a legal abortion if . . . (Percent "Yes").

	Total Sample	Gender Women	Men	Diff. (W–M)
The woman's own health is seriously endangered by the pregnancy?	89%	89%	89%	0
She became pregnant as a result of rape?	78	78	78	0
There is a strong chance of defect in the baby?	76	76	77	−1
She is married and does not want any more children?	43	42	45	−3
The family has a very low income and cannot afford any more children?	43	41	44	−3
She is not married and does not want to marry the man?	41	39	43	−4
The woman wants it for any reason?	42	40	43	−3
Sample Size	*923*	*427*	*496*	

Source: 2002 General Social Survey.

occasionally large, differences in their votes, partisan loyalties, and political opinions. The gender differences are important and are on the order of the differences in income, although for different issues. While Reagan's conservative stands have often been credited for being the catalyst to spark growing differences between men and women, these differences appeared before Reagan and have persisted since. The gender gap has appeared in all five presidential elections since Reagan.

What is the future of the gender gap? President Bush promised compassionate conservatism in his first run for the presidency; this seems that it would

TABLE 8.13A. Racial Issues by Gender.

Issue Position	White Women	Men	Black Women	Men
Government should see to it blacks get fair treatment in jobs	46%	50%	92%	89%
Government should see to school integration	51	42	76	80
The U.S. should have affirmative action	50	45	81	87
Government should aid blacks (1–2 on a 1–7 scale)	16	14	41	50

TABLE 8.13B. Differences Between Groups.

Issue Position	White Women and White Men (W–M)	Black Women and Black Men (W–M)	Black Women and White Women (B–W)	Black Men and White Men (B–W)
The government should see to it blacks get fair treatment in jobs	−4	3	46	39
The government should see to school integration	9	−4	25	38
The U.S. should have affirmative action	5	−6	31	42
Government should aid blacks (1–2 on a 1–7 scale)	2	−9	25	36

Source: 2000 National Election Study.

appeal to the women's compassionate inclinations. But in his second presidential campaign, Bush forged a coalition of voters in opposition to abortion and homosexuality (what he called family values) and in support of the war in Iraq—issue stands not at all aimed at the female side of the gender gap. Because of the president's convincing victory in 2004, there is no clear reason for him to change his stands. We shall see what effect Bush's policies have on the gender gap.

RACE AND RACIAL ISSUES

Ever since the first slaves were brought to what is now Florida in the 1570s and to Virginia in 1619, race has been an important issue in American politics. For hundreds of years, African Americans were not allowed to participate in politics, and any opinions they had barely mattered in the political arena. Slavery was followed by Jim Crow laws in the South and segregation in the North. As we have seen in the previous chapter, when survey research began in the 1930s, white Americans tended to believe in the innate inferiority of African Americans and supported segregationist laws. After the 1960s, support for segregation and discrimination diminished to the point that only a small minority of whites now support the Jim Crow system. But segregation remains in the United States, and there is a clear division in the beliefs of white and black Americans.

Table 8.14 shows the differences between white, black, and Latino Americans in terms of their party identification.

TABLE 8.14. Party Identification by Ethnic Group.

		Ethnic Group		
	Total Sample	White	Black	Latino
Party Identification				
Democrat	32%	25%	61%	42%
Independent	33	33	34	31
Republican	29	36	2	15
Other/None	7	7	4	13
Sample Size	*1,212*	*865*	*191*	*88*

Source: 2004 National Election Study.

We can see massive differences that we did not see when looking at different income groups and women and men. Whites are somewhat evenly distributed among the three party groupings, with more Republicans and independents than Democrats. Latinos are more Democratic than Republican, while African Americans are overwhelmingly Democratic. Almost two-thirds of black respondents in 2004 were Democrats, while only 2 percent were Republicans.

Racial Inequality

The disparities between black and white Americans in terms of income and wealth are quite substantial. Here, as we look at black and white perceptions, we will see great differences in perceptions of why the inequalities exist. Lee Sigelman and Susan Welch explored racial inequalities and analyzed the different explanations that black and white respondents use to explain the jobs/income gap.[21] Using polls from ABC News and the *Washington Post*, as well as the General Social Survey, they found that whites were more likely than blacks to blame inequality on blacks' personal shortcomings, which Sigelman and Welch called "dispositional" reasons. They also found that blacks were more likely than whites to blame the American racial system—what they called "situational" reasons. They concluded:

> Most blacks place the primary responsibility for racial inequality on whites or on shortcomings of American society, giving lesser credence to explanations that blame blacks themselves. By contrast, whites give shorter shrift to explanations that place the primary blame on whites or on American society in general."[22]

Using NES data from 2002, we see some of the same thing (see Table 8.15). When asked to explain why whites have better jobs and higher incomes (or why blacks have worse jobs and lower incomes), there is a clear difference between the dispositional and situational reasons. Looking at dispositional reasons first, we see that there are no large differences; whites and blacks tend to have similar answers. Neither whites nor blacks were likely to say that in-born ability, work habits, job choices, or divine order were reasons for racial economic inequality. In fact, for three of the four reasons, blacks were slightly more likely to say they were "very" or "somewhat" important.

But we see a different picture when it comes to situational reasons. Although blacks and whites tend to see lack of educational access about the same (about two-thirds cited that reason), we see very different views on discrimination and government policies. Majorities of both blacks and whites attribute economic inequality to discrimination, but a much larger percent of blacks (88 percent versus 64 percent) give that reason. In terms of government policies, blacks are nearly twice as likely to say that is a "very" or "somewhat" important reason (67 percent versus 36 percent).

Spending Priorities

We saw differences in the spending priorities of the three income groups and between women and men, but while some differences were large, most were

TABLE 8.15. Reasons for Racial Inequality: Why Whites Have Better Jobs and Higher Incomes (Percent Saying Each Reason Is "Very Important" or "Somewhat Important").

	Ethnic Group		Difference
Issue	Black	White	(B–W)
Personal, or "Dispositional" Reasons			
Whites have more in-born ability to learn*	20%	21	−1
Blacks just don't work as hard	35	33	2
Blacks just choose low-paying jobs	42	36	6
God made people different from one another	36	25	11
Societal, or "Situational" Reasons			
Blacks don't get a chance to get a good education	70	64	6
Discrimination holds blacks back	88	64	24
Government policies have helped whites more	67	36	31

* Note: Each reason was given to respondents in two ways. A randomly selected half of the respondents were asked for the reasons that whites have better jobs and higher incomes, while the other half were asked why blacks have worse jobs and lower incomes. There was not much difference between the two versions, and they are combined in this table.

Source: 2002 National Election Study.

only modest. But we see a completely different pattern when we look at race. Table 8.16 shows that there is a large gap between white and black opinions on government spending. The gap between white and black desire to increase spending is very high for programs benefiting blacks: 59 percent for "aid to blacks" and 48 percent for "preschool and early education for black children." It is also quite large for other social welfare programs that do not necessarily involve black recipients: "aid to poor people" (39 percent); "Social Security" (30 percent); and "big city schools" (33 percent). In fact, more blacks than whites want to increase spending for eighteen of the twenty programs—all but "tightening border security" and "war on terrorism." But even for these two programs, over half of black respondents want spending increased.

Table 8.16 also reminds us of Americans' dislike of welfare. Even among blacks, who overwhelmingly support increases in spending for aid to poor people (90 percent) and the working poor (80 percent), only 38 percent support increasing welfare spending.

TABLE 8.16. Federal Spending Priorities by Ethnicity.

		Ethnicity		
Budget Item		Black	White	Diff. (B–W)
1	Public schools	80%	77%	3
2	Preschool and early education for poor children	95	70	25
3	Tightening border security	66	73	–7
4	Social Security	92	62	30
5	Dealing with crime	73	63	10
6	Child care	82	60	22
7	Homeland security	70	63	7
8	Aid to the working poor	80	59	21
9	War on terrorism	51	60	–9
10	Big city schools	86	53	33
11	Aid to poor people	90	51	39
12	Preventing infant mortality	61	51	10
13	Preschool and early education for black children	96	48	48
14	AIDS research	71	42	29
15	Environmental protection	45	39	6
16	Unemployment insurance	55	35	20
17	Highways	43	31	12
18	Welfare	38	21	17
19	Aid to blacks	72	13	59
20	Foreign aid	23	8	15

Source: 2002 National Election Study.

Issue Positions

There is a great deal of literature on the large differences between opinions of black and white Americans, particularly on issues involving race or social welfare. Many observers have pointed out that the black-white opinion differences are larger than the differences between Americans with different levels of income. We have already seen very large and consistent differences earlier in this chapter between the perceptions and federal spending priorities of black and white Americans. Here, we will look at issue opinions, beginning with racial and social welfare issues.

Donald R. Kinder and Nicholas Winter said the "general pattern" of opinions on racial and social welfare issues has been characterized by "overwhelming majorities of black Americans supporting the liberal option; majorities of white Americans opposing it."[23] They wrote:

> Black and white Americans disagree consistently and often substantially in their views on national policy. This racial divide is most pronounced on policies that intrude conspicuously on the fortunes of blacks and whites, but it is also apparent on a wide array of social welfare issues where race is less obviously in play."[24]

They also wrote, "On these matters, opinion difference between blacks and whites add up to more than a gap or disagreement. They constitute a *divide*" (emphasis in original).[25]

In their analysis, they used respondents' answers from the 1992 National Election Study. In Table 8.17, we have used equivalent data from the 2000 and 2004 NES surveys, and we see that there are indeed consistent, large differences between black and white respondents on racial and social welfare issues. Kinder's and Winter's analysis holds even when we use data collected eight and twelve years later. On the racial issues, black respondents are at least 30 percentage points more likely to give the liberal answers. On social welfare issues, African American respondents are 12 percentage points more liberal on one issue and 23 percentage points more liberal on the other two issues.

Kinder and Winter did not claim there was a large racial gap for other types of issues, and we do not see one in 2004 when we look at social, foreign policy, and environmental issues in Table 8.18. On the social issues, sometimes blacks are more liberal on opposing the death penalty (54 percent versus 23 percent) and favoring gun control (69 percent versus 53 percent), but whites are more liberal on the other four issues. Likewise, there are small or inconsistent differences on foreign policy and environmental issues.

Affirmative Action

We have deferred discussion of the most controversial racial issue in order to discuss it more at length. That controversial issue is, of course, **affirmative action**. The term affirmative action in its present meaning has been around

TABLE 8.17. Opinions on Political Issues: Racial and Social Welfare Issues (Percent Liberal Answers by Ethnicity).

Issue	Ethnic Group		Difference (B–W)
	Black	White	
Racial Issues			
Government should see to it blacks get fair treatment in jobs	91%	48 %	43
Government should see to school desegregation	78	47	31
Government should aid blacks (1–2 on a 1–7 scale)	45	15	30
Social Welfare Issues			
The government should guarantee a job and good standard of living (1–2 on a 1–7 scale)	39	16	23
The government should provide health insurance (1–2 on a 1–7 scale)	42	30	12
Pro-service on a "cut spending v. more services" scale (6–7 on a 1–7 scale)	46	23	23

Source: 2000 National Election Study (racial issues); 2004 National Election Study (social welfare issues).

TABLE 8.18. Opinions on Political Issues: Social, Foreign Policy, and Environmental Issues (Percent Liberal Answers by Ethnicity).

Issue	Ethnic Group		Difference (B–W)
	Black	White	
Social Issues			
Abortion should always be obtainable	32	37	−5
Allow homosexual couples to marry	29	33	−4
Allow homosexual couples to adopt children	39	49	−10
Men and women should have equal roles	69	74	−5
Government should make it harder to buy a gun	69	53	16
Oppose death penalty	54	23	31
Foreign Policy Issues			
Reduce defense spending	15	8	7
Try to solve world's problems (not isolation)	72	81	−9
Environmental Issue			
Pro-environment on an environment v. jobs scale (1–2 on a 1–7 scale)	27	26	1

Source: 2004 National Election Study.

since the 1960s.[26] But what is affirmative action? Albert Mosley and Nicholas Capaldi have written a history of the issue for the past forty years that convincingly shows that affirmative action, properly understood in all its complexity, cannot be summarized briefly or simply. You may recall from Chapter 2 that Lee Sigelman and Susan Welch showed that support for affirmative action among both blacks and whites varied tremendously depending on the specific question asked. In Table 8.19 we have updated Sigelman's and Welch's table with the results of several questions on affirmative action asked since 2000. When answers for white, black, or Latino respondents are available, they are shown in the table. We have divided the table into four sections, and, like Sigelman and Welch, we see quite different results depending on how affirmative action is conceptualized.

The first part of the table shows that overall support for affirmative action in general ranges from 49 percent to 58 percent, with 65 percent (in the fourth question) wanting to increase affirmative action or keep it the same. In the second part of the table, support for affirmative action for college and law school admission declines to 39 percent, and support slips further to 27 percent when faced with the prospect of considering racial and ethnic background as well as merit. The third section in the table shows that about half the respondents, including 50 percent and 40 percent of the white respondents respectively, support requiring companies with histories of discriminating against blacks to have affirmative action with preferences for blacks.

But in the fourth section, survey respondents, especially whites, clearly oppose blacks getting preference in hiring and promotions because of generic past discrimination. Only one in ten white respondents supports preferences for blacks. In fact, only about half of the black respondents (58 percent, 49 percent, and 44 percent) support preferences simply "because of past discrimination."

Table 8.19 provides some clear lessons. First, black respondents are more favorable to affirmative action than white respondents are; Latino respondents

TABLE 8.19. Support for Affirmative Action: Alternative Conceptions (Percent).

| | Total | Ethnic Group | | |
Questions About Affirmative Action	Sample	White	Black	Latino
1. Abstract Affirmative Action				
"Do you generally favor or oppose affirmative action programs for racial minorities?"[1]				
● Favor	49	44	70	63
● Oppose	43	49	21	28

TABLE 8.19.—*Cont'd*

Questions About Affirmative Action	Total Sample	Ethnic Group		
		White	Black	Latino
"Do you generally favor or oppose affirmative action programs for women and minorities?"[7]				
● Favor	58	na	na	na
● Oppose	33	na	na	na
"Do you think affirmative action programs that provide advantages or preferences for blacks, Hispanics and other minorities in hiring, promoting and college admissions should be continued, or do you think these affirmative action programs should be abolished?"[5]				
● Should be continued	53	na	na	na
● Should be abolished	35	na	na	na
"In general, do you think we need to increase, keep the same, or decrease affirmative action programs in this country?"[2]				
● Increase	28	22	58	na
● Keep the same	37	40	26	na
● Decrease	26	28	8	na

2. Affirmative Action in College and Law School Admissions

	Total Sample	White	Black	Latino
"Do you approve or disapprove of affirmative action admissions programs at colleges and law schools that give racial preferences to minority applicants?"[6]				
● Approve	39	na	na	na
● Disapprove	54	na	na	na
"Which comes closer to your view about evaluating students for admission into a college or university—applicants should be admitted solely on the basis of merit, even if that results in few minority students being admitted, or an applicant's racial and ethnic background should be considered to help promote diversity on college campuses, even if that means admitting some minority students who otherwise would not be admitted?"[1]				
● Racial/ethnic background considered	27	22	49	36
● Solely on merit	69	75	44	59

3. Preferences for Blacks

	Total Sample	White	Black	Latino
"Some people think that if a company has a history of discriminating against blacks when making hiring decisions, then they should be required to have an affirmative action program that gives blacks preference in hiring. What do you think? Should companies that have discriminated against blacks have to have an affirmative action program?"[3]				
● Should have to have affirmative action	53	50	79	54
● Should not have to have affirmative action	40	42	18	40

Continued

TABLE 8.19.—Cont'd

Questions About Affirmative Action	Total Sample	Ethnic Group		
		White	Black	Latino

"Some people think that if a company has a history of discriminating against blacks when making hiring decisions, then they should be required to have an affirmative action program that gives blacks preference in hiring. What do you think? Should companies that have discriminated against blacks have to have an affirmative action program or should companies not have to have an affirmative action program?"[3]

• Should have to have affirmative action	48	40	83	67
• Should not have to have affirmative action	46	54	14	26

4. Affirmative Action to Remedy Past Discrimination

"Some people say that because of past discrimination, blacks should be given preference in hiring and promotion. Others say that such preference in hiring and promotion of blacks is wrong because it gives blacks advantages they haven't earned. What about your opinion—are you for or against preferential hiring and promotion of blacks?"[3]

• For preferential hiring and promotion	17	9	58	26
• Against preferential hiring and promotion	78	86	32	72

"Some people say that because of past discrimination, blacks should be given preference in hiring and promotion. Others say that such preference in hiring and promotion of blacks is wrong because it gives blacks advantages they haven't earned. What about your opinion—are you for or against preferential hiring and promotion of blacks?"[8]

• For preferential hiring and promotion	18	12	49	18
• Against preferential hiring and promotion	78	86	43	79

"Some people say that because of past discrimination, blacks should be given preference in hiring and promotion. Others say that such preference in hiring and promotion of blacks is wrong because it discriminates against whites. What about your opinion—are you for or against preferential hiring and promotion of blacks?"[4]

• Favor preferential hiring and promotion	16	10	44	21
• Oppose preferential hiring and promotion	84	90	56	79

na = Data not available
[1]Gallup, June 2003 (www.gallup.com).
[2]Gallup, December 2002–February 2003 (www.gallup.com).
[3]NES, 2000.
[4]GSS, 2002.
[5]Associated Press, February–March 2003 (www.pollingreport.com/ract.htm).
[6]Time/CNN Poll, January 2003 (www.pollingreport.com/ract.htm).
[7]CNN/Gallup/USA Today Poll, January 2000 (www.pollingreport.com/ract.htm).
[8]NES, 2004.

fall between blacks and whites. Second, white respondents are not uniformly opposed to affirmative action; about half the whites favor affirmative action in certain circumstances, such as "generally" favoring, wanting to increase it or keep it the same, and wanting to impose it on companies with histories of discrimination. But, third, white respondents are definitely opposed to racial considerations in place of merit in deciding school admissions and are opposed to preferences given simply because of generic discrimination. Finally, black respondents are not always in favor of affirmative action. Almost half (44 percent) oppose using racial criteria for school admissions, and 32 percent (or 43 percent or 56 percent, depending on the question) oppose preferences for generic past discrimination.

IS THERE A "PRINCIPLE-IMPLEMENTATION GAP" AMONG WHITES?

In looking at the data of white opinion on racial issues in this chapter and the previous one, we have seen some contradictory and puzzling trends in white opinions over the years. On one hand, we saw that white support for some antiblack measures has dropped dramatically. There is very little white support of preference for whites in hiring, laws prohibiting interracial marriage, racially restrictive housing laws, and segregated schools—or segregation itself. We have also seen evidence that white respondents do not attribute inferior characteristics to blacks; for example, in Table 8.15, where respondents identified reasons for blacks having worse jobs and lower salaries, whites were actually a little less likely than African American respondents to cite individual, personal failings.

On the other hand, we have also seen massive differences between whites and blacks on government programs that could reduce the black-white disparities. We have seen that many fewer whites want to increase spending on federal programs that could address economic inequalities. We have also seen less white support for governmental actions to deal with the effects of racism—such as ensuring equal employment opportunity, the government "seeing to" school desegregation, and making special efforts to help blacks. In addition, whites are much less supportive of social welfare programs that could help African Americans, such as programs to ensure jobs and good standards of living and government health insurance. And it is *only* on issues of race and social welfare that whites and blacks exhibit great differences; on social issues, foreign policy issues, and environmental issues, there are only small and inconsistent differences.

Many students of public opinion have looked at the gap between whites' acceptance of black equality and repudiation of Jim Crow attitudes, and their minimal, or at best lukewarm, support for governmental policies to address remaining inequalities and reduce them. The difference between this white philosophical acceptance of black equality, paired with resistance to programs that could effect black equality, is sometimes called the **principle-implementation gap**. There are many schools of thought concerning these gaps, but three are particularly important.[27] One school emphasizes the existence of a new or symbolic racism. This school holds that many white Americans still exhibit many racist attitudes that are evident in the way they answer survey questions. They may have abandoned the old-fashioned Jim Crow racism of legally segregated neighborhoods and schools, but they still have negative feelings for African Americans and feel they should not receive special favorable treatment from the government. People with such attitudes would not call themselves racists and have no desire to return to the old days of segregation and racial oppression. But they are likely to say that the problems of racism have been overcome and that racism is not a major problem in the United States today. They are also likely to claim that African Americans just need to work harder, and not make excessive demands on the political system and not try to get some unfair advantage through affirmative action.

According to this school, many whites perceive blacks as violating important social norms, such as the work ethic. These whites perceive most welfare money going to lazy blacks who could get good jobs if they really tried, but who, instead, have decided to sponge off hardworking Americans as they have more babies to qualify for more welfare.

These symbolic racist whites give the socially acceptable answers against segregation and blatant forms of racial discrimination, but they oppose programs to end segregation and discrimination. Whites who say they are not racists but believe the stereotypes of lazy blacks cheating the American taxpayers are more likely to oppose government programs to improve the conditions of African Americans.[28]

A second school of thought holds that many whites oppose affirmative action and other pro-black programs because they perceive those programs as threats to their own privileged positions—if African Americans receive more in government benefits, they, the whites, will receive less. Lawrence Bobo has summarized this position by explaining that "many whites will oppose affirmative action . . . because they perceive blacks as competitive threats for valued social resources, status, and privileges."[29] Political scientists arguing along these lines claim that accusations of racism miss the point of opposition to programs like affirmative action and mire political discussion in moralistic rhetoric. It would be more productive, they say, to approach racial issues from the point of view of opposing interests, the same way that most politics is approached.[30]

A third school of thought asserts that opposition to affirmative action does not necessarily come from any racial animus at all.[31] Political scientists who have this point of view say that there is nothing inconsistent about a large majority of whites favoring black and white children going to the same school while only one-fourth of whites say the government in Washington should see to it that black and white children go to the same schools. There is a difference between thinking a situation is a good one and believing that it is the government's business to make it happen. After all, it has been the position of conservatives for centuries to oppose governmental action in many spheres, not just in racial areas. Conservatives are *supposed to* oppose increasing the size and scope of government; that is what makes them conservatives.

Advocates of this school of thought also say that opposition to affirmative action may come from a desire to treat all races equally. While liberals may insist that affirmative action promotes equality and stops discrimination, conservatives may disagree. These political scientists say that there are several racial issues, not just one, so that it should not be surprising if some white people give liberal answers to some racial questions and conservative answers to others.

Proponents of this view do not say that racism has disappeared. Racism is still with us and is an important factor in American politics. But, they say, racism is not the only reason to oppose affirmative action and is not necessarily the cause of white resistance to government programs with racial components. Proponents of this view ask, if opposition to affirmative action implies racism, why do African Americans oppose it? In the last question of Table 8.19, 56 percent of black respondents opposed giving blacks preference in hiring and promotion.

We have seen in this chapter that differences in race divide the American people more clearly than differences in income or gender. In one sense, this is not surprising; we surely expected that race would be a major dividing line between respondents on racial issues. But we might take pause at the fact that race divides Americans on economic and social welfare spending priorities and issue opinions more than on income. After all, the modern party system, and the modern conceptions of liberal and conservative, come to us from the New Deal, which was based on divisions of income and social class. In addition, white prejudice as shown in survey responses has decreased dramatically in the last generation. Yet racial differences as shown by answers to issue questions has persisted. We will examine some theories about race and issue opinions in the next part of this chapter.

THE ISSUE DOMAINS TODAY AND THE AMERICAN PARTY SYSTEM

Many political scientists have investigated the link between public opinion and the American party system over the last twenty years or so. A **party system** is the arrangement of issues, public opinion, partisan alignments, and voting that characterize politics at any one time in history. Understanding the party system is vital to understanding the role of public opinion in the politics of the day. The party system is a very important factor in determining how public opinion is converted into public policy.

In its long history since the 1780s, the United States has experienced several party systems, each lasting several decades. Most of these party systems changed, usually rather suddenly, as a result of changing political conditions and political issues. The party systems, and their approximate dates of existence, were (1) the original system, 1788–1828; (2) the Jacksonian system, 1828–1860; (3) the Civil War and post-war system, 1860–1896; (4) the period of Republican dominance, 1896–1932; and (5) the New Deal system, 1932 to the present.

Typically, one or two issue domains have dominant roles in arranging public opinion and how the people and political leaders perceive political events. For example, in the first party system, the main issue domain was establishing the government. In the second party system, before the Civil War, the main issue domains were race and the extension of slavery. The party system defines the issues that are fought over and is very influential in determining who wins and who loses in the political system.

Our current party system began in the 1930s with the election of Franklin Roosevelt as president and the establishment of the New Deal. The New Deal alignment placed primary emphasis on economic and social welfare issues as the basis of the current party system. Most analysts would agree with the assessment of Edward G. Carmines and James A. Stimson about the importance of the New Deal and its primary focus:

> The New Deal, we all agree, is the basis of the current party alignment. . . . No single issue position portrays the New Deal realignment . . . [but] if one issue had to be chosen, it would be the fundamental disagreement over the proper role of government intrusions into the marketplace to provide jobs for those who wanted to work.[32]

The first four party systems lasted about thirty to forty years, but the New Deal system has hung on for over seventy years. Since it is clear to everybody that the system has changed since 1932, analysts are looking for the ways in which it has changed. The elections that had previously heralded the new party systems—such as 1860, 1896, and 1932—have been dubbed *critical elections*, and the sudden realignments have been called *critical realignments*.

The change of the current party system has been gradual, rather than cataclysmic; this sort of change is often called a *secular realignment*. Some have referred to the gradual change of issue opinions and the slow transformation of issue opinions as **issue evolution**. We will now examine some descriptions of how the current party system is changing, as well as explanations for those changes.

"Issue Evolution" and Racial Explanations

Some political scientists have looked at the gradually changing party system and have developed racial explanations, pointing to the link between race and social welfare programs, especially programs classified as welfare. They have asserted that racial issues and social welfare issues have become entangled, especially in the minds of white Americans. We have already seen that although the modern party system was developed on the axis of class and social welfare issues, opinions on social welfare issues are now better defined by Americans' race than by economic situations.

Carmines and Stimson have looked at Congressional elections and have shown that the party system was changed by the elections and actions of political elites in the 1950s and 1960s. Throughout the 1950s, the Republican Party was moderate on race, while the Democrats were divided between mostly liberal northerners and pro-segregation southerners. But changes in the late 1950s and 1960s caused a realignment of the parties based primarily on race. Beginning in 1958 and continuing into the 1960s, some liberal Republican senators were defeated by liberal Democratic challengers. During the civil rights movement of the early 1960s, the Democratic Party became more sympathetic to the cause of racial equality, while the Republican Party made serious efforts to appeal to white southerners. In 1964, Barry Goldwater, who had voted against the Civil Rights Act of 1964 in the Senate, ran on the Republican ticket and won southern states that had been off limits to most Republicans since the 1870s. In 1968, Richard Nixon ran with a law and order Southern Strategy, appealing to southern white voters. Nixon won every southern state in 1972, a feat that would have been unthinkable for any Republican during Franklin Roosevelt's lifetime.

As southern whites moved to the Republican Party, southern blacks, who began voting in large numbers after the Voting Rights Act of 1965 was passed, entered the Democratic Party. The party system experienced a sort of realignment in which race was mixed with economics as the defining cleavage. As Carmines and Stimson wrote:

> The American party system, in sum, was fundamentally transformed during the mid-1960s. The progressive racial tradition in the Republican party gave way to racial conservatism, and the Democratic party firmly embraced racial liberalism."[33]

Other political scientists have accepted this racial theme for changes in public opinion. For example, Paul M. Kellstedt examined people's opinions on welfare-state issues, or social welfare issues, and their opinions on racial issues from 1958 through 1996. He found that before the 1960s, there was very little correlation between the two sets of issues. But since the mid-1960s, the economic and racial issue domains have fused into one. He wrote:

> The evidence presented here points to the fact that racial policy preferences and welfare-state preferences were once unrelated at the aggregate level, but that within a short period of time their over-time dynamics became virtually indistinguishable, and have remained so ever since."[34]

Other analysts have found that there is a racial link between white Americans' support for social welfare programs and their opposition to welfare. (We saw this phenomenon in the tables on spending priorities earlier in this chapter.) Some of these analysts have concluded that there are two principal reasons that people oppose welfare. First, many white people see welfare as a "wasteful program that encourages sloth and sponging."[35] In addition, many oppose it because they see it as helping blacks and other minorities. In his book, *Why Americans Hate Welfare*, Martin Gilens concluded the following:

> First, the [white] American public thinks that most people who receive welfare are black, and second, the public thinks that blacks are less committed to the work ethic than are other Americans. . . . [W]hite Americans' attitudes toward welfare can only be understood in connection with their beliefs about blacks—especially their judgments about the causes of racial inequality and the extent to which blacks' problems stem from their own lack of effort. . . . [T]he centuries-old stereotype of blacks as lazy remains credible for large numbers of white Americans. . . . For most white Americans . . . race-based opposition to welfare stems from the specific perception that, as a group, African Americans are not committed to the work ethic. . . . Whites oppose welfare not because it primarily benefits blacks, but because they think it benefits blacks who prefer to live off the government rather than work.[36]

Some analysts have also found that many whites' opinions on welfare are influenced by their beliefs in stereotypes. Mark Peffley and colleagues looked at the 1991 Race and Politics Study, a survey conducted to study racial issues, and the 1992 National Election Study. They found that in the Race and Politics study, 31 percent of whites said blacks were lazy, and 60 percent agreed that "most black parents don't teach their children the self-discipline and skills it takes to get ahead in America." In the NES, 37 percent of whites said blacks were lazy (1–3 on a 7-point scale). Peffley and colleagues found that "Whites holding negative stereotypes [of African Americans] are substantially more likely to judge blacks more harshly than similarly described whites in the areas of welfare and crime policy. . . ."[37]

Other Sources of Gradual Realignment

Still other analysts have studied public opinion over the same time period and have found different processes in progress. For example, Greg D. Adams found opinions on abortion to be important in effecting change in the partisan alignment. He found that both political elites (members of Congress) and the mass public now more closely link their opinions on abortion and their partisan positions than previously. Using NES data from 1972 to 1992, he found that pro-choice people are more likely to be Democrats while pro-life people are more likely to be Republicans than was previously the case.[38]

James A. Stimson, writing after Adams's article, reviewed new data on issue evolution and agreed with Adams about the importance of abortion. He wrote:

With these data in hand, I concur with Adams that we are witnessing an issue evolution. That predicts a future in which *liberal* will come to mean *pro-choice*, *conservative* to mean *pro-life*, and vice versa (emphasis in original).[39]

Alan I. Abramowitz looked at reasons that whites had left the Democratic Party and found that opinions on social welfare and defense issues were more important than opinions on racial issues.[40]

Abramowitz and Kyle L. Saunders studied changes in people's support for the two major parties. According to them, ordinary Americans were linking their liberal or conservative ideologies more closely with their party loyalties than their parents had. Comparing respondents in 1978 and 1994, they found that liberals with Republican parents were more likely to be Democrats in 1994 than their counterparts had been in 1978. Likewise, conservatives raised by Democrats were more likely to be Republicans in 1994 than they had been in 1978. While Abramowitz and Saunders agreed with the idea of an "issue evolution," they disagreed with parts of Carmines's and Stimson's description of it. They attributed the change largely to President Reagan's "tax cuts, increased military spending, and reductions in domestic social programs [that] divide the nation along ideological lines."[41] They did not identify any one issue domain as a reason for more ideological thinking, writing instead "that civil rights was only one of a host of issues involved in the realignment."[42]

The Class Explanation

Other political scientists have found that the role of social class has actually not diminished. Some have found that racial and social issues have been important but not dominant. Clem Brooks and Jeff Manza divided the American population into six social classes based on occupation and found that from 1952 to 1992 two of the classes had become more Democratic (professionals and routine white collar workers), two had become more Republican (managers and self-employed people), and two had remained Democrats but not as strongly (skilled workers and unskilled workers). They concluded that:

> while class politics increasingly competes with other salient bases of voting behavior, the political impact of social issue attitudes has not displaced the class cleavage in recent presidential elections. . . . [T]he class cleavage has not (contrary to most scholars' expectations) been eroded by voters' attitudes toward social issues (including race), but is instead largely unrelated to these concerns.[43]

Jeffrey M. Stonecash looked at the transformation of partisan alignments since the 1950s and found evidence that social class divisions have not decreased in importance in the last fifty years and, in fact, have increased. His evidence showed that as economic inequality increased, the Democratic Party took "policy positions that are more responsive to minority needs and relatively less-affluent people" while the Republican Party took "conservative positions that are more responsive to the needs and concerns of the more affluent and business." He argued that "the combination of growing inequality and very different party responses to inequality has resulted in growing class political divisions in American politics."[44]

He also compared the South to the rest of the country. He said that politics in both sections of the country had become more class related. In the South, although both high-income and low-income whites had defected from the Democratic Party, those with low incomes were more likely to be Democrats. Outside the South, "Democratic support among low-income whites . . . has steadily increased. . . . [T]he result has been an increase in political divisions outside the South."[45] He concluded:

> The evidence appears clear: Class divisions have not declined in American politics. Instead, the trend is a steady increase in class differences in support for Democrats.[46]

CONCLUSION

So where are we? We have examined people's opinions classified by three variables—income, gender, and race. We have seen how each grouping of Americans sees the issue domains. We have also seen how they explain inequality and what their spending priorities are. We have explored how different political scientists see the issue domains today.

As we attempt to connect public opinion to public policy through voting and the political party system, we see some agreements among political analysts. They agree that important changes are occurring in the political dynamic that is changing the New Deal party system. They also agree that the economic or social welfare issue domain is being challenged by other issue domains as the defining cleavage in American politics. But they do not agree about what is happening. Carmines, Stimson, Kellstedt, and Gilens place special emphasis on the racial issue domain. Adams emphasizes abortion, and Stimson later agrees with him. Abramowitz and Saunders emphasize a variety of issues, Brooks and Manza write about both social issues and class, while Stonecash stresses class.

The New Deal system has not gone away and shows no sign of completely disappearing any time soon. If the social welfare issue domain is decreasing in importance to the American public—which is not necessarily the case— what is replacing it? Is "replacing" the correct word, or are other forces at work?

What difference does it all make, and how do all the parts of this chapter fit together? It makes a difference first in terms of the *democratic dialogue*. It matters not only what political attitudes and opinions the American people have, but also who has them. The greatest differences we see are between African Americans and whites. Since whites outnumber blacks nationally—in every state and most congressional districts—they have more ability to enact their opinions into law. If the political system is centered around racial divisions, the political decision makers may hear more racially oriented demands, and the whites may be more willing and likely to take advantage of their numerical superiority.

If, however, the political system is focused on social class, the middle and working classes may be able to use their numerical superiority to achieve class-related aspirations. This has been a dream of populist organizers for a long time. The differences in opinion between the three income groups we examined are not large, but small differences in taxing or spending can have important consequences.

But if the political system revolves around social issues, the fight might be between social conservatives of all classes against feminists, homosexuals, or other social groups.

This brings us to the *democratic dilemma*. Are some political alignments more conducive to improper use of governmental power to the detriment of those out of power? Do some arrangements of issues hurt the democratic process? For example, could a party system based on social issues prove detrimental to those with alternate lifestyles? Could a party system based on social issues distract lower-income Americans from their own economic interests and subject them to manipulation by their better-educated "allies"? Could a party system based on race prevent interracial class coalitions and allow the wealthy to change the tax system to their advantage?

The shape of political alignments will go a long way in determining whose opinions are heard and, ultimately, what public policies are enacted. But it is not the only thing that matters. Another important factor, in addition to who holds what opinions, is who voices those opinions to governmental decision makers. The political leaders cannot hear political opinions unless somebody says something. In the next chapter, we turn to political participation. To understand the relationship between public opinion and public policy, we must know more than who *thinks* what. We must know who *says* what.

Suggested Reading

Carmines, Edward G., and James A. Stimson. *Issue Evolution: Race and the Transformation of American Politics*. Princeton: Princeton University Press, 1989.

Gilens, Martin. *Why Americans Hate Welfare: Race, Media, and the Politics of Antipoverty Politics*. Chicago: University of Chicago Press, 1999.

Hurwitz, Jon, and Shannon Smithey. "Gender Differences on Crime and Punishment." *Political Research Quarterly* 51 (1998): 89–115.

Sears, David O., Jim Sidanius, and Lawrence Bobo, eds. *Racialized Politics: The Debate About Racism in America*. Chicago: University of Chicago Press, 2000.

Shapiro, Robert Y., and Harpreet Mahajan. "Gender Differences in Policy Preferences: A Summary of Trends From the 1960s to the 1980s." *Public Opinion Quarterly* 50 (1986): 42–61.

Stonecash, Jeffrey M. *Class and Party in American Politics*. Boulder, CO: Westview Press, 2000.

WWW ▶▶▶ Interactive Learning Exercise:

Analyzing Public Opinion

In this exercise, you will analyze data from the 2002 or the 2004 National Election Study. Four SPSS data sets are available to be downloaded from the *Public Opinion in the 21st Century* Web site. Each data set has been excerpted from either the 2002 NES or the 2004 NES. Each data set is completely labeled and is ready for use. Two of the data sets are small enough to be used on the SPSS Student Version.

Notes

1. V. O. Key, Jr., *Southern Politics in State and Nation* (New York: Alfred A. Knopf, 1949), p. 307.

2. A very useful discussion of the various ways to define social class, and their advantages and disadvantages, can be found in Jeffrey M. Stonecash, *Class and Party in American Politics* (Boulder, CO: Westview Press, 2000), pp. 147–150.

3. Martin Gilens, "'Race Coding' and White Opposition to Welfare," *American Political Science Review* 90 (1996): 595.

4. We borrowed this approach from Lee Sigelman and Susan Welch, *Black Americans' Views of Racial Inequality: The Dream Deferred* (Cambridge: Cambridge University Press, 1991), chapter 5.

5. Key, *Southern Politics*, p. 307.

6. Robert Y. Shapiro and John T. Young, "Public Opinion and the Welfare State: The United States in Comparative Perspective," *Political Science Quarterly* 104 (1989): 60.

7. See William G. Jacoby, "Public Attitudes toward Governmental Spending," *American Journal of Political Science* 38 (1994): 336–361.

8. Gilens, "'Race Coding,'" pp. 593–594.

9. Key, *Southern Politics*, p. 307.

10. Karen M. Kaufmann and John R. Petrocik, "The Changing Politics of American Men: Understanding the Sources of the Gender Gap," *American Journal of Political Science* 43 (1999): 865.

11. Institute for Women's Policy Research, http://www.iwpr.org/pdf/C350updated.pdf.

12. Lynne E. Ford, *Women and Politics: The Pursuit of Equality* (Boston: Houghton Mifflin, 2002), pp. 75–76.

13. Sidney Verba, Kay Lehman Schlozman, and Henry E. Brady, *Voice and Equality: Civic Voluntarism in American Politics* (Cambridge, MA: Harvard University Press, 1995), pp. 251–252. See also Kay Lehman Schlozman, Nancy Burns, Sidney Verba, and Jesse Donahue, "Gender and Citizen Participation: Is There a Different Voice," *American Journal of Political Science* 39 (1995): 270.

14. Robert Y. Shapiro and Harpreet Mahajan, "Gender Differences in Policy Preferences: A Summary of Trends From the 1960s to the 1980s," *Public Opinion Quarterly* 50 (1986): 42–61.

15. Morris P. Fiorina, with Samuel J. Abrams and Jeremy C. Pope, *Culture War? The Myth of a Polarized America* (New York: Pearson Longman, 2005), p. 50.

16. We have listed the aspects of the gender gap that have been found repeatedly and on which there is a consensus that they exist. Individual studies have found additional components of the gender gap. For reviews of this literature, see Shapiro and Mahajan, "Gender Differences"; Jon Hurwitz and Shannon Smithey, "Gender Differences on Crime and Punishment," *Political Research Quarterly* 51 (1998): 89–115; and Janet M. Box-Steffensmeier, Suzanna DeBoef, and Tse-min Lin, "The Dynamics of the Partisan Gender Gap," *The American Political Science Review* 98 (2004): 515–528.

17. For two reviews of this literature, see Susan E. Howell and Christine Day, "Complexities of the Gender Gap," *The Journal of Politics* 62 (2000): 858–874; and Kristi Andersen, "The Gender Gap and Experiences with the Welfare State," *PS: Political Science and Politics* 32 (1999): 17–19.

18. For an extended discussion of women as nurturing and men as rule-bound, see Carol Gilligan, *In a Different Voice: Psychological Theory and Women's Development* (Cambridge, MA: Harvard University Press, 1993).

19. For an explanation of the autonomy thesis, see Susan J. Carroll, "Women's Autonomy and the Gender Gap: 1980 and 1982," in Carol M. Mueller, ed., *The Politics of the Gender Gap: The Social Construction of Political Influence* (Newbury Park, CA: Sage, 1988).

20. For reviews of timing of the gender gap, see Susan E. Howell and Christine Day, "Complexities of the Gender Gap," *The Journal of Politics* 62 (2000): 858–874; and Elizabeth Adell Cook and Clyde Wilcox, "Feminism and the Gender Gap—A Second Look," *The Journal of Politics* 53 (1991): 1111–1122.

21. Lee Sigelman and Susan Welch, *Black Americans' Views of Racial Inequality: The Dream Deferred* (Cambridge: Cambridge University Press, 1991), chapter 5.

22. Ibid., p. 99.

23. Donald R. Kinder and Nicholas Winter, "Exploring the Racial Divide: Blacks, Whites, and Opinion on National Policy," *American Journal of Political Science,* 45 (2001): 440.

24. Ibid., p. 439.

25. Ibid., p. 440.

26. Albert G. Mosley and Nicholas Capaldi, *Affirmative Action* (New York: Rowman and Littlefield, 1996).

27. For a description and analysis of the schools of thought, see David O. Sears, Jim Sidanius, and Lawrence Bobo, eds., *Racialized Politics: The Debate About Racism*

in America (Chicago: University of Chicago Press, 2000), chapter 1. This volume is a collection of articles from a variety of viewpoints, including the three main schools of thought.

28. David O. Sears, Colette Van Laar, Mary Carrillo, and Rick Kosterman, "Is It Really Racism?: The Origins of White Americans' Opposition to Race-targeted Policies," *Public Opinion Quarterly* 61 (1997): 16–53.

29. Lawrence Bobo, "Race and Beliefs about Affirmative Action," in Sears, Sidanius, and Bobo, *Racialized Politics*, pp. 142–143.

30. Ibid., p. 164.

31. Paul M. Sniderman, Gretchen C. Crosby, and William G. Howell, "The Politics of Race," in Sears, Sidanius, and Bobo, *Racialized Politics*, pp. 236–279. See also Paul M. Sniderman and Thomas Piazza, *The Scar of Race* (Cambridge, MA: Belknap Press of Harvard University Press, 1993).

32. Edward G. Carmines and James A. Stimson, *Issue Evolution: Race and the Transformation of American Politics* (Princeton: Princeton University Press, 1989), pp. 145–146.

33. Ibid., p. 58.

34. Paul M. Kellstedt, *The Mass Media and the Dynamics of American Racial Attitudes* (Cambridge: Cambridge University Press, 2003), p. 127.

35. Tom W. Smith, "That Which We Call Welfare by Any Other Name Would Smell Sweeter: An Analysis of the Impact of Question Wording on Response Patterns," *The Public Opinion Quarterly* 51 (1987): 79.

36. Martin Gilens, *Why Americans Hate Welfare: Race, Media, and the Politics of Antipoverty Politics* (Chicago: University of Chicago Press, 1999), pp. 3–4.

37. Mark Peffley, John Hurwitz, and Paul M. Sniderman, *American Journal of Political Science* 41 (1997): 30.

38. Greg D. Adams, "Abortion: Evidence of an Issue Evolution," *American Journal of Political Science* 41 (1997): 718–737.

39. James A. Stimson, *Public Opinion in America: Moods, Cycles and Swings*, 2nd ed. (Boulder, CO: Westview Press, 1999), p. 91.

40. Alan I. Abramowitz, "Issue Evolution Reconsidered: Racial Attitudes and Partisanship in the U.S. Electorate," *American Journal of Political Science* 38 (1994): 1–24.

41. Alan I. Abramowitz and Kyle L. Saunders, "Ideological Realignment in the U.S. Electorate," *The Journal of Politics* 60 (1998): 636–637.

42. Ibid., p. 648.

43. Clem Brooks and Jeff Manza, "Class Politics and Political Change in the United States, 1952–1992," *Social Forces* 76 (1997): 379–381.

44. Jeffrey M. Stonecash, *Class and Party in American Politics* (Boulder, CO: Westview Press, 2000), p. 15.

45. Ibid., p. 112.

46. Ibid.

The People Speak: Expressing Public Opinion in Practice

9

Speaking Up: The People Tell the Government What They Think

The dumbest thing we can ever do is vote for all these guys, send them off, and never tell them again what we think.

—Pamela McLean[1]

Questions to Think About

In the last two chapters, we covered the history of public opinion and the state of public opinion in the United States today. In this chapter, we consider which, or more specifically, whose opinions get carried through to the governmental decision makers. After all, public opinion does not matter to anybody except political scientists unless it goes forward to public policymakers. Put a different way, public opinion is not worth studying unless it matters. But, as we point out in this chapter, not everybody's opinions advance to policymakers. As you read this chapter, think about these questions:

- What opinions are most likely to be voiced and have the opportunity to be heard by government policymakers? Whose opinions are most likely to enter the political arena, so that they can be noticed by policymakers?
- Why does it matter what opinions, and whose opinions, are advanced in the political system?

- Are your opinions carried forward? Do the government officials have a chance to hear your opinions? Why is that? What do you think about that?
- What implications does it have for democratic government if some people's opinions are voiced more frequently, or more effectively, than other people's opinions? Do you care?

SO FAR in this book, we have described how Americans have come to have the political opinions they do and what those opinions are. As we progress, we should keep in mind that a main focus of this book is to trace how opinions get translated into public policy. In this chapter we examine how people make their opinions known through participating in the political system.

Political participation is an important prerequisite of a democratic society. Political officeholders cannot read their constituents' minds. Of course, there are political polls, and they are very useful, which is why we have devoted so much space to them in this book. But while useful, they are not adequate. Political leaders cannot count on the proper polls being conducted among the proper constituents at the proper times.

Verba and colleagues explain the importance of political activity:

> [P]olitical participation matters because it constitutes the voice of the people; it provides citizens with a means of communicating information about their preferences to those who govern and generating pressure to comply.[2]

In the same book, they say that political participation is likely to influence public policy:

> Through political activity citizens have an opportunity to communicate their concerns and wishes to political leaders and to influence public outcomes. Those in public life are more likely to be aware of, and to pay attention to, the needs and preferences of those who are active.[3]

TYPES OF POLITICAL ENGAGEMENT AND PARTICIPATION

In order for political leaders to know what their constituents think, those constituents must let their leaders know. In this chapter, we examine four modes of political participation, using a classification scheme from *Participation in America: Political Democracy and Social Equality* by Sidney Verba and Norman H. Nie[4] (1972). We will use results from the 2004 American National Election Study (NES) in our examination of four types of participation.

- The first activity we will examine is *voting*. Voting is the only active political thing that a majority of people in the United States perform. Voting is the basic political action.
- Second, we will study *campaigning;* people can campaign in a number of ways, such as wearing campaign buttons, attending campaign rallies, or contributing money to a candidate or party.
- Third, we will look at *cooperative behavior,* including working with others in the community to achieve political goals. We include the "cooperative" act of protesting in this category.
- Fourth, we will examine the act of *contacting political officials.*

First, we will briefly examine Americans' levels of political participation. Most of this chapter is devoted to comparing varied amounts of activity by different subgroups in the population and the consequent **participatory distortion**—the term Verba and colleagues give to the phenomenon in which some kinds of people participate more and, presumably, are heard more by governmental decision makers. But first, in order to set a frame of reference, we will look at overall levels of participation. We will divide the four types of participation into two tables here for ease of explanation, but we will use just one table for subsequent parts of the chapter.

Voting and Campaigning

One of the most basic actions that people can take to influence the political system—to convert their opinions into governmental policies—is to vote. Respondents to the 2004 NES were asked after the election if they had voted. In Table 9.1, we can see that 73 percent of them said they had. An alert reader may find this number improbable, considering that the turnout rate for presidential elections has been in the neighborhood of 50–60 percent.[5] Yes, the number is too high; people either forgot whether they had voted, or they lied about it. Voting is the socially accepted thing to do, and many people say they voted when in fact they did not.

Most people voted, but only a few engaged in campaigning. Only about one-half even tried to influence the votes of other people. For the other campaigning activities, the proportions were much lower. One in five wore a button or displayed a sticker, and 7 percent went to political meetings or rallies.

Cooperative Activities and Contacting

Much political activity takes place at the local level. Local governments have great influence over the lives of ordinary people. They have the dominant voice in important issues like public education, police and fire protection, traffic laws,

Photo 9.1. Voting is probably the most direct and well-known form of opinion expression. Here, Dade County, Florida voters in 2004 use some of the first electronic voting machines. © Roberto Schmidt/Getty Images.

zoning, and road construction. Table 9.2 shows that about one-fourth of Americans participated locally by either attending a meeting about their communities or schools or by working with other people on community issues.

TABLE 9.1. Voting and Campaigning.

Voting Turnout in 2004	
Yes, voted	73%
No, did not vote	27
Sample Size	*528*
Political Participation—Campaigning	
Tried to influence vote of others	48%
Displayed button, sticker, etc.	21
Went to a meeting or rally	7
Did any other campaign work	3
Contributed to a candidate	9
Gave money to a party	9
Gave money to a group supporting or opposing a candidate	6

Source: 2004 National Election Study.

TABLE 9.2. Cooperative Activities and Contacting.

Cooperative Activities	
Attended community meeting in past year	27%
Worked on a community issue in last year	27
Took part in protest or march in last year	4
Contacting	
Contacted public official in past year	19%

Source: 2004 National Election Study.

Taking part in a protest is a sort of cooperative activity. It may address any level of government, from very specific local matters to national issues, to the World Trade Organization. Only 4 percent of NES respondents said they had participated in a protest or march in the previous year.

Many Americans participate in the political system by contacting public officials. This contact may be initiated for a variety of reasons, from locating a lost Social Security check to objecting to a new tax law. In 2004, 19 percent of the NES sample said they had contacted public officials in the past year.

POLITICAL ENGAGEMENT AND PARTICIPATION BY GROUPS

Officials in the government are more likely to notice and hear the opinions and needs of the people who communicate with them by participating in the political system. If participants were simply a subset of the entire population—and had the same opinions and needs as nonparticipants—governmental leaders would hear equally from all segments of the people, and policies would probably reflect the opinions and needs of everybody. However, people who participate are not like those who do not. They differ in important and predictable ways. Verba and colleagues pointed out that if some kinds of people participate more than others, those people are better represented in the government, and their needs are better reflected in governmental policies. They said that differential participation leads to "representational distortions."

> Because participants are not representative—in their policy preferences and, especially, their demographic characteristics and political needs—activists communicate, implicitly and explicitly, a distorted set of messages to public officials.[6]

In this section, we will look at Americans classified by education, race or ethnicity, and gender as a way to show who speaks most loudly to the government.

Education

Educational level is probably the most important variable for distinguishing people's levels of political participation. Education is closely linked to political participation for several reasons. One can see the effects of education most easily by looking at the college or university experience. First, students learn how to recognize, process, understand, and use information. Much of the information is abstract, just as much of political information is abstract. Although writing a term paper on Chaucer may not seem very relevant to political activity, writing the paper teaches a student to gather, interpret, and analyze information in a comprehensible way. Second, students become accustomed to working with others to solve problems or analyze data. Although some college courses may merely require students to memorize for tests, most courses include class discussions when students can explain and defend their points of view. Some courses even involve students working in groups on large or small projects, in which they learn to work cooperatively, an important skill in political activity.

Third, students learn to communicate effectively. Practically all colleges require students to write essays on a variety of topics; regardless of the topic, students get practice in communicating their ideas in writing. When students participate in discussions or make speeches or presentations, they also develop their ability to communicate orally.

Fourth, college students learn many politically relevant facts. Many students take introductory political science or American government courses in which they learn the basics of American politics. Although many students may forget many of the facts by the time they engage politically, they have learned the main outlines and frameworks of government. Fifth, students widen their horizons in college, since they are required to take national and global perspectives in their courses. This more expansive perspective helps them understand their own places in their immediate society as well as the rest of the world. Students learn that what happens in the political world affects their own lives. Sixth, college teaches students important democratic values, such as tolerance for opposing viewpoints or lifestyles. It also instills in many students a public ethic and a desire to participate in politics.

After formal education is complete, these advantages are likely to be reinforced and magnified in two ways—employment and political recruitment. First, college graduates are likely to hold jobs in which they analyze data or other information, thereby strengthening their analytical ability. They are very likely to get jobs in which they work with other people on group projects, thereby strengthening their social interaction ability. Within a few years, they are also likely to become supervisors or managers and use their problem-solving abilities. In their nonwork lives, they are more likely to join and be active in private organizations, where they practice the very skills that are effective in politics.

College graduates are also likely to get jobs that pay well and lead them to meet people who are politically important or powerful. They are also more likely than less-educated people to engage in discussion about politics and about their political interests. Consequently, they are more likely to recognize their political interests.

In short, educated people, when compared to uneducated people, are more likely to know what they want, how to get it, whom to talk to, what to say, and how to say it. Their advantages are reinforced by their greater wealth and their acquaintance with powerful people. As a result of the abilities they have developed and enhanced in their professional lives, and their social positions, those with more education are more likely to be steered in a political direction. Because they have high-level abilities and know influential people, they are much more likely to be recruited into action by political parties, candidates, interest groups, and other political activists.[7] Politicians, parties, and interest groups who **mobilize** individuals into political activity do so because they, the politicians and parties, gain something— to win an election, pass a bill, or another goal. As a result, they tend to recruit those who can be most useful to them, who are the best educated— with all the resources that education entails. In sum, education itself provides a tremendous advantage, which is enhanced by professional experience and magnified by recruitment.

Political scientists have remarked on the importance of education for many years. Philip Converse explained its importance over thirty years ago:

> There is probably no single variable in the survey repertoire that generates as substantial correlations in such variety of directions in political behavior material as level of formal education. . . . But the true domain of education as a predictor has to do with the large class of indicators of popular involvement and participation in politics. Whether one is dealing with cognitive matters such as level of factual information about politics or conceptual sophistication in its assessment; or such motivational matters as degree of attention paid to politics and emotional involvement in political affairs; or questions of actual behavior, such as engagements in any of a variety of political activities from party work to vote turnout itself: education is everywhere the universal solvent, and the relationship is always in the same direction.[8]

Because income and social standing are closely related to educational level, people with more education are likely to speak with more of an upper-class voice than other people are. Thus, in the cacophony of voices in the political world, the largest number are likely to be those of people who have the interests of the upper classes.

Steven J. Rosenstone and John Mark Hansen used data from the National Election Studies from 1952 through 1988 to calculate Participation Ratios and Indexes of Equality. Table 9.3 shows clearly that for voting and four types of electoral participation, those with lower levels of education participate at much lower rates than those with more education. The smallest differences are with voting, while the largest are with contributing money. Elected officials are much more indebted to the people with more education because they are more responsible for the officials winning their offices—and they are more likely to be influenced by their opinions.

TABLE 9.3. Inequality in Participation in Electoral Politics, 1952–1988.

Activity	Total Percentage Participating	Representation Ratios* Years of Education					Index of Equality
		0–8	9–11	12	13–15	16+	
Voted	66.1	.85	.83	1.00	1.12	1.26	.67
Influenced others	26.7	.61	.75	.94	1.33	1.61	.38
Contributed money	8.9	.33	.51	.87	1.37	2.41	.15
Attended meetings	7.8	.48	.50	.85	1.43	2.14	.24
Worked on campaign	4.6	.48	.50	.87	1.33	2.25	.23

*A "Representation Ratio" (RR) is the ratio of percentage of participants in an educational grouping to the grouping's percentage in the population; for example, if Group A makes up 10% of the participants in an activity but 20% of the population, that grouping's RR would be 10/20, or .50. The "Index of Equality" is the ratio of the lowest group's RR to the highest group's RR. For example, if the lowest educational grouping had an RR or .50 and the highest grouping had an RR of 2.00, the Index of Equality would be .50/2.00, or .25.

Source: Steven J. Rosenstone and John Mark Hansen, *Mobilization, Participation, and Democracy in America* (New York: Longman, 2003), p. 237. Copyright © 2003. Reprinted by permission of Pearson Education, Inc.

Looking at data from 2004 in Table 9.4, we see that 73 percent of the NES respondents said they had voted in the 2000 election. We know that this percentage is too high, but research has found that different kinds of people tend to exaggerate their voting in about the same proportions.[9] So while the percentages are too high, we can realistically compare the turnout rates of different subgroups. Those with more education voted more often than those with less education. There is a difference of 35 percentage points (89 versus 54) for those without high school degrees and those with advanced degrees.

People with more education do more campaigning. Compared to the least-educated, the most-educated were more likely to try to influence somebody else's vote or to attend political meetings or rallies (although there was not much difference in wearing political buttons or displaying political signs). When it came to giving money, the most educated are at least six times more likely.

About one-fourth of all the people attended community meetings or worked on community issues. As we have come to expect, more educated people were more likely to engage in both activities. Even if we look at protest marches, which one might think would be an important weapon that even the poor and uneducated could use, the most educated were six times as likely to participate as the least educated (7 percent versus 1 percent).

Although all types of Americans have reason to contact public officials, we might suppose that the least educated, who tend to be in the poorest financial shape and are most likely to receive needs-based government payments, would have the most reason to contact government representatives. However, contacting public officials shows the familiar pattern; people with graduate degrees

TABLE 9.4. Political Participation by Educational Level.

		Educational Level				
	Total Sample	Less than High School Education	High School Graduate	Some College or Associate's Degree	Bachelor's Degree (4 year degree)	Advanced Degree
Voting Turnout in 2004						
Voted	73%	54%	68%	74%	87%	89%
Campaigning						
Tried to influence vote of others	48%	38%	44%	51%	52%	59%
Displayed button, sticker, etc.	21	19	19	23	21	21
Went to a meeting or rally	7	5	2	9	9	16
Did any other campaign work	3	—	1	6	2	8
Contributed to a candidate	9	2	6	9	11	26
Gave money to a party	9	4	6	8	10	24
Gave money to a group supporting or opposing a candidate	6	2	3	5	6	22
Cooperative Activities						
Attended community meeting in past year	27%	22%	15%	27%	39%	51%
Worked on a community issue in last year	27	18	18	27	38	53
Took part in protest or march in last year	4	1	2	5	5	7
Contacting						
Contacted public official in past year	19	12	11	21	29	35

Source: 2004 National Election Study.

are almost three times more likely to contact officials than are those without high school degrees (35 percent versus 12 percent).

Gender

The different levels of political participation by men and women have been studied extensively since the 1970s. While not usually considered part of the gender

BOX 9.1

Increased Education Without Increased Participation

Over the past fifty years, the educational level of Americans has increased dramatically. At the same time, the prevalence of attitudes associated with increased education has increased. For example, as we saw in Chapter 7, opinions in the social issue domain have become more accepting of homosexuality and have increasingly supported women running for president and having equal roles with men. In the racial issue domain, whites have become more accepting of open housing, interracial marriages, and school integration.

Yet, during this time, political participation, which is also linked to higher education, has not increased. Whether we look at voting, campaigning, or other types of political participation, we see very little change over the past fifty years.

Looking at the following table, we see that in the 1948 National Election Study, none of the respondents had four-year college degrees, and in 1952, 6 percent did. But by the 2000 study, 24 percent did. The proportion of respondents with some college or more increased from 15 percent to 52 percent, while the percent without high school degrees decreased from 44 percent in 1948 to 4 percent in 2000.

In that same table, we see that in the 1948 and 1952 NES studies, 64 percent and 73 percent of the respondents reported voting. In the 1996 and 2000 NES studies, 73 percent reported voting each time. The proportion who wore political buttons or put political stickers on their cars, worked for parties or candidates, or attended political meetings, clearly did not increase from the 1950s to 2000.

Educational Levels and Political Participation, 1948–2000 (Percent).

	Year													
	48	52	56	60	64	68	72	76	80	84	88	92	96	00
Four-year college education	0	6	8	10	11	13	13	15	16	17	20	23	22	24
Some college or more	15	14	19	22	24	27	29	33	37	42	42	46	49	52
Less than high school diploma	44	41	31	30	25	23	20	17	12	11	10	8	5	4
Voting turnout	64	73	73	79	78	76	73	72	71	74	70	75	73	73
Wore button or sticker on car	–	–	16	21	16	15	14	8	7	9	9	11	10	10
Worked for party or candidate	–	3	3	6	5	6	5	4	4	4	3	3	2	3
Attended political meeting	–	7	7	8	9	9	9	6	8	8	7	8	5	5

Source: National Election Studies, 1948–2000.

Continued

BOX 9.1—*Cont'd*

The question is, if the educational levels of Americans have increased so dramatically and attitudes on social issues and racial issues have also changed, why haven't the participation levels also increased?

Norman Nie, Jane Junn, and Kenneth Stehlik-Barry addressed this issue in their 1996 book *Education and Democratic Citizenship in America.* They concluded that educational experience acts differently for two different dimensions of citizenship—political enlightenment and political engagement. For *political enlightenment,* education encourages "understanding and adherence to norms and principles of democracy."[1] Educated people understand democratic politics better and understand the rules of the game, such as the need for the First Amendment freedoms and the need to value, or at least tolerate, diversity in the society. That is why we see educated respondents with more tolerant opinions.

But, according to Nie and colleagues education works differently with political engagement. When it comes to *political engagement,* education enables "citizens to pursue and protect self-interest in politics."[2] Politics is a very competitive enterprise, and education gives people the intellectual tools to be successful in it. The more educated people are more successful in politics, and the less educated people are less successful.

By being competitive, political engagement works differently from political enlightenment. A person can become politically enlightened without making someone else less enlightened. There is plenty of enlightenment to go around. But because political engagement is competitive, a person cannot be more successful unless somebody else is less successful. There are not plenty of political rewards, such as tax breaks or government services, to go around; there is a finite quantity of payoffs that government can deliver. If a person gets a reward, somebody else does not get it. According to Nie and colleagues:

> Because there are always more demands from individuals than even the most responsive government can process, let alone satisfy, making oneself heard is a highly competitive business. Those at the periphery are much more likely to be discouraged from participation. For these citizens, the costs of figuring out the issues and who to petition are not only greater, but the probability of actually being heard is also much smaller.[3]

For political enlightenment, it is the *absolute amount* of education that matters; more educated people are, on the average, more enlightened. If more people become educated, more people become enlightened, but uneducated people are not affected. But for political engagement, it is the *relative amount* of education that matters. More educated people compete more successfully for the limited rewards that politics offers. If more people become educated, they compete more successfully, and uneducated people compete less successfully. According to Nie and colleagues, "formal education works as a sorting mechanism, assigning ranks on the basis of the citizen's *relative* educational attainment."[4]

Political enlightenment, then, increases over time as educational achievement increases over time because enlightenment is an individual noncompetitive characteristic. But political engagement does not increase because the most educated people will participate the most. As the absolute level of education goes up, the relative position of any one educational level goes down. If, for example, very few people have high school degrees, high school graduates will participate a great deal. But if a high school education is common and many people have college degrees, a high school graduate will not participate very much.

It does not matter whether the most educated have high school or college educations; whoever has the greatest resources will be the most successful and will participate the most. The less-educated, dispirited because they correctly recognize that they are less likely to succeed in the political system, do not try as often. Political participation in this sense works like the employment market. If you and other applicants are competing for a job requiring education and you have a high school degree while your competitors do not, you will probably get the job. But if you have a high school education and your competitors have college degrees, you will probably not get the job.

Following this logic, education can successfully elevate the level of political discourse, but it can never equalize the level of participation. Education cannot make society less hierarchical because education creates the hierarchy.

Notes

1. Norman H. Nie, Jane Junn, and Kenneth Stehlik-Barry, *Education and Democratic Citizenship in America* (Chicago: University of Chicago Press, 1996) p. 6.
2. Ibid., p. 5
3. Ibid., p. 63.
4. Ibid., p. 6.

gap because it does not involve people's opinions or votes, the fact that men consistently participate more in the political realm than women has prompted great concern and study. One of the most important studies on political participation by gender is *The Private Roots of Public Action: Gender, Equality, and Political Participation* by Nancy Burns, Kay Lehman Schlozman, and Sidney Verba. An important figure from that study is included here at Figure 9.1. It shows that for eight types of political participation (voting, working in a campaign, making a campaign contribution, working informally in the community, serving on a local governing board, contacting a governmental official, attending a protest, and affiliating with a political organization), men participated more often than women in seven of the eight activities (men and women were equally likely to attend a protest).

When we look at these eight political acts, we find that women, on the average, participated in 1.96 acts while men participated in 2.27. The difference is .31 political actions. While an average of less than one-third of a political act may not seem especially large, the study's authors point out that if one projects that small difference to the entire American polity, "the participatory deficit translates each year into

- 2,000,000 fewer phone calls or letters to public officials from women than men;
- 3,000,000 fewer women than men involved in informal efforts to solve community problems;

- 7,000,000 fewer campaign contributions from women than men; and
- 9,000,000 fewer women than men affiliated with a political organization."[10]

The reasons why men participated more were the same reasons that more-educated people participate more than less-educated people. That is, men tended to have more education, more money, to have developed more politically applicable skills in their jobs (especially organizational and communication skills), and to be recruited more often to political involvement. Burns and colleagues found that the factors that lead men to participation also lead women to action. When women and men had the same resources, they participated at the same levels.

However, Burns and colleagues found two factors that increased women's participation but did not increase participation by men. First, women who had been sexually harassed participated more than those who had not, while men who reported being sexually harassed did not participate at higher levels than men who had not. Second, and more important, women living in states where women ran as major party candidates for major state-wide campaigns (for governor, lieutenant governor, or senator), tended to be more active in politics than women who lived in other states.

As we examine our familiar table from the 2004 NES (Table 9.5), we see a different pattern. We see that men and women participated at about the same

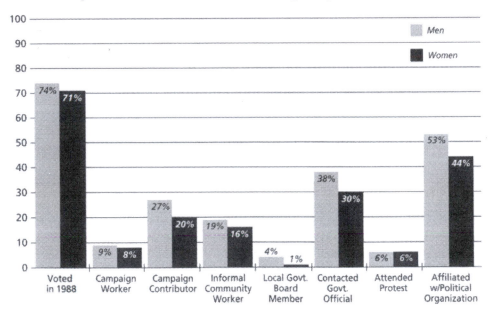

FIGURE 9.1. Political Activities by Gender.

Source: Reprinted by permission of the publisher from *The Private Roots of Public Action: Gender, Equality, and Political Participation* by Nancy E. Burns, Kay Lehman Schlozman, and Sidney Verba, p. 65 (Cambridge, MA: Harvard University Press). Copyright © 2001 by the President and Fellows of Harvard College.

TABLE 9.5. Political Participation by Gender.

| | Total Sample | Gender | |
		Male	Female
Voting Turnout in 2004			
Voted	73%	69%	76%
Political Participation—Campaigning			
Tried to influence vote of others	48%	50%	45%
Displayed button, sticker, etc.	21	22	19
Went to a meeting or rally	7	7	7
Did any other campaign work	3	3	3
Contributed to a candidate	9	8	9
Gave money to a party	9	9	9
Gave money to a group supporting or opposing a candidate	6	6	6
Cooperative Participation			
Attended community meeting in past year	27%	27%	26%
Worked on a community issue in last year	27	25	30
Took part in protest or march in last year	4	4	4
Contacting			
Contacted public official in past year	19	21	18

Source: 2004 National Election Study.

rates. Men were more active in some types of political participation, while women were more active in others. Whereas men were slightly more likely to try to influence others' votes and to display campaign buttons or stickers, women were more likely to vote. Wherever we look on Table 9.5, we see almost exactly the same levels of participation by both genders, and the differences favor men sometimes and women other times.

For advocates of gender equity, these findings about political participation are heartening. We shall see in future studies if they hold up.

Ethnic Groups

As we noted in the previous chapter, whites, blacks, and Latinos have very different opinions on many issues, particularly those related to economic and ethnic issues. Government officials are likely to hear different messages from members of these three groups. If members of one group were to participate more than members of another group, government officials would hear one

TABLE 9.6. Political Activities by Ethnicity.

Activity	White	Black	Latino All Latinos	Latino Citizens Only
Vote	73	65	41	52
Associated with a political organization	52	38	24	27
Contact public officials	37	24	14	17
Gave money to a political campaign	25	22	11	12
Worked informally in the community	17	19	12	14
Campaign activity	8	12	7	8
Protest	5	9	4	4
Board membership	4	2	4	5
Average number of activities	2.2	1.9	1.2	1.4

Source: Sidney Verba, Kay Lehman Schlozman, and Henry E. Brady, *Voice and Equality: Civic Voluntarism in American Politics* (Cambridge, MA: Harvard University Press, 1995), pp. 232–233.

side more than another; the message would be distorted. In fact, there are sizeable differences in participation levels among members of the three ethnic groups. Table 9.6 shows results from the Civic Participation Study, the same one used by Burns and colleagues.

We can see clear differences; whites and blacks participate at about the same levels, with whites exhibiting much higher levels for two types of participation, contacting public officials and affiliation with political organizations. While whites do, on the average, participate more than blacks, the participation rates of the two groups are quite close—within 4 percentage points—on five of the measures, and blacks are higher on three of them.

Both groups are more active than Latinos. Latinos who are American citizens are shown separately in the table because many Latinos living in the United States are not citizens, and noncitizens cannot vote. The table shows that, except for voting, Latino citizens participate at only slightly higher levels than all Latinos. But even the Latino citizens participate at much lower levels than white and black respondents.

We now turn to the same four types of participation we have been examining in this chapter. Table 9.7 shows that white and black respondents reported voting in 2004 in about the same proportions: 74 percent and 73 percent. Latinos reported voting at a lower level of 66 percent. Concerning campaigning activities, there are usually not large differences between members of the three ethnic groups. The largest difference is that white respondents were more likely than blacks or Latinos to contribute money to candidates, parties, or groups.

TABLE 9.7. Political Participation by Race and Ethnicity.

| | Total Sample | Ethnic Group | | |
		White	Black	Latino
Voting Turnout in 2004				
Voted	73%	74%	73%	66%
Political Participation—Campaigning				
Tried to influence vote of others	48%	51%	38%	41%
Displayed button, sticker, etc.	21	21	21	18
Went to a meeting or rally	7	7	4	9
Did any other campaign work	3	4	1	3
Contributed to a candidate	9	10	6	3
Gave money to a party	9	11	4	1
Gave money to a group supporting or opposing a candidate	6	7	1	1
Cooperative Activities				
Attended community meeting in past year	27%	25%	29%	36%
Worked on a community issue in last year	27	28	23	26
Took part in protest or march in last year	4	4	3	5
Contacting				
Contacted public official in past year	19	21	10	19

Source: 2004 National Election Study.

There were few large differences among the three ethnic groups in their cooperative activities and contacting political officials. The only sizeable differences were that Latinos were more likely to attend community meetings, and African Americans were slightly less likely to contact officials.

PARTICIPANTS' OPINIONS VERSUS NONPARTICIPANTS' OPINIONS

"So what?" you say. "What does this have to do with public opinion?" The whole point of this chapter, and the reason we have studied all these tables, is that we want to examine which opinions go further than the people holding them. What opinions are expressed so that governmental leaders have opportunities to notice them?

In this section of the chapter, we look at the opinions of those people who participate in politics and compare them to the opinions of those who do not participate. We use eleven of the issues we used in previous chapters: (1) the government guaranteeing everybody a job and standard of living; (2) national health insurance; (3) "more services" on a "cut spending v. more services" scale; (4) government helping blacks; (5) government seeing to it blacks get fair treatment in jobs; (6) abortion; (7) equal role for women; (8) the death penalty; (9) same-sex marriage; (10) level of defense spending; and (11) the environment. To make the tables easier to read, we display only the liberal opinion for each issue.

In the following tables, we compare the opinions of participants with those of nonparticipants. We use two types of participation:

- Voted in 2004: This is the only activity that most people perform.
- Contributed money to a candidate, party, or group supporting or opposing candidates: Only a few people engage in this activity.

Each table shows the opinions of those who participated in the first column of data, and it shows the opinions of those did not participate in the second column. The third column contains the difference between the two percents. For example, if 15 percent of the participants have Opinion X and 10 percent of the nonparticipants have Opinion X, the difference will be 5. A positive number means that participants are more likely to have that opinion; a negative number indicates that nonparticipants are more likely to have that opinion. Differences of +/– 10 or larger are **bolded**.

Table 9.8 shows the opinions of people who voted in the 2004 election and the opinions of those who did not vote. We can see that nonvoters tend to be more liberal than voters in all the social welfare and racial issues. The first line of data shows that 18 percent of the voters thought the government should guarantee a job and good standard of living for everybody (answered a 1 or a 2 on the 1 to 7 scale). We also see that 30 percent of the nonvoters shared that opinion. The difference between the two percents is 12 percentage points. We see the same pattern with national health insurance. Nonvoters are considerably more liberal than voters; nonvoters are 13 percentage points more likely than voters to give the most liberal answers of 1 or 2 on this question. The pattern repeats itself with "more services" on a "cut spending versus more services" scale; nonvoters are 12 percentage points more liberal. The message that candidates would derive from voters on social welfare issues would be more conservative than it would be from nonvoters, and from the public as a whole. Voter opinion is therefore more conservative than public opinion on social welfare issues.

On the racial issues, we see that nonvoters are also more liberal than voters, but the differences are not always as great. Voters are 4 percentage points less likely to say that the government should see to it that black and white children go to the same schools. Voters are less likely (–17) to favor the federal government seeing to it that blacks get fair treatment in their jobs.

But on the four social issues presented here, voters tend to be slightly more liberal. They are 6 percentage points more likely to say that a woman should

TABLE 9.8. Issue Opinions by Levels of Participation (Percent Liberal Responses).

Issue	Voted in 2004		
	Yes	No	Difference
Sample Size	*813*	*254*	
Government should guarantee job and good standard of living*	18%	30%	*-12*
Government should provide national health insurance*	30	43	*-13*
Pro-service on a "cut spending v. more services" scale (6–7 on a 1–7 scale)	25	37	*-12*
Government should help blacks*	13	17	−4
Government should see to it blacks get fair treatment in jobs	50	67	*-17*
A woman should always be able to obtain an abortion	37	31	6
Women should have equal role with men in running business, industry, and government*	74	74	0
Oppose death penalty	30	24	6
Allow homosexual couples to marry	33	35	−2
Decrease defense spending	9	10	−1
Pro-environment on an environment v. jobs scale*	27	23	4

* 1–2 on 1–7 scale

Source: 2004 National Election Study.

always be able to obtain an abortion, equally likely to say that women and men should have equal roles in society, and 6 percentage points more likely to oppose the death penalty. There are only tiny differences on same-sex marriages, defense spending, and the environment.

One might expect that people who gave money to political candidates, parties, or groups supporting or opposing candidates would be more conservative on economic issues. After all, they probably have more money, which is why they can afford to make political donations, and they would probably support policies that would help them keep their money. As Table 9.9 shows, if one thought that, one would be correct. We see large differences between the opinions of participants and nonparticipants here.

Donors are less likely to say that the government should guarantee jobs and good standards of livings (−10), to favor national health insurance (−14), and to favor more services over spending cuts (−8). The donors are also more conservative racially, although not by as much. They are slightly less likely to say the government should help blacks (−2) and see to it that blacks get fair treatment in their jobs (−7).

Donors are more likely to say a woman should always be able to obtain an abortion (+14). There are only small, or no, differences between donors and nondonors on the remaining social issues, defense spending, or the environment.

TABLE 9.9. Issue Opinions by Levels of Participation (Percent Liberal Responses).

Issue	Contributed Money to Campaign in 2004		
	Yes	No	Difference
Sample Size	*165*	*898*	
Government should guarantee job and good standard of living*	12	22	−10
Government should provide national health insurance*	21	35	−14
Pro-service on a "cut spending v. more services" scale (6–7 on a 1–7 scale)	21	29	−8
Government should help blacks*	12	14	−2
Government should see to it blacks get fair treatment in jobs	48	55	−7
A woman should always be able to obtain an abortion	48	34	**14**
Women should have equal role with men in running business, industry, and government*	74	74	0
Oppose death penalty	26	29	−3
Allow homosexual couples to marry	35	33	2
Decrease defense spending	10	9	1
Pro-environment on an environment v. jobs scale*	27	26	1

* 1–2 on 1–7 scale.

Source: 2004 National Election Study.

What does all this mean? It means that although participants are neither uniformly more liberal nor more conservative than nonparticipants, they are different in reasonably predictable ways. When elected officials listen to voters and donors, they tend to hear a message that is more conservative on social welfare and racial issues, especially social welfare issues. They also tend to hear a message that is more liberal on social issues, especially abortion. Is this good or bad? If one is an economic conservative, a racial conservative, or a social liberal, it is good. But if one is an economic liberal, a racial liberal, or a social conservative, it is not good.

CONCLUSION

The public has opinions. According to classical democratic theory, those opinions should influence the government and its public policies. But governmental leaders cannot take opinions into account if they do not know what those opinions are. Polls are one way that political leaders learn about public opinion, but they are not enough. Politicians need other ways to listen to the people, but they can listen only if somebody else speaks. To speak, somebody needs to do something. As we have seen, that somebody tends to be much better educated than other people. Other studies have shown that men were more likely to participate than women, although we saw equivalent levels of participation in the 2004 NES data. We also saw basically the same levels of participation for whites, blacks, and Latinos, although we did see that whites are much more likely to give money to candidates, parties, and political groups.

What we saw most clearly in the 2004 data is that those people who participate in the political system by voting or contributing money are much more conservative on social welfare issues and somewhat more conservative on racial issues. On the other hand, participants are more liberal on social issues; this difference is most evident on abortion where voters are 6 percentage points more likely than nonvoters—and financial contributors are 14 percentage points more likely—to say a woman should always be able to obtain an abortion.

From the perspective of the *democratic dialogue*, the dialogue itself takes place between the government and an unrepresentative set of citizens. It is a dialogue, but it is not quite democratic. In the words of Verba and colleagues, the dialogue is characterized by "participatory distortion" because the groups of activists are "unrepresentative of the public with respect to some politically relevant characteristic."[11] We have seen that activists are unrepresentative both demographically and attitudinally, although not necessarily in a simple way. Government officials are likely to hear more conservative voices on social welfare and racial issues, but a more liberal voice on social issues.

This brings us to the *democratic dilemma*. Although we have no evidence in this chapter about the relationship between public opinion and public policy, it seems reasonable to hypothesize that unrepresentative dialogue will lead to unrepresentative policy. At least the participants think so. After all, why would they bother if they did not think it would help them? With that in mind, we will close this chapter with a quotation from a particularly famous financial contributor and convicted felon, Charles Keating. When he was asked if his contributions to five U.S. senators had led to favorable banking regulations, Keating answered, "I certainly hope so."[12]

Suggested Reading

Burns, Nancy, Kay Lehman Schlozman, and Sidney Verba. *The Private Roots of Public Action: Gender, Equality, and Political Participation.* Cambridge, MA: Harvard University Press, 2001.

Hill, Kim Quaile, and Jan E. Leighley. "The Policy Consequences of Class Bias in State Elections." *American Journal of Political Science* 36 (1992): 351–365.

Hill, Kim Quaile, Jan E. Leighley, and Angela Hinton-Andersson. "Lower-Class Mobilization and Policy Linkage in the U.S. States." *American Journal of Political Science* 39 (1995): 75–86.

Hughes, John E., and M. Margaret Conway. "Public Opinion and Political Participation." In Barbara Norrander and Clyde Wilcox, eds. *Understanding Public Opinion*. Washington, DC: CQ Press, 1997.

Nie, Norman H., Jane Junn, and Kenneth Stehlik-Barry. *Education and Democratic Citizenship in America*. Chicago: University of Chicago Press, 1996.

Rosenstone, Steven J., and John Mark Hansen. *Mobilization, Participation, and Democracy in America*. New York: Longman, 2003.

Verba, Sidney, Kay Lehman Schlozman, and Henry E. Brady. *Voice and Equality: Civic Voluntarism in American Politics*. Cambridge, MA: Harvard University Press, 1995.

WWW ▶▶▶ Interactive Learning Exercise:

Political Socialization and Political Participation

One of the principal organizing themes of the book is examining how public opinion gets translated into public policy. For people's opinions to influence governmental policies, the people must make those opinions known through political participation. This exercise is designed to acquaint you with the main forces of political socialization as they relate to political participation. The exercise looks like a self-administered quantitative questionnaire, but we have used it as a device to start you thinking about the political forces in your life that have led you to participate, or not participate, politically. After completing the questionnaire, you can discuss your answers in small groups and then in the class as a whole.

Notes

1. Pamela McLean is a fictitious name given to a real participant, in Jennifer Hochschild, *What's Fair: American Beliefs About Distributive Justice* (Cambridge, MA: Harvard University Press, 1981), p. 158.

2. Sidney Verba, Kay Lehman Schlozman, and Henry E. Brady, *Voice and Equality: Civic Voluntarism in American Politics* (Cambridge, MA: Harvard University Press, 1995), p. 275.

3. Ibid., p. 163.

4. Sidney Verba and Norman H. Nie, *Participation in America: Political Democracy and Social Equality* (New York: Harper & Row, 1972).

5. The Center for Voting and Democracy calculated that approximately 60% of the eligible voters voted in the 2004 presidential election (see http://www.fairvote.org/turnout/general). The 2004 NES asked the voting question in two ways. The two versions yielded two answers: 80% and 73%. We are using the lower number because it is more realistic.

6. Verba et al., *Voice and Equality*, p. 464.

7. Rosenstone, Steven J., and John Mark Hansen, *Mobilization, Participation, and Democracy in America* (New York: Longman, 2003), chapter 6.

8. Philip E. Converse, "Change in the American Electorate," in Angus Campbell and Philip E. Converse, eds., *The Human Meaning of Social Change* (New York: Russell Sage Foundation, 1972), p. 324, cited in Norman H. Nie, Jane Junn, and Kenneth Stehlik-Barry, *Education and Democratic Citizenship in America* (Chicago: The University of Chicago Press, 1996), p. 3.

9. Warren E. Miller and J. Merrill Shanks, *The New American Voter* (Cambridge, MA: Harvard University Press, 1996).

10. Verba et al., *Voice and Equality*, pp. 1–2.

11. Ibid., p. 15.

12. This quotation is available from many places. We obtained this one from http://www.anecdotage.com/index.php?aid=1774.

The Government Listens: Taking the Pulse of the People

I never paid any attention to polls myself because in my judgment they did not represent a true cross section of American opinion. . . . A man who is influenced by the polls or is afraid to make a decision which may make him unpopular is not a man to represent the welfare of the country.

Harry S Truman[1]

Questions to Think About

In the last chapter, we discussed how people communicate their opinions to the government and to governmental officials. In this chapter, we discuss how those officials try to learn about public opinion. We will look at polling and focus groups. The main irony in this chapter is that people want their leaders to listen to them, but they also want their leaders to use their judgment and to do the right thing, even if it contradicts public opinion. Officials say they listen to the people. They also frequently conduct polls and focus groups, but they claim to pay no attention to those sources of information when they make their decisions. In fact, politicians can become quite indignant when denying that they listen to the polls. As you read this chapter, think about these questions:

- Should elected leaders listen to the polls and focus groups when deciding on public policy? If "yes," how much weight should they place on poll data and focus group results, especially in comparison to their own convictions and the wishes of their constituents as expressed through other means, such as letters and interest group lobbying? If "no," whom should they listen to?

- Since political officials claim they do not listen to the polls and focus groups when developing policy, why do they conduct them?
- What is the proper role for information from polls and focus groups in a democratic political system?

IN THE previous chapter, we discussed how the public conveys its interests and opinions to people in the government. In that chapter, the public was the active party while the government was the recipient of the people's communications. In this chapter, we will change the focus 180 degrees; here, we will discuss government officials and political candidates asking the people what they think.

In this chapter, we will look principally at politicians as they specifically seek to learn public opinion, usually through political polls or focus groups. We are not saying that public opinion research is the *only* or even the *main* way that politicians attempt to learn how people think. Recall that in Chapter 3 we included several informal methods for learning about public opinion, including voting analysis, interest group lobbying, the media, and feedback from constituents. However, polls and focus groups are important ways to ascertain the public mind, and politicians use them regularly.

THE HISTORY OF POLLING

The most important formal research method that politicians use today to learn about public opinion is the telephone sample survey—also known as polling. Modern surveys based on scientifically drawn samples became available to politicians in the 1930s. In this section, we will trace the history of polling, from the prescientific measurements conducted 200 years ago to modern presidential polling.

Straw Polls

Before modern scientific polling came into use in the 1930s, politicians sampled public opinion. They used a methodology we call **straw polling**.[2] The main difference between modern polling and straw polling is the nature of the sample of people who are questioned. In a scientific survey, the people to be questioned are selected randomly. But in a straw poll, the people to be questioned are chosen mainly because they are easy to find. Even with straw polls involving very large numbers of respondents, the samples do not reflect the larger population—and conclusions drawn from straw polls cannot be legitimately generalized to the larger population. But they have been used, nevertheless, for almost 200 years and are still used today.

Tom W. Smith has traced straw polls back to at least 1824. In order to predict the likely winner of the presidential election, politicians surveyed potential voters where they could be easily found—generally in large groups. For example, straw polls were conducted at regular public meetings that were held for other purposes, such as militia musters and grand juries. Militia musters were good opportunities to get white men aged twenty-one to forty-five together, the majority of the eligible electorate at that time.

Straw polls were also conducted at meetings specifically called to determine popular opinion. Sometimes, these were very similar to partisan political rallies. A straw poll taken at a rally organized by supporters of Andrew Jackson, for example, might find that a clear majority of those surveyed planned to vote for General Jackson. Not surprisingly, other candidates often claimed—correctly—that these straw polls were biased. Another way of conducting straw polls was to leave poll books in public places, such as taverns, for men to write down their preferences. Finally, some straw polls were conducted during elections for other offices; as long as the voters were assembled to vote, they were asked for their preferences for offices not on the ballot, such as the presidency. Men were also straw polled in a variety of other settings. Sometimes newspapers picked up the straw poll results and reported them.[3]

Subsequent presidents used straw polls to help them gauge public opinion. President Herbert Hoover, the last president to serve before modern polls based on sampling theory became available, used very large straw polls. In 1932, The Houser Associates, a research firm, conducted approximately 5,000 face-to-face interviews for the Hoover campaign.[4] Probably the most famous straw poll was the *Literary Digest* poll in 1936, which predicted that Alfred Landon would defeat Franklin Roosevelt. (This is the poll that was used as the perfect bad example in Chapter 2.)

Presidential straw polls are still taken at party meetings, sometimes a year or more before elections, to guess who the nominee will be. Today, members of Congress routinely mail questionnaires for their constituents to mail back. Members of Congress, if they are wise, do not expect the responses to these surveys to accurately reflect their constituents' opinions. Only a tiny proportion of constituents return these questionnaires, and those who do are definitely not randomly selected. In addition, many of these surveys ask questions in a very biased manner, practically commanding the respondents how to answer. But even these unrepresentative and biased answers may serve a purpose, by indicating problems or the existence of some constituents with strong feelings on certain issues. At the very least, these straw polls do give some constituents the opportunity to tell their representatives what they think. Some give constituents opportunities to contribute money to the survey sponsor's reelection effort, and the questionnaires include handy contribution forms.

TABLE 10.1. Example of an Internet Straw Poll: Howard Dean Ahead in Democratic Presidential Race.

Candidate	Number of Votes	Percent of Votes
Howard Dean	139,360	44%
Dennis Kucinich	76,000	24
John Kerry	49,973	16
John Edwards	10,146	3
Dick Gephardt	7,755	2
Bob Graham	7,113	2
Carol Moseley Braun	7,021	2
Joe Lieberman	6,095	2
Al Sharpton	1,677	1
Other	6,121	2
Undecided	6,378	2
TOTAL	317,639	100%

Source: Example of an Internet Straw Poll from moveonpac.org website.

Today, of course, many straw polls involve the Internet. In one of the first important Internet straw polls, Howard Dean rose to prominence among Democratic presidential candidates when he won an Internet straw poll on June 24 and 25, 2003, conducted by MoveOn.org, a liberal group. The straw poll results are shown in Table 10.1.

One can see the problems with straw polls from the results of this one. MoveOn.org is a liberal organization, and people who responded to its poll were very likely also liberal—not at all a representative sample of voters in Democratic primaries. Howard Dean, of course, did not fare well in the 2004 Democratic primaries and caucuses, winning only one state—his own Vermont. Dennis Kucinich survived well into the primary season but did not win any primaries or caucuses, or even come close. Third-place John Kerry eventually won the nomination. (In fairness, however, even a perfectly run scientific poll would be unlikely to accurately predict the winner six months before the primary season begins.)

The Promise of Polling

Modern scientific polling was developed during the 1920s and became available to politicians in the 1930s. George Gallup promoted his polling method in the 1936 presidential election by predicting that his poll would be more accurate than the *Literary Digest*'s poll. Of course it was, and scientific sample polling replaced straw polls as the preferred method of reading public opinion in elections.

Gallup and others made impressive claims and projected great possibilities for polling. One of the greatest advantages of polling is that it would be more accurate and unbiased than information from interest groups that politicians would get otherwise. In the first issue of *Public Opinion Quarterly*, pollster Archibald Crossley said polling gave lawmakers a choice of "reliable information" instead of "unreliable information supplied by pressure groups."[5]

In a 1940 book, Gallup and Saul Forbes Rae wrote that public opinion research was a "necessary and valuable aid to truly representative government." They said that

> representatives will be better able to represent if they have an accurate measure of the wishes, aspirations, and needs of different groups within the general public, rather than the distorted picture sent them by telegram enthusiasts and overzealous pressure groups who claim to speak for all the people, but actually speak only for themselves."[6]

Presidential Polling: Roosevelt to Bush

A wide variety of politicians use polling, including most members of Congress running in competitive races, many governors, and many other candidates running for other offices. According to Kenneth F. Warren, a pollster himself, most candidates for minor offices, such as city council or state representative, do not have enough money for polls, but "virtually all candidates for major offices spend a lot of money on polls."[7] But the most sophisticated polling that is conducted for politicians—and the subject of most political science research about politician polling—is conducted for presidents and presidential candidates.

Franklin Roosevelt was the first president to use polling, and every president since, except Harry Truman, has used it. Roosevelt used polls conducted by Hadley Cantril as well as straw polls conducted by Emil Hurja. Polling under FDR was quite informal by today's standards, with the president seeing polls "from time to time."[8]

In the beginning of presidential polling, the surveys tended to be rather inexpensive because polling operations were not formally and regularly conducted; in addition, questions were often added, or piggybacked, on other polls that somebody else was paying for (frequently without the knowledge of the survey's sponsor). Polling by Roosevelt and virtually all presidential polling since has been paid for privately, often by the president's national party. From the beginning, tax money has seldom been used.

After Roosevelt's death in 1945, polling fell into disfavor in the White House. Harry Truman did not like and did not use polls, and Dwight D Eisenhower made only minimal use of them. John F. Kennedy used polls successfully in his election to the presidency in 1960 and continued to use them after his election. President Lyndon Johnson also used polls, frequently carrying the results with

Photo 10.1. Pollsters have become influential presidential advisers. Here, President Gerald Ford meets with Republican pollster Robert Teeter in the Oval Office, while a young Dick Cheney (then White House Chief of Staff) looks on. Courtesy Gerald R. Ford Library.

him and quoting them when they served his needs. Johnson's polling operation was more intensive than any had been before. But, by today's standards, it was informal and limited. Richard Nixon expanded and improved the use of White House polling. According to Lawrence R. Jacobs and Robert Y. Shapiro, "the surveys conducted for Nixon were qualitatively superior to those available to his predecessors."[9]

The Ford White House expanded the use of focus groups, measuring the reactions of different population segments to speeches, campaign ads, and policy proposals, as well as helping Ford prepare for debates with Jimmy Carter. Focus group members were given dials to turn; as they watched a debate they would turn the dials in positive or negative directions, depending on their reactions to Ford's or Carter's comments. In addition, focus groups were used to help prepare questions for traditional polls.[10]

The quality of presidential polling declined in the Carter administration. Whereas the Nixon and Ford administrations had used teams of pollsters and sophisticated analysts, Carter used only one pollster, Patrick Caddell. Critics have later claimed that Carter's reliance on Caddell was naïve and disastrous, because Caddell conflated his own opinions and survey results and gave Carter poor advice.[11]

In Ronald Reagan's administration, the quality of polling returned to a higher level. Diane Heith noted, "As with the Nixon administration, the Reagan White House staffers possessed sophisticated knowledge of public opinion analysis."[12] Heith summarized the state of presidential polling in the Reagan and George H. W. Bush administrations:

> By the time of the Bush administration, the Republicans were quite skilled and accustomed to incorporating public opinion into the White House structure. Public opinion usage was habitual and expert. . . . Republican pollsters were skilled in working with both the sophisticated and the untrained user of poll data.[13]

The Clinton White House conducted regular polling (enough to be ridiculed for it) and increased the use of focus groups.[14] Clinton received data from his own pollsters and poll analysis from them and from consultants outside the White House. According to Heith, the high level of data analysis showed that "poll analysis skills were not the sole purview of the Republican Party." According to Heith, "The Clinton White House staffers were awash in public opinion data."[15]

President George W. Bush has used polls extensively, although not as much as President Clinton did. *The Washington Monthly* magazine used public records and their own research to estimate that the Bush administration had spent up to about $1 million in the first year in office. While that is a sizeable sum, it is only about half of what the Clinton administration had spent in its first year.[16]

USES OF POLITICAL POLLING AND FOCUS GROUPS

Presidents and other politicians have used political polls and focus groups for a variety of purposes. In this section, we explore ways that politicians use public opinion research—in campaigning, in marketing themselves and their programs, and in seeking guidance for policymaking.

Campaigning

Politicians need to get elected before they can do anything else. Polls and focus groups are used extensively to help them win, first, the primaries, and then the general election. The applicability of polls to electoral campaigns is clear. Kenneth F. Warren wrote:

> Polls provide valuable information to candidates and their staffs that helps the campaign organization decide practically anything from whether a potential candidate should actually get into the race to what attack ads to run against an opponent to whether the candidate should drop out of the election contest.[17]

Polls can tell a candidate which issue stands are popular and which are not. They can reveal which geographic areas are safe, which are hopeless, and which can be swayed. They can show which arguments will be convincing to the voters and which will not. This information can be translated into how the candidate should spend limited funds for television or newspaper ads, what the ads should say, and where the candidate should travel. For example, if polls show that a state is out of reach for a candidate, that candidate can save resources and campaign somewhere else. If the polls show that a certain argument is not working, a different argument can be used, or the issue can be ignored altogether. Polling data can also be used to find whether possible problems actually do exist.

You may recall that in the 2004 presidential election, pre-election polls showed that some states were safe for President Bush (such as Texas, most of the South, and most states between Iowa and Nevada), and some were safe for Senator Kerry (such as New York, Illinois, and California). Each candidate spent the bulk of his resources and time in the states that were competitive—the so-called battleground states. It was an odd election where the three states with the most electoral votes (California, 55; Texas, 34; and New York, 31) were virtually ignored, while smaller states (like Wisconsin, 10; Iowa, 7; New Mexico 5) were pursued vigorously. The candidates chose which states to campaign in through poll results. (Of course, states that were both large and competitive, such as Florida [27], Pennsylvania [21], and Ohio [20], received particularly intense campaigning.)

Focus groups are also used extensively by candidates. Warren wrote that focus groups allow the candidates to get past the superficial answers of quantitative polls and really see what is on voters' minds. He said that "candidates who favor the use of focus groups believe that such groups can be used to provide more insights into the classic 'Yes, but . . .' response."[18] An example will show how candidates use focus group results to guide their campaign messages. In the 1988 presidential campaign, George H. W. Bush's organization conducted several focus groups in New Jersey to explore vulnerabilities in Michael Dukakis, the Democratic candidate, who was then the governor of Massachusetts. One potential issue they examined was the case of Willie Horton. Horton was a black convict in Massachusetts who had been temporarily released from prison on a furlough program. He escaped and later raped a white woman. The Bush focus group researchers found that if they brought up the subject of Horton in a focus group and explained that Dukakis, as governor, was responsible for lax incarceration policies in Massachusetts and therefore responsible for Horton's crime, that several focus group members who had planned to vote for Dukakis changed their votes to Bush. Candidate Bush then attacked Dukakis as being responsible for Horton's crime and made Horton one of his main campaign themes. The Willie Horton ad campaign is now famous for its success and, critics assert, for its appeal to racist white prejudice.[19]

Measuring Popularity and Success

After winning office, one common way presidents use polls and focus groups is to rate their own popularity, asking how much the public approves of them,

---

BOX 10.1

Passing the Test

Several years ago, one of the authors of this book worked as a marketing research analyst, or pollster, for the *Chicago Tribune*. In one poll conducted by your author during a primary election campaign, the totals for a candidate in a statewide race were very low. The *Tribune's* managing editor realized that information has power; he thought that if the *Tribune* printed the results, the candidate would drop out of the race. In order to assure himself that the poll results were credible, the managing editor called Robert Teeter, the Republican pollster who had worked in the Ford and Reagan administrations, and read the questions to him over the telephone. He knew that Teeter would be able to say if the survey methodology and questions were good. Teeter said everything was proper and that the editor could print the results. The *Tribune* printed the story the next day, and the candidate dropped out of the race.

Your intrepid author did not learn of this telephone call until several months later—and from reporters, not the managing editor. He was somewhat disappointed that the managing editor had checked up on him, but mostly he was glad that he had passed the test.

---

their activities, and their policies. Much popularity polling is already done by Gallup, as well as by several media polls. Presidents use this information, but they typically want more specific measures of popularity and success than media sources are likely to provide. Diane Heith listed several ways that presidents have used polls to assess their popularity and success.[20] First, they use polls and focus groups simply to determine how popular they are overall and how popular their programs are. Second, they can measure the success of their public relations campaigns—for example, after a series of presidential speeches or advertisements, did support for a presidential proposal increase, decrease, or stay about the same? Third, they measure public reactions to events, both expected and unexpected. How did the public react to the latest presidential trip to Europe or Asia? What did people think about the State of the Union address? What was the popular reaction to the president's actions surrounding a recent crisis? Finally, they use polls and focus groups to try to ascertain why their ratings have improved or declined. They attempt to find the most popular aspects of their programs and the areas that need to be altered or abandoned.

Presidents can also use polls and focus groups to find out about the popularity of their opponents and their opponents' proposals. They can try to ascertain what caused their opponents' ratings to increase or decline.

Some officeholders, including presidents, use polls to identify segments of the population friendly—and not friendly—to them. President Ronald Reagan's pollsters used their polls to classify Americans into three groups, based on their support of the president. The three groups are described in Table 10.2.

TABLE 10.2. Level of Support for President Ronald Reagan.

	Level of Support	
Strong	**Mixed**	**Low**
35–54 years old	55–64 years old, 25–34 years old	65+ years old and nonaffluent, 24 years old and under
College educated	Post-graduates, high school graduates	Less than high school graduates
$20,000+ income earners	$10,000–$20,000 income earners	Less than $10,000 income earners
Nonunion workers, professionals, managers, owners, farmers, and white-collar (clerical and sales) workers	Blue-collar workers	Union members
White, Anglo-Saxon Protestants (Teutonic and Scandinavian)	Some ethnics; Hispanics and Anglo Catholics	Ethnics; southern and eastern Europeans, Jews, non-Anglo Catholics, blacks Women*

* Men do not appear in this table. We can only assume that if women showed "low" levels of support, men must have shown "strong" levels. After all, Ronald Reagan was a very popular president.

Source: From *Polling to Govern* by Diane Heith, Stanford University Press, p. 65. From *Presidential Power* by Shapiro et al. Copyright © 2000. Reprinted by permission of Columbia University Press.

Politicians also use polls to identify groups based on attitudes that might provide potential support for them. President Nixon, for example, was very successful in identifying middle-class voters as the Silent Majority.[21]

Marketing the President and His Programs

Presidents and other politicians also use information from public opinion research to help them explain policies that they favor, so that the people will favor those policies as well. In fact, insight into marketing, or selling, a program is probably the most important noncampaign use of polls and focus groups. As in campaigning, public opinion research is used to influence opinion when the successful candidate is in office. Dick Morris, one of President Clinton's most important political advisors, said:

> We used polling not to determine what positions he would take but to figure out which of the positions he had already taken were the most popular. I would always draw the distinction between deciding on policy and identifying certain issues for emphasis.[22]

Heith studied four cases involving four different presidents trying to sell their programs to the American people. The presidents were Carter (his energy policy), Reagan (his economic recovery proposal), Bush (his plan to encourage planting trees), and Clinton (how to balance the federal budget). She found that in the first three cases, the presidents were unwilling to change their policies—they just wanted to market them better. Heith wrote, "All of them defined victory in terms of passage of their legislative agenda, and refused to compromise with the public in the face of waning coalition support simply to produce victory." Only Clinton actually used public opinion data to affect his actions. In a showdown between him and House Speaker Newt Gingrich, in which the federal government was officially shut down, Clinton monitored the polls to see how the public reacting to the conflict. He saw that he was coming across as the good guy and Gingrich as the bad guy. According to one of his top advisors, Clinton agreed to a deal with the Republicans when the polls began to show that the public was growing impatient with the stalemate.[23]

Jacobs and Shapiro studied two important sales campaigns in the 1990s—President Clinton's effort to sell health care reform in 1993 and 1994, and Gingrich's effort to sell his Republican Contract With America in 1994 and 1995.[24] Jacobs and Shapiro found that neither Clinton nor Gingrich was willing to adjust their policies to win more popular support. Both engaged in a strategy Jacobs and Shapiro call "crafted talk." Jacobs and Shapiro said that with crafted talk politicians adjust "how they present their policy stances in order to attract favorable press coverage and 'win' public support for what they desire."[25] In other words, instead of adjusting their positions to suit public opinion, politicians attempt to adjust public opinion to favor their positions. Both Clinton and Gingrich were unsuccessful in their efforts; health care reform was not passed, and Gingrich's coalition centered around his Contract With America quickly fell apart.

Jacobs and Shapiro showed that both Clinton and Gingrich overestimated the effectiveness of their campaigns to sell their programs. Jacobs and Shapiro also pointed out that Gingrich and the Republicans made the serious methodological error of treating focus group results as if they were from random samples and could be projected to the larger American public:

> In place of polls, political activists (namely, social conservatives and interest groups representing business) and, especially, Republicans turned to focus groups, which are unstructured conversations with a dozen or so "ordinary" Americans. Although the findings from focus groups are not (by design) representative of the views of the entire country, they have nonetheless been treated as such by political activists.[26]

Like presidents before him, George W. Bush typically does not use polls or focus groups to determine his policies; instead, he uses them to help him sell his policies. As one journalist said of Bush, "He . . . takes policies favored by his conservative base and polls on how to make them seem palatable to mainstream voters."[27]

To Guide Policymaking

Polls and focus groups can also be used for guidance in policymaking—to help decide which positions to take on controversial issues, which policies to support or oppose, and which programs to champion and which to ignore. In one sense, it is essential in democratic government for elected officials to listen to their constituents. If the political officeholders are going to lead a government for the people, they need to listen to the people so they can find out what the people want.

Yet the use of polling and focus group research to guide policymaking is generally considered to be a bad thing—officeholders should do what is right regardless of popular sentiment. Acting on popular opinion is often known as pandering to public opinion. Officeholders should not follow public opinion if it conflicts with their own judgment of what should be done. A famous admonition from the eighteenth-century political philosopher Edmund Burke holds that: "Your representative owes you, not his industry only, but his judgment, and he betrays instead of serving you if he sacrifices it to your opinion."[28]

President George W. Bush echoed this sentiment in his first acceptance speech at the Republican national convention in 2000: "I believe great decisions are made with care, made with conviction, not made with polls, I do not need to take your pulse before I know my own mind."[29]

This widespread belief that the officeholders should operate from their convictions and personal judgment makes sense for a number of reasons. First, the elected officeholders, especially the president, have more information and they have given more thought to complicated issues than most people in the general public have.

Second, officials are elected with pre-existing policy positions. Most people would consider it unethical to run for office with one position and then change it once in office in response to polling data. Third, successful candidates have made deals with interest groups in return for their support; no interest group would be satisfied with an officeholder who had a change of heart after a new poll.

Fourth, officeholders know that they will ultimately be judged by voters and by history according to the success or failure of their policies, not by how many people agreed with those policies in the beginning. In a particularly stark example, President Lyndon Johnson enjoyed widespread support for intervening in the Vietnam War in 1964 and 1965, but that support is scarcely remembered today in light of the debacle that came later.

Fifth, the public is often a bad source for specific policy information. Many people simply do not have positions on issues, or they are completely clueless about the subject matter of the question—but ignorance does not always stop them from answering questions. They might answer interviewers' questions on the telephone, but without understanding the meanings of their answers. For example, Robert Weissberg[30] has documented that survey respondents are very willing to say they favor very expensive programs without any real idea of how much the programs cost or how they will affect taxes. Finally, even with respondents who are aware of the issues involved and have thoughtful opinions, the issues are frequently too complicated to communicate a meaningful opinion over the telephone in response to survey questions or in a focus group.

The reasons for ignoring public opinion research in policymaking—and doing the right thing—seem overwhelming. Certainly, no president would forthrightly assert that he had violated his judgment and made a decision he, himself, considers unwise because he wanted to curry favor with the public by following polling results.

Consider, for example, the following speech that President George W. Bush did not give before the American invasion of Iraq in 2003:

> The Iraqi regime . . . possesses and produces chemical and biological weapons. It is seeking nuclear weapons. It has given shelter and support to terrorism. . . . The danger is already significant, and it grows worse with time. If we know Saddam Hussein has dangerous weapons today—and we do—does it make any sense for the world to wait . . . for the final proof, the smoking gun that could come in the form of a mushroom cloud? It is imperative that we act quickly to ensure the peace of the world by removing Saddam Hussein from power. However, I have also studied polls and focus groups from around the nation very carefully and must admit that most Americans do not want a war in Iraq. Therefore, I have decided to let the whole thing drop and hope for the best.*

What do you think would be the reaction to this speech? Outrage from people supporting an invasion? Confusion from everybody? Calls for impeachment? Probably. It would be completely unacceptable for any political leader to say he or she is acting against the best interests of the people in order to conform to polling results.[31]

Yet we would not like to have a president or other officeholder announce that he was not going to take public opinion into account. A president who informed the nation that he would resolutely ignore public opinion during his term in office would not be received much better than one who said he would be ruled by it. People want their leaders to lead them—but also to listen to them.

We should keep in mind that the thought of an elected official bowing to public pressure is not exactly horrific. Jacobs and Shapiro point out, "It is surely odd in a democracy to consider responsiveness to public opinion as disreputable."[32] In 1988, Congress passed the Medicare Catastrophic Coverage Act. A short time later, senior citizens loudly voiced their objections to the law, and within sixteen months, it was repealed.[33] In 2003, Congress passed, and President George W. Bush signed, a revision in the tax code that would give tax refunds to millions of Americans with children—except those with incomes under about $28,000. After an outcry about the unfairness of denying a tax break to those who need it the most, Congress passed, and President Bush signed, a new law extending the tax break to millions of families that had

---

* Actually, President Bush did give *part* of this speech in 2002—from the beginning to ". . . in the form of a mushroom cloud."

been excluded from the previous legislation. We do not know if President Bush commissioned polls or focus groups on the subject, but whether he did or not, one could hardly claim that he was being irresponsible by signing a law that was passed in response to great public pressure.

But this level of responsiveness seems to be unusual. With some exceptions, political science literature for the most part supports politicians' claims that they do not use polls and focus groups to determine which policies to favor. Whatever the advantages of pandering (as some would call it) or responsiveness (as others would call it), politicians are seldom guilty of doing it. Jacobs and Shapiro studied the issue extensively in *Politicians Don't Pander*. They concluded that although presidents conduct a great deal of public opinion research, it is not aimed at guiding the development of their policies but rather at the marketing of those policies. According to Jacobs and Shapiro, presidents use the research to try to convince voters to favor their own policy alternatives, not to ascertain the people's policy preferences. In reference to President Bill Clinton's public opinion research on his massive health care reform package that was the centerpiece of the first two years of his administration in 1993 and 1994, they wrote:

> the president and his aides used polls and focus groups to craft their presentations in order to most effectively "win" public backing. . . . Public opinion research, then, did not guide policymaking; rather, policy decisions guided the research on public opinion in order to identify the language, arguments, and symbols most likely to persuade Americans.[34]

Jacobs and Shapiro quoted one White House staffer: "We didn't poll the policy [to discover what] people wanted policy-wise. We polled the presentation."[35]

CONCLUSION

Polling by politicians has been with us for about seventy years, and political focus groups have been around for about thirty. They are both here to stay for the foreseeable future. Presidential candidates would scarcely consider running without conducting their own research. Generally, polls and focus groups are considered legitimate, and inevitable, for candidates.

Although most officeholders claim to listen to the public, they deny making up their minds based on research they conduct to ascertain the public's opinions. Political scientists generally support them on this claim. The political science literature shows a few cases of politicians shaping their actions on poll or focus group results, but it reveals many more examples of politicians using research to discover better ways to sell policies they have already decided.

With a few exceptions, then, polls and focus groups are communications from the people to the politicians for the purpose of the politicians' manipulating the people. No politicians we are aware of say they conduct polls or focus groups in order to sell their policies better. But no politicians say they conduct polls or focus groups in order to shape policies.

In one sense, politicians' use of public opinion research does not seem problematic from the perspective of the *democratic dialogue*. We established in the previous chapter that some types of people tend to offer their opinions and make demands on the government more than other people do. In this chapter, we have described a way around the participatory distortion described before. If officeholders cannot hear from a representative sample of the population, they will ask a representative sample themselves.

But in another sense, politicians' use of public opinion research is certainly problematic from the perspective of the *democratic dilemma*. If politicians can use focus group and poll results to guide them in making public policy, should they? There are powerful democratic arguments that officeholders should listen to the people as they formulate policy, but there are also important reasons to ignore public opinion when, in the opinion of the officeholders, it is ill-informed or unwise.

So should officeholders listen to public opinion? We can answer that clearly: yes they should, and no they should not. That is, yes, they should be *responsive* to the people's legitimate desires, but no, they should not *pander* to popular prejudice. Politicians, of course, insist they are responsive. And although they conduct massive amounts of public opinion research, they insist they do not use it. Of course.

Suggested Reading

Altschuler, Bruce E. "Lyndon Johnson and the Public Polls." *Public Opinion Quarterly* 50 (1986): 285–299.

Eisinger, Robert M. *The Evolution of Presidential Polling*. Cambridge: Cambridge University Press, 2003.

Heith, Diane J. *Polling to Govern*. Stanford: Stanford University Press, 2004.

———. "Staffing the White House Public Opinion Apparatus 1969–1988." *Public Opinion Quarterly* 62 (1988): 165–189.

Jacobs, Lawrence R. "The Recoil Effect: Public Opinion and Policymaking in the U.S. and Britain." *Comparative Politics* 24 (1992): 199–217.

———, and Robert Y. Shapiro. *Politicians Don't Pander: Political Manipulation and the Loss of Democratic Responsiveness*. Chicago: University of Chicago Press, 2000.

———, and Robert Y. Shapiro. "Presidential Manipulation of Polls and Public Opinion: The Nixon Administration and the Pollsters." *Political Science Quarterly* 110 (1995–1996): 519–538.

———, and Robert Y. Shapiro. "The Rise of Presidential Polling: The Nixon White House in Historical Perspective." *Public Opinion Quarterly* 59 (1995): 163–195.

———, and Robert Y. Shapiro. "Issues, Candidate Image, and Priming: The Use of Private Polls in Kennedy's 1960 Presidential Campaign." *The American Political Science Review* 88 (1994): 527–540.

Smith, Tom W. "The First Straw?: A Study of the Origins of Election Polls." *Public Opinion Quarterly* 54 (1990): 21–36.

`www` ▶▶▶ Interactive Learning Exercise:

Analysis of Opinions on Drunk Driving

This exercise requires you to analyze real-world data and make recommendations to a committee of a state legislature. You examine data from the general public and from experts on drunk driving. A principal issue in this chapter is how much the government listens to the people in formulating public policies. In this exercise, you can play the role of governmental decision makers and determine how much you want to use public opinion—and expert opinion—in developing policies related to drunk driving. All the data in this exercise are real, and most of it *really was* collected to help a state legislature develop laws about drunk driving.

Notes

1. Quoted in Robert M. Eisinger, *The Evolution of Presidential Polling* (Cambridge: Cambridge University Press, 2003), p. 45.

2. What is the origin of the term, "straw polls?" According to Kathleen Frankovic, a pollster for CBS, the term "apparently derived from throwing straws into the wind to tell which way it was blowing." See Kathleen Frankovic, "Public Opinion and Polling," in Doris Graber, Denis McQuail, and Pippa Norris, eds., *The Politics of News, the News of Politics* (Washington, DC: CQ Press, 1998), p. 152.

3. Tom W. Smith, "The First Straw?: A Study of the Origins of Election Polls," *Public Opinion Quarterly* 54 (1990): 25–27.

4. Eisinger, *Evolution of Presidential Polling*, p. 77.

5. Archibald M. Crossley, "Straw Polls in 1936," *Public Opinion Quarterly* 1 (1937): 34. Quoted in Eisinger, *Evolution of Presidential Polling*, p. 11.

6. George Gallup and Saul Forbes Rae, *The Pulse of Democracy: The Public-Opinion Poll and How It Works* (New York: Simon and Schuster, 1940), p. 25, quoted in Eisinger, *Evolution of Presidential Polling*, p. 12.

7. Kenneth F. Warren, *In Defense of Public Opinion Polling* (Cambridge, MA: Westview Press, 2001), p. 199.

8. Eisinger, *Evolution of Presidential Polling*, p. 45.

9. Lawrence R. Jacobs and Robert Y. Shapiro, "The Rise of Presidential Polling: The Nixon White House in Historical Perspective," *Public Opinion Quarterly* 59 (1995): 163–195.

10. Eisinger, *Evolution of Presidential Polling*, pp. 150–151.

11. Diane J. Heith, "Staffing the White House Public Opinion Apparatus 1969–1988," *Public Opinion Quarterly* 62 (1998): 183; Diane J. Heith, *Polling to Govern* (Stanford: Stanford University Press, 2004), pp. 37–38.

12. Heith, *Polling to Govern*, p. 33.

13. Ibid., p. 33.

14. Eisinger, *Evolution of Presidential Polling,* pp. 173–181.

15. Heith, *Polling to Govern,* p. 34.

16. Joshua Green, "The Other War Room: President Bush Doesn't Believe in Polling—Just Ask His Pollsters," *Washington Monthly* 34, 2002, p. 16.

17. Warren, *In Defense of Public Opinion Polling,* pp. 198–199.

18. Ibid., p. 205.

19. David W. Moore, *The Superpollsters* (New York: Four Walls Eight Windows, 1995), pp. 235–238; Bob Schieffer and Gary Paul Gates, *The Acting President* (New York: Dutton, 1989), pp. 360–363.

20. Heith, *Polling to Govern,* pp. 94–99.

21. Ibid., p. 61.

22. Ibid., p. 1.

23. Ibid., p. 118.

24. Lawrence R. Jacobs and Robert Y. Shapiro, *Politicians Don't Pander: Political Manipulation and the Loss of Democratic Responsiveness* (Chicago: University of Chicago Press, 2000).

25. Ibid., p. 27.

26. Ibid., p. 267.

27. Green, "The Other War Room," p. 16.

28. Edmund Burke (1729-1797), Irish philosopher, statesman, Speech to the Electors of Bristol, Nov. 3, 1774, in Philip B. Kurland and Ralph Lerner, eds., *The Founders' Constitution* (Chicago: University of Chicago Press, 1987), V. 1, Chapter 13, Document 7.

29. Quoted in Heith, *Polling to Govern,* p. x.

30. Robert Weissberg, *Polling, Policy, and Public Opinion: The Case Against Heeding the "Voice of the People"* (New York: Palgrave Macmillan, 2002).

31. Although we wrote this "speech," we got the idea from Kenneth Prewitt and Alan Stone, who wrote a similar "speech" for President Richard Nixon concerning the American decision to invade Cambodia in 1970. See Kenneth Prewitt and Alan Stone, *The Ruling Elites: Elite Theory, Power, and American Democracy* (New York: Harper & Row, 1973), p. 206.

32. Jacobs and Shapiro, *Politicians Don't Pander,* p. xiv.

33. Bruce C. Wolpe and Bertram J. Levine, *Lobbying Congress: How the System Works,* 2nd ed. (Washington, DC: CQ Press, 1996), pp. 154–162.

34. Jacobs and Shapiro, *Politicians Don't Pander,* p. 76.

35. Ibid., p. 108.

Listening to the People? Government Responsiveness to Public Opinion

Should Government Listen? The Democratic Dilemma

It makes a great deal of difference to political theory and political life whether or not public opinion behaves in a rational fashion. According to a central strand of democratic theory, the policy preferences of ordinary citizens are supposed to form the core of government decision-making.

Benjamin Page and Robert Shapiro[1]

Questions to Think About

Previous chapters discussed how the public's wants and views can be expressed in practice, and how politicians try to discern what the people want. This chapter addresses the rather sticky question of how wise the public's voice really is, and just how much the government should listen to what the people are saying. It touches on questions such as these:

- What does democracy require of the citizen? In theory, how should the public think and behave politically? Is there a standard of democratic competency when it comes to politics?
- Do people know and care about politics? Do they think and reason about politics? If so, how do they do so?
- How have social scientists answered these questions? Where do they come down on the question of *should government listen?*

THE POLITICAL CAPACITY OF THE PUBLIC

A key question concerning the public's role in democratic government is whether ordinary citizens are capable of governing themselves. If people are generally ignorant, incompetent, or both when it comes to politics, then having the government follow public opinion may not be such a good idea. Indeed, if that is the case, then the views of government officials or experts who know better should carry greater weight than those of the citizenry. Assessing the political capacity of the public is therefore crucial to determining whether, or how much, the government should listen to the people.

The debate over this issue goes all the way back to the ancient Greeks, the originators of democracy. As previously mentioned, the Framers of the U.S. Constitution struggled with it as well, believing that government should be accountable to the people, but at the same time being wary of giving complete control to the masses, who were presumed to be generally ignorant and easily swayed. As Delli Carpini and Keeter put it: "This combination of fear and faith in the public's collective wisdom has resulted in political institutions and processes designed to allow citizens to have a voice in their own governance, while at the same time limiting the impact of that voice."[2]

Other questions have likewise been raised about the democratic character of the public, namely whether the public itself may actually be a threat to democratic government. If the people fail to support democratic ideals of majority rule, fair play, tolerance of dissent, and other related values, then unfettered public opinion will lead to majority tyranny or mobocracy. Another reason the Framers put checks on pure majority rule was not only their concern about the folly of the masses, but also their fear that those in the majority might favor repressing those who disagreed with them.

Arguments over the quality of public opinion have continued to this day, with modern social scientists joining the fray. Much of this chapter is devoted to presenting and analyzing the scholarly evidence in this debate.

This chapter will first review the ideal portrait of the public from democratic theory as a benchmark for judging the public's performance—and the research—on this topic. Then, it will present the case made by each of the two sides in the public competency debate. The chapter then examines the related issue of public support for the values and practices underlying democratic government, under the assumption that people must first support the ideals of democracy if they are to be able to practice it. The chapter then concludes with a compromise approach, and some things to think about in coming to your opinion about whether government should listen to the people.

The Democratic Citizen Revisited

In order to determine whether citizens are capable of governing themselves, it is first necessary to examine what democracy requires of the citizen. Traditional majoritarian democratic theory, including such principles as majority rule, political equality, and popular control of government—or in Lincoln's words, "government of, by, and for the people"—places great importance, and burdens, on the ordinary citizen. There are several related expectations of the public in this model. First, the model assumes that citizens are interested and involved in politics. Similarly, they will be informed about public issues, and know where they stand on them. Furthermore, they should consider, and be tolerant of, alternative viewpoints, and think about politics in a coherent fashion, so as to make reasoned and informed choices. After doing all this, citizens should also know where candidates and officials stand on the issues, and use this information in making their political decisions.

Such expectations may be a tall order for many people. One might also question whether this ideal is realistic, much less completely necessary for a proper functioning of democratic government. It was the Framers' very doubts about the ability of ordinary people to perform their citizenly duties that led them to favor barriers to voting and participation, and to place institutional checks on majority rule. Nevertheless, the ideal at least gives us a guideline by which to judge the American public.

Given its importance to democratic government, the question of public competence has also been taken up by modern social scientists. Prior to the 1940s, and the advent of survey research, most work on the study of public opinion in general, and the capacity of the citizens in particular, was anecdotal. When scholars were finally able to better assess whether people met the standards of democratic citizenship, they discovered, much to their dismay, that large percentages of the populace failed to pass the test.

This perspective has dominated academia for much of the last fifty years, although in the last two decades or so new research has emerged that presents a brighter view of the public. We address the substance of this debate in the next section. Since the negative view of the public's political competence historically developed first, we begin with a discussion of that side.

THE CASE AGAINST THE PUBLIC (OR THE INCOMPETENT PUBLIC)

The pessimistic view of the public's capacity revolves around four major areas, roughly approximating those encompassed in the model of the ideal democratic citizen advanced above. These are the degrees of political interest and involvement by the public; the amount and level of political knowledge; the extent to which most people use a coherent belief system for thinking about

PEARLS BEFORE SWINE.

PEARLS BEFORE SWINE © Stephan Pastis/Dist. by United Feature Syndicate, Inc.

politics, along with whether people link their values or value frameworks to their opinions; and lastly, the degree of issue voting (whether people vote based on issues, or other factors).

Lack of Interest and Involvement in Politics

Do people really care about politics? Are they interested in political affairs, and do they exercise that interest through participation? The answer appears to be no, or not much anyway. Early studies of voting behavior in the 1940s and 1950s found relatively low levels of interest in election campaigns. Subsequent examinations haven't brightened the picture much, although there is some variation in the amount of attention to campaigns, depending upon the election year and what is happening. For example, in 2000, only 26 percent said they were "very interested" in the presidential election, according to the National Election Study. This number isn't atypical: The 1952–2002 average is 30 percent (see Table 11.1). Polls surveying general political interest have also consistently shown that for most people, politics isn't a high priority in their lives.

When one examines public attention to news items, one discovers that political stories don't always rank very highly. For example, polls conducted by the Pew Center for Research on Politics and the Press consistently find that more Americans follow sports and weather than national, and even local, politics. Of course, that depends upon the stories in a given year. In 2001, many followed news about the terror attacks of September 11 closely, and in 2003, many followed reports about the War in Iraq. But even in these years, nonpolitical disaster and celebrity stories still rank high; in fact, Pew surveys show that despite the events of September 11 and its aftermath, interest in international news did not increase very much in the following year. (See Table 11.2.)

When it comes to involvement in politics, most Americans do not come close to fully exercising their citizenship rights and obligations. The mere act of voting, the easiest mode of participation, is not widespread. Approximately half

TABLE 11.1. Level of Interest in Election Campaigns.

The NES Guide to Public Opinion and Electoral Behavior

Interest in Current Campaign 1952–2002

	'52	'54	'56	'58	'60	'62	'64	'66	'68	'70	'72	'74	'76	'78	'80	'82	'84	'86	'88	'90	'92	'94	'96	'98	'00	'02
Not Much Interested																										
	29	**	31	41	25	26	25	29	21	24	27	**	21	34	26	30	25	33	25	33	17	27	25	31	24	27
Somewhat Interested																										
	34	**	40	33	37	38	37	40	40	43	41	**	42	45	44	44	47	44	47	46	44	47	50	48	50	53
Very Much Interested																										
	37	**	30	27	38	36	38	30	39	34	31	**	37	22	30	26	28	22	28	21	39	27	25	21	26	20
Don't Know																										
	0	**	0	0	0	0	0	0	0	0	0	**	0	0	0	0	0	0	0	0	0	0	0	0	0	0
N																										
	1776	1754	1812	1919	1294	1565	1272	1546	1506	2699	2857	2300	1567	1415	2251	2172	2036	1978	2478	1777	1714	1281	1807	1507		

QUESTION TEXT
"Some people don't pay much attention to the political campaigns. How about you, would you say that you have been/were very much interested, somewhat interested, or not much interested in following the political campaigns (so far) this year?"

TABLE 11.2. Interest in Types of News Stories.

	Trend in News Interest	
Type of News followed "very closely"	% in 2000	% in 2002
Community	26	31
Crime	30	30
Health news	29	26
Sports	27	25
Local government	20	22
Washington news	17	21
International affairs	14	21
Religion	21	19
Science and technology	18	17
Business and finance	14	15
Entertainment	15	14
Consumer news	12	12
Culture and the arts	10	9

Source: "Trends in News Interest" from "Public's News Habits Changed Little by 9/11," from June 9, 2002 Pew Research Center for People and the Press press release; accessed at http://people-press.org/reports/index.php3 ?TopicID=1. Reprinted by permission of Pew Research Center for the People and the Press.

don't vote in the quadrennial presidential elections, a large majority (over 60 percent) do not vote in most congressional elections, and even more fail to do so in many state and local elections. Americans participate at higher rates in other ways (involvement in campaigns, writing their representatives, and so forth) than people in other countries, but even so, only small minorities of the population engage in these activities. While there are many reasons for these behaviors, Americans are clearly not as interested or as involved in politics as most of us would like, nor as democratic theory would dictate. Harsh critics would even say we are apathetic, lazy, or both. A more charitable description would be that politics does not appear to be of crucial importance to most of us. Either way, on this score the picture that this perspective paints is not encouraging.

Low Levels of Political Knowledge

Those who take a dim view of the public's civic capacity also point to many people's low level of knowledge about politics, politicians, and the like. As Phillip Converse, a leading proponent of this perspective, put it: "The most familiar fact to arise from sample surveys is that popular levels of information about public affairs are, from the point of an informed observer, astonishingly low."[3]

It is hard to say exactly what citizens should know to be considered informed, or at least minimally competent. But if one examines polls querying how much the public knows, one can see why the conventional wisdom agrees with Converse that the public is woefully ignorant.

In Tables 11.3 to 11.6, we give some examples of public knowledge on political topics from selected polls. Following the categorization of Delli Carpini and Keeter (1996), we have divided them into four sections: Institutions and Processes; People; Domestic Politics; and Foreign Affairs.

In their exhaustive study of political knowledge from 1940 to 1994, Delli Carpini and Keeter examined a historical database of over 3,500 questions. They found that "only 13 percent of the more than 2000 political questions examined could be answered correctly by 75 percent or more of those asked, and only 41 percent could be answered correctly by more than half the public."[4] Russell Neuman, who also studied this subject, came to similar conclusions. "The available data show overwhelmingly that even the basic facts of political history, the fundamental structure of political institutions, and current political figures and events escape the cognizance of the great majority of the electorate."[5]

(To see how well you'd do, try the interactive exercise at the end of the section, and on the book's Web site.)

TABLE 11.3. Knowledge of Institutions and Processes ("What Government Is").

Item	% Correct	Year
Length of president's term	93	1952*
Define presidential veto	89	1989*
U.S. is a democracy	88	1948*
Right to trial by jury	83	1986*
Treaties need Senate approval	79	1986*
First Amendment protects speech/press	75	1985*
Define party platform	71	1952*
# of senators from each state	60	2001**
Who determines law's constitutionality	58	1992*
Accused are presumed innocent	50	1983*
Define "liberal"/"conservative"	46	1957*
Congress declares war	45	1987*
Substance of *Roe v. Wade*	30	1986*
Length of House term	30	1978*
Define "bipartisan foreign policy"	26	1950*
Length of senator's term	25	1991*
Name all three branches of government	19	1952*
Define "politically correct"	7	1991*

* = Cited in Delli Carpini and Keeter; ** = Gallup survey (June 28, 2001).

TABLE 11.4. Knowledge of People ("Who Government Is").

Item	% Correct	Year
Name the president	99	1986*
Name your governor	86	1970*
Leader of Iraq (Saddam Hussein)	75	1990*
Which party controls U.S. House	71	1978*
Who are the "Freedom Riders"	61	1961*
Know whether governor is a Democrat or Republican	59	1985*
Republican Party more conservative	57	1988*
Name the secretary of state	57	1958*
Recognized Warren Burger as chief justice	51	1984*
Know president of Russia	47	1994*
Incumbent House candidate	46	1966*
—may use NES avg '52–02:	56	
Name both your senators	35	1985*
President of France	34	1986*
Know your state senator	28	1965*
Attorney general	24	1970*
Secretary general of the UN	10	1953*
Name the chief justice of the Supreme Court	6	1996***
President of Mexico	3	1991*

Source: * = (polls compiled by) Michael X. Delli Carpini and Scott Keeter, *What Americans Know About Politics and Why It Matters* (New York: Oxford University Press, 1996), pp. 69–95; *** = Princeton Survey Research Associates (August 14, 1996).

Popular culture has also contributed to the conventional wisdom that the public is uninformed. Comedian Jay Leno, host of the popular late-night television program *The Tonight Show,* has a regular segment called "Jaywalking" where he demonstrates the cluelessness of many people about current events through his humorous person-in-the-street interviews. As an illustration, Leno recounts, "I remember one lady who owned a computer company, and I asked her who the President was before Bill Clinton. She said. 'I'm not into politics.'"[6]

On the bright side, as we have seen there are certain facts that almost the entire public knows, and others that large majorities do. These include such items as the length of the president's term, the meaning of a presidential veto, that Social Security doesn't provide job training, and that the depletion of the ozone layer affects the whole world. Yet, on the other hand, if much of the public doesn't know what political party their governor belongs to, which party is politically more conservative, that Social Security is a major part of the federal budget, and who U.S. friends and foes in the world are, and so forth, how can these people use the information they do have to participate effectively and make wise political decisions?

TABLE 11.5. Knowledge of Domestic Affairs ("What Government Does").

Item	% Correct	Year
Social Security doesn't provide job training	89	1974*
Budget deficit increased since 1981	83	1985*
Oil is in short supply	81	1974*
What is National Health Insurance	76	1978*
Medicare doesn't cover all medical costs	72	1987*
Voting rights legislation passed	67	1965*
Public school curricula vary by state	61	1989*
What is Watergate about	54	1973*
Number of Americans unemployed	37	1984*
What is affirmative action	31	1985*
Social Security one of top 2 federal budget expenses	27	1989*
What is acid rain	26	1980*
Government regulates radio ownership	18	1945*
Percentage of population below poverty line	18	1989*
Average yearly dollars to treat AIDS patient	9	1987*
Size of federal budget	6	1951*

Source:* = (polls compiled by) Michael X. Delli Carpini and Scott Keeter, *What Americans Know About Politics and Why It Matters* (New York: Oxford University Press, 1996), pp. 69–95.

TABLE 11.6. Knowledge of Foreign Affairs ("What Government Does").

Item	% Correct	Year
Ozone damage affects whole world	94	1988*
Name one country with nuclear weapons	93	1988*
Volkswagen is a foreign company	87	1978*
Cuba is Communist	82	1988*
China is Communist	77	1985*
Not all Indians are Hindus	72	1978*
Japan has free elections	57	1982*
U.S. only nation to use nuclear weapons	49	1986*
Kuwait not a democracy	42	1991*
Soviets are in Warsaw Pact	37	1988*
Describe aspect of U.S. immigration policy	35	1985*
Two nations in SALT (treaty)	30	1979*
Shell Oil a foreign company	19	1986*
Israel gets largest percentage of U.S. aid	18	1986*
U.S.'s largest trading partner	8	1991*

Source: * = (polls compiled by) Michael X. Delli Carpini and Scott Keeter, *What Americans Know About Politics and Why It Matters* (New York: Oxford University Press, 1996), pp. 69–95.

Consider the case of public opinion about the Comprehensive Nuclear Test Ban Treaty. This treaty would have banned all nuclear testing by all countries (at least, signatories), including the United States. It was arguably the most important arms control agreement of the past twenty years. Although signed by President Clinton a few years before, the Republican-controlled U.S. Senate voted against ratifying the treaty on October 13, 1999.

The rejection of the treaty—it didn't even get a majority vote in the Senate, much less the two-thirds majority necessary—was remarkable in many ways. It was the first major treaty since 1920, and the first arms control treaty ever, to fail to be ratified. Its defeat shocked and angered U.S. allies, and dealt a blow to American global leadership on nuclear issues.[7] Debate on the treaty took place in an atmosphere of extreme partisanship, unusual in foreign policy issues, in the aftermath of the Clinton impeachment saga. Democrats attacked Republicans for playing politics with the issue, arguing they merely wanted to deny Clinton a historic success in his final years in office as revenge for his acquittal over the Monica Lewinsky affair. They vowed to make it a campaign issue in the 2000 election.

What was the public's view on all of this? Interestingly, a Gallup poll taken a week after the Senate vote found that 65 percent of the public said they had heard something about the treaty. More specifically, 38 percent said they had followed the arguments on both sides "very" or "somewhat" closely; 22 percent "not so closely;" and the remaining 5 percent, "not at all." However, the rest of the poll showed just how closely the public actually was following the treaty, or at least, what it knew about its ultimate fate. Gallup then asked respondents whether they were aware of what the Senate had done. Only 26 percent correctly knew that the Senate had defeated the treaty; 4 percent inaccurately said (likely guessed) it had ratified the treaty; 1 percent gave a different answer altogether; but 60 percent were unaware and 9 percent had "no opinion"—probably refusing to give an answer at all.

In other words, on a major arms control agreement that had the (apparent) attention of a majority of the public, only slightly more than one in four Americans knew what happened to it the week after it was voted upon! More troubling than this, perhaps, were the implications of the treaty defeat for the public's policy preferences. The poll finally asked people what they thought the Senate should have done, regardless of what it actually did do: 59 percent believed the treaty should have been ratified, versus only 29 percent who wanted it defeated. Therefore, people's lack of knowledge about the treaty ratification likely meant that they didn't even know the Senate had gone against their apparent wishes. (Granted, given their low levels of knowledge on the treaty ratification, we can't say for sure their support of the treaty was based upon a fully informed opinion, either. But the basic conclusion one draws from the poll results is that most of the public wanted the treaty to be ratified, yet didn't even know their government had failed to do so.) Furthermore, this lack of information also meant that most people couldn't use the knowledge of the treaty defeat in forming their opinion about the performance of the Senate, or likely even their own Senator, when they went to vote in the next election. Not surprisingly, in the 2000 election the issue of the Nuclear Test Ban wasn't high on the agenda of the media, or of presidential candidates Al Gore and George Bush.

Cases like this one call popular control of government in the United States into question. How can people hold their representatives accountable for major decisions like arms control agreements if they don't even know what those decisions are? This rhetorical question is the basic conclusion of the incompetent public side concerning political knowledge.

Lack of a Coherent Ideology or Belief System; Opinion Instability

Other questions were raised about the public's capacity for coherent and consistent political thought. Emerging from early studies of voting behavior, some scholars turned their attention to examining how people mentally organized their opinions. In an influential piece of research, Phillip Converse argued that a large portion of the public in fact did not have a coherent "belief system" (he didn't feel the term ideology was appropriate) that structured their underlying attitudes, and similarly their level of ideological thinking was sketchy and simplistic. Using survey responses from the 1956 presidential election, Converse examined the extent to which people used abstract ideological concepts to make sense of the political world and how they would vote in the election, and the degree to which they understood the meaning of the ideological labels liberal and conservative.

On the first score, voters were classified into five different categories, based on how they appeared to think about politics. "Ideologues" were the most sophisticated, and used a coherent, organized, and well-understood system of interlocking beliefs to come to their decisions. "Near ideologues" were people who mentioned ideological concepts in the abstract but didn't appear to fully comprehend or use them. People who appeared to rely on their cues or associations with relevant social groups (such as workers who claimed that a candidate was good to labor as the reason for their choice) were members of a "group interest" category. "Nature of the times" voters were those who based their evaluations of candidates and parties on how things were going and whether they would be better or worse off if a particular side prevailed. In the final group were the "apoliticals," whose views of the political scene had no issue content whatsoever. Converse, along with similar studies by other researchers, found that true ideologues made up an extremely small portion (less than 5 percent) of the electorate, and even with the generous inclusion of near ideologues, at best about one-sixth of the population was reasonably sophisticated. A slightly larger portion fell at the opposite, apolitical extreme, with the bulk of the population in the other categories.[8] Further research also showed that the better-educated were more likely to think in ideological terms, adding credence to the view that nonideologues were less sophisticated.[9]

Likewise, on the second dimension, only about 10 percent of the public effectively understood the meaning of the labels liberal and conservative and what they stood for.[10] Such results led Converse to some jarring conclusions. In his view, since the vast majority of the public could not talk about their policy and candidate stands in abstract, ideological terms, and often failed to relate politics to policy altogether, the mass public didn't have a structured belief system about politics. Instead, they made up their minds on a case-by-case, issue-by-issue basis or by relying on their group identifications with others. A fairly large subset of the population didn't even have a simplistic form of belief system to think politically with at all! As he put it, "large portions of the electorate do not have meaningful beliefs, even on issues that have formed the basis for intense political controversy among elites for some time."[11]

Debate over the meaning of Converse's findings raged back and forth for several decades. Some argued his results were an artifact of the 1950s, when there were few issues of ideological importance. Surveys in the 1960s and 1970s, during an era of sharp ideological division over civil rights and Vietnam, purportedly showed an increase in the public's ideological thinking. Others in turn attacked the methodology of these findings, pointing out that the questions on these latter surveys were different from those of the 1956 survey, which led to the different results. Another group (whom we mention in more detail below) felt that focusing so much attention on the elite-driven left/right concept of ideology missed some of the actual coherence of the beliefs of the lesser-educated. Still others essentially agreed with the original perspective. For example, Luttbeg and Grant, examining data from the 1980 election, found that about 40 percent of the respondents were unable to clearly articulate the meaning of liberal and conservative, and even for those that did, knowing the labels appeared to be of little aid to voters in how they made up their minds. A multielection study by M. Kent Jennings reiterated that better-educated, more aware respondents had more coherent belief systems, while the opinions of those without "were more likely to be characterized by misunderstandings, top-of-the-head responses, other effects, poor retention, and satisficing ["good enough," educated guess] strategies."[12] Despite some scholarly confusion, the image that emerged still left the strong impression that most people's opinions on political issues were idiosyncratic and didn't hang together in any larger logical fashion.

Converse added to his grim view of civic competence with other research examining the consistency of people's policy opinions. He analyzed panel studies (where respondents are asked the same question over time) on political issues from several elections and found that many people failed to keep the same position in every survey. In fact, Converse surmised that only about 20 percent of the public kept the same views, while a large majority of the public essentially guessed or answered questions at random. He supposed that these people gave doorstep opinions so as to not look ignorant to their questioners. Thus, instead of consistent opinions, many Americans had **nonattitudes** toward most political issues.[13]

Therefore, if large numbers of people failed to have a coherent belief system, misunderstood or were largely unable to utilize ideological labels, and changed their opinion often (or, really, appeared to have no opinion but merely wanted to look as though they did to pollsters or others when asked), how could one argue the government should listen to them? Such discoveries also raised troubling questions as to whether public opinion could be said to actually exist.

Limited Issue Voting; Reliance on Simplistic Cues

Another indirect indication of the public's civic capability was how they voted. Did people vote based on issues, or other factors? Were they aware of the major issues of the campaign, did they know where the candidates and they themselves stood on those issues, and finally did they use all of that information in making their decision?

Again, the answer seemed to be no. Most voters were poorly informed about the candidates and issues, and possessed only rudimentary understandings of the positions of the two major parties. The major studies of voting from the 1940s to the 1970s may have disagreed about whether people used sociological (such as group cues and identities), or individual psychological bases (such as party identification and candidate characteristics) for making their voting decision, but the studies essentially agreed that the level of pure issue voting was low. Most voters followed simple cues such as their party identification or group affiliation in deciding how to cast their ballots.[14]

In essence, the voting studies in this tradition (although chronologically begun earlier) meshed well with the above three components to paint an unflattering portrait of the mass public. As Delli Carpini and Keeter summarize this perspective:

> the average citizen was portrayed as apathetic, uninterested in politics, unconcerned about who wins or loses presidential elections, only marginally interested in voting. The public also held few strong political opinions, and the opinions they did hold conflicted with each other and changed in seemingly random ways over time. In addition, opinions were not particularly influential in determining how most citizens voted.[15]

THE REBUTTAL: THE RATIONAL PUBLIC

Despite the dominance of the incompetent public perspective in academic and popular circles, other scholars have disputed its premises and results. Particularly in the last twenty-five years or so, new bodies of research have come along to stick up for the public and to argue that the picture may not be as bad as the detractors paint it.

Interest and Involvement: Rational Disengagement

On the issue of the public's apparent lack of interest and involvement in politics, critics of the pessimistic view respond by arguing that some researchers may have unreasonably high expectations of the average person. Not everyone can be an ideal citizen, and civic engagement takes time, effort, and opportunity. Most people are occupied with their lives, jobs, families, and other commitments, and so have little time left over for politics. Furthermore, as political economist Anthony Downs pointed out long ago, from a purely self-interested perspective, it doesn't make a lot of sense to put much effort into political matters.[16] Take voting, for example: The odds of one person's vote making a difference in terms of which candidate wins or loses (especially in a large election such as for big-city mayor, state governor, or president) are incredibly small. Why then should someone spend a lot of time following the campaign and learning about where the candidates stand on all the issues? Unless someone is a political junkie, like current or former political science majors or people who enjoy politics, the costs of being interested, informed, and involved aren't worth the likely benefits (such as the likelihood that you individually will make a difference). In fact, more people participate in and follow politics than a pure "Downsian" economic calculation would predict, suggesting that for a number of Americans, being at least minimally engaged in politics is part of their civic duty.

One can also make the argument that lack of participation, such as low turnout rates in elections, isn't necessarily equivalent to lack of concern or ignorance. Plus, given the large number of elections in the United States—national, state, and local, including both elected offices and ballot propositions—Americans probably do more voting than people in other countries.[17]

None of these considerations, however, lets the public off the hook. After all, Downs's theory could also help explain the findings of Converse and others in the pessimistic school, thereby telling us why we shouldn't be surprised people aren't more politically interested and involved. But these considerations do suggest that expecting most Americans to behave like political science majors or professors may be setting the bar too high. Just because most Americans aren't as passionate about politics as political elites doesn't necessarily mean they don't care at all. For example, if one examines the same National Election Survey question about interest in the current election campaign, and combines the number of people who were both "somewhat interested" with the "very interested," one finds that over the last fifty years or so, over two-thirds of the public have some interest in elections. The 1952–2002 average is 73 percent, a respectable number.

Political Knowledge: Issue Publics and Collective Wisdom

Similarly, regarding the public's political knowledge, this perspective retorts that there are understandable reasons for these apparent shortcomings, and there's more to the public's knowledge than first meets the eye. Again, the limited impact of each individual citizen, coupled with demands on time from other areas of life, probably constrains widespread learning about politics. Some attack the very validity of many of these measures of knowledge, arguing that many of the questions "amount to little more than political trivia quizzes."[18] How important is it to know the name of your senator or the length of their term of office off the top of your head? As long as you know an election is coming up, and you know something about their performance and basic political orientations (and similar things about their opponent[s]) when you fill out your ballot, that may be enough to perform your basic, democratic civic duties. Or, for example, what if much of the public doesn't know specific abbreviations or acronyms, as in the ABM (antiballistic missile) Treaty, but knows where they stand on the issue of building a national missile defense? Isn't that more crucial?

The public also may not be as ignorant as they appear. Far more people do recognize the name of their representative in Congress (as they would have to do in the voting booth in a real election) than can name them outright.[19] An experiment in the 1998 National Election Study also found that the phrasing of political knowledge questions may mask the real extent of knowledge in the population. It compared results on political knowledge questions where those who weren't sure were asked to give it their best guess, versus an identical survey in which they were not so encouraged. The study discovered increases in the number getting questions right by a few to over 10 percentage points, depending upon the question.[20]

Delli Carpini and Keeter, in conducting their national political knowledge test survey in 1989, uncovered other evidence that the public may be more informed than pure percentages of right and wrong questions would suggest. They noted some cases where people strained to remember, being angry with themselves for not knowing the answer, which was on the tip of their tongue. These kinds of responses suggest that given a different context, say in a political discussion with friends and not a political pop quiz, knowledge would be greater. They also found that on average fewer citizens gave out-and-out wrong answers than honestly admitted they did not know. We saw that such was indeed the case with the earlier example of the Nuclear Test Ban Treaty.

When they examined cases where incorrect answers were numerous, they identified two main types of errors. The first suggested the public was closer to the truth than at first glance, and the second, that people were wrong due to patterns of incorrect or misleading information provided to them. In the first, some of the knowledge questions bordered on opinion and not fact, or were vague enough that it was understandable why many in the public gave completely incorrect answers. Other mistakes were ones that appeared to be cases of lags in public awareness, such as people continuing to think that Margaret Thatcher was prime minister of Great Britain the year after she left office; identifying Warren Burger as Chief Justice of the Supreme Court after he stepped down; or responding that the previous majority party in the Senate was still in power after a change in control.

In the second type of error, significant portions of the public made projections, assuming the best about American politics. This category of errors included believing the U.S. Constitution guarantees a person a job or a high school education, for example. In other cases, people apparently gave wrong answers due to opinion manipulation or misinformation. An apparent example of manipulation was the finding that on the eve of the 1991 Persian Gulf War, 80 percent of the public knew Iraqi leader Saddam Hussein used chemical weapons in the war with Iran, but only 4 percent knew that Kuwait's stand on oil prices threatened Iraq's economy (a possible reason for Iraq's attack). Cases of misinformation included a majority thinking the president had the power to declare war, not Congress (incorrect but understandable given the post–World War Two presidency's numerous military involvements abroad); or the substantial minority in the 1980s who thought the Soviet Union fought against the United States in World War Two (also understandable, given the Cold War animosity between the two countries).[21]

These latter findings suggest, as scholars Benjamin Page and Robert Shapiro argue, that public ignorance may be as much the fault of political elites—the media, politicians, and the like—as it is the public.[22] If politicians would not be so ambiguous about their issue positions, or mislead the public with bad information, and if the mass media would cover more substantive issues about politics rather than sensationalism, scandal, and trivia—so this side argues— public knowledge might increase. As an example, Box 11.1 examines the apparent ignorance of the public about some key issues in the 2003 war with Iraq; it can actually be used as an illustration of both sides in this debate.

In fact, learning can and does take place. Over the course of a presidential campaign, large numbers of the population learn who the major-party presidential and vice-presidential candidates are. And, given media attention, political knowledge does increase. For example, in mid-January 2003, 45 percent of the public correctly named Trent Lott as the person who had resigned as Senate majority leader two weeks earlier, following a highly publicized controversy over racially charged remarks he made at a birthday party for fellow Senator Strom Thurmond. This number is undoubtedly much higher than the usual percentage of Americans who know the Senate leader (we don't have any previous examples of such a question for direct comparison, but the number of those who know the speaker of the house is in the 25–35 percent range, so it's probably similar).[23]

Beyond these objections is the more sophisticated point made by some in the rational public school that the collective whole of the public is greater than its individual parts. Public opinion as a whole may be wiser than individual citizens within it—for two main reasons: the role of opinion aggregation and the process of collective deliberation. First, collective opinion reflects the logic of information pooling: If each person has a reasonably good, but imperfect, chance of judging whether something is true, then by simple probability, a majority of independent-judging individuals has a greater chance of being right.[24] Second, the public benefits from a process of collective deliberation. Namely, the informed subset on any given issue constitutes an issue public that both knows more and has clearer opinions on a particular issue.

BOX 11.1

Abject Ignorance or Understandable Confusion? Public Knowledge About the War in Iraq

Along with the terrorist attacks of September 11, 2001, the subject of war with Iraq was one of the major political issues of the early twenty-first century. Going to war and fighting one are serious undertakings, regardless of the circumstances. It's also the kind of issue voters should care about, since it clearly strikes home and affects them. The Iraq war in particular was heavily debated for months in late 2002 through early 2003, and the invasion and subsequent U.S. occupation were covered heavily by many media outlets for weeks thereafter. So, one would think that it would be an issue about which there would be great public knowledge.

These reasons make the number of misperceptions that segments of the population had about major issues of the war all the more surprising and disturbing. For example, three different surveys in the summer of 2003—from one to several months after President Bush declared "major combat over" in May—revealed the following:

- About one-fourth (24 percent) of the public mistakenly believed Iraq used chemical or biological weapons against U.S. forces in the just-concluded war (62% rightly knew they did not);[1]
- A similar number (27% percent) believed evidence of weapons of mass destruction (chemical, biological, or nuclear materials) had been uncovered in Iraq, despite the fact that this was not the case, and the administration's own weapons report admitted as much (although it did say the potential may have been there);[2]
- A stunning 72 percent said they believed the Iraqi regime was "harboring Al Qaeda terrorists and helping them develop chemical weapons."[3] While some supposed training camps were discovered in Northern Iraq (outside effective control of the Iraqi government), none were directly linked to the Al Qaeda group. In fact, in September, President Bush himself forcefully admitted that at least there were no direct links between Hussein and the September 11, 2001, attacks, generally attributed to Al Qaeda and their leader Osama Bin Laden.

Granted, on the first two issues, a majority of the public got them right, and the third issue is itself a bit less clear. Still, given widespread media coverage of the war and the issues involved in it, how could even a small segment of the public *not* know these facts? And why were there many who were not just ignorant, but who actually thought something that wasn't true or proven at that point?

Therefore, such evidence gives weight to the view that the public is unwise—or at least, that the public is easily confused or doesn't pay attention. This may also be a case of nonattitudes, in which members of the public, not to appear ignorant, instead chose to project the worst on official American enemies or the best in America's case.

On the other hand, taking the rational public position, the level of public mistakes is instead easily attributable to government and media misinformation. At the very least, such results convey understandable confusion, given the information environment surrounding the war.

After all, President Bush and members of his administration spent months blanketing the media with charges against Iraq in order to make the case for war. The most forceful of these arguments was that Iraq was developing weapons of mass destruction (or was capable of doing so) and might deliver them to terrorists to use against the United States. (Whether the administration intentionally misled the public is an issue revisited in Chapter 12.) The main aim of the war was to disarm Iraq, and Bush officials—at least, after no weapons were initially found—also justified the Iraq action as part of the war on terrorism. Vice President Cheney, in particular, was adamant about Hussein's ties to Al Qaeda and Osama Bin Laden, and his desire to obtain nuclear weapons—all charges that have not been substantiated.

Nationalistic, pro-war and pro-Administration media coverage may also have played a role in those who appear to have been misinformed. Discussion, tapes or file footage of Iraq's use of chemical weapons in previous wars, for example, coupled with the administration's fearful rhetoric, may have led some to the mistaken conclusion that WMDs were used in the 2003 war or were uncovered after it. In fact, the administration attempted to tout some initial, minor, and sketchy discoveries as vindicating evidence. Also, government claims of training camps and contacts between terror groups and Iraq's government, coupled with some Americans' natural inclinations to assume the best about their own side and the worst about others, could explain why many thought a connection had been found (or they believed there was one, even if evidence was missing). Some Americans may even have chosen to invent such connections in a post-hoc fashion, to help them justify the war in their own minds.

Further evidence for this perspective comes from a different set of poll results. Researchers from the Program on International Policy Attitudes (a joint project of several academic centers) and Knowledge Networks, a polling firm, also were interested in public misperceptions about the war and explanations for them. Throughout the summer of 2003, they also found similar misperceptions: 48 percent of Americans believed hard evidence of connections between Al Qaeda and Hussein had been uncovered; 22 percent thought WMDs had been found in Iraq; and 25 percent believed that most people in other countries had backed the U.S. war against Iraq (also not true). In addition, 60 percent of all respondents believed one of the three mistaken assertions; 8 percent believed all of them. The researchers then asked where respondents got their news, and linked news sources to the level of misinformation. Eighty percent of viewers of Fox Network news believed at least one of these untruths; 45 percent believed all three; 71 percent of viewers of CBS news believed in one, though only 15 percent believed all three. The comparative numbers for viewers of PBS and listeners of National Public Radio were lower at 23 percent and 4 percent, respectively.[4] Thus, part of the problem with public understanding may have been due to their sources of information.

In any case, this perspective would argue the public is not solely responsible for such mistakes. Elite discourse and a faulty information environment should share some of the blame.

Regardless of the explanation for them, these public misperceptions did have real political consequences. Another PIPA poll done on the eve of the 2004 election found stark differences between Bush and Kerry supporters on these facts. As late as October 2004, and after the final report of Charles Duelfer that Iraq did not have weapons of mass destruction, 72 percent of Bush supporters believed Iraq had WMD or a substantial program to develop them; 57 percent believed Duelfer had found such evidence; 75 percent

Continued

BOX 11.1—*Cont'd*

believed Iraq was providing support for Al Qaeda, and 63 percent that support for such a case had actually been found; 55 percent of Bush supporters believed, incorrectly, that this was a conclusion of the 9/11 Commission. Kerry supporters believed exactly the opposite on all these scores.[5]

Few Bush supporters also correctly knew that most of the world opposed the Iraq war (31 percent), whereas 74 percent of Kerry supporters did. Bush supporters also misperceived Bush's own foreign policy positions on a number of major issues, such as the Kyoto Treaty on global warming, the Comprehensive Nuclear Test Ban Treaty, and labor and environmental restrictions in trade agreements; furthermore, they believed his views were actually in line with their own. Steven Kull, the lead researcher, thinks these misperceptions were due to "the traumatic experience of 9/11 and the pitch-perfect leadership Bush showed in its wake. This created a powerful bond between Bush and his supporters, an idealized image of the President that makes it difficult for his supporters to imagine that he could have made incorrect judgments before the war, that world public opinion could be critical of his policies, or that the President could hold foreign policy positions at odds with his supporters."[6]

Thus, arguably these misperceptions among the Bush faithful may have led them to vote for a president who actually disagreed with them on many issues and was engaging in a war that was not what it appeared.

This case study, as with other examples of public knowledge, provides fodder for both sides in the public competency debate. Which side you come down on philosophically may influence which set of evidence you choose to emphasize. Facts can often be used to fit one's own values.

Notes

1. ABC News/*Washington Post* survey, released June 23, 2003.
2. Harris Poll, released August 22, 2003.
3. Princeton Survey Research Associates poll conducted for *Newsweek,* released July 26, 2003.
4. Poll results cited in Harold Meyerson, "Fact-Free News," *Washington Post National Weekly*, October 20–26, 2003, p. 26.
5. See the Program on International Policy Attitudes report by Steven Kull, "The Separate Realities of Bush and Kerry Supporters," released on October 21, 2004, accessed at www.pipa.org.
6. Kull, "The Separate Realities of Bush and Kerry Supporters," pp. 13–14.

Other, less-informed members of the public may take cues from them, thus benefiting from an informational division of labor. While this characteristic does not explain away or excuse public ignorance (and indeed, as is discussed below, is more important for the actual content of the public's opinions on political issues rather than its factual knowledge), it does make a strong case that public opinion is less ignorant than isolated, individual opinion.

There are downsides to low levels of political information, however. Delli Carpini and Keeter also show that people with less political knowledge are more likely to misperceive candidate stands or the effects of particular policies, and so may support the wrong candidate or policy position for them.[25] Scott Althaus likewise uncovered evidence that the unequal distribution of knowledge in the population has political and policy consequences. Because political knowledge is concentrated among the economically and socially advantaged— and in particular, because the older, white, male and educated in the population are more likely to express an opinion (in other words, the "no opinions" and uninformed in surveys are not randomly distributed, but are more likely the poorer, younger, minority population)—public opinion polls are likely to distort the public's policy preferences. To estimate these effects, Althaus simulated full information, or what the public *would want* if it was fully informed, by comparing the responses of lesser informed individuals with demographically similar knowledgeable ones. Using data from the 1988 and 1992 National Election Studies, he concludes that

> the uneven social distribution of political knowledge causes the mass public to consistently appear more progressive on some issues and more conservative on others than might be the case if all citizens were equally well informed about politics. To the extent that opinion polls influence democratic politics, this finding suggests that information effects may impair the democratic responsiveness of governments to their citizens.[26]

To summarize: People may know enough to make reasonable decisions and be decent citizens, especially if they take cues from other more informed members of the public or political elites they trust. The public may not be as informed as ideal visions of a democratic citizenry would want, but neither is it as ignorant as some fear.

Real Attitudes, Underlying Values, and a Stable, Rational Collective Public

Other scholars have attacked the notion that most of the public does not possess a coherent belief system or ideology. Robert Lane, in his book *Political Ideology* (which we briefly discussed in Chapter 3), argued that most members of the public do have underlying value structures, but not ones that easily correspond to the liberal-conservative framework used by elites. In his in-depth interviews of ordinary working people, Lane found that they did have basic value frameworks, but these were more morsels of a political theory rather than an abstract, clearly identifiable whole.[27] Scholars in this research tradition have continued to find visible patterns in the public's core values.[28] While these may not fit Converse's definition of a belief system, nevertheless the public isn't completely apolitical, either. Therefore, just because people do not employ well-defined and sophisticated conceptualizations about politics, like political leaders or other elite segments of the population, does not mean they are incapable of thinking coherently about politics.

Further research in the rational public tradition likewise discredits the ideas of nonattitudes and capricious opinion change. Page and Shapiro, among others, counter that this conclusion, too, is a mistake driven by focusing on *individual* rather than *collective* opinion. They examined series of questions over time—with precisely the same phrasing, to avoid errors based on question wording—on a huge variety of political issues. What they found was that rather than great fluctuation and instability, instead the policy preferences of the public were real, stable, sensible, and relevant. When public opinion did change, it did so in understandable ways, given the political and information environment of the time. How can this be? As noted above, much of this is due to the unique characteristics of public opinion *as a whole*. First, error, instability, and randomness (the nonattitude guessing of Converse) at the individual level essentially *cancels each other out*. So, for example, for every person who, rather than honestly admitting he doesn't know about an issue, chooses one side, it's equally likely another such person will choose the other side.

Second, the collective whole is greater than its parts due to a process of **collective deliberation**. Other less informed members of the public, rather than guessing or having no opinion, may choose to rely on others who are more informed—opinion leaders or members of a specialized issue public. They take their cues on political issues from these opinion leaders, trusting their judgment rather than developing their own fully informed opinion. While they might not have all the background information, they do nevertheless have a real, actual opinion, based on their views and values. For example, you might not know much about President Bush's "no child left behind" education policy, but your mother the high school principal does, and you might take her word, and position, on that issue as your own. The result is a stable, real public opinion.

Similarly, if new information comes to light—say, government statistics showing the success of Bush's education policy on raising test scores—public opinion will respond to that, based on the credibility of the evidence or the cues provided by opinion leaders. These more attentive members of the public in turn likely take cues from political elites such as politicians, experts, or media commentators, as was mentioned in Chapter 6 on the media.[29]

Another point of view takes a middle position by granting that most people do not have firm, readymade opinions on most political issues, yet they do have underlying predispositions which inform the opinions they express. This view has been most forcefully expressed by John Zaller and Stanley Feldman.[30] They said that while some people do have opinions, most people carry in their heads what they called *considerations* about issues, politicians, and other political objects. Considerations can be ideas, evaluations, or other thoughts. Some considerations are positive, and some are negative. These considerations may be contradictory, but most people really don't examine them, so they don't notice. When most people are polled, they cannot reveal their true opinion on an issue because they don't have one. Instead, they have several opinions, and the one they give to the interviewer is the one at the top of their mind, which could reflect the last thing the person has heard or thought on the issue.

These are not Converse's random nonattitudes; there may be patterns to them. An example might be a question on defense spending. One person may read a newspaper article about the Air Force buying $600 toilet seats, which would lead to a negative consideration about wasteful military spending. This same person may also see a television show about the American infantry soldiers not having enough armor on their vehicles, which would lead to a consideration about the necessity of defense spending. According to Zaller and Feldman, when most people are asked survey questions, they are most likely to sample the considerations at the top of their heads, which tend to be the most recent or the easiest to retrieve, or the ones triggered by the question wording. If our hypothetical respondent had just seen the story about American troops in Iraq not having enough armored Humvees, he might say that defense spending should be increased. In Zaller's and Feldman's view, people can give wildly different responses to the same question asked twice in a short time if their mix of considerations changes or if different considerations are at the top of their heads at the time the question is asked. Nevertheless, these are linked to an underlying value structure and cues that members of the public take from elite political debates. A respondent who was generally against defense spending, for example, might interpret the top of the head issue of armor for Humvees differently from someone generally in favor of increased spending.

R. Michael Alvarez and John Brehm later built on Zaller's and Feldman's work. They argue that, rather than a comprehensive framework, people develop *predispositions* about political objects in response to a complex political world. These predispositions may include (1) values, such as egalitarianism, individualism, authoritarianism, or racism; (2) affective relationships with groups, such as positive feelings for the military or prejudice against Mexicans; and (3) expectations about the performance of political actors. People's survey responses are not random or haphazard answers, but a complex interaction of predispositions and the actions of political elites' attempts to influence public opinion. In fact,

> [w]hat happens at the doorstep or over the phone is that the survey respondent *constructs* answers to the questions asked by the interviewer. But if these are "doorstep opinions," they are not created out of thin air or "made up as they go along," but constructed using a toolkit of predispositions [emphasis in original].[31]

Alvarez and Brehm also said "the range and complexity of predispositions argues against an expectation of a consistent left-right political ideology."[32] In addition, people's complex sets of predispositions are unlikely to be elicited by survey research questions because respondents are not given enough time to reflect on their ideas. Consequently, respondents could appear to be answering haphazardly when, in fact, they are being forced to relate their complex answers to simple questions and cannot do so consistently. Alvarez and Brehm concluded that "neither lack of information nor response variability necessarily implies a public incapable of reasoning about politics."[33]

The public, therefore, does possess real attitudes about politics. This public opinion does exist, and can be measured through instruments such as public opinion surveys.

Retrospective Voting, Gut Rationality, and Heuristics

Finally, other scholars have stood up for the public in the debate over issue voting. V. O. Key, for example, while accepting many of the conclusions of Converse and others about the limitations of the public, argued nevertheless that people make sense of politics and vote as best they can. In examining poll data on elections, he found clear connections between voters' general predispositions, their sense of the candidates' characters, their attitudes toward the general state of the political system, and how they ultimately voted. He emphasized that much of the electorate's confusion about where candidates stood was due to the fuzziness of the candidates themselves. "In the large, the electorate behaves about as rationally and responsibly as we should expect, given the clarity of the alternatives presented to it and the character of information available to it."[34]

This line of thinking has been extended to include the notion of *retrospective* (that is, backward-looking) voting by the public.[35] Many voters, especially those truly independent of party affiliation and others who cross party lines, while being uninformed about detailed candidate positions and policy issues, instead vote based on how things are going at the time, using such performance-based measures as the economy, wars, and the general state of the nation. If times are good, they vote to reelect the incumbent or party in power; if times are bad, they vote to throw them out of office. While not conforming to the model of the ideal electorate, such behavior is far from random, ignorant, or capricious. Indeed, given that candidates may intentionally blur their policy positions or even lie or promise things they can't deliver, focusing on past performance seems to be a reasonable fall-back strategy.

Samuel Popkin takes a similar position on elections and voting to that of Page and Shapiro about public opinion on policy issues. He also admits that voters are not extremely sophisticated and lack detailed information. But, based on his research on voting and election campaigns, he thinks voters make reasonable judgments within their own levels of information based on **gut rationality**: the accumulation of a variety of signals they receive about the candidates, the current political climate, and other tidbits. Voters learn about candidates and the campaign from the media and conversations with others. In so doing, they thereby increase their knowledge about the candidates and the election, crystallizing their voting choice as the campaign progresses toward Election Day. The basis of his argument is that voters take shortcuts by employing what are known as **heuristics**—mental rules-of-thumb that allow them to come to a reasonable decision based on little information. Voters use their life experiences and previous knowledge to make up their minds about how to vote. The political campaigns (and their coverage by the media) tap into this storehouse of knowledge, triggering connections so that voters can link the issues and candidates of the day to their long-held political predispositions.[36] For example, if a candidate has trouble within his campaign—in-fighting with staff, campaign event problems, battles with the press, and so on—voters may take this seemingly irrelevant information and use it to conclude that if elected, that person would have similar problems running things once in office. Al Gore's apparent penchant for exaggerating his achievements during the 2000 campaign likely set off alarm bells in some voters' heads that he could not tell the full truth, thus further linking him to the perceived less-than-honest Clinton White House. George W. Bush's mangled and incoherent speaking style likely helped convince other voters that he wasn't smart enough to be president.

There are consequences to such an approach, however. Voters are still reliant on the media portrayals of the campaign, and on candidate campaign appeals, and so may be misled or encouraged to focus on trivial issues. In the case of Al Gore's tall tales in 2000, in fact several of these could have instead been cases of media exaggeration or inaccuracy. His widely repeated, supposedly ridiculous claim of "inventing the Internet" masked the fact that he was one of the earliest congressional supporters of creating a government-funded computer network; his incorrect claims of visiting a Texas disaster site with the director of FEMA during the first presidential debate may have been due to confusing it with a similar visit to a different location.[37] Likewise, the general media tendency to report the unusual, the negative, and even the humorous may have meant they overemphasized Bush's malapropisms and ignored those parts of his campaign speeches where he spoke correctly or presented sophisticated ideas.

In fact, studies have shown reliance on heuristic shortcuts can lead to errors. Lau and Redlawsk, in an experimental study simulating an actual election, found that while heuristics were employed by almost all voters, the least sophisticated voters were more likely to employ them in such a way as to vote for the wrong candidate, while the more politically sophisticated utilized them to come to the right choice. So, ironically, in complicated situations, heuristics are actually most beneficial to those who arguably need them the least.[38]

In the conclusion, we address the consequences of both the original and revisionist perspectives in more detail. The point here is that the public is still able to make reasonable decisions based on less-than-perfect information, much like the overworked college student has a good chance of getting the answer right on a test despite not having enough time to study.

PUBLIC SUPPORT FOR DEMOCRACY

Another area of importance to the question of "should government listen to the people?" concerns the public's own commitment to democracy. If the masses don't support democratic values—such as majority rule, equality, and in particular, the civil liberties of minorities (be they ethnic, religious, or political), then the Founders' fears about mob rule may be justified. After all, how can government function in a democratic way if the public itself is undemocratic? In this section, we examine support for democratic principles among the American public.

Support for Democracy in the Abstract, Not Specifics

The very idea of democracy is widely accepted and supported by the American people. Indeed, democracy along with its related democratic values of popular sovereignty (rule by the people, majority rule, and so forth), political equality, and individual freedom are all favored by large segments of the population, enough so that they make up an integral part of the American political culture. For example, Americans rank highly when compared with other citizens of other Western countries on the question of whether "democracy is the best form of government."[39]

Similar results are found when one examines certain elements of democracy. Americans strongly support competitive elections and other democratic decision-making mechanisms. Americans also favor egalitarianism and the idea of political equality. For example, 69 percent of the public supported giving everyone the right to vote, no matter their level of ignorance, and about the same number (63 percent) disagreed with the statement that "only people with at least five years of schooling should be allowed to vote."[40] When it comes to social and economic equality, Americans favor equality of opportunity over equality of outcome. Nevertheless, there is a strong commitment among the bulk of the population to the basic political equality of all citizens.

Liberty appears more ingrained as a widespread value than almost any other. Indeed, Americans are a freedom-loving people. When asked whether personal freedom or equality was more important, Americans preferred freedom over equality by a 50 percent margin, 72 to 20 percent; for Western Europeans, by comparison, it was 49 to 35 percent.[41]

However, there is a nagging paradox about public support for democracy: Public opinion researchers have long noticed that Americans appear to support abstract democratic principles far more than they support the *application* of those principles in specific instances. For example, large numbers of Americans say they support free speech, but that support often withers when specific groups, like the Ku Klux Klan or Communists, are used as examples. Similarly, more people are tolerant of homosexuals in general than would allow them to marry or teach in school.

Stouffer's research in the 1950s on deviant groups of that time was one of the most notable studies to uncover this phenomenon of public opinion. He found that large majorities said that an admitted Communist should not be permitted to speak publicly, to teach in school or college, or have the same work rights as others. Support was also expressed for having such people's

Public Opinion in the 21st Century

Let the People Speak?

BOX 11.2

Wartime Is a Tough Time for Democracy in America

One might imagine that when the United States is attacked, or goes to war to defend democracy, that Americans would be even more supportive of it at home. But history shows this is often not the case. Tolerance toward particular groups, and support for civil liberties in general, declines during wars and crises, as people feel threatened. Thus, it was perhaps no surprise that following the terrorist attacks of September 11, 2001, Americans' support for democratic values like freedom and equality was called into question.

Indeed, in the immediate aftermath of the attacks polls confirmed increasing intolerance towards people of Middle Eastern descent, even American citizens; support for racial profiling of such people; and decreasing support for civil liberties like criminal procedures and free speech. Although such sentiments seemed to have declined over time, they were clear in the subsequent months as the United States absorbed the impact of the blow, and the government developed its response.

A few days after the attacks, a Gallup poll found that Americans supported singling out Arabs for special security measures. In the survey, 58 percent supported requiring all Arabs, even American citizens, to undergo more intensive screening procedures at airports; 49 percent supported having them carry special identification cards, and 32 percent supported placing such people under special surveillance by the government. Surprisingly, the poll found blacks supported these racial profiling measures even more than whites did. Despite the obvious misgivings some minorities had, they too still found themselves looking at such people differently. For example, Jermaine Johnson, a nineteen-year old community college student in Tennessee, said, "I've seen prejudice all my life, with me growing up an African-American male. I try not to judge." But he added, "I would not feel comfortable at all if an Arab-looking person sat next to me on a plane. I would be nervous, and right now it could be anyone . . . I don't feel comfortable with ones I don't know—it's hard to know who to trust."[1]

The Bush administration took several decisive steps following 9/11 in what it called a new "War on Terrorism." Some elements of the government's response raised objections from civil libertarians. For example, the administration held a large number of Middle Eastern aliens in custody without trial; announced they would treat terror suspects as "enemy combatants" and try them in military courts; and it succeeded in getting Congress to pass the USA PATRIOT Act (discussed in Chapter 1), giving the government new legal, surveillance, and investigative powers. Despite possible infringements on freedom, polls showed the public supported such efforts. In one survey, 60 percent agreed with Bush that suspected terrorists should go to military tribunals; 73 percent that it should be legal for the federal government to wiretap conversations between suspected terrorists and their attorneys; and almost 90 percent that the United States was justified in detaining indefinitely thousands of foreign nationals for violating immigration laws.

There appeared to be a feeling in the country that sacrifices had to be made for greater security. As one Manhattan woman even put it, "If we keep going the way we're going with civil liberties, other countries are going to see us as a patsy. You have to change with the times." She also had little sympathy for those held for possible connection to the attacks. "They should torture them. Sometimes you have to do things that are uncivilized," she said.[2]

Some did express reservations about freedom, such as a retired librarian who said, "I'm concerned that we not become a runaway train when it comes to civil liberties. . . . It's always harder to get these basic freedoms back once we relinquish them."[3]

But public opinion experts, such as George Marcus, Professor of Political Science at Williams College, were not surprised. "In periods of high stress and threat, support for civil liberties goes down. Most Americans don't think of rights as unqualified or universal."[4]

Support for other freedoms was likewise weak. Another survey indicated popular support for government control of the news media and restrictions on a free press. Two months after 9/11, the Pew Center for Research on the People and the Press found slight majorities favoring official censorship of news if the government believed it represented a threat to national security, and for giving the military more control over how war news was reported. These numbers were similar to findings on the eve of the 1991 Persian Gulf War, but higher than an identical survey in the nonwar year of 1985.[5]

Some of these sentiments persisted long after the events of September 11. A Cornell University poll in December 2004 found nearly half—44 percent—favored at least one type of restriction on the civil liberties of Muslim Americans, while 48 percent did not. More specifically, 27 percent of respondents supported requiring all Muslim Americans to register with the federal government; 22 percent favored racial profiling to identify terrorist threats; and 28 percent thought undercover agents should infiltrate Muslim civic and volunteer organizations to keeps tabs on their activities and fund-raising. Republicans, highly religious people, and heavy television news viewers were more likely to favor such restrictions.[6]

Professor Marcus's point is well taken: Threats from abroad and within have often brought stronger government measures, and as we have seen, intolerance is often aimed at groups currently out of favor. However, one might argue that the picture today isn't as bad as it seems, or at least may be milder, historically speaking. Those who claim Americans are more tolerant today (at least, of racial minorities) might have a leg to stand on.

Consider policies and attitudes toward Japanese Americans in the aftermath of the attack on Pearl Harbor in 1941. Anti-Asian sentiment had been strong on the West Coast of the United States for decades, and grew to a fever pitch as war with Japan came. Fear of Japanese saboteurs, disloyalty, and general war and racial hysteria led to an official U.S. policy of detaining thousands of Americans of Japanese ancestry. They were placed in detention centers (what amounted to concentration camps) in the western interior of the country, stripping them of their rights, liberties, property, and livelihoods. The bulk of them remained there for the duration of the war. We can only assume that this action was taken with public support.

In an early poll in December 1942, the public was asked if they thought the Japanese who were moved inland should be allowed to return to the Pacific Coast after the war; a plurality of 48 percent thought they should not (only 35 percent said yes, with 16 percent having no opinion). To those who said "no," a follow-up question asked about what should be done with them. Of these people, 63 percent thought the interned people should either be "put out of the country" or "sent back to Japan"; another 10 percent that "they should leave them where they are," coupled with 4 percent saying "remain somewhere inland"; 7 percent said "kill them, get rid of them, destroy them"; and 4 percent responded, "if U.S. citizens, they can stay, otherwise send them back to Japan."[7]

Further evidence of intolerance was found later in the war. On the issue of loyalty, Americans were asked, "of the Japanese who are American citizens, how many of them would do something against the U.S. if they had the chance?" Only 19 percent answered "practically none of them." 15 percent said "practically all," 9 percent "most of them," and

Continued

BOX 11.1—*Cont'd*

another 9 "about half," for a half-or-more total of 33 percent. Thirty-four percent, the plurality, answered "a few of them."[8] Incidentally, no evidence of disloyalty or sabotage was ever found against the Japanese American population.

Examining these results, one might be proud to be living now. On the other hand, perhaps some Americans today feel similarly about Arabs, but are unwilling to say so publicly. But such a comparison seems to bolster the argument that Americans are relatively more tolerant today than in previous decades.

Furthermore, in the case of the aftermath of September 11, the picture of a fearful, antidemocratic public, weakly committed to civil liberties and tolerance, may be an oversimplified one. Two political scientists analyzing the civil liberties versus security tradeoff in a national survey in the months after the terrorist attacks did indeed find that the greater people's sense of threat, the lower their support for civil liberties. However, this effect interacted with the respondents' level of political trust: The lower someone's level of trust in government, the less likely they were to favor sacrificing civil liberties in return for greater security provided by the government. African Americans were also less likely to trade liberty for security than whites or Latinos, perhaps reflecting their history of struggle.[9]

Once again, perhaps people are more sophisticated, and public opinion more complicated, than it appears at first glance. Still, the researchers concluded that "the results indicate that Americans' commitment to democratic values is highly contingent on other concerns, and that the context of a large-scale threat to national or personal security can induce a substantial willingness to give up rights."[10]

These two cases of America attacked (Pearl Harbor and September 11, 2001), may be extreme examples, but they do highlight the general truth that when threats or fear drive people, intolerance and support for harsh measures may follow. Perhaps the lesson of these examples is that Americans need to be ever vigilant in the defense of liberty, and in times of crisis especially so.

Notes

1. Sam Howe Verhovek, "A Nation Challenged: Civil Liberties; Americans Give in to Race Profiling," *New York Times*, September 23, 2001, p. A1.
2. Richard Morin and Claudia Deane, "Most Americans Back U.S. Tactics; Poll Finds Little Worry Over Rights," *Washington Post*, November 29, 2001, p. A1.
3. Morin and Deane, "Most Americans Back U.S. Tactics," p. A1.
4. Ibid.
5. November 28, 2001 Pew Center for Politics and the Press poll, cited in "Civil Liberties in Wartime," *CQ Researcher* 11 No. 43 (December 14, 2001): 1020.
6. William Kates, "In U.S., 44 Percent Say Restrict Muslims," AP Wire, December 17, 2004; actual survey is discussed in "Fear Factor: 44 Percent of Americans Queried in Cornell National Poll Favor Curtailing Some Liberties for Muslim Americans," at http://www.news.cornell. edu/releases/Dec04/Muslim.Poll.bpf.html.
7. Gallup poll, December 1942.
8. National Opinion Research Center poll, April 1945.
9. Darren W. Davis and Brian D. Silver, "Civil Liberties vs. Security: Public Opinion in the Context of the Terrorist Attacks on America," *American Journal of Political Science* 48 No. 1 (January 2004): 28–46.
10. Ibid., p. 28.

TABLE 11.7. Increasing Tolerance and Support for Free Speech.

	1954	1973
Percentage willing to grant freedom of speech to:		
admitted Communists	27	53
persons against religions and churches	37	62
persons favoring government ownership of the railroads and big industry	58	72

Source: Adapted from Clyde A. Nunn, Harry J. Crockett, and J. Allen Williams, *Tolerance for Non-Conformity* (San Francisco, CA: Jossey-Bass, 1978), chap. 3.

However, these findings too, may be misleading. Critics of the evolving tolerance thesis instead argue that the changing results may be because the groups mentioned in the polls (leftist ones primarily), seen as threatening in the 1950s, had become less so by the 1970s, so that in fact perhaps the public had become more tolerant toward these particular groups rather than more tolerant in general. One study testing this proposition indicates that this may indeed be the explanation. As an experiment, they first asked people to choose a group they were opposed to from a list of extremist organizations. Most Americans picked one or more. The researchers then asked whether they favored democratic rights for these groups, and found, in numbers comparable to those about Communists in the 1950s, that most Americans were opposed to granting rights to groups they disfavored. When asked, people justified their intolerance as a defense against undemocratic groups that threaten their rights, or in other words people are intolerant toward groups they view as intolerant. Therefore, the researchers argued, "claims that the public is now [in late 1970s] more tolerant than in the 1950s are either untrue or greatly exaggerated."[45] Or, as the title of one book put it, perhaps Americans favor "free speech for me, but not for thee."[46]

Public Disdain for Democratic Practices and Procedures

In similar fashion, many Americans disapprove of certain essential attributes of democracy in practice, such as policy differences and battles between political parties, dissent and conflict over political issues, and the general need for negotiation and compromise in order to make democratic government function. One set of scholars found that much of the negative public perceptions of Congress are rooted in the very democratic operations of a legislative body: The public dislikes the typical partisan fighting and the compromising, deal-laden world of the legislative process.[47] Further research in the same vein discovered that much of the public was either uninterested in, or annoyed by, democracy in practice. According to a national survey, almost half of the public would prefer that decisions be made either by business leaders or unelected experts rather than by elected politicians or even by the people themselves. In fact most people didn't want more political responsibility. Many of those polled also wanted politics to be easy, neat, and clean—unlike the classic democratic notions of heated debate and competition between politicians, parties, and ideas. For example, in one study, participants were divided into three groups: One group read a description of a heated political debate; the second read a description of a pleasant debate; and the third read a description of a political discussion in which the politicians weren't disagreeing. Not only did people prefer the pleasant debate to the heated one, most telling was the fact that they preferred *no debate* at all![48]

In some ways, these sentiments may be off-shoots of people's general lack of interest in, and distaste for, politics. "We're not saying that people aren't capable of engaging in politics," said John Hibbing, one of the researchers. "The truth is, they don't want to."[49] Sizable numbers of people dislike how democratic politics actually works and in effect favor others to make decisions for them in undemocratic ways; such a situation is not exactly a ringing endorsement for government by the people.

Explaining the Survival of Democracy: Democratic Elitism

The lack of strong public support for democratic values in practice has led some to wonder how democracy has been so relatively successful in the United States. The answer is perhaps surprising: according to one line of thinking, it is not the support of the public, but rather the support of the elites, that is critical.

According to polls, political elites, both leaders (government officials and the like) and members of the educated public, have been found to be more tolerant, more supportive of democratic values and practices, and so forth, than the public as a whole. For example, compare the results of polls listed in Table 11.8.

TABLE 11.8. Differences Between Community Leaders and the Mass Public on Certain Democratic Values.

Question	General Public	Community Influentials
Books that preach overthrow of the government should be banned from the public library	50	13*
Censoring obscene books is necessary to protect community standards (agree)	50	39*
People ought to be allowed to vote even if they can't do so intelligently (agree)	48	66**
Most people don't have enough sense to pick their own leaders wisely (agree)	48	28***

Source: Herbert McCloskey and John Zaller, *The Democratic Ethos: Public Attitudes Toward Capitalism and Democracy,* * = p. 38; ** = p. 75; *** = p. 78.

These findings have led some to the idea of **democratic elitism:** Democracy survives because the major players in the political game are more knowledgeable and supportive of democratic politics than are the masses, and therefore the elites play by the democratic rules rather than undermining them.[50] Hence, when Al Gore lost the contentious presidential election of 2000, despite numerous legal challenges and possibly dubious court decisions, he and the Democratic Party accepted the victory of George W. Bush, rather than taking up arms or staging a revolt.

This attribute is part of what Thomas Dye and Harmon Zeigler have called the "irony of democracy": that democratic government exists to the degree it does in America is due more to its acceptance and basic support by political elites rather than the mass public.[51] Indeed, some might argue that it was elite intervention—namely, leaders like President George W. Bush and members of Congress—speaking out against intolerance towards Arabs and Muslims that has helped stunt backlashes against these groups in the aftermath of the terrorist attacks of September 11, 2001. Of course, the McCarthy-era witch hunts against Communists in the 1950s and the internment of Japanese Americans in World War Two provide examples where elites failed to uphold democratic values and went along with intolerant public sentiments. Indeed, some evidence suggests that elites are no more tolerant than the masses, and, for example, the degree of repressive policies adopted by state governments during the 1950s was more due to the level of *elite intolerance* toward Communists than it was to mass opinion.[52]

Still, if democracy may be dependent for its existence on the favor of elites, what does that say about the role of the public, the supposed bedrock of democracy? Such a question adds to the puzzle of whether the government should listen to us. Below, we attempt to forge a compromise solution to the *democratic dilemma*.

CONCLUSION

After all the evidence has been sifted, and the arguments weighed, what can we say definitively about the political capacity of the public? Are we, the people, really fit to rule?

Clearly, there is no easy answer to such a question. Both sides have points in their favor. For example, those who argue that the public is basically rational are probably correct, that the voters aren't the incompetent boobs they are portrayed to be by their critics, and that public opinion as a whole does contain characteristics different from and superior to its atomistic individual parts. But the critics of the public's competence are right that Americans don't live up to civic ideals and that their opponents may instead just be lowering the bar. Lack of widespread, strong support for democratic values in practice is also cause for concern.

However, none of these arguments proves that the public isn't capable of governing itself, at least at some basic level. And it is probably safe, albeit not very exciting, to conclude that the public as a whole is neither a wise sage nor the village idiot.

Along these same lines, there is no question that the public's political competence could be greater, and democratic government improved. Clearly, better political education, including explicit lessons in citizenship, a more informative and critical media, and the like, would make public opinion a more accurate and crucial factor in government, and lead to a more democratic system. A better understanding of democracy and how it works in practice, so that more of the public would appreciate the nitty-gritty of democratic politics, would likewise be all for the better.[53]

Public intolerance and lack of specific support for democratic values is disturbing, and should and can be increased through political education. But even here, one can argue that things aren't as bad as they seem. Declining support for civil liberties for groups one dislikes, or when the nation is at war, is certainly understandable, even if it is at the same time regrettable. Public distaste for the processes of democracy is also somewhat understandable, given the negative portrayal of politics and politicians in recent years. It may also reflect a naïve desire for consensus and cooperation in politics, something that rarely happens, since politics is at root about differing conceptions of values and what government should do about various problems.

Besides, if one chooses to take a dim view of the public, which implies that government shouldn't listen to the masses, the question then arises: To whom should government listen instead? We must rely on the public. However, the extent to which we should do so remains an open question. How much should short-term mass opinion on specific issues—like the kind expressed through polls—guide day-to-day government decision making, as opposed to more general or long-range expressions of public sentiment (like latent opinion or retrospective judgments that are exhibited after politicians have been given leeway to set policy)? In the end, the final answer depends on your *informed* response to the question, should government listen?

Suggested Readings

Converse, Phillip. "Public Opinion and Voting Behavior." In Fred I. Greenstein and Nelson B. Polsby, eds. *Handbook of Political Science.* Reading, MA: Addison Wesley, 1975.

Delli Carpini, Michael X., and Scott Keeter. *What Americans Know About Politics and Why It Matters.* New Haven: Yale University Press, 1996.

Hibbing, John R., and Elizabeth Theiss-Morse. *Stealth Democracy: Americans' Beliefs About How Government Should Work.* New York: Cambridge University Press, 2002.

McClosky, Herbert, and John Zaller. *The American Ethos: Public Attitudes Toward Capitalism and Democracy.* Cambridge, MA: Harvard University Press, 1984.

Neuman, W. Russell. *The Paradox of Mass Politics: Knowledge and Opinion in the American Electorate*. Cambridge, MA: Harvard University Press, 1986.

Page, Benjamin I., and Robert Y. Shapiro. *The Rational Public: Fifty Years of Trends in Americans' Policy Preferences*. Chicago: University of Chicago Press, 1992.

Zaller, John. *The Nature and Origins of Mass Opinion*. New York: Cambridge University Press, 1992.

⧉ **www** ▶ ▶ ▶ Interactive Learning Exercise:

Test Your Political Knowledge

One of the key elements in the public competency debate is the level of political knowledge possessed by average citizens. How do you stack up? To find out, you can go to the book's Web site under Chapter 11 and take our Political Knowledge Quiz. In it, you will answer several questions testing your knowledge of political facts. As a point of comparison, you will also be shown the percentage of the general public that got each question right. You may also be asked to forward your results electronically to your instructor. Alternatively, your instructor may provide, or may have already provided, a paper survey asking you such questions in class.

Notes

1. Benjamin I. Page and Robert Y. Shapiro, *The Rational Public: Fifty Years of Trends in Americans' Policy Preferences* (Chicago: University of Chicago Press, 1992), p. 1.

2. Michael X. Delli Carpini and Scott Keeter, *What Americans Know About Politics and Why It Matters* (New York: Oxford University Press, 1996), p. 2.

3. Phillip Converse, "Public Opinion and Voting Behavior," in Fred I. Greenstein and Nelson W. Polsby, eds., *Handbook of Political Science* (Reading, MA: Addison-Wesley, 1975), p. 79.

4. Delli Carpini and Keeter, *What Americans Know*, p. 101.

5. W. Russell Neuman, *The Paradox of Mass Politics: Knowledge and Opinion in the American Electorate* (Cambridge, MA: Harvard University Press, 1986). p. 15.

6. Jay Leno, quoted in Emily Bonden, "Not so Chin-tzy: Just Jay Talking," *Central Washington Observer*, October 9, 2003, p. 10.

7. For the political context surrounding this case, see Edward S. Greenberg and Benjamin I. Page, *The Struggle for Democracy*, 5th ed. (New York: Longman Publishers, 2001), p. 533.

8. Angus Campbell, Philip E. Converse, Warren E. Miller, and Donald E. Stokes, *The American Voter* (New York: John Wiley, 1960).

9. M. Kent Jennings, "Ideology Among Mass Publics and Political Elites," *Public Opinion Quarterly* 56 (Winter 1992): 419–441.

10. Philip Converse, "The Nature of Belief Systems in Mass Publics," in David E. Apter, ed., *Ideology and Discontent* (New York: Free Press, 1964).

11. Ibid., p. 245.

12. Jennings, "Ideology Among Mass Publics and Political Elites," pp. 419–441.

13. See Phillip Converse, "Attitudes and Non-attitudes: Continuation of a Dialogue," in Edward R. Tufte, ed., *The Quantitative Analysis of Social Problems* (Reading, MA: Addison-Wesley, 1970), pp. 168–189; "Non-attitudes and Public Opinion: Comment: The Status Nonattitudes," *The American Political Science Review* 68 No. 2 (June 1974): 650–660; and Phillip Converse and Gregory Marcus, "Plus ca change . . . : The New CPS Election Study Panel," *The American Political Science Review* 73 No. 1 (March 1979): 32–49.

14. See, for example, Bernard R. Berelson, Paul F. Lazarsfeld, and William N. McPhee, *Voting: A Study of Opinion Formation in a Presidential Campaign* (Chicago: University of Chicago Press, 1954), and Campbell et al., *The American Voter*.

15. Delli Carpini and Keeter, *What Americans Know*, p. 41.

16. Anthony Downs, *An Economic Theory of Democracy* (New York: Harper and Row, 1957); see also the discussion of "rational ignorance" in Page and Shapiro, *The Rational Public*, p. 14.

17. For the evidence and reasoning behind this argument, see Ivor Crewe, "Electoral Participation," in David Butler, Howard R. Penniman, and Austin Ranney, eds., *Democracy at the Polls: A Comparative Study of Competitive National Elections* (Washington, DC: American Enterprise Institute, 1981), p. 219–232.

18. Page and Shapiro, *The Rational Public*, p. 12.

19. See, for example, Gary Jacobsen, *The Politics of Congressional Elections*, 5th ed. (New York: Addison-Wesley-Longman, 2001), pp. 110–116.

20. 1998 National Election Study pilot; see www.umich.edu/~nes.

21. Delli Carpini and Keeter, *What Americans Know*, pp. 95–100.

22. Page and Shapiro, *The Rational Public*, pp. 397–398.

23. Pew Research Center for People and the Press, News Interest Index Poll, January 16, 2003.

24. Page and Shapiro, *The Rational Public*, p. 388.

25. Delli Carpini and Ketter, *What Americans Know*, pp. 238–267.

26. Scott L. Althaus, "Information Effects in Collective Preferences," *American Political Science Review* 92 No. 3 (September 1998), p. 545; article is 545–558.

27. Robert Lane, *Political Ideology* (New York: Free Press, 1962).

28. Jennifer Hochschild, *What's Fair? American Beliefs About Distributive Justice* (Cambridge, MA: Harvard University Press, 1981).

29. Page and Shapiro, *The Rational Public*, pp. 383–393.

30. John R. Zaller, *The Nature and Origins of Mass Opinion* (Cambridge: Cambridge University Press, 1992); and John R. Zaller and Stanley Feldman, "A Simple Model of the Survey Response," *American Journal of Political Science* 36 (1992): 579–616.

31. R. Michael Alvarez and John Brehm, *Hard Choices, Easy Answers: Values, Information, and American Public Opinion* (Princeton: Princeton University Press, 2002), p. 218.

32. Ibid., p. 218.

33. Ibid., p. 224.

34. V. O. Key, *The Responsible Electorate: Rationality in Presidential Voting 1936–1960* (New York: Vintage, 1966), p. x.

35. Morris P. Fiorina, *Retrospective Voting in American National Elections* (New Haven: Yale University Press, 1981).

36. Samuel Popkin, *The Reasoning Voter: Communication and Persuasion in Presidential Campaigns* (Chicago: University of Chicago Press, 1991).

37. Maria LaGanga and Elizabeth Shogren, "Bush and Gore Campaigns Tally Up Post-Debate Scores," *Los Angeles Times*, October 5, 2000, p. 22; and Bennett Roth, "Gore Says Criticism Designed to Detract From Relevant Issues," *Houston Chronicle*, October 8, 2000, p. A8; see also the discussion in Al Franken, *Lies and the Lying Liars Who Tell Them* (New York: Dutton Press, 2003), p. 2.

38. Richard R. Lau and David P. Redlawsk, "Advantages and Disadvantages of Cognitive Heuristics in Political Decisionmaking," *American Journal of Political Science* 45 No. 4 (October 2001): 951–971.

39. See Russell Dalton, "Political Support in Advanced Industrial Democracies," in Pippa Norris, ed., *Critical Citizens: Global Support for Democratic Government* (New York: Oxford University Press, 1999), pp. 69–70. Eighty-eight percent of Americans agreed with the statement "democracy is the best form of government," which tied for sixth place (with Japan) among nineteen primarily Western, democratic nations.

40. Herbert McClosky and John Zaller, *The American Ethos: Public Attitudes Toward Capitalism and Democracy* (Cambridge, MA: Harvard University Press, 1984), p. 73–86.

41. Ibid., p. 18.

42. Samuel Stouffer, *Communism, Conformity, and Civil Liberties* (New York: Doubleday, 1955).

43. Robert Chandler, *Public Opinion: Changing Attitudes on Contemporary Political and Social Issues* (New York: R.R. Bowker Co., 1972), pp. 5–6.

44. Allen J. Williams, Jr., Clyde Z. Nunn, and Louis St. Peter, "Origins of Tolerance: Findings from a Replication of Stouffer's *Communism, Conformity, and Civil Liberties*," *Social Forces* 44 (December 1976): 394–408.

45. John L. Sullivan, James Piereson, and George E. Marcus, *Political Tolerance and American Democracy* (Chicago: University of Chicago Press, 1982), p. 250.

46. Nat Hentoff, *Free Speech for Me, but not for Thee: How the American Left and Right Relentlessly Censor Each Other* (New York: HarperPerennial, 1993).

47. John R. Hibbing and Elizabeth Theiss-Morse, *Congress as Public Enemy* (New York: Cambridge University Press, 1995).

48. John R. Hibbing and Elizabeth Theiss-Morse, *Stealth Democracy: Americans' Beliefs About How Government Should Work* (New York: Cambridge University

Press, 2002); see also Richard Morin, "Leave-Us-Alone Democracy," *Washington Post*, February 2, 2003, p. B5.

49. John Hibbing quoted in Morin, "Leave-Us-Alone Democracy," p. B5.

50. Herbert McClosky, "Consensus and Ideology in American Politics," *American Political Science Review* 58 No. 2 (June 1964): 361–382.

51. See Thomas R. Dye and Harmon Zeigler, *The Irony of Democracy: An Uncommon Introduction to American Politics*, 12th ed. (Belmont, CA: Thomson-Wadsworth, 2003).

52. James L. Gibson, "Political Intolerance and Political Repression During the McCarthy Era Red Scare," *American Political Science Review* 82 No. 2 (June 1988): 511–529.

53. See Page and Shapiro, *The Rational Public*, pp. 397–398; and Delli Carpini and Keeter, *What Americans Know*, pp. 287–290, op.cit.

Does the Government Listen? The Democratic Dialogue

At a general level, the key question is whether public opinion processes in their natural operation are democratic . . . in other words, whether "true" public opinion, or that which influences policy choices, is in reality shaped by an egalitarian, bottom-up communication of public concerns and ideas to policymakers.

—Vincent Price[1]

Questions to Think About

In the last chapter, we explored the question of whether the public was competent and able to govern itself. Here, we will examine whether the government does listen to the people, the fundamental implication of the *democratic dialogue*. We ask you to consider the following as you read:

- What is the connection between public opinion and public policy in basic democratic theory? How easy is it to put such notions into practice?
- What do social science researchers have to say about how often, and under what conditions, government listens to the people? How have scholars gone about trying to study the public opinion–policy link, and what have they found?
- What can we conclude about how the democratic dialogue works? In the end, how responsive is government to the people's wishes?

THE RELATIONSHIP BETWEEN PUBLIC OPINION AND PUBLIC POLICY

Beyond the normative or evaluative question of whether the government *should* listen to the public (explored in the last chapter) lies the more empirical or explanatory one of whether the government actually *does* listen. Of course, one's position on the quality of public opinion influences the way one looks at the findings of governmental responsiveness to opinion. If one holds a dim view of the public, then if it is found that the government doesn't follow public opinion very often, one might be pleased; if it is found that public opinion has a great influence on policy, one might be distressed. The reverse is also true. Nevertheless, understanding the effect of public opinion on public policy is vital in its own right. "The responsiveness of governmental institutions to the citizen's preferences is central to democratic theory and practice."[2] Indeed, in order to tell whether the people rule, one must determine whether the government listens to the people instead of other voices.

In this chapter, we first review what role public opinion ought to play in policymaking, according to democratic theory. The second part of the chapter discusses the scholarly evidence about whether the government actually does listen to the people.

Public Opinion and Public Policy in Democratic Theory

According to classic majoritarian democratic theory, government should do what its citizens, defined more practically as a *majority* of its citizens, want. If democracy truly is rule by the people, then in a perfect democracy, government policy should always reflect majority will.

Likewise, in this model political leaders should for the most part *follow* public opinion, rather than their own views or other influences. Politicians would be in essence, slaves to opinion. The people would speak, letting their officials know what they wanted, and politicians would listen, acting to create and execute policies mirroring or at least close to public sentiment. Politicians could also legitimately lead opinion by convincing a majority of the public to either change their minds or to adopt a new course of action promoted by them. The politicians would still in essence follow what the people wanted; it's just that their own preferences, and those of the public, would now be one and the same.

Difficulties with the Majoritarian Model of Opinion-Policy Linkage

Nevertheless, the basic idea of government following the will of the majority, attractive as it may be, is actually more complicated in practice. In some instances, it may be very difficult to just do exactly what the majority wants.

The process of translating the people's opinions into policies isn't always so easy and straightforward. Consider the following points.

First, what about the minority? There may be instances where limits must be put on the will of the majority to protect minority (and everyone else's) rights. Majority sentiment may favor, for example, putting some dissidents in prison simply for expressing their opinions in public, which not only would be repressive but ironically would limit the ability of the public to be exposed to new ideas with which it might later agree. In fact, these situations are exactly why the Framers of our Constitution and others sought to limit the power of the majority, through such protections as the Bill of Rights. The larger point is that in such cases the government may be prohibited from or may reasonably choose not to follow the will of the people.

Or, if the minority is sizable, and the majority small, should the government do exactly what the majority wants? Compromising or not going as far as the majority wants might be more prudent for government policymakers.

What if the majority is apathetic or unsure? Such a situation is especially difficult when there may be intense minorities. In such cases, government may well choose to give greater weight to the minority voices, such as has historically been the case with the gun control issue.

Or what if, as in the case of multifaceted issues, the public is split, such as when there are several positions of opinion, each with a sizable number of adherents? Then, perhaps the plurality (one with the most) should rule, or perhaps the government should do nothing, which of course may not be an option.

Finally, government may not be able to give the people what they want because sometimes the people may want incompatible things. For example, polls show most Americans do not favor paying higher taxes, and sometimes even support tax cuts. At the same time, they also want spending on various government programs, like education, Social Security, transportation, and so forth, to expand, and certainly not to be cut. Yet simultaneously, they favor a balanced budget to boot! The point here is that there may be reasons why government policy might not follow public opinion beyond the assumption that politicians don't care what the people want.

Although the idea of government policy simply reflecting the popular will isn't so simple, nevertheless it at least provides a basic framework for us to think about government responsiveness to opinion. The rest of the chapter is devoted to presenting and assessing the state of the debate about how much effect public opinion has on public policy.

DOES THE GOVERNMENT LISTEN TO THE PEOPLE? THREE COMPETING VIEWS

Despite the importance of determining whether government does what the people want, scholars studying this question have been unable to come up with a definitive answer. A major reason for this lack of consensus is that proving that opinion in fact caused policy is exceedingly difficult. Even if government does appear to do what a majority of the people want (assuming we can accurately measure this), how do we know that public opinion was the reason? For example, if polls show public support for a government-sponsored prescription drug plan, and a plan of that type later passes Congress, how do we know that the government acted in response to the polls? Part of the problem also stems from the fact that one's findings depend upon how one studies and measures the effect of opinion on policy, and how one interprets those results—something that is true about all kinds of scientific and scholarly pursuits.

Three main schools of thought have emerged in recent years in the research on public opinion–policy linkages.[3] The first school basically answers in the affirmative, seeing large and enduring effects of public opinion on policy. The second school, on the other hand, sees minimal impacts of public opinion on public policy—either the public has few real opinions that can be translated into policy; elites can influence, manipulate, or misread public opinion; or the apparent responsiveness found by the first school is due to other factors. The third school takes a middle position, arguing that in some instances, in some types of policies, at some times, public opinion does influence policy, but that in others it does not. We examine each view in turn below, before attempting to come to a tentative conclusion about them.

Does Government Listen? It Appears So

A fairly large body of research has indeed found that what the public wants eventually becomes what the government does. This evidence comes from both large, multi-issue **quantitative studies** and in-depth **qualitative case studies** of specific policy issues. Quantitative studies attempt to find a statistical or mathematical relationship between two variables (in this case, public opinion on the one hand and government policy on the other) across a large number of cases. Qualitative approaches examine one or more cases in detail, relying upon archival materials or other non-numeric sources, such as interviews with policymakers, to determine their effects. Lastly, other journalistic and anecdotal evidence also seems to point to an increase in concern for what the public wants and in the use of polling information by politicians—by extension making public opinion a bigger influence in public policymaking.

Apparent Responsiveness Across Many Cases

First, several quantitative studies examining the connection between public opinion on a variety of issues (measured through polls) and public policy (measured via government action such as laws, court decisions, executive actions, and so forth) on precisely the same topics have found some strong parallels. In one of the earliest research efforts, Miller and Stokes tried to find connections between U.S. House members' views, their constituents' views, and their votes on issues. They compared the opinions of a sample of constituents from 116 districts with the roll-call voting record and policy positions of the members who represented them. Their research uncovered modest, but variable, links. Members were much closer to their publics on civil rights than on domestic, and especially foreign, policy issues, but overall appeared somewhat responsive.[4] Subsequent studies using different methods extended Miller and Stokes's work, finding stronger constituency influences on members of Congress.[5]

Other evidence for a public opinion–policy link comes from the state level. Erikson and colleagues came up with a simple and powerful way of determining the connection between public opinion and policy. Their basic hypothesis was that if public opinion influenced state policy, then the more liberal a state's population, the more liberal its policies would be. To test this proposition, they first developed measures of the liberalness of each state's population, based on poll questions on ideological self-identification. They then examined state policies on a number of different issues, creating a numerical index of state policy liberalness, and statistically compared the two scores for each state. In fact, their suspicions were confirmed: More liberal states like California and Massachusetts on average did have more liberal policies than conservative states like Oklahoma and South Carolina, as democratic responsiveness would predict. While not perfect, nevertheless the strength of the relationship was quite strong (a correlation measure of .81, where 1.0 would be a perfect correlation or match).[6]

Further evidence for a national impact of public opinion comes from time series studies examining whether what the public wants at one point in time is related to governmental policy afterward. In an ambitious research agenda, Erikson, MacKuen, and Stimson have examined historical evidence of changes in the national opinion moods with the output of national legislation and Supreme Court decisions.[7] They don't presume the public is well-informed on issues, but that nevertheless government officials can discern broad ideological mood shifts in public opinion to which they respond. From national surveys on political issues since 1956, they derived a measure of the public's degree of liberalism or conservatism and charted it over time. They then developed a parallel ideological measure of government policy output from each of the three branches, with various time lags, and in turn compared it to the public opinion data. Their data painted a picture of governmental responsiveness: They conclude that as mood shifts into a more liberal position, more liberal policies are enacted, and vice versa. Thus, in broad terms at least, the public appears to get what it wants from government. Erikson and his colleagues go so far as to liken officials to antelopes in the field, sniffing the air for danger (the public mood), and moving with changes in the wind (opinion changes).[8]

Other researchers, using different data and methods, also conclude that government largely moves in line with public wishes. Monroe drew links between majority-opinion views toward changes in specific policies and over 500 parallel cases where new policies were adopted: 63 percent of the time, policy moved in the direction the majority wanted.[9] Page and Shapiro identified 357 instances of change in public opinion on a policy issue, and then determined whether government policy on that issue indeed did change a year or more later. Their study found that 43 percent of the time change occurred along the lines of what the public wanted; 33 percent of the time there was no policy change; and 22 percent of the time policy changed in a way inconsistent with public sentiment. However, in a more streamlined design, removing cases where policy changes the public favored were impossible, and allowing for a longer lag time for change to occur, they found (similar to Monroe) that 66 percent of the time, policy changes reflected public opinion.[10] So, it appears that approximately two out of every three times the public changes its mind, the government changes its policy along similar lines.

Evidence from Case Study Analyses

Qualitative studies exploring individual, in-depth case studies of specific policy domains, using historical and archival materials, interviews with policy-makers, and the like, have also uncovered strong evidence of the influence of public opinion. One comprehensive review of this body of work found that, out of twenty case studies from the 1970s to the 1990s, only one did *not* show a strong relationship between public opinion and subsequent policy in its issue area.[11] A number of more recent studies also document close links between public opinion and policy. In domestic policy, Jacobs found archival evidence showing that perceptions of public support aided passage of Medicare in Congress in 1965,[12] and Burstein's studies of equal opportunity employment legislation and related policies found Congress in tune with changing public perceptions about blacks, women, and the disabled in the workplace.[13] Quirk and Hinchliffe found public opinion influenced policy changes to one degree or another in several different domestic policy domains such as petroleum policy, tax policy, business regulation, and Social Security.[14]

In foreign policy, the evidence is more limited, but still clear. Some of the best indications of public influence concern U.S. defense spending, where a number of researchers have uncovered links between the public's attitudes on changing the current level of spending, and subsequent changes in actual spending.[15] For example, spending dropped after the Vietnam War in concert with decreased public support, and in similar fashion increased in the late 1970s and early 1980s, following the Soviet invasion of Afghanistan and other events, in tune with changing public ideas supporting higher spending. Other research exploring foreign policy decision making also finds public opinion playing a significant part. Sobel, after examining a number of cases of proposed and actual U.S. military interventions since Vietnam, concludes that "despite minimizing the role of public opinion, officials were aware of public attitudes and recognized the central importance of public support for their policies. Both [administration officials and members of Congress] recognized existing or anticipated constraints in public opinion on their decisions."[16]

More informally, one also sees instances of policymakers altering course in the face of adverse public reactions. Ronald Reagan's scuttling of his proposed eligibility and funding changes to Medicare and Social Security in the 1980s, the failure of Bill Clinton's health care reform plan in 1994, and Harry Truman's and Lyndon Johnson's de-escalation of the Korean and Vietnam Wars (coupled with their decisions not to run for reelection, and their successors' continued policy changes), are cases in point. A more recent example was President George W. Bush's decision making concerning the creation of a new cabinet-level Homeland Security Department in late 2002. Initially, Bush was opposed to the idea, wanting merely to continue with the small White House office he created soon after the September 11, 2001, terrorist attacks. However, following heavy media and elite criticism of how his government had handled the attacks, and public disapproval of his position, the administration hurriedly announced a new proposal for such a department. Perhaps not coincidentally, the announcement of this reversal in position was made the week following the biggest drop in his job approval ratings since 9/11.[17] On the other hand, there are also times when politicians embrace popular policies seemingly at odds with their own political bases, giving strong indications of responsiveness to popular opinion. Some notable examples are Republican Richard Nixon's support for greater environmental regulation in the early 1970s, Democrat Bill Clinton's support of welfare reform in the mid-1990s, and Republican George W. Bush's push for a prescription drug benefit plan under Medicare in 2002–2003.

Increased Awareness and Importance of Public Opinion to Policymakers

Lastly, others point to the great increase in readily available information about public wishes as inherently increasing government responsiveness. As noted earlier, widespread polling in the news media, and by political candidates, political parties, and officeholders, has given politicians more information about public preferences. As pollster Kenneth Warren puts it, "Overwhelming evidence exists that virtually all of our elected leaders, from local officials to the President of the United States consult and employ polls regularly, and have done so for many years."[18] With access to better information about what the public wants, and a political incentive for most politicians to deliver, presumably government can now more easily do so. Many journalistic accounts have documented politicians' reliance on polls, though often disdainfully portraying them as slaves to public opinion polls. Still, in his research on the relationship between politicians and polls, Geer asserts that the more officials know about public opinion, the more likely they are to follow it: "well-informed politicians behave differently than their lesser-informed counterparts, even when their motivations are the same."[19]

Does Government Listen? Not Exactly

A second school of thought, which sees only minimal effects of public opinion on policy, retorts that the positive picture of public influence on policy presented by the above evidence is misleading, and in fact public opinion has less power than it appears. These critics, and their research, make several points. One is that studies documenting a link between the two probably overemphasize the degree to which public opinion really is the driving, causal force behind the policy. Another is that in fact leaders and political elites may influence public desires first, so that the public ends up wanting the same thing, and the politicians then give it to them. Therefore, political leaders tell the people what to think rather than listening to them. Finally, other scholars even argue that politicians, in an honest attempt to do what they think the people want, instead misread opinion and end up being nonresponsive.

Overstating the Influence of Public Opinion

Some argue that public opinion isn't coherent enough to influence policy in the first place. Building on the incompetent public arguments advanced in the previous chapter, they claim that the policy preferences of most citizens are so weak that they can either be easily influenced by politicians or readily ignored. Furthermore, although "public opinion" can be constructed through polls, the fact that these measures may be similar to what government does is no evidence for their influence.

Other scholars advance the scientific argument that *correlation does not equal causation*. In other words, the evidence of public opinion and public policy congruence touted by the affirmative school does not prove that opinion *caused* policy.[20] Studies finding such a linkage, even when they do show that opinion came first, then the corresponding policy, still do not take into consideration other factors that may be the actual reason for policy change. For example, perhaps a third force—say, mass media coverage, political events, and so on—influenced both the public and the government in the same direction. Or perhaps government officials or other political elites influenced public opinion first, to build public support or acceptance, and then changed or created the policy. Or, more unlikely but even more problematic, perhaps officials made new policy or policy changes for reasons having nothing to do with public opinion, but the policies just happened to coincide with public desires. Researchers call these latter kinds of factors **spurious causation**.

Even in-depth case studies, which can directly document the influence of public opinion on policymakers, may suffer from a positive effects bias in case selection. As Paul Burstein, a case study researcher himself, points out, one problem with case studies is that the cases researchers select are likely to be ones where public opinion on the issue can be easily identified (there are polls, protest demonstrations, news accounts, and so on). Therefore, they tend to be high profile and major issues, where it is more likely that policymakers will be aware of public opinion and be more afraid to ignore it, as opposed to other issues, which receive little media attention and/or are ones where the public is less-informed and where responsiveness might be much lower.[21] The end result is that again scholars may give a misleading impression of how strongly public opinion really does influence policy.

Leading, Misleading, and Manipulating Opinion

A number of scholars emphasize the ability of elites to influence, lead, or manipulate public opinion to bring it in line with their policies. In this view, public opinion is more a dependent than an independent force on policy.

Here, it is important to make a distinction between leading and manipulating opinion. It is unrealistic to think politicians should only follow public opinion; they also have a legitimate role in leading public opinion by educating the public about possible future policy directions. In our view, if elites make factual, truthful arguments to the public in a successful attempt to persuade them, they have exercised responsible opinion leadership. Such instances should not trouble us, since the public is making a decision for itself. However, if elites present information that is knowingly deceptive, inaccurate, false, or misleading, and convince the public of their position, based wholly or in part on such information, we can say they have manipulated the public.[22] They thus have led the public (or a majority) to favor a position that, had they known the whole truth, they might not have supported. In either case, the attempt at persuasion must be successful. Failed attempts at leadership or manipulation are of no concern for the subsequent influence on public opinion and policy.

Two notable and interesting examples of the issues involved in assessing opinion *leadership* versus *manipulation* concern America's wars with the Iraqi regime of Saddam Hussein under the two President Bushes (see Boxes 12.1 and 12.2).

Nevertheless, for gauging the influence of public opinion on policy, one could argue, it makes little difference: If elites influence the public, and then do what the public wants, then public opinion is not directly affecting public policy.

Given the important role of the mass media in influencing public opinion, members of this branch of the minimal effects of opinion school point to elites' use of information in the media to sway the public to support their policies. As Margolis and Mauser note, "It is clear that the ideas and policies promoted by

BOX 12.1

Taken by Storm: Elite Manipulation in the Persian Gulf War[1]

Sometimes, because of their control over information and their ability to frame issues, elites may be able to use misleading or slanted information to persuade the public to adopt their policy positions. To a large extent, this may have been what happened before and during the Persian Gulf War with Iraq in 1991. As political communication scholar W. Lance Bennett puts it, this case "illustrates how political elites who favored going to war against Iraq used sophisticated public relations, news management, and marketing techniques" to exploit the media and public and "sell a war to the American people."[2]

The crisis began in August 1990 when Iraq, under President Saddam Hussein, invaded its tiny, oil-rich neighbor Kuwait. In response, U.S. President George H. W. Bush sent American troops, eventually numbering near 500,000, to defend nearby Saudi Arabia from a similar fate, in what was called "Operation Desert Shield." Bush then went about building an international coalition of countries and got a United Nations resolution calling for a full Iraqi withdrawal from Kuwait by January 15, 1991. If Iraq did not comply, the implication was that a U.S.-led military expedition would expel them by force. Bush argued he had drawn a line in the sand with Iraq and would not let the invasion of Kuwait stand.

President Bush and other advocates for military action after the January 15 deadline faced a somewhat divided public and a skeptical Congress. Though by November, some polls were showing over 60 percent of Americans favored "using all means necessary, including military force" if Iraq did not withdraw voluntarily, other polls showed support for Bush's military option was not that strong. For example, an ABC News poll asking the public if, in the event economic sanctions failed, the United States should attack Iraq, only 52 percent agreed; a Gallup poll found that 51 percent were actually opposed to war "if the situation in Iraq did not change by January," and another found that 70 percent supported waiting to see if sanctions worked.[3] Congressional Democrats, who were then in the majority, strongly considered letting economic sanctions against Iraq and other diplomatic efforts continue. In response, the administration went on a public relations blitz to win public and congressional backing for war.

As it played out, Bush succeeded in winning over both Congress, who passed a narrow resolution authorizing the president to use force, and the public. An ABC News poll on January 13, after the congressional vote but before the UN deadline, found 69 percent of the public in favor of war if Iraq did not withdraw.

The administration, along with other elements of the U.S. government, was also able to manage the war so as to maintain high popular support. It also helped that the war was over in roughly one hundred days, and was a smashing victory for U.S.-led forces. They drove the Iraqi military out of Kuwait with relatively few American deaths.

However, in the process of selling and conducting the war, the Bush administration and other like-minded elites engaged in a number of deceptions that raise the specter of *opinion manipulation*. These incidents came to light much later, too late to have affected the outcome.

First, some people argue President Bush overstated the threat posed by Iraq when he initiated Operation Desert Shield. He claimed Iraq had over 300,000 troops and several tank divisions in Kuwait, when in fact declassified Soviet satellite intelligence from that era showed the number was much lower.[4]

Second, in their pre-war public relations campaign, pro-war adherents slanted and distorted information to gain congressional and public support for their position. They played up the threat and barbarity of Saddam Hussein, likening him to Adolf Hitler in many news accounts.[5] This portrayal was an exaggeration, but it was undertaken mainly because market research using polls and focus groups showed this was an effective persuasive device.

Most devious of all were the efforts of public relations firm Hill and Knowlton, which was paid $11 million by the Kuwaiti government in exile to win American support for the war. Their behind-the-scenes efforts included getting Nayirah, a young Kuwaiti health worker, to testify in front of Congress during the debate on the war. She related a dramatic and shocking story of Iraqi atrocities, including Iraqi soldiers throwing babies out of incubators to die while they looted a Kuwaiti hospital. Not only was her testimony broadcast nationally, but Hill and Knowlton disseminated a video news release of the event, ready-made for local television news, insuring that many Americans heard the tale.

Unfortunately, it wasn't exactly so. Nayirah was actually the daughter of the Kuwaiti ambassador to the United States. Further journalistic investigation after the war also showed that there had been no incubator story, and other corroborating testimony was actually retracted. None of this was known at the time.[6]

The administration also carried out the war—dramatically dubbed "Operation Desert Storm"—with a heavy emphasis on public relations. The Pentagon tightly controlled media access to the battlefield and the flow of information the American people received about the war. They forced journalists into press pools with a heavy military presence, controlling when and where they could go. To compensate, and further manage the message, the military fed journalists information through official briefings after the fact, and with flashy video imagery of high-tech weapons. Much of the information provided gave a rosy picture of the war, which appeared all the more credible as a result of the swift American victory. These public relations efforts included stories about the accuracy of American precision weapons, U.S. technological superiority, and the lack of civilian casualties. One notable example was the amazing success of the Patriot antiballistic missile in shooting down Iraqi Scuds (as the Army, not the Iraqis, termed them).

Some of these reports later turned out to be inaccurate, if not complete falsehoods. For example, the Patriot was not very successful at knocking out enemy missiles, and the U.S. bombing campaign was not so precise and humane.[7] Furthermore, the military also used psychological warfare and false reports about U.S. activities to fool the Iraqis about what was going on, but in the process also misled Americans.[8]

All in all, the American public didn't seem to mind. Polls showed strong support for the war, even support for government censorship; patriotism was back in vogue, and President Bush's approval ratings soared to record levels.

Still, this case does raise the issue of whether majority support for the war was genuine, or artificially created. How might public opinion have been different if the American people had known Hill and Knowlton had been paid to convince the public to go to war, or if they had known the war was not as successful as it was being portrayed?

Continued

BOX 12.1—*Cont'd*

As Bennett puts it, "The question here is not whether the war against Iraq was a good idea, but whether the American people received the kind of information they needed to decide that question in a critical way."[9] The evidence would suggest they did not.

Notes

1. This title comes from W. Lance Bennett and David L. Paletz, eds., *Taken By Storm: The Media, Public Opinion, and U.S. Foreign Policy in the Gulf War* (Chicago: University of Chicago Press, 1994).
2. W. Lance Bennett, *News: The Politics of Illusion,* 3rd ed. (New York: Longman Publishing, 1996), p. 42.
3. ABC News poll, November 6, 1990; Gallup Poll, November 16–18, 1990.
4. Peter Zimmerman, "The Bush Deceit," *Washington Post,* August 14, 2003, p. A19. A subsequent letter to the editor in response argued Iraq also had troops massed along the Iraq-Saudi border, and thus were a threat, and that the fewer the Iraqi troops, the easier to remove, but this additional information in no way disputes that Bush had exaggerated their number.
5. William Dorman and Steven Livingston, "News and Historical Content: The Establishing Phase of the Persian Gulf Policy Debate," in Bennett and Paletz, *Taken By Storm,* pp. 63–81.
6. Jarol B. Manheim, "Strategic Public Diplomacy: Managing Kuwait's Image During the Gulf Crisis," in Bennett and Paletz, *Taken by Storm,* pp. 131–148; John MacArthur, *Second Front: Censorship and Propaganda in the Gulf War* (New York: Hill and Wang, 1992). There was some negative fallout from this effort. Once the truth was revealed, Hill and Knowlton lost so much credibility in the eyes of potential clients that it went out of business. In fact, the case (including other elements of Hill and Knowlton's campaign) is even used to teach about ethics in public relations. See "Case 30: Hill and Knowlton and Citizens for a Free Kuwait," in Raymond Simon and Frank W. Wylie, *Cases in Public Relations Management* (Lincolnwood, IL: NTC Business Books, 1994), pp. 273–300.
7. Mark Crispin Miller, "Operation Desert Sham," *New York Times,* June 24, 1992, p. A21.
8. Tim Weiner, "Masters of the Art of Deception," *Des Moines Register,* August 10, 1991, p. T1; it also appeared as "Our Secret Weapon: Illusion," *Miami Herald,* July 28, 1991, p. C1.
9. W. Lance Bennett, *News: The Politics of Illusion,* 4th ed. (New York: Longman, 2001), p. 47.

established elites—business leaders, public officials, televangelists and the like—have greater access to the media than do those of others and that they receive more favorable coverage than do those of dissident elites or the public."[23]

Presidents and other political actors, including interest groups as well as other politicians, now engage heavily in various media and public relations

BOX 12.2

Taken Again? George W. Bush's Justifications for a Second War with Iraq

History eerily repeated itself eleven years later as another George Bush (W., the son) pushed for war with Saddam Hussein's Iraq. This time, circumstances were different.

For a decade after its defeat in 1991, Iraq remained a defiant, rogue regime, albeit one weakened by United Nations economic sanctions and a United States–enforced no fly zone over much of its territory. Although it had not yet attacked another country, in 2002 President George W. Bush argued that Iraq constituted a grave threat to U.S. and world security. In particular, Bush made claims about Iraq's possession of weapons of mass destruction (WMDs—chemical, biological, or nuclear weapons) and the regime's links to terrorist organizations, arguing in turn that such weapons could be used against the United States or Iraq's neighbors. Following the terrorist attacks of September 11, 2001, and the subsequent military actions against Afghanistan, Bush turned the nation's attention toward Iraq as a similar danger, which only preemption—attacking first, before the opponent has a chance to attack—could prevent.

Like his father before him, Bush undertook a public relations offensive to convince the public, and especially Congress, of the need for military action. Again, Hussein's brutal rule, his use of chemical weapons in previous wars and against his own people, and his general untrustworthiness, were part of the story. And, much like the elder Bush's in 1991, the effort was successful. Making Iraq and national security a campaign issue in the 2002 midterm congressional elections, Bush used his post-9/11 popularity to put pressure on Congress and especially the opposition Democrats. Polls also showed most Americans supported the President's tough stand on Iraq. Not wanting to look weak on national security in an election year, in October congressional Democrats went along with Republicans and an authorization to use military force passed both the House and the Senate. In March 2003, after Bush's hand was further strengthened by Republican gains in Congress from the election, Operation Iraqi Freedom was launched. Iraq's military and its regime quickly crumbled, Hussein went into hiding, and U.S. forces took effective control of the country in late April. Although guerilla warfare and other problems in occupying Iraq continued thereafter, in the short run at least, it was clearly a military and political victory for the president.

However, questions arose soon after the war's end, when no WMDs were found. Even more controversial was the discovery that one of Bush's most startling claims—that Iraq in fact was trying to restart its nuclear weapons program, and had indeed tried to buy uranium "yellowcake," a crucial component, from the African country of Niger—was proven to be totally false.

While hinting at Iraq's ability to produce a nuclear device as part of its overall case that Iraq was a threat, it wasn't until a nationally televised address that Bush made the link explicit. In his State of the Union Message of January 2003, making his case to the American people, Bush said, "The British government has learned that Saddam Hussein recently sought significant quantities of uranium from Africa."

In fact, no such thing had occurred. Apparently, in 2001 Italian intelligence obtained what were actually forged documents from Niger (and not even good forgeries at that) supposedly showing Iraqi attempts to buy uranium. These in turn ended up in British hands, and the British report was passed on to the United States.[1]

Continued

BOX 12.2—Cont'd

The Niger story was discounted within some branches of the intelligence community. But in February 2002, after Vice-President Dick Cheney came across a reference to it, he became strongly interested in it, asking the CIA to give him more information. The CIA sent Joseph Wilson, former ambassador to Gabon (and a member of the U.S. embassy in Iraq before the 1991 war) to Niger to investigate. Upon his return, Wilson reported to the CIA that based on his work there, he believed the allegations to be "bogus and unrealistic." Some members of the State Department also objected to the claim, noting Niger had no national interest in selling such material to Hussein's Iraq. These objections were noted in Bush's intelligence briefing in October, although along with the British charge. Nevertheless, members of the White House staff chose to go with the British version in Bush's speech.

Secretary of State Colin Powell also intentionally chose not to mention the Niger evidence in his speech to the United Nations outlining the case for war in February 2003. Powell later said he didn't repeat the charge because he "didn't think it was solid enough to present to the world."

The administration publicly admitted as much later, but claimed it did not know for certain that the evidence was false (just disputed—although it never mentioned that earlier). Bush supporters and staffers instead blamed the CIA and other agencies charged with insuring the accuracy of presidential statements for not contradicting the sixteen words in Bush's speech before its delivery. Critics, on the other hand, charged that the Bush administration had intentionally deceived the American people, or at the very least had politicized intelligence by leading certain agencies to tell them what they wanted to hear and ignoring dissenting voices.

Defenders of the president argued that Bush didn't know for certain the information was false, and that the responsibility of insuring the quality of information in the president's speech fell to other members of the administration, such as National Security Adviser Condoleezza Rice and CIA Director George Tenet. Likewise, Bush cited British government sources, and it was they who claimed the evidence was solid.

Other pre-war administration claims also failed to be confirmed after the U.S. occupation. These included claims that Iraq had close ties to the terrorist group Al Qaeda (in September 2003, Bush even admitted openly that there was no evidence of a link between Hussein and the events of 9/11, though other links were still possible); that Iraq had unmanned drone aircraft designed for delivering WMDs (they did not, although they had worked on some); and that Iraq had several mobile-chemical weapons labs (two suspicious trailers were discovered, but there was no conclusive proof they were put to such uses).[2] Later, even the administration's own chief weapons inspector, David Kay, admitted that Iraq had no WMDs, and that intelligence estimates suggesting otherwise were largely wrong. A follow-up report in October 2004 by Charles Duelfer, who succeeded Kay, did say that the Hussein regime had the desire to build or obtain these weapons, but not the capacity.

Was the Bush case for war another example of opinion manipulation? After all, an Iraq with nuclear capabilities was certainly a frightening prospect, especially when coupled with supposed terrorist ties. Were the American people misled into supporting the war?

The charge of manipulation is somewhat more difficult to prove in this instance than in the first war with Iraq. Part of this is due to uncertainty over what Bush really knew, and part due to whether or not the issue of Iraq's nuclear capability was all that important in forming the public's opinion supporting military action.

The evidence (at least, at the time of this writing) does not definitively show that George W. Bush or other members of his administration knowingly lied to and misled the public, although some clearly pushed the point more than others. It appears they may have chosen to rely on the most alarming assessments of Iraq because those fit more easily with their pre-existing beliefs. Instead, Bush and other top officials passed on bad information, so that the public was given an inaccurate and incomplete picture of the Iraqi threat. More evidence may be revealed that disputes this conclusion, however.

Furthermore, it is hard to know whether the truth (or in any event, the lack of the nuclear claim) would have made any difference in public attitudes about going to war. In a *Time* magazine poll taken four weeks before the war, 83 percent of Americans thought war was justified on the grounds that "Saddam Hussein is a dictator who has killed many citizens of his Iraq." That claim was undisputed, and was also a large part of Bush's case for war. In the same poll, 72 percent did say that the war was justified because it "will help eliminate WMDs from Iraq."[3] Nevertheless, the political controversy over this matter raged on through the summer and into the fall of 2003, hurting Bush's and America's credibility at home and abroad.

Despite the inconclusive evidence of manipulation, this case still highlights the fact that in order to win policy debates, political elites will sometimes use whatever information supports their case, no matter how questionable. Therefore, the public should be inherently skeptical of the factual claims of all sides. It also underscores the extent to which *good information*—provided by an independent, critical media—is necessary for the public to come to its own conclusions about policy choices. High-quality debate, discussion, and information is crucial for creating a genuine public opinion on which government policy should be based.

Notes

1. See Seymour M. Hersh, "The Stovepipe," *The New Yorker*, October 27, 2003.
2. See the summary of CIA Director George Tenet's views reviewed in "Iraqi Weapons: Before and After," *Seattle Post-Intelligencer*, February 6, 2004, p. A16.
3. Michael Duffy, "A Question of Trust," *Time*, July 21, 2003, pp. 22–24.

activities to influence public opinion. Studies have shown that such efforts can have some effect on policy, though two limits on their success are the public's limited attention span and elite competition over policies.

Elite influence on public opinion is most powerful when media attention is high, and elites are unified in their positions, making it difficult for the public to get additional, contrary information. For example, following the events of September 11, the Bush administration was able to dominate the political agenda and public discourse about terrorism policy, and other elites (journalists, members of Congress, interest groups) went along with many administration actions. One specific result of such opinion shaping was passage of the USA PATRIOT Act discussed in Chapter 1. The Bush administration took advantage of the climate of opinion in the country and its dominance over public discourse in the media to push for new terrorism legislation, getting Congress to pass the law quickly with little debate or discussion. In cases like these, it is difficult to claim that "public opinion drove policy."

Power elite studies have long made the case that business and other established interests have an advantage in getting their viewpoints heard and inculcating their values into the public mind. Scholars such as Domhoff, Dye, and others have documented the massive efforts of business groups, through funding think tanks, research studies, running advertisements, and the like, to influence opinion on economic and regulatory policy.[24]

Others see the increase of polling and interest in public opinion by elites not as inherently increasing democratic responsiveness, but rather giving political elites better political intelligence to manage opinion. Jacobs and Shapiro note that presidential polling is more likely to be used to help elites develop *crafted talk*—targeted rhetoric to get the public to accept policy positions the elites have already decided upon—rather than as tools for following public opinion, although polls do give presidents an idea of how far they can go.[25] Even more damning are those who say polls have in a sense made it easier for elites to get their way, or to avoid political disasters that would lead to massive public outcries. Ginsberg argues polling makes it easier for elites to manage democracy: "Rather than promote governmental responsiveness to popular sentiment, polls serve to pacify or domesticate opinion, in effect helping to make public opinion safer for government."[26] According to Ginsberg's thinking, polls give politicians an early warning system to anticipate public reactions, thus making it easier for them to persuade the public to accept their policies. In a slightly different take, Justin Lewis argues that polls allow the media to "construct public opinion" so as to make it appear in line with the range of elite debate about issues. This process in turn allows policymakers to seem more democratic than they actually are. "What is particularly striking is the degree to which a whole range of apparently popular opinions can be ignored if they fall outside the general political framework advanced by political elites."[27] Through what questions do and don't get asked by the pollsters, government can likewise avoid listening to the true desires of the public.

Misinterpreting the Public Will

Less insidiously, another set of scholars in this school see politicians as simply misinterpreting or misreading public opinion, so that even in trying to follow it they inadvertently ignore it. In a sense, they try to listen to the public, but they don't hear it correctly.

First, officials apparently have rather limited success at predicting or guessing the views of the public. Studies of state legislators asking them to predict what their constituents' views on certain issues were (and then comparing them to either surveys of opinion or actual direct votes on legislation), have found that representatives are sometimes way off the mark.[28] One study in particular found legislators to be poor estimators of their constituents' wishes. It surveyed state legislators from all fifty states on their perceptions of their constituents' views on ten different policy issues. These results were then compared to simulated measures of constituency opinion, derived from matching state populations demographically with the results of national Gallup polls on those same issues. In other words, the researchers derived state-level opinion by revising the national-level data to fit each state's population demographics, so that if a state's population had a higher proportion of blacks than the nation as a whole, for example, they weighted the data to reflect that. This comparison revealed that the legislators' guesses were off by an average of 20 percentage points. Their perceptions of public opinion were so far off, that in fact the researchers concluded the legislators would have done a better job of representing constituency opinion if they just acted on their own beliefs rather than according to their flawed estimations of what their constituents wanted![29] Success at accurately seeing opinion does vary, however, by issue, with more accurate perceptions coming on salient issues than on obscure ones. We saw evidence of this earlier in the discussion of the Miller and Stokes study of congressional representatives: They were much closer on civil rights issues, then highly important in the early 1960s, than they were on foreign policy issues.

Second, the sources of public opinion for policymakers may lead them to misinterpret what the people want. For example, Herbst asked state-level policy managers (staffers in the Illinois legislature) how they conceived of public opinion and what their sources of information about discerning public opinion were. She discovered they relied upon constituent letters, letters to the editor, and other media sources, along with interest group voices—ironically because they viewed these sources as more representative than the results of public opinion polls.[30] Kull and colleagues,[31] in a series of studies of foreign-policy makers (executive branch officials, members of Congress, staffers, other elites), discovered that these officials rarely sought out public opinion about foreign policy matters, in part due to general disdain for the public's knowledge of foreign affairs. They also found that policymakers relied upon media and congressional opinion as accurate indicators of what the people want. They argue these attitudes and sources in turn led to certain misperceptions among elites about public opinion, such as the belief that Americans had become more isolationist and inward-looking after the end of the Cold War in the early 1990s, when in fact polls showed strong evidence that this was not the case.

Of course, while arguably nonpoll sources might be unrepresentative or biased measures of what the people think, there are good reasons for politicians to use them. Individuals that directly contact officials, write letters to the editor, and so forth, are more likely to vote and be involved in politics, and thus may be more representative of people who really count in the political process. Also, such people may be opinion leaders who in turn influence others. Taeku Lee also points out that such sources can actually be more useful to politicians than polls. He argues that during the civil rights era, the content and thrust of letters to the president provided a better source of information about quickly changing racial attitudes than did polls.[32] Nevertheless, heavy reliance on such sources for their information about public desires may be another source of nonresponsiveness in practice.

Does Government Listen? Sometimes Yes, and Sometimes No

A third school of thought argues in favor of a contingency approach. Scholars in this camp believe that the effect on policy is not an all-or-nothing proposition; rather, responsiveness will likely vary, depending upon the type and nature of the issue, the institutions involved, the political context, and so on. For example, high-profile issues are likely different from low-profile ones; foreign policy may be different from domestic; policy made by Congress may be different from policy made by the president; and so on. Therefore, the goal of research is to uncover and explain this variation.[33]

Cook and Barrett's study of members of the U.S. House of Representatives found that representatives used different guides in deciding how to vote, depending upon the situation. How much weight they gave to constituency opinion in their districts varied, depending upon the issue and political context.[34] Remember, in the 1963 Miller and Stokes study mentioned earlier, representatives were closer to their constituents on civil rights issues than on foreign policy ones, with economic issues in between.

What might determine the level of responsiveness? There are several factors that logically would appear to affect the public opinion–policy connection.

Institutional Sources of Variation

First, there are variations in institutions' formal relationships with the public. The three different branches of American government—legislative, executive, and judicial—each make policy in different ways, using different mechanisms, and are even designed with different incentives for listening to the public. The federal courts, for example, decide cases based on legal matters and are unelected, whereas Congress for the most part conducts policy openly, operates in a democratic fashion, and is elected. Some studies have shown that the Supreme Court, for example, acts in accordance with public opinion slightly less often than the other branches (although others argue it is roughly comparable). Still other evidence suggests that, even if the Court is responsive, there tends to be a time lag in its responsiveness, as one would expect with a body appointed by elected officials.[35] More telling, studies comparing state court rulings on such high-profile issues as the death penalty and abortion, for example, have found that judges in states where they are elected are significantly more likely to issue rulings on those issues in line with the climate of opinion in their states than are judges in states with uncompetitive elections or where judges are appointed.[36] Therefore, these inherent institutional differences may lead to variations in governmental responsiveness to opinion.

Variations in Proximity

A second factor is where policy takes place within the federal framework of government in the United States: the national, state or local levels. In other words the *degree of separation* from the public is a key factor. The level at which policymaking occurs might influence the degree of responsiveness to opinion. Local officials presumably are closer to the people, and so might mirror popular concerns more closely than national ones. Alternatively, however, some have argued that because the public knows more about the activities of the federal government than about state and local ones—recall our surveys of political knowledge in the previous chapter—policy may actually be more responsive to public opinion at the national level. While some studies of state-level policy have shown a fairly close relationship to opinion, as we mentioned earlier, there is almost no research on the local level, and strong evidence to believe that officials may be more sensitive to organized interests like real estate developers and local businesses.[37]

Issue-Specific Variations

A third factor is variation in the *salience* of issues. Presumably, the greater the attention to an issue, the more responsive the policy, because the public knows what the government is doing and voices its concerns more clearly. On issues with low salience, however, officials can more safely ignore opinion (or not know what it is) and instead listen to their own views or the positions of organized interest groups.[38] Recent research by Vincent Hutchings shows that statewide representatives like governors and U.S. senators are more likely to be responsive on higher salience issues thought to be of concern to motivated issue publics within the electorate. He concludes that representatives are very concerned about their votes on certain issues out of fear of latent opinion, as we discussed in the feature about the recall of Tom Ament in Chapter 1. He conceives of the public as a collection of sleeping giants that politicians don't want to disturb. However, on low-salience issues that do not receive much attention from the mass media or from motivated political elites such as party leaders or interest groups, there is little likelihood that the giants will stir, allowing politicians to get away with being less responsive.[39]

There are also inherent differences between issue domains, based on a combination of all of these factors. The public appears to have a stronger voice on domestic rather than foreign policy issues. One reason foreign policy issues may have less congruence than domestic ones is because the public knows little and cares less about foreign policy, and policymaking is dominated by a small set of officials mostly in the executive branch at the national level of government.[40] Similarly, government may lead public opinion instead of following it more on foreign policy issues.

Some issue domains may be crowded with a number of established interest groups or players with a vested interest in the current policy, thus making it difficult to change, as opposed to new or emerging issues, which might be more amenable to policies the public favors. For example, in her study of domestic policymaking in six issue areas (criminal justice, pornography, affirmative action, abortion, welfare, and Social Security), Sharp found large variations in responsiveness, with issues such as welfare and Social Security more responsive than affirmative action or abortion.[41]

The structure of opinion on issues also affects the degree of responsiveness. For example, as we mentioned earlier in the chapter, it's harder to do what the people want in cases where opinion is strongly and evenly divided than on issues with a clear majority or large plurality. A good example is the abortion issue, where opinion is split in several different directions.[42]

Variations over Time

Finally, there can even be variations in responsiveness over time, with the government listening more to the people at some times, or in some eras, than others. A number of scholars, for example, have found that general responsiveness has declined over time, particularly since the 1970s.[43] One explanation for this phenomenon may be increased partisan polarization in Congress, with the Democrats becoming more uniformly liberal and the Republicans more conservative since the 1960s. This development likely means that legislation passed under Democratic control from 1975 to 1995 in general was more liberal, and legislation under Republican control since 1995 has been more conservative, than what the public may have wanted.

A recent study highlights the multiple forces that can influence how and how often public opinion affects policy. Canes-Wrone and Shott compared public opinion about government spending (whether the government should increase, decrease, or maintain the same level of spending) on various policy issues to presidents' actual budget proposals on those same issue areas from 1972 to 1999. They discovered a pattern of "conditional responsiveness" in presidential policymaking. First, they found that presidents are more likely to take popular positions on issues that voters are more likely to encounter in their daily lives such as crime, health care, and Social Security, rather than on more obscure issue areas like national parks or space exploration. Second, presidents are more likely to be in tune with the public's spending preferences in the last two years of their first term, when reelection is imminent. Third, presidents who are very popular or unpopular (have high or low standings in their job approval ratings) are less likely to advocate spending choices in line with popular sentiment than are presidents with average approval ratings, similarly suggesting that presidents are more in tune with the people when they need them most. Furthermore, the individual presidents under the period of the study varied in the degree to which they heeded public opinion overall.[44]

Given the large variety of factors that may come into play, then, there is strong reason to believe that the impact of public opinion on policy varies. This conditional perspective, however, is more recent and still emerging, and thus has less research to back it up. But the contingency approach presupposes that one must first understand the context within which policy is made before one can fully assess how much influence public opinion has in any given instance. Therefore, "rather than debating whether policy is responsive to public opinion overall . . . scholars [should] work toward the development of theories of the sources of contingency to better understand the factors that explain variation in the opinion-policy link."[45] In that respect, we are a long way from our goal.

CONCLUSION

In the end, what can we say about the effects of public opinion on policy? The three perspectives presented in this chapter make it difficult to definitively answer the question of does the government listen to the public?

We, the authors, can't tell you which side is right, nor is it our wish to do so. Just as there are competing opinions about political issues, so are there about the public's influence on policy. Your job, as an independent-thinking person, is to weigh the arguments and evidence on each side and decide for yourself, a task that is no different in academic questions of political science than in day-to-day political questions.

We will simply say that the process of the democratic dialogue—how the people speak, who speaks, what the government hears, and whether they listen—is enormously complex, and doesn't function the same in any one instance. Likewise, studying governmental responsiveness isn't easy. It is very hard to tell whether government actors did something because they wanted to please the public, or for different reasons (though they could do both).

Public opinion undoubtedly does influence policy; the government does listen to us, but how often, how much, and how accurately, it is difficult to say. Even some of the proponents of the idea that government generally listens to the public admit that it doesn't do so perfectly or all the time. Leading, influencing, and even manipulating the public also happens, but probably not often, given the difficulty of doing so. The larger point may be that, on a number of issues, especially low-salience ones, leaders may be able to ignore public opinion or may not even know what it is. The strength of the contingency perspective is that it wisely hedges its bets. There are strong reasons to believe that the government is responsive, but also good reasons as to why it isn't and can't be completely so, an issue which we will revisit in the final chapter.

Suggested Reading

Erikson, Robert S., Michael B. MacKuen, and James A. Stimson. *The Macropolity.* New York: Cambridge University Press, 2002.

Jacobs, Lawrence R., and Robert Y. Shapiro. *Politicians Don't Pander: Political Manipulation and the Loss of Democratic Responsiveness.* Chicago: University of Chicago Press, 2000.

Lewis, Justin. *Constructing Public Opinion: How Political Elites Do What They Want and Why We Seem to Go Along With It.* New York: Columbia University Press, 2001.

Manza, Jeff, Fay Lomax Cook, and Benjamin I. Page, eds. *Navigating Public Opinion.* New York: Oxford University Press, 2002.

Margolis, Michael, and Gary A. Mauser, eds. *Manipulating Public Opinion: Essays on Public Opinion as a Dependent Variable.* Belmont, CA: Brooks/Cole, 1989.

Sobel, Richard. *The Impact of Public Opinion on U.S. Foreign Policy Since Vietnam* New York: Oxford University Press, 2001.

Notes

1. Vincent Price, *Public Opinion* (Newbury Park, CA: Sage, 1992), pp. 21–22.

2. Jeff Manza, Fay Lomax Cook, and Benjamin I. Page, "Navigating Public Opinion: An Introduction," in Jeff Manza, Fay Lomax Cook, and Benjamin I. Page, eds., *Navigating Public Opinion: Polls, Policy and the Future of American Democracy* (New York: Oxford University Press, 2002), p. 3.

3. This section relies heavily upon the framework developed by Jeff Manza and Fay Lomax Cook in their excellent review, "The Impact of Public Opinion on Public Policy: The State of the Debate," in Manza, Cook, and Page, *Navigating Public Opinion,* though the discussion and material here differs in some respects. The stylistic format of the discussion below also is similar to one in Edward S. Greenberg and Benjamin I. Page, *The Struggle for Democracy,* 6th ed. (New York: Longman Publishing, 2003), p. 141–143, although it also differs in content.

4. Warren E. Miller and Donald E. Stokes, "Constituency Influence in Congress," *American Political Science Review* 57 No. 1 (March 1963): 45–56.

5. Christopher Achen, "Measuring Representation," *American Journal of Political Science* 22 (1978): 475–510; Robert S. Erikson, "Constituency Opinion and Congressional Behavior: A Reexamination of the Miller-Stokes Representation Data," *American Journal of Political Science* 22 (1978): 511–535.

6. Gerald Wright, Robert S. Erikson, and John P. McIver, "Public Opinion and Policy Liberalism in the American States," *American Journal of Political Science* 31, No. 4 (November 1987): 980–1001; and Robert S. Erikson, Gerald C. Wright, and John P. McIver, *Statehouse Democracy: Public Opinion and Policy in the American States* (New York: Cambridge University Press, 1993).

7. James A. Stimson, Michael B. MacKuen, and Robert S. Erikson, "Opinion and Policy: A Global View," *PS: Political Science and Politics* 27 No. 1 (March 1994): 29–35; James A. Stimson, Robert S. Erikson, and Michael B. MacKuen, "Dynamic Representation," *American Political Science Review* 89 (1995): 543–565; Robert S. Erikson, Michael B. MacKuen, and James A. Stimson, *The Macro Polity* (New York: Oxford University Press, 2002).

8. Stimson et al., 1995, p. 559; see also their "Panderers or Shirkers? Politicians and Public Opinion," in Manza, Cook and Page, *Navigating Public Opinion*, p. 82.

9. Alan D. Monroe, "Consistency Between Public Preferences and National Policy Decisions," *American Politics Quarterly* 7 (1979): 3–19.

10. Benjamin I. Page and Robert Y. Shapiro, "Effects of Public Opinion on Policy," *American Political Science Review* 77 (1983): 175–190.

11. Paul Burstein, "Bringing the Public Back In: Should Sociologists Consider the Impact of Public Opinion on Policy?" *Social Forces* 77 (1998): 27–62.

12. Lawrence Jacobs, *The Health of Nations: Public Opinion and the Making of American and British Health Policy* (Ithaca, NY: Cornell University Press, 1993).

13. Paul Burstein, *Discrimination, Jobs, and Politics: The Struggle for Equal Opportunity Employment in the U.S. Since the New Deal* (Chicago: University of Chicago Press, 1998); and "Public Opinion and Congressional Action on Labor Market Opportunities, 1942–2000," in Manza, Cook, and Page, *Navigating Public Opinion*.

14. Paul Quirk and Joseph Hinchliffe, "The Rising Hegemony of Mass Opinion," *Journal of Policy History* 10 (1998): 19–50.

15. Christopher Jencks, "Methodological Problems in Studying 'Military Keynesianism,'" *American Journal of Sociology* 91 (1985): 373–379; Thomas Hartley and Bruce Russett, "Public Opinion and the Common Defense," *American Political Science Review* 96 (1992): 905–915; and Bruce Russett, *Controlling the Sword: Democratic Governance of National Security* (Cambridge, MA: Harvard University Press, 1990).

16. Richard Sobel, *The Impact of Public Opinion on U.S. Foreign Policy Since Vietnam* (New York: Oxford University Press, 2001), p. 234.

17. See the discussion of this case in George C. Edwards III, "Riding High in the Polls: George W. Bush and Public Opinion," in Colin Campbell and Bert Rockman, eds., *The George W. Bush Presidency: Appraisals and Prospects* (Washington, DC: CQ Press, 2004), p. 29; polls during 2002 showed around 70 percent support for such a department.

18. Kenneth F. Warren, *In Defense of Public Opinion Polling* (Boulder, CO: Westview Press, 2001), p. 198.

19. John G. Geer, *From Tea Leaves to Opinion Polls: A Theory of Democratic Leadership* (New York: Columbia University Press, 1996), p. 2.

20. See Benjamin I. Page, "Democratic Responsiveness?" *PS: Political Science and Politics* 27 No. 1 (March 1994): 25–29, for a discussion.

21. Paul Burstein, "Public Opinion and Congressional Support for Policy Change," paper presented at the Annual Meeting of the American Political Science Association, San Francisco, CA, August 2001.

22. See Benjamin I. Page and Robert Y. Shapiro, "Educating and Manipulating the Public," in Michael Margolis and Gary A. Mauser, eds., *Manipulating Public Opinion: Essays on Public Opinion as a Dependent Variable* (Belmont, CA: Brooks/Cole, 1989), pp. 294–320.

23. Michael Margolis and Gary Mauser, "Public Opinion as a Dependent Variable: An Empirical and Normative Assessment," in Margolis and Mauser, *Manipulating Public Opinion*, p. 365.

24. Cf. William G. Domhoff, *Who Rules America?* (Englewood Cliffs, NJ: Prentice-Hall, 1967), and various updated editions; Thomas Dye, *Who's Running America?* (Englewood Cliffs, NJ: Prentice-Hall, 1976), and various updated editions; Patrick Akard, "Corporate Mobilization and Political Power: The Transformation of American Economic Policy in the 1970s," *American Sociological Review* No. 57 (1992): 597–615; all of these derive in part from the classic by C. Wright Mills, *The Power Elite* (London: Oxford University Press, 1959).

25. Lawrence R. Jacobs and Robert Y. Shapiro, *Politicians Don't Pander: Political Manipulation and the Loss of Democratic Responsiveness* (Chicago: University Chicago Press, 2000).

26. Benjamin Ginsberg, *The Captive Public: How Mass Opinion Promotes State Power* (New York: Basic Books, 1986).

27. Justin Lewis, *Constructing Public Opinion: How Political Elites Do What They Want and Why We Seem to Go Along With It* (New York: Columbia University Press, 2001), p. 200.

28. Ronald D. Hedlund and H. Paul Friesema, "Representatives' Perceptions of Constituency Opinion," *Journal of Politics* 34 (August 1972): 527–542.

29. Eric M. Uslaner and Ronald E. Weber, "U.S. State Legislators' Opinions and Perceptions of Constituency Attitudes," *Legislative Studies Quarterly* 4 No. 4 (November 1979): 563–585.

30. Susan Herbst, *Reading Public Opinion* (Chicago: University Chicago Press, 1998).

31. Stephen Kull, I. M. Destler, and Clay Ramsay, *The Foreign Policy Gap: How Policymakers Misread the Public* (College Park: Center for International Security Studies, University of Maryland, 1997); Stephen Kull and I. M. Destler, *Misreading the Public: The Myth of a New Isolationism* (Washington, DC: Brookings Press, 1999); and Stephen Kull and Clay Ramsay, "Elite Misperceptions of U.S. Public Opinion and Foreign Policy," in Brigitte L. Nacos, Robert Y. Shapiro, and Pierangelo Isernia, eds., *Decisionmaking in a Glass House: Mass Media, Public Opinion, and American and European Foreign Policy in the 21st Century* (Latham, MD: Rowman and Littlefield, 2000), pp. 954–110.

32. Taeku Lee, *Mobilizing Public Opinion: Black Insurgency and Racial Attitudes on Civil Rights* (Chicago: University Chicago Press, 2002).

33. Jeff Manza and Fay Lomax Cook, "The Impact of Public Opinion on Public Policy: The State of the Debate," in Manza, Cook, and Page, *Navigating Public Opinion,* p. 27.

34. Fay Lomax Cook and Edith Barrett, *Support for the American Welfare State: The Views of Congress and the Public* (New York: Columbia University Press, 1992).

35. For research suggesting the Court is less responsive, see Jay Casper, "The Supreme Court and National Policy Making," *American Political Science Review* 70 (1976): 50–63; and David Barnum, "The Supreme Court and Public Opinion: Judicial Decision Making in the Post-New Deal Period," *Journal of Politics* 47 (1985): 652–666; for evidence that courts are essentially no different from other branches, see Page and Shapiro, "Effects of Public Opinion on Policy," p. 183; Thomas R. Marshall, "Public Opinion, Representation, and the Modern Supreme Court," *American Politics Quarterly* 16 (1988): 296–316. Another study (William Mishler and Reginald Sheehan, "The Supreme Court as a Countermajoritarian Institution? The Impact of Public Opinion on Supreme Court Decisions," *American Political Science Review* 87 No. 1 [March 1993]: 87–101), takes the position that the Court is responsive to opinion, in a delayed sort of way.

36. Paul Brace and Melinda Gann Hall, "Studying Courts Comparatively: The View From the American States," *Political Research Quarterly* 48 No. 1 (March 1995): 5–29; and Paul Brace and Melinda Gann Hall, "The Interplay of Preferences, Case Facts, Context, and Rules in the Politics of Judicial Choice," *The Journal of Politics* 59 No. 4 (November 1997): 1206–1231.

37. See, for example, Susan E. Clarke, "More Autonomous Policy Orientations: An Analytic Framework," in Clarence N. Stone and Heywood T. Sanders, eds., *The Politics of Urban Development* (Lawrence: University of Kansas Press, 1987), pp. 105–124.

38. John W. Kingdon, *Agendas, Alternatives, and Public Policies* (New York: HarperCollins, 1984); Lawrence Jacobs, *The Health of Nations: Public Opinion and the Making of American and British Health Policy* (Ithaca: Cornell University Press, 1993); Paul Burstein, *Discrimination, Jobs, and Politics: The Struggle for Equal Opportunity Employment in the U.S. Since the New Deal* (Chicago: University Chicago Press, 1998).

39. Vincent L. Hutchings, *Public Opinion and Democratic Accountability* (Princeton: Princeton University Press, 2003).

40. See, for example, Page and Shapiro, *The Rational Public,* pp. 366–372.

41. Elaine B. Sharp, *The Sometime Connection: Public Opinion and Social Policy* (Albany: SUNY Press, 1999).

42. Ruth A. Strickland and Marcia L. Whicker, "Political and Socioeconomic Indicators of State Restrictiveness Toward Abortion," *Policy Studies Journal* 20 (1992): 598–620.

43. Stephen D. Ansolabehere, James M. Snyder, Jr., and Charles Stewart III, "Candidate Positioning in U.S. House Elections," *American Journal of Political Science* 45 (2001): 136–159; Jacobs and Shapiro, *Politicians Don't Pander;* Alan D. Monroe, "Public Opinion and Public Policy, 1980–1993," *Public Opinion Quarterly* 62 No. 1 (1998): 6–28.

44. Brandice Canes-Wrone and Kenneth W. Shotts, "The Conditional Nature of Presidential Responsiveness to Public Opinion," *American Journal of Political Science* 48 No. 4 (October 2004): 690–706.

45. Jeff Manza and Fay Lomax Cook, "A Democratic Polity? Three Views of Policy Responsiveness to Public Opinion in the United States," *American Politics Research* 30 No. 6 (November 2002): 658.

The "New Referendum": Presidential Approval

Presidents no longer govern for four years on the strength of one election; today, the electoral mandate is continually updated and reviewed by public-opinion polls.

—Paul Brace and Barbara Hinckley[1]

Questions to Think About

This chapter investigates presidential approval ratings, a particularly notable type of connection between the public and government. It addresses such questions as

- Why has the relationship between the public and the president become closer and more politically significant?
- What factors best explain variation in polls on the president's job performance?
- How has the focus on presidential approval ratings by presidents, the press, and the mass public affected presidential governance?
- Has this focus made presidential politics more responsive, or not?

GOVERNMENT RESPONSIVENESS to public opinion includes public officials as well as public policies. In a representative democracy, one measure of whether officials are acting in accord with public opinion is whether the public supports the job they are doing. Thus, one indication of how well the democratic dialogue is working is the degree of popular support public officials enjoy. In theory, such approval is measured at election time—but as noted earlier, elections are imperfect, intermittent ways of judging whether officials are successfully conducting the people's business. One can make the case that it is equally important to tell how government is performing in between elections.

PUBLIC OPINION AND PRESIDENTIAL PERFORMANCE

Nowhere has the increasing importance of public opinion in American politics become more evident than in assessments of the president's job performance. This chapter examines why public support has become more important, as well as how and why the public judges presidential performance the way it does. It ends with a discussion of the implications of this measure for the presidency and American politics.

The Rise of the Public Presidency and the New Referendum

Since the early twentieth century, presidents have become closer to the public and more concerned with public opinion. As the economic, military, and political superpower status of the United States grew, the power, prestige, and importance of the American presidency grew with it. The rise of the national media also increased public attention on the presidency at the expense of other actors and institutions in American government.[2] Together, these trends made

"No, I don't want to know what my approval rating is."

the president the nation's preeminent politician. At the same time, public expectations of the office increased, perhaps exceeding presidents' abilities to satisfy them.[3]

The Framers of the Constitution did not anticipate a close relationship between the president and the people. In fact, they had in part attempted to insulate the office from the public by design, by way of indirect election of the president through the Electoral College and through checks on presidential power.[4] However, ambitious presidents sought to increase the power of the office and believed public support was one means for doing so. Presidents such as Teddy Roosevelt, Woodrow Wilson, and Franklin D. Roosevelt in particular saw public opinion as an important resource for presidential leadership.[5] The bond between president and public was further strengthened by two other changes: the development of a more popular-based electoral system (electors were directly pledged by popular vote in each state, and by the 1970s party delegates in the nominating process were popularly chosen), along with a mass media (radio and television) that made direct communication with the public possible.[6] As a consequence of these developments, presidents in the modern era became more concerned with public opinion.

Another key element of this new public presidency was the advent of public opinion polling in the 1930s. This made it possible to measure what the people thought, not just about particular issues, but also about presidential performance overall. Beginning in Franklin Roosevelt's administration, the Gallup Organization has asked a sample of the public the simple question "Do you approve or disapprove of the way X [name of the incumbent] is handling his job as President?" All presidents since Truman in the late 1940s have been regularly surveyed throughout their terms in office. Other polling and news organizations have followed suit, building on the popularity of the Gallup question. The net result has been that the frequency of polling on this question has grown dramatically over time. According to one count, from the occasional querying of the populace in the 1940s, the number of these polls increased to an average of twelve per year in the period after 1953, and then reached twenty-plus after 1977.[7] It is safe to say that today random samples of the public express their view of the president almost weekly, and even more if one counts multiple polling organizations that ask the same question or similar ones. Sometimes, the public is also asked not only how good an overall job the president is doing, but also about the president's performance in specific policy areas (foreign, domestic, the economy, the environment, health care, and so on).

Presidential approval polls now attract a great deal of attention from pollsters, journalists, scholars, presidents, and other politicians. Every new poll essentially provides a new barometer reading of the president's popular standing. Paul Brace and Barbara Hinckley label this dynamic process "the new referendum,"[8] and Godfrey Hodgson "the perpetual election,"[9] since rather than every four years, presidents now are publicly evaluated almost constantly.

Just because such a measure of support is publicized and of interest to various members of the body politic does not mean presidential approval is of any substantive political significance, however. One might ask: so what? Do presidential approval ratings really matter?

In fact, the president's standing in approval polls appears to have real political consequences. First, the approval rating is directly related to election outcomes. Presidents who are popular (at 55 percent or higher in June of the election year) are significantly more likely to be reelected than those who are not.[10] Furthermore, presidents' level of popular support in the final polls before the election is loosely related to the percentage of the popular vote they actually receive; the higher their popularity, the higher their vote share. Popular support may also help members of their own party when the presidents themselves are lame ducks unable to run for reelection.[11] In 1988, for example, then-Vice-President George H. W. Bush probably benefited from Ronald Reagan's late-term resurgence in the polls. Al Gore apparently got less of a boost from Bill Clinton in 2000, although without Clinton's popularity, he might have done worse.

Presidential approval also apparently affects the fortunes of the president's fellow partisans in congressional elections. Recent declines in popular support, or especially sheer unpopularity (below 50 percent), appear to be tied to the number of seats the president's party loses in midterm House and Senate elections.[12] Interestingly, although they occurred after most studies examining this connection, the only times in the post–World War Two era when a president's party *gained* seats in Congress after a midterm contest were in 1998 and 2002; in both cases, the president enjoyed relatively high approval ratings. In 1998, despite the Monica Lewinsky scandal, Bill Clinton rode high in the polls with a rating in the high sixties, and in 2002, George W. Bush had comparable ratings months after his record highs during the War on Terrorism. Other forces were undoubtedly at work as well, but support for the president, as head of his party's team, likely played a role in these election results.

Second, poll ratings also impact a president's relations with Congress. Although the relationship is not strong, and is complicated by other factors, popular presidents tend to have greater success getting their legislative measures adopted, and also tend to propose more legislation, than unpopular ones.[13] Lastly, popular presidents seem to have more success moving public opinion itself, although this may not win them policy success in Washington.[14]

Besides, as Brody succinctly puts it: "Presidential poll ratings are important because they are thought to be important. They are thought to be important because political leaders look for indications of when it is safe or dangerous to oppose their policy interests or career ambitions to those of the president."[15] So, because of their perceived importance by other political elites, presidential approval ratings can help or hurt a president's relationship with other Washington power brokers, such as members of Congress, party and interest group leaders, and the like.[16]

We will return to the issue of the political ramifications of presidential approval at the end of the chapter. But given its obvious importance, not only to president watchers but to presidents themselves, it is likewise important to understand the dynamics of presidential approval ratings and the patterns in public support for the president.

ANALYZING PRESIDENTIAL APPROVAL

As an indicator of government performance and public satisfaction, presidential approval ratings are one measure of governmental responsiveness to public opinion. Yet that begs the questions: Just exactly what are the ingredients of popular support for the president? When do these ratings change, and what causes them to do so? In this section, we examine the extensive research on presidential approval.

Figure 13.1 graphs the raw job approval ratings of Presidents Eisenhower through Bush. As you can see, there is considerable variation and change over time. The undulating curves of approval graphs over time, or the periodic announcements of the president's latest standing by the media, hide some notable underlying patterns in the public's assessment of the president. Detailed examinations of these ratings over several presidencies have revealed certain commonalities, despite the unique differences of each.

Most presidents start out with relatively high ratings in their early months in office, when approval may even slightly increase. They then begin losing support, although their first year in office is generally still above 50 percent. Support continues to drop significantly, with some fluctuations, through the second year, before bottoming out at a low equilibrium point in the third. From this point,

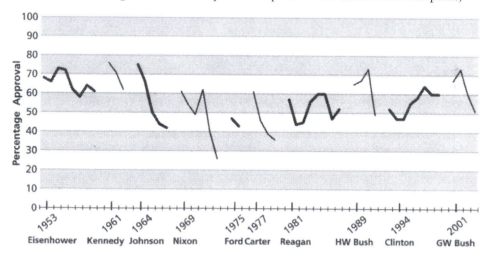

FIGURE 13.1. Approval Ratings of Presidents Eisenhower through George W. Bush.

Source: Data for Eisenhower through H. W. Bush comes from Lyn Ragsdale, *Vital Statistics on the Presidency* (Washington DC: CQ Press, 1996), pp. 189–192. Data for Clinton through G. W. Bush (Dec. 2004) is from averaging period Gallup polls.

presidents generally gain support as they go into their reelection year, when presumably they benefit by comparison to their potential rivals for the job. This rebound, however, is not always enough to save them from electoral defeat.[17]

The pattern for presidents is depicted in Figure 13.2, which plots the trends in approval ratings over the length of the first term. This graphically depicts the general downward trends presidents face, with gains in the months before the election. As Brace and Hinckley describe it, "All presidents, it seems must contend with this decay of support, caused by public expectations and the boundaries of a four-year term."[18]

For example, the average yearly approval for first-term presidents from Eisenhower through Clinton (including Johnson for the last year of Kennedy) was 63 percent for the first year, 57 percent for the second, 55 percent for the third, and 56 percent for the fourth. Only Eisenhower and Bush (the elder) had ratings that were higher in their third year than in their second, and in Eisenhower's case, they were higher still in the fourth (he was reelected) whereas Bush's dropped significantly (he was defeated for reelection).

The second term appears to be similar to the first, although the decline in the early months is somewhat steeper. Presidents, too, seem to benefit in their

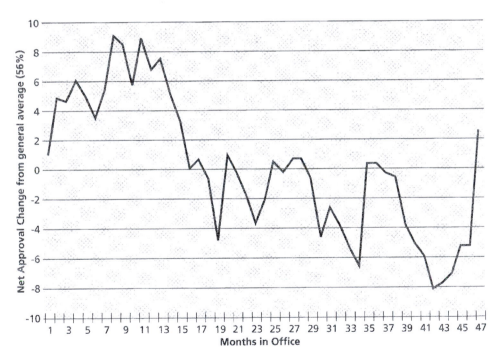

FIGURE 13.2. First-Term Presidential Approval Ratings.

Source: Data for Eisenhower through H. W. Bush comes from Lyn Ragsdale, *Vital Statistics on the Presidency* (Washington DC: CQ Press, 1996), p. 193. Data for Clinton through G. W. Bush (Dec. 2004) is from averaging period Gallup polls.

final year, despite being lame ducks, unable to run for a third term. However, since the advent of polling we have had few complete second-term presidencies (Eisenhower, Reagan, and Clinton), so it is difficult to know how accurate these patterns are.

Nevertheless, these general trends mask substantial monthly, and in some cases, even weekly variation. Explaining the ups and downs of presidential popularity has become the subject of much analysis and speculation by political scientists.

Real World Events and the Political Context

From a variety of different studies and methodologies, research has uncovered several different factors that appear to affect the public's evaluation of the president. Two main approaches have developed among scholars: one that sees the public as responding to various real world indicators of presidential performance and another that instead believes the mass media coverage of those events, and how newsmakers respond to them, is the driving force behind changes in approval ratings.

First, we will discuss the real world cues or environmental perspective. Studies in this vein have developed statistical models using various measures of the state of the country (such as peace and prosperity) and the state of the president (such as foreign trips, speeches, scandals, and the like) and related them to changes in the president's standing in the polls.

The Honeymoon

As noted above, scholars noticed that presidents generally start out their terms with high and even occasionally increasing approval ratings during the first six months to a year, a period they dubbed the "presidential honeymoon." Why does this happen? Scholars surmised that the unifying symbol of the president as our sole national leader, along with the prestige of the office and the pomp and ceremony of the inauguration, lead Americans to put the acrimony of the election behind them and to give the new president the benefit of the doubt. This reaction is likely linked to a "positivity bias" among Americans, who tend to infer positive rather than negative relationships from ambiguous situations.[19] Furthermore, because the president hasn't actually done anything yet, there is nothing to disapprove of.

This honeymoon with the public, like the supposed warmth between newlyweds, wears off after a time as the electorate becomes more familiar and unhappy with the new president. In fact, according to this view, presidents in a sense inevitably alienate some parts of the public simply by doing their jobs: As they make decisions, take stands on issues, sign or veto bills, and so forth, they make some constituents angry and lose their support. Mueller hypothesized that this downward slide was due to the building of a "coalition of minorities" as new groups or issue publics disapprove of presidential decisions over time.[20] In other words, you can't please everybody.

The Economy

Other various real world indicators of presidential policy success were also found to influence presidential approval ratings. After the honeymoon wears off, the president's popular support is linked to various fluctuations in the state of the country. According to this argument, Americans expect presidents to deliver good times, and hold them particularly responsible for the economy.

Although debate has raged over how to precisely gauge economic performance, and which statistics best explain changes in approval ratings, there is consensus that the health of the economy does impact the president's standing with the public. Studies generally show that when the economy is bad—especially when inflation, or unemployment, or both (called the misery index) is high—presidential approval declines; when the economy is doing well, and these measures are lower, presidential approval usually increases or remains higher.

For example, Jimmy Carter's approval ratings remained dismal in the late 1970s as the country struggled through a period of high inflation and high unemployment. His successor, Ronald Reagan, although elected in part because of Carter's bad times, also saw his early high ratings fall as the recession worsened in the early 1980s; as the economy improved, so too did Reagan's poll ratings. Similarly, Bill Clinton's poll numbers rebounded at the end of his first term and continued throughout much of his second in connection with historically low inflation, low unemployment, and a booming stock market during the mid-to-late 1990s.

Interestingly, the public does not appear to hold presidents accountable for their own economic situation, but rather for the state of the country as a whole. Instead of asking, "what have you done for me lately?" they ask, "what have you done for the nation?" Such attitudes make some sense, since the president is arguably more responsible for larger, national economic trends than for whether a given individual gets a job or a raise.[21]

Scholars within this tradition, however, have been unable to come to agreement as to how the public develops its views about the economy, or whether they rely on current or past conditions, or instead use their future prognoses, in coming to their assessment. Still, there is a strong evidence that the public's beliefs about the direction the nation's economy is headed, based in part on information from economic experts, is related to changes in the president's job approval rating.[22]

International Crises and the Rally Effect

One of the largest and most positive types of effects on the president's approval rating is an international crisis and/or a quick use of force by the president. In order to trigger such an effect, these events must be international, dramatic, sharply focused, and "presidentially relevant."[23] For example, the launching of the satellite *Sputnik* by the USSR in 1957, the Cuban Missile Crisis in 1962, and the seizing of the U.S. Embassy in Teheran, which began the Iranian Hostage Crisis in 1979, all saw an increase in approval ratings for the incumbent president; the invasions of the Dominican Republic in 1964, Grenada in 1983, and Panama in 1989, along with the start of the Gulf War in 1991, did likewise. Perhaps most dramatically, in the aftermath of the terrorist attacks of September 11, 2001, the percentage of the public approving of George W. Bush's job skyrocketed from the low fifties before the attack to the high eighties soon thereafter.

In fact, there doesn't even have to be successful resolution of the crisis for such results to occur. Kennedy's approval rating went up ten points following the failed attempt to overthrow Cuba's Fidel Castro at the Bay of Pigs in 1961. This led Kennedy to quip, "The worse I do, the more popular I get."

Why would the public behave this way? The real world events perspective posits that the increase is primarily due to patriotism and an us versus them mentality that leads some citizens to rally round the flag (hence the name *rally events* to describe this phenomenon). The president, as the nation's most preeminent symbol and personification of the country, thus benefits from this patriotic, nationalistic reaction.

Similarly, victory in war also leads to an uptick in approval. Truman's highest ratings occurred shortly after the surrender of Germany in World War Two, and George H. W. Bush's ratings climbed to then-record levels shortly after the Persian Gulf War in 1991 ended with the U.S.-led military coalition freeing Kuwait and driving Iraqi forces back. Again, the idea is that the president, as national leader, benefits from the national pride that accompanies the successful end of military hostilities.

These increases are short-lived, however, with approval ratings again moving back toward their prerally levels within a couple of months or so—if not sooner. Arguably, once the crisis has passed, and the president has bathed in the glow, new issues arise, or the public goes back to judging the president as they had before. Prior opponents of the president in particular are the most likely to abandon their support for the president, since they were also ones who contributed most to the rally.[24]

Other events also have been found to have positive, short-term effects on approval, although usually not much. These may include major presidential addresses, trips abroad, peace treaties, and even presidential health crises. President Nixon's historic trip to China and the Camp David Peace Accords between Egypt and Israel, brokered by President Carter, both increased their ratings slightly. Polls after Eisenhower's heart attack in 1955 and the assassination attempt on Reagan in 1981 both showed around 7 percent gains.[25]

Again, it is the nature of the events themselves that appear to boost the president. Speeches, health crises, and trips abroad presumably elicit rallylike notions of the president as national leader, whereas peace treaties and the like are presidential successes in their own right.

"Negative" Events: Scandals, War Deaths, and Policy Failures

If certain events appear to be a boon to presidents and their approval ratings, others seem to have the opposite effect. Most notable among these are presidential scandals: When official wrongdoing or bad policy decisions are revealed to have happened in the White House, approval drops. For example, over the course of a year and a half, Nixon's approval rating declined from the upper fifties into the mid-twenties over Watergate, until he finally resigned under the threat of impeachment. More dramatically, Reagan lost 16 percentage points in less than a month in late 1986 following the initial revelations in the Iran-Contra scandal that his administration had secretly sold arms to Iran in a botched hostage-release effort, and then had illegally diverted the profits to rebels fighting in Nicaragua. His ratings stayed at similar levels for a number of months afterward as the scandal developed.

Other events can also be negatives for the president. When wars drag on or go badly, support declines. Scholars found negative correlations between approval ratings and battle deaths, particularly during the Korean and Vietnam Wars.[26] As we noted earlier, President Bush's approval ratings declined from his post–September 11 and early Iraq War highs, and disapproval of his job increased in the summer and fall of 2003 as the American death toll climbed during the extended American occupation. Although it went up and down slightly thereafter, his approval rating hovered around the 50 percent mark for months afterward.

Domestic crises may also hurt the president. Lyndon Johnson lost some support during severe race riots in the mid-1960s. Bill Clinton's approval ratings dropped several percentage points following the disastrous FBI raid on the Branch Davidian sect's compound in Waco, Texas, in 1993 and the subsequent criticism he and his administration received.

The general point here is that presidential approval ratings fluctuate in response to good or bad events. When things go well (prosperity, peace, victory), ratings go up; and when things go poorly (economic recession, stagnating wars, scandals, and policy disasters), ratings go down.[27]

Mediated Events: The Effects of News Coverage and Interpretation

Other scholars have instead focused on the media as an important filtering factor that influences presidential approval ratings. In particular, Richard Brody and some of his colleagues propose that media coverage of events, and in particular how other politicians (as news sources) respond to those events, is primarily what moves public opinion on presidential performance.[28] So, according to this view, it is not the events themselves but how those events are *portrayed* and *interpreted* that influences the public.

How does this process work? Essentially, the public responds to the tone of news about presidential performance: When the news is bad, ratings tend to fall, and when the news is good, ratings tend to increase.

However, some people are more resistant to change than others. Those who affiliate with the president's party are more likely to support the president, and opposition partisans more likely to oppose.

A key question for this perspective is thus what determines the tone of the news. Brody notes that the tenor of news coverage doesn't come just from the facts such as what the unemployment rate is, how many troops died in combat that day, whether the stock market went up or down, and so forth, but how political elites respond to those facts. Why? Because these elites—such as members of Congress, administration officials, party leaders, and the like—are important news sources for the media in building their story. Their comments are thus transmitted to the public, shaping the tone of news. Again, we see the important role of opinion leaders in the political elite, transmitted by the media, in influencing public opinion. When elites—especially politicians of the opposite party—support, praise, or at least fail to criticize the president, the news is more positive; when they criticize the president, news is more negative. Subsequently, some people in the population (perhaps using heuristics) take cues from this tone of coverage. Below, we examine how the mediated politics perspective explains the various influences on presidential approval mentioned previously.

Why a Honeymoon?

This perspective argues that the presidential honeymoon has more to do with the nature of news coverage during the early days than it does with some natural inclination of the American people to automatically support the new president. For example, while all presidents begin their terms with high approval ratings, there is considerable variation in how great their honeymoon is and how long it lasts. John F. Kennedy's first approval rating was 72 percent, and he maintained ratings in the seventies for almost eighteen months. George H. W. Bush started out with 57 percent in January 1989, and then kept up 60 to 70 percent support until October 1990, when he again dropped into the fifties. On the other hand, Ronald Reagan began with a rating of 51 percent, and although it went up for several months following the assassination attempt on his life a few weeks thereafter, it was back down to 52 percent in August, a period of just eight months. In fact, Bill Clinton received almost no honeymoon at all. He began with a near-average rating of 58 percent, but rather than maintaining or even increasing it, he basically lost support over the next several months, until a mere 38 percent approved of his job performance in June 1993.[29]

The real existence of the honeymoon may be due instead to how other political elites respond to the new president and how the media cover the early days. During this period, the mass media generally give the president favorable coverage, for two main reasons. First, members of the media want access to the new administration and to build a favorable working relationship with it, and so they generally avoid criticism. Second, more importantly, other political elites tend to be more positive or, at least, refrain from being negative, toward the new government, as they wait for the administration to make its initial moves.[30] Since the public has yet little information on which to base a decision on presidential performance, in a way they are positive by default. As Brody puts it, "in the early stages of a presidential term, people in other parts of the political system do little to disabuse the mass public of its positive response to the new president."[31]

One of the reasons Bill Clinton's honeymoon was so short, for example, may have been because he made many early mistakes with the press, and, more importantly, his policy decisions drew fire from other political elites. First, to fulfill one of his campaign promises, Clinton moved quickly to lift a ban on gays in the military. This move was controversial, undoubtedly more so than Clinton expected, and led to dissension not only from Republicans, but also from fellow Democrats like Sam Nunn of Georgia, the influential chair of the Armed Services Committee. Although Clinton eventually achieved his "don't ask, don't tell" compromise, the issue largely was negative. In addition, the gays-in-the-military flap exploded in the midst of attempts by him to "focus like a laser beam" on the economy and may have hampered his ability to get an emergency economic stimulus package through Congress, an attempt that ultimately failed. Other problems with Congress, such as his difficulties getting his first two choices for attorney general confirmed by the Senate, and poor relations with the White House press corps generally, also plagued him.[32] In essence, Clinton just received more bad news than most presidents in his first few months in office.

George H. W. Bush, on the other hand, had a relatively longer honeymoon than most because he advanced few programs in his first one hundred days in office, and was the fortunate benefactor of the fall of Communism in Eastern Europe in 1989–1990, with the positive news it heralded. Nevertheless, regardless of luck or skill of the president, the positive atmosphere of the early days cannot last forever, particularly in the American political system where presidents are expected to lead and develop policy proposals to address the nation's problems. The length of the honeymoon, therefore, is determined more by the news coverage that follows subsequent presidential decisions or other events.

Rally Effects That Aren't Always There

The mediated events perspective also offers an alternative explanation for the rally effect. Rather than giving a robotic, patriotic response, instead the public again largely responds to the information with which it is presented, within the context of partisan affiliation.

First, international crises themselves are not always positive for the president. Although it is true that even policy failures can trigger a rally, such as Kennedy's Bay of Pigs fiasco, there are other times where approval drops, and others still where even a relatively successful operation simply fails to stimulate an increase in support. Clinton got no boost in the polls from a threatened invasion of Haiti in 1994, which led, without firing a shot, to an abdication of power by the military rulers there and a successful restoration of democracy. One would think that avoiding the risk to American lives, coupled with a positive political outcome, would have led to an increase in his approval rating.

More questionable for the natural rally explanation, is the fact that very similar international crisis events can have very different effects on presidential approval, with some sparking rallies, and others not. Consider the stories of two ships, the *Mayaguez* and the *Pueblo*. The *Mayaguez*, an American merchant ship, was seized by the Cambodian navy in the Gulf of Thailand in May 1975. President Ford responded with a successful military raid to free the ship and crew. Although in the ensuing rescue mission, thirty-nine U.S. Marines and airmen were killed, plus an additional fifty were wounded bringing back the thirty-eight crew members, and the action sparked a diplomatic flap with Thailand and Laos, Ford's approval rating rose from 40 percent before to 51 percent after the event, a notable increase. By all standards, this event led to a classic rally effect.

The *Pueblo* incident bears a close resemblance to the *Mayaguez*, yet the public failed to rally behind President Johnson the way they later would with Ford. On January 23, 1968, the U.S. Navy's *Pueblo* was captured by North Korea. Like the *Mayaguez*, it was an American ship seized by an Asian Communist country in international waters. However, no rescue mission was launched; instead, the North Koreans put on a show trial of the captain and kept the *Pueblo*, but thereafter returned the entire crew unharmed to the United States. According to Gallup polls before and after this event, Johnson's approval rating actually declined from 49 to 41 percent, rather than increasing as the rally phenomenon would lead one to expect. One could argue that the *Pueblo* was a failure, and the *Mayaguez*, a success, but both resulted in the successful release of the crew, and in the case of the *Pueblo*, no Americans died.[33] Nevertheless, one would think that if the public automatically and patriotically rallies around the president during crises, one ship seizure would be as good as another.

According to Brody's formulation, the rally effect is due not to the *public* rallying behind the president, but rather political elites doing so. It is the lack of criticism of the president voiced in the news that allows presidential interpretations, naturally more favorable to the president, to be conveyed to the public unhindered. And this in turn leads to the rally effect. When certain international crises occur, political elites (such as members of Congress from the opposition party to the president) fear speaking out against the president, or may even side with him. Therefore, media accounts of the situation are unusually positive and convey bipartisan support, or at least acquiescence.

These other elites in essence provide opinion leadership for the public, who take their cues from them. "When they rally behind the president, or run for cover, the public will be given the explicit or implicit message 'any appearances to the contrary notwithstanding, the president is doing his job well.'"[34] Given this message, it is not surprising that in the main the public rallies also, with more Americans approving of the president's job performance. On the other hand, in crisis situations where elites fail to unite behind the president, the rally in public opinion fails to develop. In still other cases, where opposition elites initially refrain from criticism but then attack the president soon thereafter, when the political waters are clearer, the rally evaporates quickly.

This process essentially explains the differences between the two ship-seizure cases mentioned above. After analyzing media coverage following both events, Brody found that elite responses, and the news coverage they generated, differed considerably. In Ford's case, no criticism of the administration's actions occurred during the entire ten-day period in which the event was a major news story; the major voices being transmitted to the public were those of the administration, justifying their action, and the news was unusually positive. In Johnson's case, however, a few days after the *Pueblo* seizure, Republican senators were quoted in major news reports expressing comments critical of the president's policy. Therefore, taking their cues from elite interpretations, the public rallied to Ford's side during the *Mayaguez* incident, but failed to do so for Johnson during the *Pueblo* crisis.[35]

Or consider George W. Bush's approval rating following the terrorist attacks of September 11, 2001, as we discussed in Chapter 4. According to this view, it was not the automatic, knee-jerk patriotism of rallying around the flag that caused Bush's approval ratings to skyrocket, but rather how that event was interpreted by the media, and how politicians reacted to it. Given the national mourning over the event as a tragedy of tremendous proportions, and its portrayal as "America attacked," elites from across the political spectrum—liberals, conservatives, Democrats, Republicans, and the like—united behind Bush, presenting a face of national unity during crisis. It was this lack of criticism, and even strong support, coupled with favorable media coverage, that presumably led to Bush's rise in the polls.

The Role of Media Coverage and Elite Discourse in Other Events and Day-to-Day Performance

The dynamics of news coverage and elite support of issues that appear on the media (and thus public) agenda are crucial determinants in the level of presidential support. The level of a president's support is based on the degree to which elites support the president on the issues of the day.

Thus, what appears in the news, as we discussed in Chapter 6, impacts the public's perceptions of national problems and political issues. It is these reports, then, that drive evaluations of the presidential performance. For example, following the 1991 Persian Gulf War, President George H. W. Bush had then–record high approval ratings in the upper 80 percent range. In the year that followed, he lost much of that support, polling in the low forties a little over a year later. In short, the main reason for his drop in support was that the news agenda shifted from coverage of foreign affairs (where the bulk of people approved of the job he was doing) to that of the economic recession (where people disapproved of his performance), thus affecting his overall approval rating.[36]

Of course, news events don't speak for themselves; the final outcome depends upon how those events are framed and interpreted by the media and other political elites. Economic statistics or trends, for example, aren't simply transmitted neutrally or completely; news reports highlight certain elements more than others, and news about the economy has been found to affect public perceptions about overall presidential performance.[37] Another recent example might be the relationship between media coverage of the war and occupation of Iraq, and George W. Bush's approval rating. Initially, media focus on Iraq and the swift American victory buoyed Bush's approval ratings, much as it had done for his father. However, heavy coverage of American casualties in the aftermath of the invasion both set the agenda (continued to make the issue of his handling of Iraq prevalent in American minds) and framed it—from positive at the end of the direct fighting with Hussein's forces in Spring 2003, to negative for the summer and fall that followed, as the occupation and rebuilding went on. These developments also emboldened Bush's opponents, such as the nine Democratic candidates running for president at the time, who aided in fomenting negative news by criticizing Bush. As a result, his overall job approval ratings dropped. When new, better news developed in the winter of 2003–2004, including the leveling off of American casualties, the establishment of a new interim government, and the capture of Saddam Hussein, Bush's approval ratings rebounded somewhat.

This dynamic also explains why presidential scandals can have such a negative effect. When they break, they often gain major news attention, making them primary components in the public's performance evaluations. Also, since they are inherently negative for presidents, their opponents take full advantage of the opportunity to attack. Journalists and media commentators may also join in, and sometimes, even members of the president's own party. These opinion leaders in turn influence some members of the public to change their evaluations of the president.

Of course, here too agenda-setting and framing arguably play a role. If a scandal doesn't catch fire with the media, or is seen as boring, unimportant, or difficult to explain, it may be ignored or downplayed. This may limit its negative impact on the president's public standing. Such characteristics may explain why Bill Clinton was never really damaged by the so-called Whitewater affair, an Arkansas land deal gone bad in which he and his wife were involved. It was an extremely complicated matter to understand, and although it went on for years, it never really captured the nation's attention the way Watergate did. Alternatively, new issues may arise that generate different stories with a different tone, so the president may be able to escape with approval intact.[38] For example, George W. Bush could have been damaged in late 2001 by the stock and bankruptcy scandal of energy giant Enron Corporation, which was a Houston-based company with close ties to his campaigns for governor and president. However, the story broke at the same time that the news agenda was focused on the aftermath of the September 11 terrorist attacks and the U.S.

BOX 13.1

The Strange Case of Bill Clinton's Approval During the Monica Lewinsky Scandal: Low-Information Rationality or Mediated Response?

Seemingly nothing does more damage to a president's job approval rating than a full-blown White House scandal. Yet oddly, such was not the case with Bill Clinton and his extramarital affair with White House intern Monica Lewinsky.

The scandal erupted on January 21, 1998, when the media revealed that Kenneth Starr, an independent counsel investigating various allegations of wrongdoing by Clinton before and during his time in office, was seeking Lewinsky because Clinton may have pressured her to lie under oath to a grand jury investigating charges of sexual harassment against Clinton. Evidence of their affair came from secret tapes of Lewinsky procured by one of her friends, Linda Tripp. Clinton had denied the relationship in his own testimony, and did so again publicly; after several months of media scrutiny and spectacle—coupled with Starr's relentless investigation—Clinton was forced to admit to a national audience in August that he had lied about the affair.

On September 10, after the Lewinsky story had dominated the news for months, Starr delivered his report to Congress, which included graphic details of Clinton and Lewinsky's White House trysts. In an atmosphere of extreme partisanship, the House of Representatives, controlled by the opposition Republicans, pushed forward with articles of impeachment against Clinton for perjury and other crimes. Two of the four articles passed. In January 1999, Clinton's case went before the U.S. Senate for trial to see whether he would remain in office. Clinton was acquitted when the Senate failed to achieve the necessary two-thirds vote on any of the articles, and his presidency survived.

During the more-than-a-year-long period of the scandal, Clinton's approval ratings not only held firm, above the 60 percent range, they actually increased on a few occasions. From spring 1998 through his impeachment acquittal by the Senate in February 1999, public support for Clinton remained strong, with the only decrease being at the very beginning of the scandal in January 1998, when it dipped to 51 percent. In January 1999, on the eve of his impeachment trial, Clinton ironically had the highest approval rating ever recorded for a president beginning his sixth year in office.

Although the story of Clinton's affair and the public deception surrounding was in no way positive for the president, and indeed news coverage of ongoing revelations portrayed him in a negative light, both the environmental and mediated events perspectives, along with conventional wisdom, would have expected his job approval rating to fall. Instead, to Clinton's ultimate benefit, they did not, perhaps saving him from being removed from office.

What accounts for this apparent anomaly in public opinion? Scholars have advanced several different explanations, depending upon the model of public opinion they subscribe to and the types of data they examine.

One interpretation for Clinton's high support, despite such negative news, is that many people may have responded to real indicators of presidential performance rather than to partisan attacks and media emphasis on sensationalism. Indeed, political scientist John Zaller believes the Lewinsky case (at least, the poll bounce-back following its initial dip) shows "not just the power of a booming economy to buttress presidential popularity . . . but the importance of political substance, as against media hype, in American politics."[1] The economy remained strong, the strongest it had been in years, with low unemployment, a booming stock market, and increases in real income for most Americans. The country was also relatively at peace, with no military conflicts or serious crises. Lastly, Clinton took popular positions on the issues, by abandoning the more liberal positions of his first term and moving squarely to the center, which all the more won him plaudits given the extreme conservatism of Republicans in Congress.[2] Hence, Clinton's support was an example of a "low information, gut rationality" public who made up its mind based on matters of peace and prosperity, or presidential results, rather than politics.

W. Lance Bennett offers an alternative perspective more closely aligned with the mediated events perspective. Bennett notes that although Clinton's approval rating stayed relatively stable, there were changes in other polls that indicated the public was responding to the media spectacle created by the scandal. He argues that "if we look to almost any issue beyond approval for how Clinton was handling his job as president, we find major opinion shifts that can only be explained by attention to events in the news."[3]

However, in the end the public's lack of support for impeachment and continued support of Clinton's job performance hinged on the private/public distinction about the affair. Early on, people came to the conclusion that it was a private, not a public, matter. Most Americans just didn't see that it was relevant to his job. But why? Bennett links it to news coverage of the event and Clinton's own media strategies, which were crucial in determining how the issue was framed:

> Deciding this question about the significance of Clinton's lying depended to an important degree on how the story became framed. Clinton's opponents tried to keep the issue of lying within the frame of breaking a legal oath. Yet the President, opinion polls, and ultimately, the bulk of news coverage, all framed his lying in the context of trying to hide a consensual sexual affair—something that many people found more excusable. . . . The private-affair frame made for a better, and more sustainable news story, and it provided a less effective context for the Republican message that lying warranted impeachment.[4]

Clinton was also definitely aided in building this news frame by the fact that congressional Democrats almost uniformly stuck behind their president. So, by this way of thinking, in the end it was media interpretation of the event, and how it was presented to the public, that influenced public opinion.

Lastly, in their analysis of this case, Dhavan Shah and colleagues build on the notion of framing but also attempt to bring in perceptions of other real-world factors like the economy, thus sort of fusing the two perspectives.[5] They measured the dominant frames the media used for the scandal and, like Bennett, argue that the way the scandal was portrayed provided cues to the public on how to judge Clinton. Most importantly, the media framed the Republican charges, along with Democratic defenses, as politically motivated attacks about a matter that was essentially a private, not a public, issue. But they also employed measures of the economy (like real disposable income) and measures of economic coverage to flesh out their model of influences, and find that it too had an impact. In essence, both prosperity and economic news, coupled with negative yet partisan Republican attacks, led to a backlash in public opinion against Clinton's opponents. As Shah and colleagues put it, "our modeling suggests that, while economic cues are important in explaining trends in presidential approval during the vast majority of Clinton's term, accounting for these trends . . .

Continued

BOX 13.1—*Cont'd*

after Lewinsky entered the public stage requires particular attention to the framing of scandal coverage in terms of conservative attacks and liberal responses."[6]

Whether the public's response to Clinton's troubles was wise or not depends upon your point of view. Those who view the public as rational might argue, like Zaller, that the public made up its mind based on real indicators of presidential performance, instead of political ones. On the other hand, others might argue that the public was simplistically led into viewing the Lewinsky matter as all about an inappropriate affair, rather than a case of lying under oath and thus an abuse of the presidential office. Or perhaps the public can effectively engage a complex political issue, but how they do so depends upon media coverage, as Bennett suggests.

1. John Zaller, "Monica Lewinsky's Contribution to Political Science," *PS: Political Science and Politics* 31 No. 2 (June 1998): 182.
2. Zaller, "Monica Lewinsky's Contribution," p. 186.
3. W. Lance Bennett, *News: The Politics of Illusion,* 4th ed. (New York: Longman, 2001), p. 228.
4. Bennett, *News,* p. 124.
5. Dhavan V. Shah, Mark D. Watts, David Domke, and David P. Fan, "News Framing and Cueing of Issue Regimes: Explaining Clinton's Public Approval in Spite of Scandal," *Public Opinion Quarterly* 66 (2002): 339–370.
6. Shah et al., "News Framing and Cueing," p. 368.

---

involvement in Afghanistan, arguably limiting its impact. Still, none of these patterns can successfully account for Bill Clinton's strong public support in the wake of the Monica Lewinsky scandal—making it a intriguing case for scholars (see Box 13.1).

THE POLITICS OF PUBLIC SUPPORT

The popular and elite interests in the president's latest poll standing have led approval polls to take on a political life all their own. The politics surrounding or involving the periodic presidential approval poll in turn has some important ramifications for the American political system.

Effects on Presidential Behavior

The importance of approval polls is not lost on presidents themselves. Concern with public support affects how presidents approach their jobs, from what they do to how and when they do things. For example, presidents appear to time major national addresses, press conferences, trips, policy proposals, and even military action based on their standing in the polls and the electoral calendar.[39]

Concern with polls, and public support more generally, also helps to explain presidents' obsession with their public image and their portrayal in the media, along with the hiring of their own pollsters, press aides, and political consultants. Some worry that this driving focus has created an "image is everything" presidency where style is more important than substance.[40] Even worse is the possibility that presidents may undertake specific actions with the polls rather than policy in mind, such as launching a military strike when they are in trouble at home, as the 1997 movie *Wag the Dog* suggested. At a minimum, the concentration on poll standings takes valuable time, effort, and resources away from the actual business of governing the nation.

Presidents appear to be limited in their ability to successfully control their ratings. Presidential speeches to the nation boost their approval a few percentage points, but only temporarily.[41] And despite the efforts of presidential stagecraft and image-making, the public appears to respond, at least most of the time, to real policy results.

In any event, one could argue presidential worrying over poll ratings is all to the good, since it drives presidents to work toward pleasing the public. On the surface, at least, approval polls do seem to have some effect on presidential behavior. Bill Clinton changed course, declaring that "big government is over," and then pushing for more moderate proposals, following his plunge in the polls and Republican gains in Congress at the end of the second year of his presidency. In similar fashion, a drop in approval ratings during 2003—especially ones concerning his handling of post-war Iraq—probably led president George W. Bush to put trusted National Security Adviser Condoleezza Rice in charge of overseeing the rebuilding efforts there, and to ask for more assistance from other countries through the United Nations.

Altering the Dynamics of Presidential Governance

The emphasis on popular support as a presidential necessity as well as a resource has also impacted the environment in which presidents operate. Presidents no longer have the leeway they once did; instead of a four-year term, they must now contend with persistent evaluations, constantly looking over their shoulder at the public's response. Pollster Irving Crespi believes that "presidential approval ratings have created a pseudo-parliamentary situation, where the president faces a monthly vote of confidence from the total electorate. While not binding in any sense, this vote of confidence is accepted by both politicians and political analysts as an indicator of the president's political clout, and therefore, his ability to govern effectively."[42] This state of affairs may drive presidents to focus on short-term goals, complicating policy planning for the long term.

Political scientist Samuel Kernell also believes that the constant cultivation of, and reliance on, popular support for governing, while giving presidents some new tools for presidential leadership, also brings with it substantial political consequences. He argues the "going public" presidency has essentially two effects on policymaking: Presidents are freer to choose which issues they sponsor, but the success of those issues depends more heavily upon the talents and fortunes of their sponsors. The first development leads to a more variable policy agenda, and the second means that coalition building behind particular policies becomes more volatile.[43]

Why? By using public appeals to gain support inside Washington for their policies, thus drawing on their job approval to achieve results, presidents' fortunes become tied more closely to their poll ratings. However, because poll ratings go up and down with events and media coverage, the ability of presidents to use the power of their popularity to get other policymakers to follow them also goes up and down. As Kernell puts it, "the effect of the president's own public standing on his ability to rally public opinion behind his policies exposes policy to extraneous and wholly unrelated events. Whatever affects the president's standing with the public will alter the prospects for those policies he sponsors."[44]

How Good an Indicator Is It?

Other people take issue with the very validity of the approval poll itself, asking what it really measures. Although we appear to know a lot about it from studying its ups and downs, as Neustadt noted long ago, "the question is unfocused; so is the response, which tells us anything or nothing about what respondents meant."[45] After all, unlike policy questions, approval polls don't tell the president, or the pollster, what we want; they only say whether we like what he (or someday she) is doing.

They may not even do that. As Brace and Hinckley note:

> Many people do not evaluate the President's job performance, however. Some respond to the President as a person, or linking two patriotic symbols, say how the nation is doing. [Also,] . . . we often evaluate Presidents based on good luck or bad luck in office. Hence, the ratings that form the basis of news stories—and set their own additional forces in motion—are an amalgam of influences, only some of which reflect a president's job performance or are even under a president's control.[46]

Perhaps all this attention on approval ratings is really misplaced. They may tell us how well the president is doing, but not *why*. Some people automatically approve, out of hard-core partisan or personal loyalty. We don't know how many of these there are at any one time, although it may be as high as 20 to 25 percent—the lowest approval ratings ever recorded. Truman, in the depths of the Korean War and with threats of Communism at home, Nixon in the final throes of Watergate, and Carter in the oil crisis-recession, all received support from at least one-fifth to one-fourth of the public. Similarly, other people are knee-jerk disapprovers for the opposite reasons, although there are an apparently smaller number of them. At the end of World War Two, the conclusion of the Persian Gulf War, and the aftermath of September 11, 2001, only around 10 to 15 percent disapproved of Truman's, H. W. Bush's, and W. Bush's job performance, respectively.

Most of us, however, seem to be responding with specific portions of the president's job in mind, rather than the whole. The logic of agenda-setting and issue salience, coupled with priming, means that the public will likely weight certain aspects of the president's job more heavily than others in forming their assessment, as noted earlier. Thus, the approval rating may be more of a barometer measuring the president's handling of the issue of the day or certain major issues rather than his actual overall performance.

As an example, let us examine in detail George W. Bush's approval ratings in January 2002, shown in Table 13.1. This time period was selected because it was the end of his first year in office, and because it was long enough after the September 11 attacks and the war in Afghanistan that his rating should have begun to return to normal. As you can see, the public rates his performance in different policy areas quite differently. He receives 79 percent support on foreign affairs, 58 percent on tax policy, 44 percent on the environment, 89 percent on terrorism, and so forth. Yet his overall rating is 83 percent. His general job approval thus is not an amalgamation of his performance in all policy areas, but more likely is based upon his performance in areas people see as most important (either in the news or to themselves). In this case, his overall rating is likely greatly influenced by his job in foreign policy and fighting terrorism. Based on this information, it appears that only about 45 percent of the public actually supports him in *all* areas. Therefore, those people who truly do rate the president overall are probably a distinct minority.

Still, one could make the case that this is no different from what people must do when they cast a ballot. Most people are forced to vote for a candidate with

TABLE 13.1. Job Approval Rating of George W. Bush in Different Areas, January 2002.

Performance in	% Approve	% Disapprove	% Don't Know/No Answer
Overall job	83	10	7
Foreign policy	79	12	9
Energy policy	45	27	28
Tax policy	58	28	14
Education policy	66	18	16
Environment	44	31	25
Managing economy	59	27	14
Dealing w/Congress	70	13	17
Fighting terrorism	89	6	5

Source: Fox News/Opinion Dynamics Poll, January 9, 2002. The order of the issues listed is the order in which they were asked in the survey.

whom they do not completely agree on all the issues, so they must prioritize the ones most important to them, or make a general choice. In this way, the approval rating does provide a similar measure of accountability. A key difference, however, is that in an election, people choose from a menu of alternatives (at least two, if not more), rather than just deciding whether they like the one dish offered. Nevertheless, as Brody notes, presidential approval ratings can be a democratic instrument. "The final verdict isn't delivered until election day, but every day during the four years before the public has been having its attention drawn to presidential performance, and has been drawing conclusions from what it sees and reads. There is a rough justice and a source of public influence in this process. A very long way from 'all power to the people,' but democracy nonetheless."[47]

CONCLUSION

Whatever the pros and cons of the new referendum on American presidential politics, it is clear that the president's popular support, as measured through opinion polls, matters. It is also clear that, whatever the approval question may actually be measuring, there are common patterns in its fluctuations. The public's responses, while not necessarily completely predictable, are understandable. Therefore, as Brace and Hinckley point out, it is important for all Americans to understand approval polls and the politics surrounding them.

If nothing else, the existence of approval polls does appear to have made the government more sensitive to public opinion. How approval polls have done so, and whether in so doing they have improved American politics, is less certain.

Measures of government performance like presidential approval provide a different type of responsiveness to the people than policy issues do. Theoretically, public officials should have popular support, and indeed, it does appear helpful to their ability to govern. Job approval, then, does contribute to whether the government does listen to the people. One would imagine that presidents' job approval ratings would in turn be related to their policy stances. In other words, a president in line with the public's policy sentiments would in turn have high job poll ratings, and vice versa. Yet, that is not necessarily the case. The degree to which presidents and other officials may be able to maintain popular support overall, while pursuing unpopular public policies, raises questions for the functioning of the democratic dialogue in practice.

Suggested Reading

Brace, Paul, and Barbara Hinckley. *Follow the Leader: Opinion Polls and the Modern Presidents*. New York: Basic Books, 1992.

Brody, Richard A. *Assessing the President: The Media, Elite Opinion, and Public Support*. Stanford: Stanford University Press, 1991.

Edwards, George, III. *The Public Presidency: The Pursuit of Popular Support*. New York: St. Martin's Press, 1983.

Kernell, Samuel. *Going Public: New Strategies of Presidential Leadership*, 3rd ed. Washington, DC: CQ Press, 1997.

Ragsdale, Lyn. *Vital Statistics on the Presidency: Washington to Clinton*. Washington, DC: CQ Press, 1996.

| www ▶ ▶ ▶ | **Interactive Learning Exercise:** |

Using Presidential Approval to Apply What You've Learned

Presidential approval ratings are useful instruments for illustrating a number of different aspects of public opinion covered in other parts of the book. In this collection of interactive exercises, you will analyze and interpret presidential approval ratings regarding the conceptual issues of opinion measurement and question wording, group differences and similarities, and the effects of mass media on public opinion. Go to the Web site under Chapter 13 and follow the instructions. Your instructor may opt to have you do all or only some of these exercises.

Notes

1. Paul Brace and Barbara Hinckley, *Follow the Leader: Opinion Polls and the Modern Presidents* (New York: Basic Books, 1992), p. 18.

2. Alan Balutis, "The Presidency and the Press: the Expanded Public Image," *Presidential Studies Quarterly* 7 (Fall 1977): 241–251; Doris Graber, *Mass Media and American Politics*, 6th ed. (Washington, DC: CQ Press, 2002), pp. 272–275.

3. Thomas E. Cronin and Michael Genovese, *The Paradoxes of the American Presidency* (New York: Oxford University Press, 1998), pp. 1–28; Arvand Raichur and Richard Waterman, "The Presidency, the Public, and the Expectations Gap," in Richard W. Waterman, ed., *The Presidency Reconsidered* (Itasca, IL: F.E. Peacock, 1993), pp. 1–21.

4. See Jeffrey K. Tulis, *The Rhetorical Presidency* (Princeton: Princeton University Press, 1987), pp. 27–45.

5. Dennis Simon and Charles Ostrom, "The Politics of Prestige: Popular Support and the Modern Presidency," *Presidential Studies Quarterly* Vol. 18, No. 4 (1988): 742–744.

6. Samuel Kernell, *Going Public: New Strategies of Presidential Leadership*, 2nd ed. (Washington, DC: CQ Press, 1993), especially pp. 23–39.

7. Simon and Ostrom, "The Politics of Prestige," p. 746.

8. Brace and Hinckley, *Follow the Leader*, pp. 18–19.

9. Godfrey Hodgson, *All Things to All Men* (New York: Touchstone, 1980), p. 210.

10. Simon and Ostrom, "The Politics of Prestige," pp. 749–750.

11. See sources in footnote 42 in Simon and Ostrom, "The Politics of Prestige."

12. See footnotes 43–45 in Simon and Ostrom, "The Politics of Prestige."

13. Jon R. Bond and Richard Fleischer, *The President in the Legislative Arena* (Chicago: University of Chicago Press, 1990); George Edwards III, *At the Margins: Presidential Leadership of Congress* (New Haven: Yale University Press, 1989).

14. Kernell, *Going Public*, pp. 164–183; Benjamin I. Page and Robert Y. Shapiro, "Presidents as Opinion Leaders: Some New Evidence," *Policy Studies Journal* 12 (1984): 649–661. Mondak et al. also have found that presidents can be powerful "source cues" for members of the public on political issues, meaning that presidents with higher approval ratings are potentially more able to influence public opinion on policy. See Jeffrey I. Mondak, Christopher J. Lewis, Jason C. Sides, Joohyun Kang, and J. Olyn Long, "Presidential Source Cues and Policy Appraisals, 1981–2000," *American Politics Research* 32 No. 2 (March 2004): 219–235.

15. Richard A. Brody, *Assessing the President* (Stanford: Stanford University Press, 1991), p. 22.

16. Richard Neustadt, *Presidential Power: The Politics of Leadership from FDR to Carter* (New York: Macmillan, 1980), pp. 67–73.

17. For a nice summary of generalizations about presidential approval, see Cronin and Genovese, *The Paradoxes of the American Presidency*, pp. 73–74.

18. Brace and Hinckley, *Follow the Leader*, p. 32.

19. See discussion in George Edwards III and Alec Gallup, *Presidential Approval: A Sourcebook* (Baltimore: Johns Hopkins University Press, 1990), p. 123.

20. John Mueller, *War, Presidents and Public Opinion* (New York: John Wiley, 1970).

21. Donald R. Kinder, "Presidents, Prosperity, and Public Opinion," *Public Opinion Quarterly* 45 (Spring 1981): 1–21; Donald R. Kinder and D. Roderick Kiewiet, "Sociotropic Politics," *British Journal of Political Science* 11 (1981): 129–161.

22. See Michael B. MacKuen, Robert S. Erikson, and James A. Stimson, "Peasants or Bankers? The American Electorate and the U.S. Economy," *American Political Science Review* 86 No. 3 (September 1992): 597–611.

23. Mueller, *War, Presidents, and Public Opinion*, pp. 208–213.

24. John Wanat, "The Dynamics of Presidential Popularity Shifts: Estimating the Degree of Opinion Shift from Aggregate Data," *American Politics Quarterly* 10 (April 1982): 181–196; Lee Sigelman and Pamela Johnston Conover, "The Dynamics of Presidential Support during International Conflict Situations: The Iranian Hostage Crisis," *Political Behavior* 3 No. 4 (1981): 303–318.

25. See the discussion in Brace and Hinckley, *Follow the Leader*, pp. 27–31, along with their review of the literature.

26. Mueller, *War, Presidents, and Public Opinion*, pp. 62–64; and Samuel Kernell, "Explaining Presidential Popularity," *American Political Science Review* 72 No. 2. (June 1978): 506–522.

27. Brace and Hinckley, *Follow the Leader*, pp. 27–31; and Charles Ostrom and Dennis Simon, "Promise and Performance: A Dynamic Model of Presidential Popularity," *American Political Science Review* (June 1985): 334–358.

28. Brody, *Assessing the President*; Timothy Haight and Richard A. Brody, "The Mass Media and Presidential Popularity," *Communication Research* 4 (1977): 41–60; Richard A. Brody and Catherine R. Shapiro, "Policy Failure and Public Support: The Iran-Contra Affair and Public Assessments of President Reagan," *Political Behavior* 11 (1989).

29. Gallup polls, January to June 1993, as reported in 1993 Gallup Poll Annual (Wilmington, DE: Scholarly Resources, 1994).

30. Brody, *Assessing the President*, pp. 37–38; Michael Baruch Grossman and Martha Joynt Kumar, *Portraying the President* (Baltimore: John Hopkins University Press, 1981).

31. Brody, *Assessing the President*, p. 29.

32. James Fallows, *Breaking the News* (New York: Vintage, 1997), pp. 171–172.

33. See Brody, *Assessing the President*, pp. 61–62

34. Ibid., p. 66

35. Ibid., p. 67.

36. George Edwards III, William Mitchell, and Reed Welch, "Explaining Presidential Approval: The Significance of Issue Salience," *American Journal of Political Science* 39 No. 1 (February 1995): 108–134.

37. Richard Nadeau, Richard G. Niemi, David P. Fan, and Timothy Amato, "Elite Economic Forecasts, Economic News, Mass Economic Judgments, and Presidential Approval," *Journal of Politics* 61 No. 1 (February 1999): 109–135.

38. See Robert M. Entman, *Democracy Without Citizens: Media and the Decay of American Politics* (New York: Oxford University Press, 1989), pp. 39–74.

39. Brace and Hinckley, *Follow the Leader*, pp. 51–55; Lyn Ragsdale, "The Politics of Presidential Speechmaking, 1949–1980," *American Political Science Review* (December 1984): 971–984.

40. Richard Waterman, Robert Wright, and Gilbert St. Clair, *The Image-is-Everything Presidency* (Boulder, CO: Westview Press, 1999).

41. Brace and Hinckley, *Follow the Leader*, pp. 56–60; Ragsdale, "The Politics of Presidential Speechmaking," pp. 979–980.

42. Irving Crespi, "The Case of Presidential Popularity," in Albert H. Cantril, ed., *Polling on the Issues* (Cabin John, MD: Seven Locks Press, 1980), p. 42.

43. Kernell, *Going Public*, p. 238.

44. Ibid., p. 239.

45. Neustadt, *Presidential Power*, p. 71.

46. Brace and Hinckley, *Follow the Leader*, p. 164.

47. Brody, *Assessing the President*, p. 176.

Conclusion

14 Public Opinion and American Politics at the Dawn of the Twenty-First Century

Why should there not be a patient confidence in the ultimate justice of the people? Is there any better or equal hope in the world?

—Abraham Lincoln[1]

THE UNDERLYING premise of this book has been that an effective understanding of public opinion is vitally important to comprehending contemporary American politics—both how it works, and how it might work better. After examining the many different facets and aspects of public opinion, it is useful to step back and reflect upon what it all means.

Here, at the end of the book, we ask you to revisit some fundamental questions. Now that you know more, what do you think—is the public wise or foolish? When the people speak, does the government listen? (At least, to your satisfaction?)

As we have said elsewhere, there are no easy answers, possibly because the questions are so important to democratic government. While we believe you should form your own, educated opinion on these matters, by way of conclusion we return to some of the vital questions with which we began the book and discuss their implications for today and the future.

REVISITING THE DEMOCRATIC DILEMMA

The idea of the people effectively ruling themselves may be an old one, but it has never been wholly accepted or without controversy. An old Roman saying, whose origin is unclear, proclaims *vox populi, vox dei*—the voice of the people is the voice of God. What it means exactly is also somewhat unclear, but it certainly suggests that the public is both wise and should be listened to. Its roots can be found in the writings of Greek poet Hesiod, who in 700 B.C. said roughly, "talk never wholly dies away when many people voice her; because the talk of many is itself divine." The prophet Isaiah echoes this theme in the Bible: "A voice of noise from the city, a voice from the temple, a voice of the Lord that renders recompense to his enemies." Others have said much the same thing—that the collective voice of the people is astute.[2]

Yet this very statement, and the basic idea it embodies, has stirred the opposite reaction from some who see in public opinion not collective wisdom, but ignorance and folly. The English theologian Alcuin, referring to it in a letter to Charlemagne in 798, wrote, "those people should not be listened to who keep saying 'the voice of the people is the voice of God,' since the clamor of the crowd is always close to madness." The German Chancellor Theobald von Bethmann-Holweig thought it was more accurate to say, "Voice of the People: voice of cattle."[3] And even our own General William Tecumseh Sherman contemptuously decried, "vox populi—vox humbug."

These sentiments are at the root the bases for what we have termed the democratic dilemma. Should the government listen to the people? If so, how much?

We believe, as we said in Chapter 11, there is reason for guarded optimism about the capacity of the public. While individual citizens may not live up to the democratic ideal, there are enough members of the populace who do, at least to a reasonable degree, so that they can act either in place of, or as cue givers for, others. Still, the quality of the public could be even better: civic literacy and political participation could be increased. All of us could be more well-informed, as well as more involved. Efforts to do both should be encouraged.

But the debate over the competence of the masses and the quality of public opinion will likely go on as long as democracy and its critics exist. This debate is healthy, especially if it leads to more positive attempts to improve popular competence.

DISTORTIONS IN THE PEOPLE'S VOICE

All things considered, what can we say about the democratic dialogue and whether the government listens to the public? Although some dispute it, modern social science has mustered impressive evidence documenting a fairly high degree of government responsiveness to public opinion. As noted in Chapter 12, approximately two-thirds of the time, what the public wants is what government eventually does. Major government policy decisions such as civil rights for African Americans and Medicare for senior citizens in the 1960s, and more recently, issues as disparate as family and medical leave (1993), a handgun purchase waiting period (1994), campaign finance reform (2002), and a ban on partial-birth abortion (2003), all became law with public support and against strong interest-group opposition.

Still, it is hard not to agree with the late V. O. Key, a political scientist who cared deeply about public opinion and democratic politics. He once stated, "The voice of the people is but an echo."[4] There are some important reasons to think that when the people speak, their voice either is not so clear or is not heard clearly. A brief review of the whole process of the democratic dialogue reveals multiple ways the public's voice can be distorted.

First, as Key recognized, public opinion may well be a political input that influences policy output, but public opinion itself is affected by other actors and forces.

> The output of an echo chamber bears an inevitable and invariable relationship to its input. As candidates and parties clamor for attention and vie for popular support, the people's verdict can be no more than a selective reflection from among the alternatives and outlooks presented to them. Even the most discriminating popular judgment can reflect only ambiguity, uncertainty, or even foolishness if those are the qualities of input into the echo chamber.[5]

Although here Key is talking about voting, where the message the public sends is less clear, his point applies equally well to the whole democratic dialogue. For example, what policy options are included in debates over legislation, how the media frame political issues, or how pollsters construct questions about them, all influence the sound of the people's voice.

What the people say is likewise deeply affected by the information they receive and how they interact with the political world. Given control over the information environment, elite leadership or manipulation of opinion can occur, sometimes (as was probably the case with the outbreak of the Vietnam and 1991 Persian Gulf Wars), against what the public might have wanted had it been fully informed. Similarly, media coverage of politics sets the agenda and influences how people think about political matters. Poor, slanted, or otherwise limited information, coverage of sensationalism and scandal, and so forth, may limit the ability of the public to speak intelligently about politics or form an effective voice.[6] Or, as Key aptly put it, "fed a steady diet of buncombe, the people may come to . . . respond with the highest predictability to buncombe."[7]

Second, the people's voice is but an echo because it is only one voice clamoring for the attention of the government. Other voices may be louder and clearer. Lack of equal participation in politics—voting, contacting officials, and so on—means that what the public appears to be saying may not be so in actual fact. Similarly, organized interest groups, or aroused, intense minority issue publics tend to have advantages in getting their message through, and politicians may choose to listen to them rather than to the majority, particularly on issues where the bulk of the public may not be paying attention. Also, for most elected officials, the need to stay in favor with donors who fund their campaigns and help keep them in office may mean the public's wishes come second in some cases. Political parties, although more majority-sensitive in that they want to get their candidates elected to office, nevertheless tend to be run and operated by activists who are more politically involved, opinionated, and ideologically extreme than the general public. Thus, candidates who emerge from party nominating processes and eventually become government officials probably are similar to their activist followers, so that policy over-steering—creating policies that are more conservative or liberal than majority public opinion—may result. Although political officials are limited as to how far they can go without losing votes to candidates of other parties, on some issues, they may choose to satisfy their base over the bulk of the citizenry, such as was the case with the House Republicans on the issue of the Clinton impeachment.

Politicians themselves may also misread or misinterpret what the people say, even in honest attempts to respond to them. In fact, as noted in studies by Herbst, Kull and Ramsay, and others, policymakers' main sources for reading public opinion often are the mass media and interest groups. While these are certainly legitimate measures of opinion expression, as we noted in Chapter 3, they likely are not representative of the entire populace. Even politicians who rely more on polls may do so, not to follow public opinion, but to determine better ways of either leading, manipulating, mollifying, or safely ignoring the public's wishes. For example, despite Ronald Reagan's failed efforts in the 1980s to move public opinion toward more American political and military involvement in Central America, his administration actually did become directly involved in the internal politics of Nicaragua and El Salvador, against public sentiment.[8] Bill Clinton tried to lead public opinion on national health care in 1993–1994 by pitching and emphasizing elements of his plan the public liked, while downplaying its unpopular aspects. Although his plan ultimately failed when Congressional and interest-group opponents essentially did the opposite against him, the point is that in the case of health care, elites chose to shape the debate and the public's response toward the ends they favored rather than asking, and then listening to, what the public wanted.[9]

In some cases, policy may even go against what the public wants because of a belief that politicians know better or that the national interest is more important than short-term, possibly uninformed majority will. A case in point was when Congress authorized President Bush's request for an $87 billion supplemental aid package to Iraq and Afghanistan in October 2003, despite the fact that polls consistently showed that 55 percent or more of the American public was opposed to the measure, and at a minimum wanted more of the money to be in the form of loans rather than grants.[10] Apparently, America's international leadership role, and the government's (and especially the Republican Party's) commitment to properly finish the job in Iraq, along with the belief of most members of Congress that such a vote wouldn't hurt them at election time, all carried more weight than public disapproval.

Finally, it must also be recognized that the American governmental system was not designed to maximize the role of public opinion in its operations. As noted in Chapter 1, since most of the framers had a dim view of the public and even feared its potential wrath, their answer to the democratic dilemma was to create a system based on popular consent but with limitations on majority rule. Our federal system of separation of powers and checks and balances means that there are a number of different ways in which the majority will can be stunted or blocked. Only if there is a strong consensus—such as after the attack on Pearl Harbor, or following the terrorist attacks of September 11—will government move quickly and decisively. At other times, public opinion may be a powerful force to be reckoned with, but there are other ways intense minorities can use the system to prevail, such as was the case with attempts at gun control legislation prior to the 1990s.

Because of all of these factors, public opinion scholar Benjamin Page argues, borrowing a phrase from the late E. E. Schattschneider, that the public is only "semi-sovereign":

> There is substantial evidence of government responsiveness to public opinion, especially on high-salience issues. But the evidence also indicates that there is considerable room for interest groups, party activists, policymakers and others to prevail against the public on many issues. Often, anti-popular policy decisions can be kept out of the spotlight or cleverly packaged to avoid offense. Sometimes public opinion can be manipulated. Moreover, the extent of responsiveness to public opinion varies by type of issue and over time.[11]

The democratic dialogue, then, is not always democratic in result.

THE PEOPLE'S VOICE GROWS

Despite controversy over the proper role of public opinion, there is no doubt that its influence, or at least attention to it, has grown in American politics since the founding. Increases in political participation, such as the breaking down of barriers to voting, election reforms, and the opening up of political party nominating processes, have all meant that the people have more of an ability to speak to the government, and for the government to listen to them. The rise of the mass media and the development of polling over the last seventy years or so has also opened up Washington, D.C., and made it more likely that politicians will be aware of, and respond to, public wishes. As we have seen, presidents and other politicians now appear to pay more attention to polls and even hire their own pollsters to find out what the people think. At the very least, media coverage of public opinion expressions has made the issue of what the people want a bigger part of the political calculations politicians must make.

There is also reason to believe, as John Dewey predicted in the 1920s, that the role of public opinion will continue to grow and be brighter in the twenty-first century. Advances in technology, such as the Internet, which is now allowing for limited, two-way communication between leaders and led, will increase opportunities for participation. Already, there have been new uses of that medium for political information and political organizing outside mainstream political institutions and organizations. For example, the almost entirely Web-based political organization MoveOn.org went from being an electronic grass-roots group opposed to the Clinton impeachment in 1998 to becoming an interactive, participatory network in liberal causes today. In the 2004 primary season, Democratic presidential candidate Howard Dean and his staff pioneered use of the Internet for grassroots networking and fundraising; other candidates of all political stripes are following suit, by providing such features as e-mail campaign updates and access to their personal blogs, or Web diaries. E-forums and electronic town hall meetings on issues of public importance are certainly possible, although whether they are desirable is another matter entirely. Real-time television and twenty-four hour cable networks devoted to politics have likewise made more outlets for information available, even if everyone doesn't take advantage of them. And media attention to and use of public opinion polls seems insatiable, increasing public awareness about public opinion.

New techniques and ways of measuring public opinion are already being developed. As mentioned in Chapter 2, Internet surveys are seen as a potentially powerful and dramatic new method of ascertaining the public's wishes. As Internet use and accessibility expands—and nonresponse rates in telephone polls increase—Internet polling may well grow in importance, even if issues of sampling, representativeness, and response rates continue. Online surveys also create new opportunities for data collection and opinion analysis through interactive formats, such as with visual or aural stimuli. Researchers can even cull information from respondents without their knowledge (as some marketers now do, for example, with commercial Web sites that track how long a visitor spends or how often a cursor passes over certain features), although this type of surveying raises ethical questions.[12] Another intriguing method is probabilistic polling, where respondents, rather than giving a direct "yes or no" response to a question, instead provide an answer in probability form—say, the percent chance they will actually vote in the next election and the percent chance they will vote for a particular candidate. This technique provides the pollster with better, more refined data as to how strongly members of a sample feel or how likely they are to do something.[13] While the immediate goal of probabilistic polling is to improve the accuracy of candidate horse race polls, it could theoretically be adapted to polls on issues, making for greater sensitivity to the nuances of public opinion. Undoubtedly, there will be other unforeseen developments that will also impact the role of public opinion in the future.

The exciting thing about technological developments like the Internet is that they promise truly interactive communication between both members of the public themselves, and the public and political officials. As one observer put it, "Unlike television, where the viewer can only absorb a message, not respond to it, the Internet promotes the exchange of ideas. Democracy is based upon the interaction of citizens for the common good, and the Internet can be its most powerful instrument if it is put to proper use."[14]

Still, these new technologies for expressing and measuring public opinion have their downsides. One is a representation bias: In terms of sheer usage, people with access to computers, text message cell phones, and the like tend to be better educated, wealthier, and younger than those without. Even though prices keep going down and the number of people with access to such technology is expanding, this does not mean that the political playing field is leveled. People who are already organized, interested, and involved in politics are still far more likely to use these technologies for political communication and activity. And specialized communications outlets like the Internet and cable or satellite television may serve instead to fragment the public even further into specialized issue or interest publics—not only in terms of gun lovers or nature lovers or "Deaniacs," but also nonpolitical home shoppers, antique buffs, etc. who now have a greater ability to shut out bothersome matters of politics altogether.

Another drawback is that faster, easier information dissemination and more diverse outlets for information retrieval in turn lead to problems of information overload and even greater amounts of distortion, inaccuracy, or sheer propaganda. For example, during the 2000 presidential election, a thirty-year-old Web designer, Zach Exley, created www.gwbush.com, a surprisingly sophisticated mock-official Web site of the Bush campaign, which raised questions about Bush's past, gave links to various allegations, and advocated his defeat. It was so good, and so close in name to Bush's own site, that some news reports even accidentally gave its address out as the link for the real Bush campaign site! Various dirty tricks and unfounded allegations have been released via the Internet by some campaign organizations, who hide behind phony group names or anonymity.[15] In 2004, John Kerry was the target of questionable charges about his military record through a Web site run by a group called "Swift Boat Veterans for Truth," who used their site to raise money for a television and radio campaign. Furthermore, what amounts to political gossip can now be put out into cyberspace, and even get into mainstream media. In 1998, Internet gossiper Matt Drudge took information from Monica Lewinsky's confidante Linda Tripp that President Clinton's adviser Vernon Jordan had asked Lewinsky to lie under oath about her affair with the president—a story that was rejected by mainstream news organizations like *Newsweek* for questionable veracity—and posted it on his site, resulting in a media feeding frenzy. It later turned out to be largely a bogus claim, and Lewinsky and Jordan both testified under oath that no such request was ever made. Although some of Drudge's revelations during the Lewinsky scandal turned out to be true, the point remains that unsubstantiated yet juicy stories can now receive widespread attention.[16]

In essence, anyone with a computer can now put any kind of information out into the ether and potentially into the news cycle, meaning that the quality of political information is more suspect, and the potential for misleading the public is even greater. "There's much to be said for the discarding of 'traditional media filters' like newspapers and television news organizations in cyberspace. But with the disappearance of information gatekeepers, Net users must learn to apply their own individual filters for falsehood and manipulation," warns one analyst.[17]

For all of these reasons, the Internet and other visions of "e-democracy" may fail to live up to their lofty potential. As political scientist and new media scholar Richard Davis puts it, "As a tool for direct democracy, the Internet, like its predecessors, will fail in that expected role. In fact, the Internet is more likely to reduce participation and increase the political system's reliance on a small number of political activists than to actually represent public opinion. Although that reliance is not new, the danger comes from the illusion of broad public involvement."[18] In the end, while public opinion may become more easily expressed, visible, and important in politics and society in coming years, many of the same issues in the democratic dilemma (like rationality and competence) and the democratic dialogue (like representativeness, distortion, and transmission) remain.

CONCLUSION

Those of us who are fortunate enough to live in a democracy, however imperfect, ought to understand the obligations of citizenship. We must be aware of public opinion and be educated consumers of information about it (news stories, polls, demonstrations, and so forth), if only because some will claim their actions are the will of the people when that may not actually be the case. We need to seek out multiple measures of opinion, for even if some may not be representative, they still may provide important cues as to what is going on or why the government is doing something.

Whatever your opinion about public opinion, it should be clear to you by now that public opinion is vitally important to contemporary politics in the United States. It is equally important that you express your beliefs (remember, an opinion doesn't really exist until it's expressed!). As a citizen, you have a civic obligation, in addition to a vested self-interest, in both knowing what is going on and voicing your concerns on the issues of the day. Even if the voice of the people is but an echo, the louder the echo, the more likely it is to be heard.

Notes

1. From Abraham Lincoln, First Inaugural Address, 1861, in Abraham Lincoln, *Speeches and Writings*, Vol. 2, edited by Don E. Fehrenbacher (Library of America, 1989), p. 223.

2. Elisabeth Noelle-Neumann, *The Spiral of Silence: Public Opinion, Our Social Skin* (Chicago: University of Chicago Press, 1984), pp. 175–176.

3. Ibid.

4. V. O. Key, *The Responsible Electorate* (Cambridge, MA: Belknap Press, 1966), p. 2.

5. Key, *The Responsible Electorate*, pp. 2–3.

6. See, for example, W. Lance Bennett, *News: The Politics of Illusion*, 4th ed. (New York: Longman, 2001); Robert M. Entman, *Democracy Without Citizens: Media and the Decay of American Politics* (New York: Oxford University Press, 1989); and Michael X. Delli Carpini and Bruce Williams, "Let Us Infotain You: Politics in the New Media Environment," in W. Lance Bennett and Robert M. Entman, eds., *Mediated Politics: Communication in the Future of Democracy* (New York: Cambridge University Press, 2001), pp. 160–181.

7. Key, *The Responsible Electorate*, p. 7.

8. See, for example, W. Lance Bennett, "Marginalizing the Majority," in Michael Margolis and Gary A. Mauser, eds., *Manipulating Public Opinion: Essays on Public Opinion as a Dependent Variable* (Belmont, CA: Brooks-Cole, 1989), pp. 321–362.

9. Lawrence R. Jacobs and Robert Y. Shapiro, "Policy and Policymaking in the Real World: Crafted Talk and the Loss of Democratic Responsiveness," in Jeff Manza, Fay Lomax Cook, and Benjamin I. Page, eds., *Navigating Public Opinion: Polls, Policy and the Future of American Democracy* (New York: Oxford University Press, 2002), pp. 54–75; see also Darrell West and Burdett Loomis, *The Sound of Money: How Political Interests Get What They Want* (New York: W.W. Norton, 1999), pp. 75–108.

10. When asked, 56 percent of respondents opposed the aid package in a Quinnipiac University poll of October 23, 2003; 57 percent opposed in a Gallup/CNN/*USA Today* poll of October 10; 59 percent opposed in a CBS News/*New York Times* poll of October 20; and 64 percent opposed in an ABC News/*Washington Post* poll of October 26 (from Roper Center polling archive in the *Lexis-Nexis* database).

11. Benjamin I. Page, "The Semi-Sovereign Public," in Manza, Cook, and Page, *Navigating Public Opinion*, p. 325.

12. James Witte and Phillip E. M. Howard, "The Future of Polling: Relational Inference and the Development of Internet Survey Instruments," in Manza, Cook, and Page, *Navigating Public Opinion*, p. 288.

13. Charles F. Manski, *Probablistic Polling*, in Manza, Cook, and Page, *Navigating Public Opinion*, pp. 251–271.

14. Graeme Browning, *Electronic Democracy*, 2nd ed. (Medford, NJ: Cyber Age Books, 2002), p. 170.

15. Ibid., pp. 86–87.

16. See Bill Dovach and Tom Rosenstiel, *Warp Speed: America in the Age of Mixed Media Culture* (New York: Century Foundation Press, 1999).

17. Browning, *Electronic Democracy*, p. 90.

18. Richard Davis, *The Web of Politics: The Internet's Impact on the American Political System* (New York: Oxford University Press, 1999), p. 185.

Glossary

activated public opinion: the opinions of the informed, engaged, and organized citizens, or the "attentive public."

affirmative action: proactive government policies to address past discrimination, usually in the areas of employment and education.

agenda-setting: influencing people's issue priorities, or what issues they think are important. Mass media coverage has been found to have an agenda-setting effect.

bandwagon effect: presumed effect of media coverage of polls, influencing some voters to "jump on the bandwagon" by switching their allegiance to the candidate leading in pre-election preference polls.

bias: a prejudiced, slanted, or non-neutral depiction of reality; a common criticism of media coverage of politics is that it is not neutral, balanced, or fair to all sides.

CATI or Computer Assisted Telephone Interviewing: a method of conducting telephone interviews in which the interviewer reads questions from a computer screen and enters the respondents' answers directly into the computer.

collective deliberation: a social system whereby the public reasons about political issues, usually by way of "opinion leaders" or the attentive public educating or providing cues to members of the mass public.

conservatism: an ideology that generally opposes government involvement in the economic and racial issue domains, favors government involvement in social issues, and favors larger defense budgets. In the left-right continuum, conservatism is to the right of center.

cross-sectional study: a "snapshot" poll that interviews one sample of a population at a single time, as opposed to a panel study where respondents are re-interviewed. Most polls are cross-sectional in design.

deliberative polling: a form of polling developed by James S. Fishkin to measure what the public would want after a period of discussion and reflection, which combines attributes of a random sample poll and a focus group. A sample is selected at random, and then polled on a variety of issues; sample members then participate in series of lectures and discussions about those issues and afterward are polled again with the same questions to see where they stand.

democratic dialogue: the process by which public opinion is translated into public policy, or the question of whether or how much the government actually does listen to the people in practice.

democratic dilemma: the question of whether, and how much, the government should listen to the people, given that the public may not live up to ideal visions of democratic theory.

democratic elitism: the ironic notion that democracy survives primarily because political elites are more supportive of democratic values like majority rule and tolerance for unpopular groups and points of view than are most of the public.

economic issues: the issue domain that involves taxes, government spending, regulation, and social welfare issues such as Social Security, welfare, unemployment benefits, food stamps, and health care.

exit poll: a survey of voters conducted at polling places immediately after respondents have voted.

focus group: a moderated, small-group discussion, where respondents, usually selected on the basis of some variable of interest, such as "pro-life" Democrats, etc., are guided through topics of interest to the researcher. Though too small and lacking representativeness to be generalizable, focus groups nevertheless can provide important qualitative, detailed context to issues, or feedback on advertising or how issues are presented in the media. Many political candidates employ them.

foreign policy issues: the issue domain involving the defense budget and negotiations and treaties with foreign countries, as well as war and peace issues.

framing: how an issue, event, or person is presented, interpreted and put into context; a media effect that influences how people process and think about political and other matters.

gender gap: the difference in voting, party identification, and political attitudes and opinions between men and women. Generally, women are more Democratic than men and have more liberal opinions, especially on issues concerning force and violence.

generational effects: the impact of events, issues, and life experiences on one particular generation's political attitudes and opinions, typically when your adults are being socialized into the political system; for example, the so-called "baby boomers" who came of age during the Vietnam-Watergate era and its effects on their views compared to those of their children and parents. Generational effects lead to generational replacement.

generational replacement: notion that as one generational cohort ages and dies, members are replaced by younger, newer generations that may have very different values based on the politics of the time they come of age. Also known as "cohort replacement."

heuristics: a decision-making model relying upon certain simplified cues to overcome a lack of information, such as using party identification as a guide to how to vote in an election where one doesn't know a lot about where all the candidates stand on issues.

honeymoon: term for the early period of a president's first term in office, usually the first several months, when presidential approval ratings tend to be higher.

horse race journalism: media coverage focusing on candidate strategies, who's ahead, and who's behind in the race, usually as measured in trial heat and candidate preference polls. Often, such coverage is at the expense of other campaign information such as candidates' experience or stands on issues.

ideology: a set of interlocking, interrelated attitudes and beliefs that fit together in a coherent structure.

in-depth interview: a form of qualitative research where the researcher gathers data from the respondents through intensive face-to-face interviews over an extended period of time.

interval sampling: a type of random sampling where the researcher selects respondents at set intervals (every *n*th person) after selecting the first one at random. For example, choosing every tenth name from your college or university phone book to call. This is the same as **systematic** sampling.

issue evolution: the gradual transformation of issue opinions over time.

laboratory experiment: a closed research design that allows the researcher to manipulate a variable of interest. In most experiments, respondents are separated into "treatment" and "control" groups. Treatment groups receive the treatment or manipulation, while the control group does not. The results are then compared to determine whether the variable of interest had any effect on the participants in the treatment group. The researcher is thus able to control for all outside factors except for the manipulated one, which increases the ability to draw conclusions about causality (that x caused y).

latent opinion: the dormant or underlying opinions of the masses before an issue goes through a period of identification, discussion, and deliberation.

liberalism: an ideology that generally supports government involvement in the economic and racial issue domains to help promote equality, opposes government involvement in social issues, and favors smaller defense budgets. In the left-right continuum, liberalism is to the left of center.

lifecycle effects: the impact upon political opinions of relatively uniform life stages or events as one ages—e.g., young adulthood "starting off," then moving into middle age with family and job, and then into old age with retirement, etc.

lifestyle issues: term for a particular set of issues in the social policy domain that have to do with how people live their lives, such as gay rights, birth control, family planning, abortion, marriage, drug use, gambling, etc.

mass opinion: the aggregation or summation of individual people's opinions through polls, referenda, or elections. Mass opinion is usually ascertained through surveys or polls.

mobilization: the process by which political elites (parties, candidates, interest groups, or other activists) attempt to induce people to participate in politics. May also be known as "recruitment."

New Deal: the package of governmental and social programs put forward by President Franklin D. Roosevelt to address the Great Depression. The New Deal defined the basis of the current party system and the modern definitions of "liberalism" and "conservatism," especially with reference to economic or social welfare issues.

nonattitudes: Philip Converse's term for the tendency of the inattentive or mass public to have no real political opinions at all, often guessing or making up "doorstep opinions" on the spot to pollsters.

operationalization: how a particular theoretical concept or hypothesis is put into practice and formally measured by the researcher. For example, if a researcher wanted to measure political interest in a survey, he or she would need to develop questions that measure interest, such as how often a respondent read political news or how much a respondent cared about an upcoming election.

panel study: a poll where the same set of sampled subjects is re-interviewed at several points in time. Panel studies allow the researcher to track changes in opinion over time. The National Election Studies have sometimes embedded panel studies in their cross-sectional time-series studies.

participatory distortion: the term Sidney Verba et al. give to the phenomenon of some kinds of people participating more and, presumably, being heard more by governmental decision makers.

party identification: a psychological attachment to, or affiliation with, a political party, which has been found to be a useful cue for organizing or connecting a variety of political opinions.

party system: the arrangement of issues, public opinion, partisan alignments, and voting that characterize politics and divisions between the major political parties at any one time of history.

perceived majorities: what majority "public opinion" is, according to the perceptions of informed observers such as journalists, politicians, and even members of the public themselves.

period effects: the impact of events or issues that affect all generations about equally; for example, the ending of the Cold War or the terrorist attacks on September 11, 2001.

persuasion: actually influencing a person's policy preferences or opinions on issues.

political efficacy: the belief that one can make a difference in politics, or that one's actions can have an impact on the political process or the political world.

political poll: a canvassing of opinion or "counting of heads" on a political topic. Usually, polls are conducted using some form of a random sample, though nonrandom polls on political matters are also done.

political socialization: the process by which people learn and develop their political values and attitudes.

population: all the people in whom the researcher is interested. For example, in a presidential election poll, the population is all the voters in the presidential election.

precision journalism: a school of journalism that believes reporters should become schooled in survey research and public opinion polling techniques, and should effectively and accurately use polls in their coverage to provide needed context and public input.

predispositions: according to John R. Zaller, individual traits, such as values, attitudes, pre-existing biases, or political inclinations, that influence how people respond to new information and form opinions.

primacy principle: idea in political socialization that "what is learned first is learned best," or that earlier learned attitudes are retained the longest.

priming: a media effect whereby media influence what issues or traits are used in people's evaluations of politicians and their policies.

principle-implementation gap: term describing certain patterns in white views about racial equality for minorities: that they support the idea of racial equality in principle, but tend to oppose specific government policies or practices aimed at promoting equality for minorities, such as affirmative action.

probability sampling: The method of selecting members of a sample so that each member of the population has a known chance (typically, an equal chance) of being selected.

projectable: the quality of a random sample survey or poll to be generalized, or projected, to the whole population. Random samples can be generalized within a set margin of error based on statistical probability.

public journalism: a journalistic reform movement that argues media organizations should cover politics and elections from the standpoint of citizens rather than politicians. In this view, journalists should use polls of the citizenry on issues to set the agenda and focus of coverage, rather than candidate statements, press releases, or campaign advertising.

public opinion: the expressed attitudes and views of ordinary people on issues of public concern.

qualitative research: research methods that rely on non-numerical data and do not use statistical or other mathematical techniques to develop generalizations. Qualitative research is usually more informal and interpretative, such as using notes and textual analysis of interviews rather than translating them into numerical scores.

quantitative research: research methods that rely on numerical data such as coded responses and use statistical and mathematical techniques to develop generalizations. quantitative research is formal and methodical, such as numerically coding interview responses into categories (such as "strongly agree," "weakly agree," "neutral," etc.) or scales so statistical analyses can be performed on them.

quota sampling: a type of non-random or non-probability sampling in which the researcher selects people based on predetermined characteristics, stopping when the "quota" for a particular group is reached.

racial issues: the issue domain involving ethnicity. Racial issues include efforts to fight discrimination, guarantee equality and fairness for minorities, and provide affirmative action for members of minority ethnic groups.

rally effect: also known as "rally 'round the flag" effect, the tendency for a president's approval rating (or the number of people approving the president's job performance) to go up during an international crisis; presumably due to patriotism or loyalty to the president as leader of the nation.

RDD or Random Digit Dialing: a method of selecting sample members of a telephone survey in which telephone numbers are chosen randomly. Telephone numbers, rather than people, are selected.

refusal rate: the percent of the drawn sample that refuses to participate in the poll. High refusal rates mean less accuracy.

response rate: the percent of the drawn sample that actually responds or agrees to participate in the poll. High response rates usually mean greater accuracy.

retrospective voting: using the record and past performance of the incumbent party or candidate in office as the main determinant of one's voting—e.g., rewarding those currently in power for doing a good job by voting to re-elect them or punishing them for doing a bad job by voting for their opponents.

sample: the people who are questioned in a survey. Sample sizes typically range from 400 to 3,000 people.

sampling error: random error produced by the sampling procedure; a statistical formula for probability samples that allows the researcher to estimate the probable difference between the drawn sample and the population.

scale: the assignment of numbers to individuals' responses based on specific rules, a form of operationalization. Numbers on a scale are related to one another to measure distance or preference. A scale may also be constructed from a series of questions on a topic. For example, the answers to several questions of feelings of political efficacy could be combined into one "political efficacy" scale. This type of scale is sometimes called an **index**.

schema: a general knowledge structure that provides a framework for organizing knowledge or political thought and which helps to interpret new knowledge and information.

selective exposure: the tendency for people to seek out media sources that already conform to their pre-existing attitudes and beliefs, thereby limiting media influence on opinion.

simple random sampling: sampling method in which potential respondents are randomly assigned numbers. A sample of them is then chosen for interviewing. This method is seldom used in large studies.

social class: one's economic and social standing in society; generally, a system used to classify people into various socioeconomic groups for the purpose of comparison. The most common criteria for determining social class are a person's income, education, and occupation. The vast majority of Americans believe they are middle class, regardless of objective criteria.

social issues: heterogeneous issue domain concerning gender and lifestyle issues—and may include immigration, crime, regulation of the environment, and civil liberties.

social welfare issues: a subset of the economic issue domain, generally concerning the degree to which government should promote economic equality and provide a "safety net" for all its citizens; includes issues such as Social Security, welfare, unemployment benefits, food stamps, health care, etc.

Spiral of Silence: theory of public opinion expression, enunciated by Elisabeth Noelle-Neumann, that people who perceive they are in the minority on an issue, in order to avoid being isolated or chastised, tend to keep silent, while those who believe they are in the majority are more likely to express their views. This leads to a spiraling effect where one view dominates, whether or not it actually represents majority sentiment; mass media coverage of issues and/or polls may help trigger such a phenomenon.

spurious causation: when a researcher mistakenly comes to the conclusion that force x causes result y, when in fact a third, unmeasured factor is the reason; some argue that just because public opinion and government policy change in congruent, or similar, ways, does not prove that opinion caused policy because policy may have changed for reasons other than changes in public opinion.

straw poll: any of a number of non-probability polls, in which respondents are not chosen at random but rather in a haphazard or arbitrary fashion like "straws in the wind"—for example, asking a certain segment of students eating in the cafeteria on a given day their position on a tuition increase, or readers of a teen girls' magazine their view on a new pop singer. Straw polls have a long history in the United States, though their results are likely to be in error because their sample is non-random.

structuring principle: idea in political socialization that early learning structures or molds later learning.

survey-based experiment: a form of experimental study conducted through sample surveys. Participants are randomly assigned to different groups, each given a different "treatment" of questions, and the results are then compared. For example, researchers may want to study the effects of question wording on respondents, and so may ask two randomly selected, comparable samples different versions to measure framing effects or better understand the nuances of opinion on an issue.

survey research: a study of a particular population relying on a sample or subset of the whole, as opposed to the entire universe or population (known as a census). Virtually all polls rely on surveys for their results.

time-series study: a type of research design in which a series of cross-sectional surveys are taken over a period of time. Two important time-series studies are the National Election Studies and the General Social Survey.

two-step flow: the idea that mass media information is further mediated by "attentive publics" or "opinion leaders" in the population, who in turn filter and transmit its meanings to other people in the mass public.

underdog effect: presumed effect of media coverage of polls, influencing some voters to "root for the underdog" by switching their allegiance to a candidate trailing in pre-election preference polls.

***Vox populi, vox Dei*:** Latin term for "the voice of the people is the voice of God," unclear but generally meaning the people speak wisely.

weighting: a statistical adjustment to raw data collected in a poll before they are analyzed, usually to make the sample more representative of the population or more accurate. For example, if a survey had a smaller percentage of African Americans in the sample than the actual population, the researcher might mathematically adjust, or weight, the responses of that sub-group more to make the survey closer to the "real" population.

Index

Made in the USA
Lexington, KY
16 August 2011